RAISING STEAKS

◆

ALSO BY BETTY FUSSELL

Mabel: Hollywood's First I-Don't-Care-Girl

Masters of American Cookery

I Hear America Cooking

Eating In

Food in Good Season

Home Plates

The Story of Corn

Crazy for Corn

Home Bistro

My Kitchen Wars

The Police Gazette, October 27, 1883, reported that "A Deadhead Passenger" on October 3 was swept up sixteen miles west of Atchison on the cowcatcher of a west-bound freight train on the Atchison, Topeka & Santa Fe line, where she traveled six miles to Nortonville before the conductor put her off because "she had no ticket and would not pay fare."

RAISING STEAKS

THE LIFE AND TIMES OF AMERICAN BEEF

Betty Fussell

HARCOURT, INC.

ORLANDO | AUSTIN | NEW YORK | SAN DIEGO | LONDON

Requests for permission to make copies of any part of the
work should be submitted online at www.harcourt.com/contact
or mailed to the following address: Permissions Department,
Houghton Mifflin Harcourt Publishing Company,
6277 Sea Harbor Drive, Orlando, Florida 32887-6777.

www.HarcourtBooks.com

Library of Congress Cataloging-in-Publication Data
Fussell, Betty Harper.
Raising steaks : the life and times of American beef /
Betty Fussell. — 1st ed.
p. cm.
Includes bibliographical references and index.
1. Beef cattle — United States — History. 2. Beef industry — United
States — History. 3. Beef — United States. 4. Cookery (Beef)
I. Title. II. Title: Life and times of American beef.
SF196.U6F87 2008 636.2'130973 — dc22 2008017310
ISBN 978-0-15-101202-2

Text set in Minion
Book design by Victoria Hartman

Printed in the United States of America
FIRST EDITION
A C E G I K J H F D B

Permissions acknowledgments appear on page 347, which
constitutes a continuation of the copyright page.

THIS BOOK IS PRINTED ON 100 PERCENT
POSTCONSUMER-WASTE RECYCLED STOCK.

For Tucky and Sam
then and now

If you ain't a cowboy, you ain't shit.

— SAM SHEPARD, *Fool for Love*

The only time to eat diet food is while you're
waiting for the steak to cook.

— JULIA CHILD

CONTENTS

◆

RAISING STEAKS

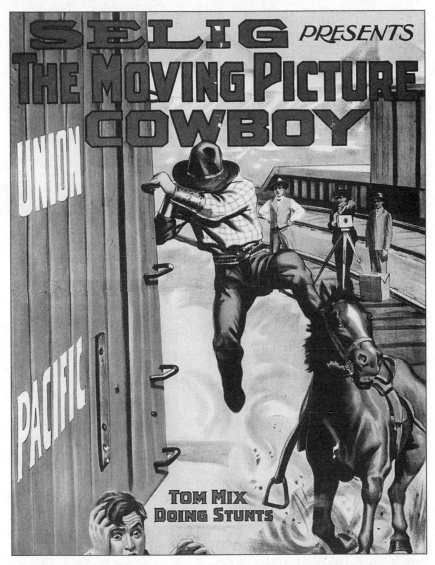

A lithograph poster of "The Moving Picture Cowboy," 1914, shows "Tom Mix Doing Stunts . . . The Way He Told the Story . . . And What He Really Did." Printed by Goes Lithography Co., Chicago. Copyright 1914, Selig Polyscope Co.

— From the Poster Collection, Prints and Photographs Division, Library of Congress

Being American is to eat a lot of beef steak, and boy, we've got a lot more beef steak than any other country, and that's why you ought to be glad you're an American.

— Kurt Vonnegut, Jr., *City Limits*

I DIDN'T GROW UP eating beefsteak. I was a child of the Depression, and our fancy meat for Sunday-noon dinner was boiled chicken or boiled beef tongue, or else a shoulder of lamb, boiled until cuttable with a spoon. Steak was a luxury for the rich, and when I ate my first steak at seventeen, in the company of college chums fed up with our dorm swill, I didn't know how to cut it. I'd never before had to cut meat with a knife in order to get a bite-size piece. Nor did I know how to chew it. The meat we cooked at home, including the rare holiday treat of Swiss steak in the pressure cooker, was designed to give way at the first touch of my grandparents' dentures. My family were enthusiastic proponents of the Puritan principle that all food aspired to liquid, so that you could flush it out of your body as rapidly as possible. Maybe this was just an elaborate rationalization for not being able to afford steak.

I did grow up American, however, in a small town in Southern California, shaped by two kinds of stories, one Spanish and the other British. Riverside, our town on the banks of the Santa Ana River, had first been mapped by Captain Juan Bautista de Anza in 1774, on his overland expedition from the Sonora desert to San Francisco. Every year everyone in town dressed up in Spanish clothes for De Anza Days, with a fine parade of horses and caballeros magnificent in black silver-studded leather, prancing before carriages of women in flounced skirts and lace mantillas. In our cheap imitative costumes, we kids danced the Mexican Hat Dance and sang *"La Golondrina"* as if to the hacienda born. Though Scotch-Irish born and bred, I didn't think this in any way odd. Our Calvary Presbyterian Church had been built in the colonial Spanish style that dominated the town's main buildings, like the famed Mission Inn with its tiled roofs and arcades. We knew that mission fathers had been followed by Hispanic *rancheros* who grew rich on cattle until the War with Mexico in 1848 shook up the land grants and an Eastern consortium tapped the Santa Ana River for water to turn the desert into orange trees. Water brought émigrés from the East and Midwest, and what started as a trickle grew in the 1920s to a flood of farmers from Iowa, Nebraska, and Kansas.

My family arrived in time to get me born there, but I was an anomaly. Nobody we knew had been born in California. My family saw California as the last frontier, the New Eden that God had promised as they journeyed from Edinburgh to Londonderry to Philadelphia and points west. The native heritage of our clan of Harpers, Erskines, Stevensons, and Kennedys was strictly British, but our relocated heritage was Spanish, and the majority of kids growing up in the 1930s in my town were, like myself, Midwestern WASPs in Mexican clothing. It seemed a happy hybrid.

It was the same hybrid, I would discover, that had produced, over the course of five hundred years, American beefsteak. Bred from both Spanish and British traditions, as well as from both Spanish and British cattle breeds, American beefsteak is more characteristic of our hybrid national identity than apple pie (which came from the English), popcorn (from the Native Americans), or the hamburger (German). True, every country has its beef, branded with chauvinism. England has its bully roast beef, evoking not only the coziness of hearth and home, but also "the marrow of political freedom," as historian Simon Schama would have it, whereby the Society of Beefeaters proclaimed that "Beef and Liberty" would vanquish the effeminate French. France, in turn, has its *entrecôte et frites*, typifying in its full-bloodedness, as literary theorist Roland Barthes would have it, "the very flesh of the French soldier." Argentina has its *parrillada,* evoking the fierce independence of the gauchos on the vast and lawless pampas. Japan has its soft-as-butter Kobe, treated as a work of art by aesthetic islanders devoted to the refinements of *umami.*

We Americans have a very different take on steak because we have a very different history. When I wrote the story of corn a couple of decades ago, looking for the most American of all foods, I discovered my indebtedness to the native cultures of the New World, who first cultivated that plant thousands of years ago. I also learned how modern America had, in the last century, changed the face of the globe by being the world's first country to fully industrialize a plant so that it could do anything petroleum could. At the time, I'd thought I'd write next about beef because it, too, seemed such an American food, so iconic of American culture. I didn't then realize that American beef had become as much an industrial by-product of corn as ethanol is.

As a Westerner who'd gone east, I was still and forever caught up in the romance of beef. I felt that when I ate steak, I was sinking my teeth into the myth of the Frontier — the Marlboro cowboy busting his bronc, the cast-iron skillet on an open fire, the smell of tobacco and burnt coffee, a soft neigh or two from a tethered horse, the clank of a metal spur, the wheeze of a harmonica, a black sky full of stars. Mine was part of the national imagination, suckled on thousands of Western novels and movies, serenaded by millions of country-western songs, clad by the fashioners of boots and jeans, ritualized in rodeos, pastoralized in dude ranches, and nourished by billions of pounds of American steak. Americans, I decided, eat steak more lustily than pot roast because steak is fast, mobile, improvised, casual, egalitarian, reliable, raw, bloody, and violent — and it tastes best outdoors. It represents both freedom and independence, and the camaraderie of campfires. It's the closest we can get to yoking the raw and the cooked, the savage and the civilized. It invokes "Home on the Range" with a pang of longing far closer to the national heart than "The Star Spangled Banner." It goes with beer or wine, bourbon or tequila, and (God help us) Coke or iced tea. If it's pricey, it's also good value, because all that protein sticks to the bones. Muscle builds

muscle, blood feeds blood. Steak denies our faith in evolutionary progress and returns us to our dark and dirty primordial roots. Let the ascetic
and self-righteous weep for the lobster and the clam, ignoring the rape of
beets and berries. Like a movie Western, steak ritualizes our appetite for
violence and purges us of its need. Let the never-too-thin or too-rich of
Eastern cities devour limp fish and vacuous chicken, white and bloodless
as paper. Real American men, women, and children eat steak because it is
red with blood, blood that pumps flavor, iron, vitality, and sex into flac-
cid bodies. For women, steak is better than spinach. For men, it's better
than Viagra. With steak, it's easy to get carried away.

I'd already learned from corn that geography is destiny. The destiny of
beef was shaped by the 100th meridian, conveniently marked by the Mississippi River. That mighty river divides the wet East from the dry West,
just as it had divided, until the nineteenth century, British-colonized territory from Spanish territory. But our minds and imaginations shape
geographical facts, and our differing expectations create different landscapes. What my British ancestors saw when they imagined the West was
a larger England, with forests and meadows just like those of the eastern
seaboard Colonies. What the Spanish saw was a larger Spain, with desert
highlands and mountains like those of Mexico. I'm sure that all a British
yeoman wanted was a cottage for his family and just enough land to
plow, while all a Spanish herdsman wanted was a nice hacienda with
peons serving the *patrón*. While Britishers looked forward to the egalitar-
ianism of a new world founded on Reason, Spaniards looked back to the
feudalism of an old world serving God, pope, and king. One vision was
utopian and utilitarian, the other monarchic and nostalgic.

And so the crazy mixed-up iconography that shaped me was the result not just of one collective fantasy but a pair of conflicting fantasies,
with a push-pull as permanent as taffy. What child of the twentieth century did not grow up worshipping cowboys? Yet the cowboy himself is
a hybrid. We got our mythic Western cowboy from Spain, a man on a
horse herding cattle; but he's got the moral stance of a Britisher, a man
who does what's right. This mixed-breed loner is both an underdog
fighting for the common man and nature's nobleman, superior to others,

a knight in chaps. But the beauty of icons is that they get to have it both ways, which is how they ride out the contradictions of history. The historical cattle drives lasted a mere twenty years in the second half of the nineteenth century, but that was long enough to fix the iconography of the Cowboy as a peculiarly American fantasy of power that clothes violence in virtue.

In fact, even when actual cowboys were herding cattle from Mexico to Wyoming, it wasn't they who controlled the destiny of the herds. It was the barons back East who owned the cattle, the railroads, the markets, and most of the land. If the Cowboy's weapon was a gun, the Technocrat's was the steam engine. The Iron Horse was another icon of power fueling our romance with the Machine, which has been every bit as vital to the raising of American beefsteak as the cowboy's lariat and saddle. We try to keep these myths, separate but equal, running on parallel tracks that double the great disconnect between pasture and plate. But they belong together, as our very first cowboy motion picture showed in 1903, when "Broncho Billy" Anderson shot up the screen in *The Great Train Robbery*, while Edwin S. Porter cranked the camera.

TO MY DISMAY, I find that one of the first questions people ask me when I say I've been working on beef is whether or not I eat it. I guess they want a quick typecasting to know whether I'm for or against the eating of cows. Well, that's easy. I love meat. I'm a full red-blooded carnivore who eats omnivorously up and down the food chain because I know that the chain is circular, and that if today I'm eating pork chops, tomorrow I'm food for worms. I've always taken the antianthropocentric but egalitarian view that all created life is equal, and that just because a raw turnip doesn't scream when I bite into it doesn't mean that a turnip is of lesser value than a pig. It is simply less like me. But does that make it okay for me to cannibalize a turnip? Ask the turnip. A more interesting question is why, since we all must eat life to live, have human beings for millennia wanted to eat meat, craved it, died for it? Why do I like the smell, taste, texture, and even the sound of a thick beefsteak sizzling on a grill?

I'm not talking about nutrition. I'm not talking about health. I'm talking about the experience. What intimacy is involved in our relationship, the steak and I?

To find out, I set out for the territories — west, east, north, and south. In the past four years, I've branded Highland cows on a ranch in Montana, stalked nilgai in Texas, watched cows butchered by hand in a slaughterhouse in Colorado, and toured a Cargill plant near Dodge City that kills 6,000 cows per hour. I've attended conventions of the National Cattlemen's Beef Association in San Antonio and of a breakaway group in Denver, applauded lectures at the American Grass-Fed Society in Indiana and whooped it up at rodeos at the National Denver Western Stock Show. I've talked with a New Jersey housewife investigating mad cow disease, with an ex–bull rider turned political activist, with an animal scientist who transformed McDonald's. I went to Florida to see Piney Woods cattle in the palmettos, to Cheyenne to "Eeeee*haaaawwww*" with the Cowgirls of the West in the Pioneer Days Parade. I even enrolled in Beef 101 at Texas A&M, in order to get some hands-on experience in how we turn cows into meat.

I am grateful to them all, for helping me to put together the steps of the process that we've disassembled and kept separate for so long: breeding, feeding, slaughtering, processing, rendering, marketing, cooking, and eating. Yet while they filled in the story of beef in a way that neither the vast literature of the West nor the vast letterpress of agribusiness could, they also told more than one story. For whether they were corporate industrialists talking efficiency or small ranchers talking calves, all of them wore cowboy clothes, talked cowboy talk, sang cowboy songs, watched cowboy movies, ate cowboy steaks, just as our president does. All of them saw themselves at once as progressive independent businessmen and also as cowboys — just as our president does. The content might be Cattle-Fax statistics, but the packaging was white Stetson and custom-made boots. I should know — I kept a pair hidden in my own closet.

So the story of beef turns out to be two stories: the story of the head and the story of the heart. And boy, am I glad I'm an American because putting them together has meant eating a lot of great steak.

Beefy Boys

"A Democratic Barbecue," from *Frank Leslie's Illustrated Newspaper*, October 18, 1884, displays "Democrats and their guests enjoying a Tammany Hall–sponsored roast at a political barbecue in Harlem."

Then there is the beefsteak. They have it in Europe, but they don't know how to cook it. Neither will they cut it right. It comes on the table in a small, round, pewter platter. It lies in the center of this platter, in a bordering bed of grease-soaked potatoes; it is the size, shape, and thickness of a man's hand with the thumb and fingers cut off.

— Mark Twain, *A Tramp Abroad*

NOVEMBER 7, 2003. I'm handed a tan apron and a mug of Brooklyn Lager as I enter chef Waldy Malouf's Beacon Restaurant at 25 West 56th Street in Manhattan. I've been warned that the Fourth Annual Beacon Beefsteak will be literally a hands-on affair, and sure enough, co-owner David Emil suggests I remove my jacket to free my arms for swilling beer and grabbing meat. I head for one of the long communal tables that stretch across both the bar and kitchen levels. From the balcony upstairs, the oompahs of a brass band compete with the chatter of the 150 or so aproned celebrants. A few people wander in off the street to find out what the occasion is, then either flee in terror or beg to stay.

Chef Malouf is remaking New York history here, reviving a ritual Joseph Mitchell described in a 1939 *New Yorker* piece, "All You Can Hold for Five Bucks." To "throw a beefsteak" was a rite of male nostalgia that began in the saloons, workingmen's clubs, and political clubs of eighteenth- and nineteenth-century New York and continued right up until World War II. Tonight someone has brought a 1915 photo that shows a group of men throwing a beefsteak at the New York Furniture Exchange. We look at men standing and sitting in white aprons and chef's hats, in front of large hunks of spit-grilled beef, soon to be cut into steaks served on slabs of bread for plates, like medieval trenchers. Beef was a man's world, and New York threw its beefsteaks in the wake of London's all-male beefeating clubs of the eighteenth and nineteenth centuries, especially the Sublime Society of Beefsteaks founded in 1736 by William Hogarth, among others. The Beefsteaks, as they called themselves, were a refinement of the Beefeaters — the Buckingham Palace Yeomen of the Guard, whose monthly ration per man in 1813 was 24 pounds of beef, 18 pounds of mutton, and 37 gallons of beer, quantities that would put tonight's boys to shame.

Beefsteak throwing in Manhattan evolved over the two centuries when the city, unlikely as it seems now, was a major center for raising, slaughtering, and butchering cattle. Just as goods mysteriously fall off the back of trucks today, extra cuts from butcher shops on the East and Hudson rivers would find their way into saloons, taverns, oyster houses, or similar cellar "dungeons" with sawdust floors, where men sat on kegs to consume their steaks and wash them down with buckets of beer. Clubs like Tammany Hall found that a competitive orgy of gluttony to determine who "drank the most beer, ate the most steak, and got the most grease on his ears" was a good way to pay off favors and increase male bonding. Women were let into the party after they got the vote, whereupon they promptly corrupted the feast with frills like cocktails, vegetable relishes, seafood starters, and — horror of horrors — table linen.

Although men far outnumber women at the Beacon Beefsteak, there are starters: wheels of cheddar cheese, along with platters of shrimp and crab remoulade. The Wall Street reporter next to me insists we eat the shredded crab with our fingers, and I'm certainly not going to be caught out in a ladyism. We also work our way through lamb kidneys wrapped in bacon, mini-burgers on tiny buns, double-rib lamb chops, and thick-cut French fries. Delicious as these burgers are, made from ground scraps from the choicest of beef cuts, the short loin, they still remind us that hamburgers are not as American as steaks. Hamburger has a foreign name and a foreign history, and the meat requires a culinary tool — a grinder — and the application of a chef's hands to shape it into patties. In any case, I need to pace myself. After all, this meal was advertised as all you can eat for $85, and it would be easy to fill up on beer alone, since every time I put down my schooner it is magically refilled.

But it's the beef I'm here for, the primal experience of the carnivorous American omnivore, sinking fingers and jaws into a chunky two-inch-thick shell steak cut from a 15-pound short loin of prime Black Angus, dry-aged 38 days. The loins are grilled on spits over roaring flames to produce a crust black as a merry-widow corset, protecting a bordello-pink interior, sliced on cutting boards by big men wielding knives, and finally dipped in a finger-licking sauce of butter, drippings, and Worcestershire sauce. Away with the effeminacy of serrated knives and foppish forks. It's every caveman for himself, clasping his meat like a hunk of mastodon, gnawing flesh that resists seductively before it yields, squirting fluids red with blood and fat over my hands and down my chin to the anomalous apron below. We are one in our carnal desire. We forget everything but vestigial echoes of cannibal rites, blood sacrifice, the communal sharing of slaughtered flesh. Elbows out, the men sitting either side of me lunge for the platter to see who can sop up the most sauce with their bread and fill their triple-sized shot glasses from the bottles of Maker's Mark that line the tables, to see who can toss down the most boilermakers. This meal is not for wimps. As we tear and chew and slurp, the band segues to jazz and then to old pop favorites like "A Bicycle Built for Two." In a moment we are all on our feet together, singing "God Bless America."

"THE BEEFSTEAK IS American," William Allen White wrote in *The Nation* in 1923. He went on to specify that an American beefsteak is big, thick, and rare — by preference, a 4-pound T-bone, broiled solo and served without condiments. "It is not regional," he said, but national and democratic, "the same on every American table," from Seattle to Palm Beach. It's the same because it is cooked primitively, above or below the flame, denuded of associations of race, class, color, or creed that appear in the cultural transformation of any food from raw to cooked. Beef is the one meat we eat nearly raw, and for some of us, the bloodier the better. As we shall see, blood matters.

Even before the resurgent nationalism that rose after Manhattan lost its two front teeth and America its prolonged innocence on September 11, 2001, there had been an outbreak of steakhouses and an increase of beefsteak on home tables everywhere in America. In New York alone, classic steakhouses like Peter Luger, Sparks, Old Homestead, Gallagher's, Keens, Frankie & Johnnie's, Smith & Wollensky, and the Palm had been jostled by upscale newcomers like BLT Steak, BLT Prime, Strip House, Nick & Stef's, and Bull & Bear. In Las Vegas, steakhouses had multiplied like poker chips, attracting celebrity chefs as diverse as Jean-Georges Vongerichten, Charlie Palmer, Tom Colicchio, Eric Klein, and Emeril Lagasse. Nationally, the success of classic steakhouse chains like Morton's and Ruth's Chris had spawned rivals as unlike as Michael Jordan's, Bobby Van's, Texas Roadhouse, Longhorn, Landry's, and Ryan's. Steakhouses seemed to be the cash cows of the 1990s. As I traveled around the country researching this book, I knew that no matter how grungy and out of the way my motel, I would never be more than half-an-hour's drive from someplace that served overcooked steak and bottled beer. And however murdered in the cooking, the steak was still going to taste better than anything I could order at the roadside clumps of fast-food outlets, exuding the smell of rancid cooking oil. One of the reasons steak is the most American of our dishes is that, in addition to being fast, steak is classy. It's an icon of something "special," whether a backyard barbecue or a night out on the town. It's part of our democratic code that everyone shall win and all shall have prizes. Steak is one of those prizes.

As White suggested eighty years ago, steak is its own category, the pinnacle of the American food chain. Last year, a research team claimed that steak eaten "as is" was the single most popular beef dish in America. "As is" presumably means unprocessed, untreated, unflavored, unmarinated, un "value-added" — the red muscle and bone thing in itself — sold in single packs labeled rib eye, sirloin, tenderloin or filet mignon, porter-house, T-bone, and strip steak, ready to be unwrapped and thrown on "the barby." Significantly, low-income consumers ate steak nearly as often as high-income consumers and ate more beef of all kinds than high-income ones did. The high price of steak is one reason the U.S. beef market is the largest revenue generator in our entire agricultural industry ($49 billion in 2005). The average consumption per person of all cuts of beef in 2005 was 66.1 pounds, second only to chicken at 84.3 pounds per person. A beefsteak, however, may cost eight times as much as chicken, so if price is not the major determinant, what is?

Not surprisingly, one answer is gender. Steak is not only guy food, but he-man food. I remember World War II as a time when we civilians ate no red meat because it all went to our fighting boys, to whom the U.S. Army issued nearly half a pound of animal protein each day. Russell Baker has described this as "beef madness . . . when richly fatted beef was force-fed into every putative American warrior," but beef was less fatted then than now, and our warriors were delighted to be fed any meat that wasn't Spam. But while few American men nowadays get to be warriors, despite the number of wars around the globe, they still eat the lion's share of the beef. In 2005 men aged 20 to 39 ate the most beef and the most steak, a substantial 86 pounds of beef per person, and out of that, nearly 25 pounds of steak. Women of the same age group ate about 52 pounds of beef, of which only 11 pounds was steak. "The more men sit at their desks all day," the nutritionist Jean Mayer points out, "the more they want to be reassured about their maleness by eating those large slabs of bleeding meat which are the last symbol of machismo."

Steak is also the one food men like to cook, because grilling a slab of bleeding meat is hardly cooking at all. It's as close to hunter-caveman cooking as you can get — a fire and a stick will do it. Civilized cooking involves a woman and a pot of bark or clay to mediate more gently between fresh-killed meat and meat softened for the teeth. Men grill, women boil. Lévi-Strauss distinguishes between boiling and roasting or grilling when he says, "Boiled food is life; roast food death." Or as Jeremy

Rifkin says, "One never thinks of cowboys and boiled beef." Perhaps that's why real men eat steaks and women eat quiche.

BUT WHERE EXACTLY did Beacon's steaks come from? They're not like anything I would find in my local supermarket, with its aisles of fluorescent-lit counters embedded with gleaming Cryovac packs of "as is" steak, which in fact means pre-cut, pre-trimmed, and frequently pre-tenderized, one thin steak at a time. As a Greenwich Village eater, however, I'm lucky because I can order my steaks from one of the last, and for me the best, butcher shops in Manhattan, the Florence Meat Market at 5 Jones Street, within walking distance of my apartment. The shop was started by Jack Ubaldi in 1936, when there were twenty-six butcher shops in Manhattan, bought by Tony Pellegrino in 1976, and by present owner Benny Pizzuco in 1996. Pizzuco gets his beef, as does the Beacon, from a handful of remaining wholesalers in the Washington Meat Market, officially known as Gansevoort, along the Hudson River between Fourteenth and Little West Twelfth streets. Even twenty-five years ago, when I stumbled over its Belgian cobblestones past beefy guys hauling carcasses, the market was but a shadow of its former self. Today, invaded by trendy boutiques, bistros, nightclubs, and glass-walled hotels, it is but a whisper of what it was in its glory days in the late 1800s, after the Hudson Railroad in 1847 laid street-level tracks along the river to keep supplies moving for 250 slaughterhouses and meat packers.

It's hard to think of Manhattan, a small rock with steel-and-glass skyscrapers perched on it, as cow country. But Manhattan was once a major cattle site for every aspect of the beef industry, and until World War II, Manhattan was the largest slaughtering/processing site on the entire Eastern seaboard and the fifth largest in the country, exceeded in volume only by Chicago, Kansas City, Omaha, and St. Louis, all of them in the far more spacious Midwest. Today the sleek slab and curves of the United Nations Headquarters overlook the East River on what was until 1946 an industrial wasteland of slaughterhouses and railroad barge loaders. The coming together of slaughterhouses and railroads was a distinctive link in the formation of American cities, and Manhattan is no exception.

By 1900 traffic was thick at Gansevoort Market, named for the fort at the end of Little West Twelfth Street, where an open-air farmers market offered local produce as well as meat, poultry, and dairy. Traffic was so thick by 1930 that the city decided to elevate the tracks to prevent civilian casualties along Tenth Avenue, better known as "Death Avenue," despite the presence of "West Side Cowboys" who rode on horseback waving red flags in front of the freight trains. Today all that remains of the High Line is twenty-two blocks of elevated concrete and scrap-iron track to nowhere, amputated at both ends, wildly overtaken by weeds, a surreal and melancholy reminder of change. Ironically, nature's subversion will be completed by man's, for new construction work has begun to transform the High Line into a tree-lined pedestrian walkway and an adjoining meat warehouse into a museum of art. Where once cattle were unloaded directly from railway cars to slaughterhouse-packers like Maggio Beef, now the Whitney Museum plans to unload artwork into a Renzo Piano–designed satellite of its uptown site. The Whitney took over from the Dia Art Foundation, after the Dia's hopes for a Meat District Museum collapsed. "In some weird way, it's the cultural people who romanticize the industrial sites," noted Michael Govan, Dia's director. "The meatpackers probably think we're crazy."

"Used to be a hundred places, now there's only three," says Raymond DeStefano, a heavy, big-talking man in his sixties who's worked for Wilmart Wholesalers on Washington Street for the last forty years. DeStefano blames Cryovac for the death of butchering. Commercial meat packers first "came over with a truck of boxed beef in Cryovac in the '80s," he remembers. "We tried to prevent them because we have a union. So we all went to jail. It didn't do any good, no good at all." He knows that butchering is a dying art, and it makes him sad. He's spent his life butchering. He came to this market with his grandfather in a horse and wagon and held the horse for him while he bought four quarters for his butcher shop on Houston Street. His grandmother was the one who taught him butchering. When he was eight, she put a pillow on a chair so that he could stuff the sausages. During the Korean War, he was a paratrooper in the 101st Airborne Division. After he was wounded, he was sent to France, where he "really learned to cut meat" for the U.S. Army commissary in Orléans. Those days of slaughtering and butchering reek of the good times he had in Paris, Orléans, Olivette. "It's very romantic. You get a flat-bottom boat, you sit in it, you go down the river nice and easy with the weeping-willow trees hitting you in the face." But here? Now? "They want to put us at Hunts Point," he said, referring to the wholesale food market in the Bronx. "There you have to take what they want to give you. Everything will be choice, not prime. The mom-and-pop stores are gone. Then, when you came into our butcher shop and said, 'I need one lamb chop,' you got it. Hands-on, nice, personal. You got home and the damn thing tasted delicious. Why? It was cut by hand in front of you."

If you cross Washington Street and look up, you see the chopped-off end of the High Line. If you look beneath it toward the river, you see a large courtyard enclosed on two sides by a red brick double-story building, with red doors punctuating the loading docks and a number of black-and-red trucks sporting the name DeBraga and Spitler, a wholesale company that has been here since the 1930s. DeBraga and Spitler were joined in the 1950s by Marc Sarrazin, a butcher from Charolles, France, home of Charolais cattle. Marc Sarrazin eventually became president of the firm, and his son inherited both his father's name and the business he'd grown up in. Marc Jr. is now in his fifties, a square-built man with quizzical eyebrows and a good smile. I'd met him first at the Beacon Beefsteak dinner because he'd provided the beef — twenty-five dry-aged bone-in strip loins of Certified Angus Beef weighing 17 pounds each or 400 pounds total, which translated into 250 to 300 net pounds of steak. For 150 beefeaters, that's a lot of beef. Marc explained to me that the strip loin (which is simply the short loin with a little piece of tenderloin removed) is the traditional steak-eater's steak. In the East, we call it "New York Strip." Marc handpicks the best of them for the event and puts them on the shelf for aging. How do you judge what's best? You begin with a guaranteed brand, like Certified Angus Beef. This country slaughters around 700,000 cattle every single week, Marc explains, and only 2 percent of those will be Certified Angus. If you select Certified Angus Prime, the amount produced is less than 0.75 percent. The same is true of Certified Angus Natural (no hormones, antibiotics, or animal by-products), which is what Chef Malouf uses now.

Marc's father joined up with the Certified Angus Beef program in 1982, and his firm became the first licensed distributor for it in the United States. His office is lined with plaques awarding Bronze Club Membership to companies "purchasing in excess of one million pounds of Certified Angus Beef per year"; these days Marc's company purchases double that amount. When the government lowered beef-grading standards twenty-five years ago, the association got the USDA to certify its standards and then trademarked them as a brand name. It was a smart piece of marketing that provoked two decades' worth of imitators pushing knockoff products, and I'd already heard lots of cynical remarks from beef producers about how every ordinary black steer was being claimed as Angus. Nowadays the association distinguishes its "Certified Angus" from mere "Angus-type cattle," and says that less than one in six meets their standards of marbling, maturing, and yield grade.

"It's very, very expensive," Marc says of Certified Angus, "but quality beef is something people want." His people are chefs and restaurants who demand the best — Daniel, Le Bernardin, Le Cirque, Bull & Bear — and his job is to get it for them. "We're the number-one white-tablecloth distributor in New York City and the Tri-state area." He's told me that most of his beef comes from a pair of midsized packers, Nebraska Beef Company and Moyer Packing, with plants in Pennsylvania and Wisconsin, who in turn are owned by the giant packer Smithfield. This is feedlot corn-fed beef, which has "the tenderness and texture that Americans want," he says. "That last hundred days on corn gives them a little more marbling, and I love the flavor, I grew up on it. That's what I'm accustomed to." Of beef in general, he says, "If I have steak, I feel I've eaten well. I don't have the same satisfaction with a piece of fish. Maybe it's the chew factor. A piece of halibut is delicious, but you chew it and it's gone."

WHEN HENRY HUDSON, hired by the Dutch East India Company in 1609 to find a trade route to India, had his first glimpse of the three rivers and a cliff that would become New York Harbor, he brought out knives, hatchets, and beads to trade with natives who on occasion became violent. "It's ironic," writes Russell Shorto in *The Island at the Center of the World*, "that immediately upon entering the watery perimeter of what would become New York City, these two things take place: trade and violence." It was trade that brought the Dutch across the Atlantic, and it was for the purposes of trade that the Dutch West India Company landed the first cattle in 1625 on the island of Nieuw Amsterdam. Within five years, the company inventoried 60 cows and 47 horses, but grain shortages from failing wheat crops diminished the herds, and new boatloads of cattle had to be sent from Holland. Although the company collapsed in 1651, the Dutch remained preeminent in the Eastern colonies as skilled butchers, while cattle pens and slaughterhouses began to crowd lower Manhattan. The small stream that ran along the palisades — *de wal* — which the Dutch had built across the lower part of the island to keep the natives out was known as Bloody Run during the winter slaughtering season, when as many as 4,000 cattle might be slaughtered on its banks. Eventually such facilities became so numerous and so odoriferous that they were ordered to move to a public facility created for them on Pearl Street, to the north of *de wal,* or Wall Street.

Wall Street is the proper name to link cattle with money. Unlike dairy cows, which pay for their room and board with milk and calves, cattle raised for meat are freeloaders until sold. The Latin word for money, *pecunia,* comes from *pecus,* or cattle, and Roman coins were often stamped with the figure of a bull; our word *capital* comes from *chattel,* meaning cattle; our phrase "bull market" comes from the potential of breeding more cattle. Anciently, then, from the domestication of Caucasian aurochs 8,000 years ago, one measure of a man's wealth was his "property in cattle," the value of which was not realized until the property was traded or sold — as meat, hide, tallow, bones. From the beginning, to talk about cattle was to talk about property and about moving that property to market. During the sixteenth and seventeenth centuries, both Spain and England enjoyed a large cattle surplus, so they were motivated in their own homelands to find ways of getting cattle to market efficiently. In Las Marismas, the marshlands of southern Spain where the Guadalquivir met the Atlantic, *vaqueros* on horseback rounded up herds of wildish Andalusian cattle and drove them to the market cities of Sevilla and Córdoba. In Britain, drovers from the Scottish Highlands herded their shaggy Highland cattle on foot along drover trails to London. Cattle were a common sight in London streets until the middle of the nineteenth century, when the Smithfield live-cattle market was finally removed to Islington. The concentration of slaughterhouses in London was a common complaint of citizens like Charles Dickens, who cataloged their evils in *Oliver Twist:* "The ground was covered, nearly ankle-deep, with filth and mire; a thick steam perpetually rising from the reeking bodies of the cattle, and mingling with the fog."

Trade was in the mind of Pilgrim Edward Winslow when in 1624 — just a year after the Dutch came to Nieuw Amsterdam — he landed the first livestock in New England: "three heifers and a bull." He wanted to establish a breeding herd of Devonshire reds, not just to supply milk and labor for his farm, but to provide a surplus for trade. Livestock was the root of England's economy and its expansion overseas, since in the seventeenth century, England had the highest ratio in Europe of livestock to people (in 1696, 4.5 million cattle, 12 million sheep, and 2 million hogs to 5.3 million people), and had already exported its surplus meat from "dry cows" and its dairy products from "milch cows" throughout Europe.

In New England, even though colonists complained about how inferior native grasses were to English ones, their herds expanded rapidly, along with markets in which to sell them. While the New England landscape wasn't suitable for monocultures like tobacco in the South or sugarcane in the West Indies, the British colonists' mixed agricultural practices encouraged a continuing surplus of cattle, which they exported live or salted. As trade increased in the 1640s, slaughtering shifted from local farms to concentrated sites in port cities. The family of Thomas Pynchon in Connecticut was typical in moving cattle down the Connecticut River to Warehouse Point, New Haven, where they would be slaughtered, packed, salted, and shipped to the West Indies.

In 1521, just two years after Cortés's first landing and a century before Winslow landed his cattle in Massachusetts, Spaniard Gregorio de Villalobos had landed the first cattle — "six heifers and a bull" — on the mainland of Mexico. But the cattle Villalobos brought with him had been born not in Andalusia, but in Hispaniola, where Columbus, on his second voyage in 1493, had landed a small number of cattle, "both for food and to assist the settlers in their work." Food first, then farm labor, then trade. In their own country, the Spanish had already established "an entrepreneurial, market-based, specialized cattle-ranching system" in Andalusia, where city fathers owned herds of cattle fed on the open range and tended by workers or slaves. A business model was in place for Spanish entrepreneurial explorers and conquistadors as they swarmed to the New World to make their fortunes. Early on, Columbus had suggested to the Court that he pay for the cattle on his second voyage by sending back "Cannibals" as slaves, but the Court declined and soon cattle were paying for themselves. Luckily, Hispaniola ecology and Andalusian cattle were a perfect match. In the wet heat of the Indies, forage grew continuously and the tough longhorn breeds loved the heat. They reproduced so quickly that within a decade hundreds had gone wild and beef had become so abundant that the animals were killed merely for tallow and hides. That cattle could be labeled personal property by branding was no small part of their charm. Cortés's brand was a triple Christian cross, although when he partnered with Antonio de Mendoza, the first viceroy of New Spain, to set up a cattle business, he had the cheeks of the natives he enslaved to tend them branded with a G for *guerra*, or war.

The first cattle to cross the present-day border between Mexico and the United States were the 500 "big and little cattle" brought by Francisco Vasquez Coronado in 1540 to feed his sizable expedition as it searched for a city glittering with gold, the fabled Cibola. After two years of wandering through New Mexico, the expedition failed, but many of the cattle and the thousand horses that also accompanied it escaped or were abandoned to the wild, so that the animals prospered even as the men did not. It is said that during the following two centuries, the spread of wild Spanish mustangs on the Plains exceeded any other introduction of a new species in a new land, and certainly it sped the transformation of nomadic Plains Indians into warriors. The first European to successfully bring in a breeding herd of any size (legend claims 7000, but 2500 was more probable) was Juan de Onate in 1598, at San Juan de los Caballeros, north of the Rio Grande, which launched the Texas cattle industry a good twenty-two years before Pilgrim Edward Winslow had even set foot on Plymouth Rock.

The American cattle industry was born nationally at the crossroads of space and speed: while nature provided a vast "free" land where untold numbers of cattle could feed, the European immigrants provided ingenious methods of crossing that land with increasingly unimaginable speed — first by horse, then by train, truck, and plane — to concentrate its slaughtering, packaging, and distributing in urban centers. "Cows and cowboys might be symbols of a rugged natural life on the western range," the historian William Cronon writes, "but beef and pork were commodities of the city."

As New York became the major city of the East Coast, writes Roger Horowitz in *Putting Meat on the American Table,* it also became its major cattle market, where cattle raised in upstate New York, New Jersey, Connecticut, and Massachusetts were shipped by boat or ferry to central stockyards on the Lower East Side (by tradition, near Bull's Head Tavern). Butchers licensed to sell in the public markets killed the cattle during the cool of night in small slaughterhouses and sold beef cut to order for customers the next day. A butcher named Thomas F. De Voe claimed that the term "porterhouse" arose in 1814 after a tavern keeper on Pearl Street, who sold a dark beer called porter, ran out of steak and was forced to cut from a large sirloin generally used for roasting. The cut proved popular and the name stuck, as did the story. In his *Market Book* (1846),

De Voe wrote that when he lived at Mulberry and Spring Streets in 1822, there were 25 to 30 slaughterhouses within 200 yards of his house. By 1850, Manhattan had 531 butcher shops across the city, in addition to public markets. As the railroads massively increased cattle traffic to Manhattan, the Pennsylvania Railroad built holding pens in New Jersey, whence barges would ferry cattle across the Hudson to slaughterhouses along Twelfth Avenue and Thirty-fourth Street. Traffic was so heavy in the 1870s that a "Cow Tunnel" was built beneath Twelfth Avenue to serve as an underground passage, and it's rumored to be there still, awaiting designation as a landmark site.

As late as 1880, Horowitz writes, "New York was still the nation's leading beef-producing center" because New York was a major beef consumer. To widely separate the place of slaughter from the point of sale and consumption was not really possible until refrigeration was added to transport. It was clear to an Easterner like Gustavus Swift, after he'd moved from Massachusetts to Chicago, that it would be far cheaper to transport butchered meat, or "dressed beef," than livestock, because meat accounts for only 60 percent of a cow's weight. Swift was the first to devise refrigerated railroad cars, cooled by ice harvested along the Great Lakes and brought to ice stations along the train routes. This was the first major step in separating the producers and packinghouse/processors of meat from the eaters of it.

THAT THE CATTLE boom in the second half of the nineteenth century coincided with our first major industrial boom was no accident. The shift from a rural small-farm economy to a giant urban industrial one was tectonic, and as permanent as the San Andreas Fault. In a mere twenty years, from 1867 to 1887, urban livestock markets shifted from the East to the Midwest, intensifying in turn the shift from the mixed farming of the East to large-scale ranching in the West as settlers, entrepreneurs, and engineers moved ever westward, gobbling up land. Between 1867 and 1880, four major railroads crossed the Plains — the Union Pacific, Kansas Pacific, Northern Pacific, and the Santa Fe. Within this period, the slaughter of America's buffalo increased in speed and efficiency so that by 1893, only 300 of the original 60 million were left. "Nobody in history consumed buffalo the way the railroads did," Ian Frazier writes. "The remaining buffalo . . . disappeared up the tracks like water up a straw." As the buffalo disappeared, they were replaced not just by iron railroad tracks — nearly 193,000 miles of them — but, as General Phil Sheridan said with glee, by "speckled cattle and the festive cowboy." Cattle drives had begun decades earlier, but the railroads opened new markets for the surplus of cattle that had gone wild in Texas during the Civil War, and the number and range of the drives increased exponentially.

I choose 1867 as the beginning of the end because it marked the creation of the first "cowtown" in Abilene, Kansas, thanks to the convergence of the Chisholm cattle trail with the Kansas Pacific branch of the Union Pacific Railroad. Abilene is the controversial destination that father John Wayne and son Montgomery Clift fight over in Howard Hawks's 1948 *Red River.* Joseph C. McCoy — no cowboy, but a fast-talking young cattle entrepreneur from Illinois — built stock pens at Abilene, then persuaded the railroad to lay down a siding, then persuaded trail herders driving the Chisholm from the Gulf Coast of Texas to push on north beyond Wichita to Abilene, where he would buy their herds and ship them north and east. In two years, 300,000 cattle had been shipped through Abilene, mostly to Chicago for slaughtering and packing.

In 1867 Armour Meat Packers opened their first plant at the Union Stock Yards in Chicago, just three years after nine railroad companies agreed to create a centralized stockyards on a 320-acre swamp at the city's edge. That same year, Parker Earle patented the first refrigerator car after he shipped 200 quarts of fresh strawberries from his farm in Cobden, Illinois, to Chicago on the Illinois Central Railroad and kept them cool with 100 pounds of ice in straw-lined chests. "Time had conspired with capital to annihilate space," Cronon writes rather grandly. But certainly time and ingenuity conspired with producer capital and consumer desire to achieve America's twin goals of speed and mobility.

These were the goals of the beef industry a century and a half ago, and they have remained unchanged from their first corporate expression in the vertically integrated Beef Trust made up of the Big Five slaughter-packers: Armour, Hammond, Swift, Morris, and Cudahy. Earlier in the nineteenth century, as soon as corn began to be planted as a monoculture in the Midwest, many railroad cities like Cincinnati, or "Porkopolis," had built industrial slaughter and packing plants in order to turn swine into pork. But the Beef Trust took the industrial model of combined operations to a new level. Within this same twenty-year period, Chicago came to control 50 percent of the cattle market in America, and by 1900 had increased its control to 90 percent, with the Trust fixing prices on both ends — for producers and consumers. At the same time, the cattle population in America more than doubled, from 15 million in 1870 to 35 million in 1900. By World War I, despite the thousand listed meat packers in the United States, the cartel of the Big Five, financed by Eastern investors, operated as the equivalent of a First World culture of capitalists exploiting a Third World workforce of agriculturalists and ranchers.

Ironically, 1867 also marked the last grand gesture of another era and another meat culture altogether, when Les Halles in Paris saw the unveiling of the architectural splendor of the abattoir called La Villette. Here each ox was killed in its own separate booth, in a long line of booths beneath the glass-domed ceiling, as if the slaughter was simply an extension of the "handicraft methods" of a traditional peasantry. France, smaller than Texas and with agricultural practices as ancient as the Celts, could absorb burgeoning industrialism without making it the model for everything else. America, the size of the whole of Europe and fired by everything new, promised to redeem the sloppiness of hand-worked agriculture by the precision of mechanics.

Nature took revenge. The Great American Cattle Bonanza was over in a mere twenty years. In the winter of 1886–87, unrelenting blizzards decimated Wyoming and Montana cattle in the "Great Die-Off," when "one could have walked for miles on the bodies of dead animals." Natural catastrophes, topping the man-made devastation wrought by overgrazing and wire fencing, lessened the enthusiasm of foreign investors, including such titled royals as the Earl of Aberdeen and Baron Tweedmouth. Most im-

portant, the disasters on the Great Plains ended the period of land grabbing by corporations, which had been encouraged by the Homestead Act
of 1862, and began the period of market grabbing by industrialists.

Yet those twenty years had etched a schism in the American imagination that paralleled the physical divide of the 100th meridian. The sudden, invasive presence of the urban Machine created a deep nostalgia
for lost Wilderness, which our stories often presented as the conflict of
Eastern capitalist against Western cowboy. But history shows that these
figures were twinned heroes in our collective fantasies of progress, as in-
terdependent as day and night. Both the man of ideas and the man of
action were driven by a vision of man triumphant over space and time.
While one relied on technical invention, the other relied on personal
virtue. One looked to the future, the other to the past, but both com-
manded motion and speed like supermen for whom violence is just stuff
that happens. This one brief historical period provided the proscenium
for our national epic rendered ambiguously, violently, and powerfully by
Western movies for the next hundred years. In the opening scene of
Dodge City in 1939, the race between the stagecoach horses and the railroad engine with its two cars enacts the paradoxical conflict and agreement between cowboy Errol Flynn and railroad baron Henry O'Neill.
"It's progress!" shouts Colonel Dodge. "Iron horses, iron men." But when
Flynn asks one of his pals what's up in Dodge City, the cowboy replies,
"Gamblin', drinkin' and killin'. Mostly killin'."

What I remember in the movies I grew up on was not the killin' but
the speed: cops chasing crooks, cowboys chasing Indians, Indians chasing buffalo, horses chasing trains, trains chasing cars, and pretty soon,
airplanes chasing anything that moved. The fantasy of moving with speed
across limitless space, grounded in the belief that good guys would inevitably win — thanks to their moral rectitude *and* their technology —
was America's bread and butter. When seventy years later I rose to join
my fellow beefsteak eaters at the Beacon in singing "God Bless America,"
there was grief in the moment as well as pride. The twin towers of the
World Trade Center had fallen but two years before. The toppling of

those towers, wrote one commentator, was like the sinking of the *Titanic*, in undermining America's belief in "the *inevitability* of progress and the *infallibility* of technology." At the very moment we were celebrating America's greatest symbol of abundance, beef, we were aware of contradictions we hadn't known before, at least not here, not in New York, that most fantastic of America's great towered cities that aspire to scrape the sky.

◆ Breaking the Wild ◆

Riding a bucking steer, bull, or bronco, turned work into sport at the roundups that became rodeos. *Frank Leslie's Illustrated Newspaper*, May 5, 1888, based this lithograph on a photograph by C. D. Kirkland of Cheyenne, Wyoming.

—————————————————————◆—————————————————————

EVEN IN MAY AT 6:00 A.M., with mist clouding the mesquite, it's hot. I crawl sweating behind Fred, a retired high-school superintendent whose camouflage suit is better suited to the job of big-game guide than my thin cotton tunic, which catches on the thorns of the catclaw bush. Through steamed glasses I can barely make out his bulk ahead. Suddenly he stops and points at the ground. The sand holds the clear imprint of a large paw. "Bigger than a bobcat's," Fred whispers. "Maybe a mountain lion — one's been reported."

I hold my breath. A few yards farther, he points again. On the ground is a cone-shaped mound of black pellets the size of goat turds. "Nilgai territorial scat," he whispers. Immediately he straightens and puts his fingers to his lips. He points directly ahead as we crawl on hands and knees toward an edge of brush where the mesquite ends and open field begins. I see the silhouettes of more than half a dozen of them, feeding. A huge blue-black male, maybe 800 pounds, is no more than thirty yards in front of me, broadside. Short horns, small tail, huge torso, a flat black profile against the sun. We are downwind, so unless I make a noise, my big guy will go on eating, unaware that we are here.

We are hunting, with Fred's skill and knowledge, a wild animal. That is Fred's job, to guide hunters, and we've spent nearly an hour in his jeep, driving around to find a group of nilgai we could sneak up on. Fred has told me that the target shot is just behind the shoulder, in order to hit lungs or heart or both. I've never shot anything in my life, don't know how to shoot, eyes aren't good enough to shoot, but at this one moment narrative has taken over and some ancient rumbling in my gut tells me to kill because I can. I want to finish the job for the simple reason that I have a perfect shot. Instead, I raise my camera and shoot.

When we get back to camp, I tell the guys that I can't believe I wanted to kill. They laugh. What they mean is, "Welcome to the club."

The club in Texas is big. Very big. I'm at Danny Butler's Camp, which is part of his 22,000-acre ranch in Hidalgo County, just north of the Rio Grande. I'm staying in a small cabin with two air conditioners and a ceiling fan, and I'm still hot. I hadn't come here for game. I'd flown down to the little airport at McAllen to find cattle and history. I found few cattle but plenty of history. This southern tip of Texas that hooks way south into Mexico is where the American beef industry began, because Mexico is where American cattle began. In fact, this border country, bounded between Laredo on the west, Brownsville on the east, and the Nueces River on the north, belonged to Mexico until a mere century and a half ago, and the oldest ranches in America still belong to Anglo-Mexican families.

Now the ranches are no longer about cattle. Instead of picturesque herds of longhorns descended from ancient *criollo*, I found a few of the usual commercial breeds, but mostly I found wild and semiwild game. Lots of deer and javelina, of course, but also herds of the bulky Indian antelope called nilgai, African lechwe antelope, scimitar-horned oryx, and even zebra. Danny tells me there are more nilgai now in Texas than in India: 20,000 at the King Ranch, 30,000 at the Kennedy Ranch. "If we don't control their numbers, they'll outeat the whitetail," Dan says. His cousins Monica and Ray Burdette, who live nearby on their several thousand acres, have gone into a combination of ecotourism, guided bird-watching, and deer hunting to preserve the family farm. Another cousin with a historic Hispanic surname, Frank Yturria, has leased one-third of his ranch as a game preserve for ocelots. It's as if this desert wilderness of prickly pear, sage, and mesquite, once described by an imaginative Spanish surveyor as inhabited by "numerous wild animals such as tigers, lions, many snakes," had reverted to its original state.

It's hard to locate yourself in this Texas flatland, where hundreds of miles of straight highway are marked by nothing but electric fences and an occasional metal gate to signify a ranch invisible on the horizon. Danny has suggested we meet at the Whattaburger in Raymondville, which has been selling whattaburgers for fifty years. A sign in the window reads "100% pure American BEEF — Just like you like it." While I'm eating mine (trimmings, fries, and ice water for $4.19), a short man comes in, round face, round brown eyes, and a rim of white hair around his bald spot. For once, no cowboy hat. Danny proves to be a talker, so all I have to do for the next three days is listen. He's just flown in from a Wildlife Confederation meeting in Coeur d'Alene. Twenty years ago, he decided to make wildlife his business, he says, to save the ranch. This was after he'd heard a lecture by noted economist Lester Thurow, who'd said that the American farmer/rancher was through because he could no longer compete globally. Other countries could produce food, as well as cars, far cheaper than we could. "It changed my life," says Dan. "If I know a train is coming, I want to be prepared for it when it hits."

Today he keeps no more than 1500 steers and 600 heifers, and with no children of his own, he'd like to get rid of his cows entirely by giving them to his two nieces and their children for Christmas. "I'm paranoid," he says. "I'm on a fast track to get my ranch changed over to wildlife because the cattle can't pay for it." But maybe ecotourism plus hunting can. Bring the whole family out to camps like his to experience the outdoors and outdoor critters. In Texas you can get a hunting license when you're eight. "Anti-hunters," Dan believes, "are city people who never grew up on a farm."

That evening we sit around an open campfire, modeled on the African hunting safari camps Dan and his family have been going to for the past thirty years. Grateful for the pine and mesquite smoke that drives away bugs, I watch the cook grill some elephant-sized beef sausages and nilgai-sized T-bones. In the shadows, a troup of javelina teeter by on tiny hooves. All kinds of birds are chattering away in the trees. Danny's wife, Shirley, joins us and then his brother, Richard, and his two daughters to swap tales about the real thing, big-game hunting in Africa. One of the girls, Quita, chic as a fashion model, laughs about stalking elands for two weeks and ending up with a leopard instead. Danny's dream, he confesses, is to shoot one of everything, and he's now trying to fill in the gaps. After four trips to Ethiopia, he finally got a mountain nyala. Next on the list is a Roberts gazelle on the Serengeti Plain.

Dan's cousin Monica Garcia Burdette is married to a hunting man who specializes in antlers, as a look at the trophies inside and out of their El Canelo Ranch will tell you. Antlers flow from interior walls, swarm up a pillar supporting the patio roof, and blossom from the branches of a large shade tree outside. "Whitetail deer is a big crop out here," says Lieutenant Colonel Ray Burdette, a tall man with a soldier's posture. "And this crop is all about racks. A small rack is worth $500, but a large one $5000." Retired from the military, Ray offers special hunting tours on their acreage. The Whitetail Buck Package, $3500 for five days, allows a hunter one buck, one doe, one hog, one javelina, and unlimited coyotes. For a couple of thousand dollars more, you can shoot an additional buck. Ray's deer hunts are unusual. Danny tells me that 99 percent of Texans hunting deer use a battery-run corn feeder that spins out a bunch of corn every hour on the hour. "A hunter sits in a stand and waits to see what comes to eat the corn and then shoots 'em."

Ray's on the board of the North American Deer Farmers Association, and a city person like myself is stunned to learn that their 13,000 members farm 700,000 fenced deer in a business worth $19 billion. Texas alone has 1,000 deer breeders, Ray says, and they've just hired a deer farmer to work in Washington as a lobbyist because "we need a guy in politics who's on the inside." Farmed deer are of three kinds: Most are native whitetail harvested for their racks, but recently Americans have begun to farm red and fallow deer for their meat, to compete with New Zealand's export to the States of 1000 tons of venison a year. U.S. deer farmers are now lobbying, Ray says, to get the same free USDA inspection of deer and buffalo that farmers of "traditional" livestock get. However much deer and buffalo are farmed, the government does not yet consider them "traditional" and since processors have to pay for their inspection, they don't want to handle them.

Ray is good at crunching numbers. Right now he has over 200 whitetails and 100 fawns in his pens, which means $2.5 million worth of deer within 40 acres. In contrast, it takes 30 acres to graze a single cow, which he can sell for only $600. Also, he can sell a doe for breeding for $6000, so what's the point of raising cows? In 1950 a calf was worth $350 and a truck $1500. Now a calf's worth $400, but the truck's worth $40,000. You have to find alternative ways to make a living, says Ray. Recently a man offered him $45,000 for one of his breeding bucks, and Ray turned him down. "Wasn't enough money." A deer farmer up the road just sold a buck for $450,000, Ray says. "And the coyotes may get it," Monica adds, "or it may get gored by another deer." But this kind of gamble is a lot better than gambling with cattle because the rewards are as disproportionate as deer racks. An Amish deer farmer in Ohio owns the biggest buck in North America, says Ray, with horns so big "they look like they'd exploded." Semen straws from this deer sell for $3500 a straw, bringing in around $3.5 million a year, so it makes sense to insure it for $15 million. With this kind of dough at stake, deer rustling is not unknown. Ten years ago, what was then the largest deer, Goliath, disappeared one night from his pen. A couple of years later, after a Deer Association member spotted a deer that looked a lot like Goliath in a pen run by a none-too-reputable farmer, the police took the buck's DNA and got a match. Now the real owner is suing the thief for all the money made from the deer's semen. Ray personally has no fear of rustlers. "In Texas the laws are so severe that they've taken all the joy out of crimes like that. Here if you steal livestock or wildlife, it's a felony. You don't want to be caught doing something wrong in Texas."

Despite losing money on their cattle, Ray and Monica still keep a few, mostly Charolais sold "ranch-to-rail," where a buyer comes to the ranch, buys the animals, and loads them directly onto a railroad car to ship to a feedlot. While this cuts out the middleman, neither consumer nor rancher benefits, says Ray. He gets more money selling calves to rodeo team ropers than to feedlots. "For many years the meat packers have driven the cost of beef," Ray tells me. "You got to remember that the NCBA [National Cattlemen's Beef Association] is not a cattle-raiser association. It's a meat-packers' association. Packers don't care where the beef comes from. If they can get it from Canada twenty cents a pound cheaper, they'll buy it, but they don't lower the market price. They just make more money. Since most of the market is for bottom-line beef, if you sell your cattle at the local livestock sale, you'll get hamburger prices for T-bone quality." He knows a few Texas producers who've now hired a custom meat packer so they can market their own product, which includes venison and bison. But at best that means a niche market. "You're never going to go to a McDonald's and say, 'Give me a double-decker bison burger.'"

The only rancher I met in these parts who was still dealing seriously with cattle was a pioneer in breeding deer as well as cattle. Jim McAllen, a courtly man in his sixties, has raised five children and ten grandchildren on one of the oldest continuous cattle ranches in the country. He's been experimenting with whitetail deer breeding for the past twenty years. "I was one of the first to raise them, in 1978," he says. "I got special permits to capture deer, raise them, breed them for antler configuration, then release them to pasture." These weren't for hunting but to improve the genetics of the herd, which takes at least twelve years, six for a doe to mature and another six to get offspring. Nor was it for meat, since whitetail are considered "wild," whether or not farm raised, and all wildlife belongs to the state. Jim gave the meat to state prisons for free distribution. Most restaurant venison, he explains, is "imported access deer," a fancy phrase for red deer, which is related to American elk and was originally imported from India. Despite the prohibition in America against selling game for meat, a lot of wild pigs from Texas end up in Europe, where they're sold as wild boar. The main way Jim makes money from his deer herds is by selling hunts. He's put up a hunting lodge, built an eight-foot "game-proof" fence to keep the deer in, and hires a full-time game manager for hunting season, November through January.

Long before deer, Jim was interested in breeding cattle, chiefly Beef-masters, having got his first Beefmaster bull in 1942 from Tom Lasater, father of Dale, who is one of the big names in grass-fed beef and prairie preservation. The Lasater family ranch in Colorado just south of Denver has become a kind of mecca for the grass-fed movement. Tom Lasater had created the Beefmaster breed by making a three-way cross among Brahman, Hereford, and Shorthorn, a radical innovation in the early 1940s, to combine the heat-resistance of Indian Brahman with the meat-building capacities of the English breeds. Jim said he'd done a perfor-mance test and found that the Beefmaster gained six pounds a day on grain, where their other steers gained only three. Now he's trying to re-duce genetically the breed's heavy dewlaps, which get so cut up by brush and cactus thorns that they must be sent to slaughter. "I got braggin' rights on the Beefmaster Sire Registry," he says, "and while Dale Lasater may call genetics 'voodoo science,' one of my bulls was recently the cover guy on the *Beefmaster Cowman.*"

A number of Beefmaster cattlemen have formed a limited partnership to produce a marketing program they've named for famous Texas base-ball pitcher Nolan Ryan. Their goal is to match the success of the Certi-fied Angus Beef program in making a breed a brand name that signifies quality. "Because of marketing, marketing, marketing, everything has gone black; everyone's going for all-black animals," complains Jim's daughter Melissa Guerra, who is herself a good marketer of Rio Grande products. But where Angus cattlemen aim for a high degree of marbling, Beefmaster cattlemen aim for tenderness, says Jim. A meat scientist named Keith Belk, whom I would later meet at Colorado State Univer-sity, has devised a way to measure scientifically the degree of tenderness of a rib eye. Belk found that the color of lean meat, calibrated by an infrared-scan camera, could indicate tenderness as measured by the Warner-Bratzler shear-force test, which is the industry's standard mea-sure for determining the amount of pressure needed to cut through a piece of meat. According to Belk's research, more important to tender-ness than fat is the quality of the lean. "Marbling is for taste," Jim asserts, "but it doesn't improve the tenderness all that much."

Marbling (and age) are the sole determinants of quality in the official USDA grading system of Prime, Choice, and Select, which in turn determines price. By applying other measures than marbling to the quality of beef muscle, the Nolan Ryan program hopes to develop and promote tenderness in Select beef, so that it will bring a better price. The program has added to genetics both mandatory aging and high-voltage electrostimulation in order to guarantee the customer tender meat or your money back. For a rancher like Jim, machinery like electrostimulation and a patented Smart MV Beef Cam (based on the camera Levi Strauss uses to measure the color of stonewashed jeans, only this one measures the color of red muscle) is as natural a part of raising cattle as genetics if you want to hold on to the ranch.

"THIS WILD HORSE Desert used to be nothing but cactus and wild grasses before cows came," says Jim. The cows "spread mesquite and huisache trees through their dung; and once the screwworm was eradicated, flora and fauna have flourished." Now there's opuntia cactus, rattail cactus, Texas persimmon, Brazil birch. In addition, Jim has planted his homeplace with ebony trees, in full white bloom in May and alive with birds — the kiskiddy flycatcher, vermilion flycatcher, suntail hawk, white-tailed hawk, black-headed oriole, the *karakara* or Mexican eagle, and buzzards they call *sopilote*. Except for the buzzards, this is quite a change from when the Spaniards called the whole stretch of land between Tampico and the San Antonio River El Desierto de los Muertos, the Desert of the Dead.

But time tends to disappear in land like this, along with arbitrary political borders, so it's not hard to imagine in this part of Texas a direct line to the cattle Gregorio de Villalobos landed at Tampico in 1521, the first brought to the mainland of Mexico for the purpose of building a herd, rather than simply supplying meat for soldiers. That same year, Ponce de León landed the first cattle to reach what is now U.S. territory, when he brought a colony of settlers to the west coast of Florida. Columbus had brought cattle with him to Hispaniola on his second voyage, in 1493, and they had so flourished on the year-round forage provided by the tropics that very quickly beef in the Spanish colonies became common food, not a luxury. This Rio Grande borderland reminds us that a century before there was a New England, there was a New Spain, whose colonists settled this land over the next four centuries, raising cattle that were all direct descendants of the *criollo* cattle from Estremadura and Andalusia that Columbus first brought from Cadiz.

But Spanish cattle were not welcomed by native Karankawa and Coahuiltecan Indians, who felt the land was theirs. Nor later by the French, who made their own claims to the western coast of the Gulf, moving south from New Orleans. It wasn't until 1749 that José de Escandón brought colonists north of the Rio Grande to settle fourteen villages, each laid out with a town plaza surrounded by fields for farming and grazing. The King of Spain had given him permission to grant leagues of land from Coahuila in the south to the Nueces River in the north, and Escandón granted them with a liberal hand, sometimes giving as many as 600,000 acres to a single claimant. He divided the land in *porciónes*, narrow strips of land about half a mile wide and sixteen miles long, running inland from the river in order to maximize access to water. So confident was he of success that he named the area Nuevo Santander, after his birthplace in Old Spain. By this time, there was an abundance of both wild horses and wild cattle, and the first ranching consisted largely of rounding up wild cattle for their tallow and hides alone. *Vaqueros* who herded cattle here became known as "brush poppers" from the sound the animals made when they drove through thorny brush. The first cattle drives also began here, when herders gathered cattle along the Rio Grande, then shipped them west to the province of Coahuila and east to the Louisiana Territory.

Tejanos culture had been established along the river for nearly a century when the first capitalist Anglos arrived to mix and match their entrepreneurship with that of the Spanish-Mexicans. The mixture was fertile but also volatile, and when Mexico warred for independence from Spain in 1821 and Texas warred for independence from Mexico in 1836, older Tejanos fled and their lands came available for possession, just as

that of the now-extinct Karankawa had been appropriated by the Tejanos. Since land wars were also race wars, no one expected hostilities to
end with the U.S. government's annexation of the Republic of Texas in
1846 or the conclusion of the war with Mexico in 1848. Nor did they.
Nearly thirty years later, after an Anglo family of ranchers was murdered
in Refugio County, five Mexicans were hanged by a mob of "Regulators,"
whose stated aim was "to make every Mexican who could not give an account of himself either leave the country or take his chances at kicking at
Texas soil with nothing to stand on."

The Rio Grande and its twin ports of Brownsville and Matamoros,
where the river debouches into the Gulf, provided a path to riches for any
number of energetic merchants who made money fast, particularly during the Civil War, and used it to buy land and cattle. Marrying a land-rich
daughter or widow was another primrose path for fortune hunters. The
group of border cattle ranchers I met up with were all descendants of enterprising Anglo-Mexican marriages. Jim McAllen's great-grandfather
was a Scotch-Irishman named John, whose wife possessed the splendid
name of Salome Balli and 95,000 acres of a Spanish land grant to her father that dated from 1767. "Salome's father was a colonel from Mexico,"
Jim told me. "The Spanish didn't want the French nosing west from New
Orleans, so they set up missions and forts and settlements. You had to
prove to Escandón's military representatives that you were improving the
land and establishing cattle, then the government would send surveyors
to the four corners of the rectangular grant. At each corner, they'd throw
sand in the air, dispense blessings and grass seed, and name it for a saint."

However barren the land, it originally provided additional income
through trading salt. A salt lake near the McAllen ranch was named Sal
del Rey and was important to the Spanish for curing hides and meat and
for extracting silver from ore. Jim's daughter Melissa, a cookbook author
and television chef, explained to me how they processed meat. "Once
skinned, the meat was cut into quarter-inch slivers of steak, salted, then
hung on a line in partial sun to help keep off flies and dust. It was called
machacado, or shredded dried beef." Her brother Jim is now marketing
this beef under his own company name, Carnes Latinas. Salt proved to

be a key ingredient in subsequent property claims. While the Treaty of Guadalupe at the end of the Mexican-American War granted settlers the mineral rights to their land, it also claimed the right to tax the salt. The Spanish had set up a salt tax of 20 percent, called the *quinto,* but after the treaty many landowners lost their land in the general legal confusion, either because they failed to pay the tax entirely or they paid on one side of the river and not the other. "Entrepreneurs would buy the land from them right there on the courthouse steps," says Jim. Many were happy to sell because a quantity of land and cattle in country like this could be a hardship. "Who wanted to live out here in this heat in a little rinky-dinky house full of scorpions and spiders and snakes?" Jim asks rhetorically. The ladies would live in town, and on the rare occasions they visited the ranch, it was with a caravan of horses and wagons and a full household staff. "This was not a fancy Southern plantation with lace umbrellas."

These Spanish salt laws are important today because they form the basis of Texan laws about mineral rights, and therefore about oil rights. Not even the Mexican War changed the Texas cattle world as violently as did the discovery of oil at a salt dome called Spindletop near Beaumont in 1901. When Patillo Higgins and Captain Anthony Lucas finally hit oil, they hit it big. Instead of the hoped-for 50 barrels a day, Spindletop produced 100,000 barrels. Red-haired Melissa, who not only grew up here but married the guy who'd grown up on his father's ranch next door, Alberto Guerra, understands about property rights. She explained that every piece of property in Texas has two ownerships: surface ownership and mineral-rights ownership, and mineral rights take precedence. "Mr. Smith may buy a ranch, but if Mrs. Jones owns the minerals on it and a company wants to extract gas on that ranch, Mr. Smith has nothing to say about it." When petroleum was discovered in Reynosa in the 1940s, land values in the Rio Grande exploded. "If you didn't own the minerals, you had to sell because surface land became an expensive liability."

Oil is hardly the dirty little secret of Texas cattle ranching and wildlife hunting; it is out there in the open, in aluminum gas tanks and tall derricks sprouting up through the mesquite. But ranchers like Danny Butler worry about their dependence on oil and gas. Those rights subsidize

Danny's ranch to the tune of $30,000 a month. "Having gas makes you seem like a whole lot smarter rancher," said a Texas woman rancher named Randee Fawcett. But since oil and gas are not renewable resources, these ranchers know they're living on borrowed time. Danny's question to himself is whether he can be a rancher and not a cattleman. There's no shortage of doctors and lawyers who want to buy up his cattle for grazing rights, he says. "It's an excuse to get out of their doctor's uniform or their lawyer's suit and buy a pair of cowboy boots and a cowboy hat and put on jeans and the big belt buckle and fly their airplane in to check on their cattle. We could make good money by leasing the ranch, but the cattle wouldn't be ours, and that's a hard thing for a rancher to say: 'I own the ranch but not my cattle.' I haven't been able to say that yet."

NO PLACE BETTER epitomizes what has happened to Texas cattle ranching than the King Ranch, which evolved over a century and a half from a camp pitched on the banks of the Santa Gertrudis Creek to a megacorporation headquartered in Houston. King Ranch today is about the size of Rhode Island, occupying some 825,000 acres in and around Nueces County, and the men who run it are not cattlemen but "land managers." The ranch is so large that helicopters do the cattle roundups that cowboys once did, and they do it in three hours rather than three weeks. And yet cattle is only a small part of the business. While the company keeps a herd of 60,000 head, hunting is beginning to bring in the same revenue as beef. Butch Thompson, Director of Security and Wildlife at the ranch, puts it this way: "I see a day when nonconsumptive wildlife ops outstrip consumptive ops, but it ain't happening yet." Both are small change ($1 to $3 million) in comparison to the company's two major sources of income: oil ($12 million) and sod ($16 million). Large farming acreage adds to the pot: 70,000 acres in citrus, 57,000 in cotton and milo, 17,800 in sugarcane.

Tourism is also big business in terms of PR. Over 15,000 head of tourists a year pay $7 plus tax to hop in a van with a guide to view a small part of the original homestead Richard King built on a Spanish land grant, Rincón de Santa Gertrudis, in 1853. An orphaned Irish boy from

New York, King ran away to sea at eleven and by sixteen had become a steamboat river pilot in Alabama, where he fought off Seminoles from the Ocochokee riverboat. Later he fought in the war against Mexico with Mifflin Kennedy, another Irish river pilot, who became his business partner. Although no more than five and a half feet tall, King was the type of rugged, determined, hard-drinking, and hot-tempered man you might expect a venture capitalist to be in the early nineteenth century. He parlayed piloting steamboats into owning steamboat fleets, adding to the company of King and Kenedy another Yankee, Charles Stillman, the founder of Brownsville in 1848. After making money shipping salt, wool, and troops for the Mexican War, the company monopolized the cotton trade during the Union blockades of the Civil War. By registering their boats under the Mexican flag, at the war's end they had shipped 300,000 bales of cotton to Matamoros and profited every step of the way.

As a businessman-rancher, King's personal destiny coincided perfectly with America's Manifest Destiny, expressed succinctly by Frederick Law Olmsted of Central Park fame, while traveling in Texas: "We saw the land lying idle; we took it." This was the same man who once spoke of Mexicans as "vermin, to be exterminated." When Olmsted spoke, there were already 70,000 Tejanos, thousands of head of livestock, and hundreds of Indians on this idle land. The Indians did not go quietly. At the time King bought the Santa Gertrudis Ranch, the place was so harassed by Comanches and Apaches that he sought help from the Texas Rangers of Gideon "Legs" Lewis, who formed a land partnership with King.

But King was unusual among Anglo land speculators, who were usually absentee landlords reliant on a foreman and seasonal workers, in that he chose to live on his land in Spanish style. In the Spanish-Mexican way, workers lived on the hacienda as serfs controlled directly by the owner, the *hacendado*. *Vaqueros* traditionally had higher status than peons because they were more mobile, but as Texans moved in, *vaqueros* became cheap labor in comparison to the better-paid Anglo cowboys. The cheapest way to get the cheapest workers was to resettle an entire Mexican village, which King did when he went to buy cattle at Tamaulipas across the border and imported the village to work for him, marching families several hundred miles north. King's workers became known as *los kineños,* "King's people." Today their descendants are often called "Ranch Mexicans," with the kind of slur implicit in "Uncle Toms."

Through the force of personality and the use of armed forces, King was one of the first Anglo cattlemen to become a romantic figure as a rancher, prefiguring cowboy heroes to come. During the Civil War he had had to defend his ranch often against Union raiders assisted by the guerrilla army of Juan Cortina, a rich Mexican rancher who championed the Mexican cause and became mythologized as "The Robin Hood of the Rio Grande." These were rough times, and in the 1870s King fought against organized rustlers in the Peelers War, so called because they killed and skinned (peeled) their stolen cattle on the spot. Mexicans accused of thievery were also killed on the spot during the Rangers War led by Captain McNelly in 1875; suspects were tortured and then hung or shot according to *la ley de fuga* ("prisoner killed trying to escape"). To a man like King for whom personal property was sacred, the loss of a single animal was a declaration of war. "King absolutely hated to have his cattle disappear into Mexico," his biographer Graham wrote, "and Mexican raiders absolutely loved it." When a reporter asked why he carried a double-barreled shotgun instead of the new Winchester rifle, King answered, "Because I'm a businessman, not a sportsman." As the power of cattle barons grew, the violence endemic to land wars and race wars became institutionalized economic wars.

King owned cattle in order to market them and make money. Two changes in the 1870s improved marketing conditions for a capital-growth businessman as radically as they deformed the face of the land: railroads and fences. The Chisholm Trail from Brownsville to Abilene, by way of Waco and Fort Worth, was transformed into a 1,000-mile Union Pacific conveyor belt to Chicago and the East for thousands upon thousands of cattle. In 1876, the year that Custer fell trying to push the Sioux onto reservations and open the West to the white man, King drove 30,000 head of cattle to market at Abilene. In that same decade, King saw the first fence "improvement" using barbed wire, and by 1874 he had fenced 70,000 of his acres, ending abruptly, at least in Texas, the idea of an open range. The expansion of railroads and of fencing effectively killed off the cattle drives, and at King's death in 1885, they were done for good. By that date, King's feudal empire was already out of date. As railroads had transformed the marketing of cattle, the drives had transformed the marketing of the cowboy-vaquero. He had become a migrant worker, seasonal and replaceable, hired for wages by a remote producer, whether a cattleman or a company, and was as dependent as they on the vagaries of finance.

In an increasingly Anglo world, King's family of *kineños* were the last of their kind, for his Spanish ranching style concealed a radical change in substance. The burgeoning American cattle industry was founded not on an agrarian social contract but on a commercial one, which fragmented each part of the process, dividing producers from laborers according to an urban industrial model. As a self-made capitalist, however, King was nostalgically attracted to the image of the *hacendado,* the generous but willful patriarch who exercised absolute power. It was a fashion adopted by many less-colorful Anglo profiteers who worked their way south to the Rio Grande, but it was particularly apt for the man named King. In 1850 he'd supported the Brownsville Separatist Movement, which aimed to create the Republic of the Rio Grande, joining land north of the river with the whole state of Tamaulipas. When King married in 1854, it was to Henrietta Chamberlain, daughter of a Presbyterian missionary. It turned out to be an excellent marriage of God and Mammon, and after King's death La Patrona, as his widow was called, dressed in mourning like Queen Victoria for the rest of her days, which were considerable. She died in 1925 at age ninety-two.

If King was the initiator of a cattle empire, his dynastic successor, Robert Justice Kleberg, was the consolidator. As one Mexican-American landowner remarked later, "King took the land and Kleberg settled it." This ambitious young lawyer had been hired by the widow of one of King's early partners in a substantial and well-substantiated land-grant claim against King. She settled for the measly sum of $5,811.75 at the urging of Kleberg, unaware that he was on retainer to King. For this and other efforts, Kleberg was rewarded with the management of King's property and the hand of his youngest daughter, Alice.

Where King ruled by gun, Kleberg ruled by science. He was one of the first to drill artesian wells and to search for the cause and cure of what we now call Texas tick fever. At his urging, his nephew, Caesar, began to restore wildlife on one of the ranches around 1900 and brought in the first nilgai. Kleberg's eldest son, Richard, became a legislator known as the Cowboy Congressman, who once hired a young aide named Lyndon Johnson. Another son, Bob, leased land to the Humble Oil Company in 1919; after the drill hit seventeen years later, he spent most of his time breeding quarter horses and Triple Crown winners, although he also developed a new breed of cattle, the Santa Gertrudis, from a Brahman bull and a Shorthorn heifer. When he died in 1974, Mister Bob was the last saddleman to run the ranch. Around a hundred King-Kleberg descendants still own shares in the company, but the town of Kingsville and the Ranch form a commodified theme park branded with the "Running W," which the Spanish called "the little snake."

The guide on the tourist van at the Visitor Center points out the original yellow-brick buildings of the Santa Gertrudis School and the 1853 carriage house and the "Colony" cottages, where thirty to forty descendant *kineño* families live now. The guide himself grew up here in a multigenerational cowboy family and tells us that at age twelve boys were permitted to begin to learn cowboying from their dads, if they'd done okay at school. After the original homestead burned to the ground, Henrietta built a new one in 1915, described as Spanish mission with "Mediterranean elements," but in fact it's a fantasy palazzo of arched colonnades and Tiffany windows with farmhouse elements like a courtyard bell to call folks to dinner and a surrounding fence to keep rattlesnakes out. In town the King Ranch Museum sports both a 1926 green Lancia with cowhide seats and a 1949 cream-colored Buick-8 convertible, custom-made into a hunting car named El Kineño. In the King Ranch Saddle Shop, I find a Mexican saddlemaker, Robert Salsas, who makes the best saddles I've seen anyplace. He starts with a wooden tree of laminated pine (stronger than fiberglass) and applies a layer of foam rubber, then multiple layers of leather. Price depends on how elaborately you want the leather carved, since at his rate of $120 an hour, designs like the

basket weave and the floral may cost you $50,000. You can choose be-
tween two main saddle styles: one with a rounded front, the other peaked,
which gives more stability for neophytes. Usually, he says, customers
want the whole package: peaked saddle, saddlebags, boot protectors,
straps, bridle, reins, and the special King Ranch chaps with big silver buttons on the sides. The Ranch used to throw in the horse for free.

ONE EVENING AT dusk, Dan Butler took me to the main white-frame
ranch house beside a lake to meet his family. His mother, Lydia, appeared
classically Spanish in silk skirt and heels, hair very black, lipstick very red,
altogether elegant at eighty-five. Dan's father, who'd been an airplane
pilot from Ohio, was still handsome at eighty-eight, with a white mustache to match his crisp white shirt. They sat on polished mahogany furniture atop Oriental carpets surrounded by hundreds of birds singing in
brass cages. The parrot had been shut in another room to spare their visitor a noisy one-sided conversation. The scene seemed light-years away
from the description by a nineteenth-century traveler to these parts:
"You cannot imagine how desolate, barren, and desert-like this country
is; not a spear of grass, nor a green shrub, with nothing but moving
clouds of sand to be seen on these once green prairies."

Maybe the country had been tamed, but the wild in this border culture is constantly being redefined. Dan had spoken of his mother's bitter-
ness at the racial prejudice she'd experienced as a Mexican throughout
her life. At the same time, she despises the current illegal Mexican immigrants her generation calls "aliens." Frank Yturria, a dapper man in his
eighties, is similarly obsessed with "the illegals swarming across that
river, across that border, thinking they own this country." A former Air
Force officer, banker, government adviser to two Republican presidents,
horse breeder, polo player, and an expert roper who once toured with
Roy Rogers, Frank can speak with authority on a range of subjects. "If
you took the fifteen million illegals we have in this country and put them
back in Mexico, what would happen? A revolution. We have a neighbor
next door that we don't want to explode on us, but talk about terrorism,

what greater terrorism could you have than thousands of kilos of cocaine coming into this country to poison our youth?"

Yturria's voice seems moderate in comparison to the voices of Ranch Rescue, a group of Texas vigilantes who threaten to close the border with machine guns and who call illegals "dog turds . . . ignorant, uneducated and desperate." The illegals regularly cut the fences on all their ranches, Dan says, but not on his because he leaves food out for them and tells them they have to keep moving because he can't harbor them legally. "These are poor people, disoriented," he says. "I found a man and his wife sleeping by one of our water holes and thought it was an animal huddled up there. I told them in Spanish not to worry, drove them to the next fence, pointed them north, and said, 'Follow that line.' The border-patrol guys are fat and the Mexicans are skinny, so when they run, the patrol can't catch 'em."

Staying in motels with signs in English and Spanish that read "No Guns or Weapons Permitted," I spent quite a bit of time driving around Brownsville looking for the Rio Grande, the iconic River I'd seen in dozens of movies but never in life. Downtown Brownsville looked like an ordinary Mexican town of small shops with Spanish names dominated by the structure of a large bridge, but even at the bridge itself, guarded by the usual armed officers, the river was nowhere visible. I asked a passerby, "Where do I have to go to see the river?"

"Go straight, turn right up a little hill, and there it is."

The hill was no more than a hillock with a patch of green grass and a picnic table. Beyond, between reeds and scruffy shrubs, ran a small green rivulet. Rio Piqueño. Many years ago, I learned, an upriver dam had re-duced the Grande to this. Jim told me there was still a hand-pulled ferry between Hidalgo on the American side and Reynosa on the Mexican side. There the river is so narrow that one man can pull a car ferry across by hand on a rope that stretches from one side to the other. But everyone had warned me not to cross. "It's too dangerous now," Jim had said. "There's a lot of bad folks down there, drug-running, people-smuggling, every once in a while a shoot-out." Last time smuggling was this big was the bootlegging days during Prohibition, which brought in the Texas

Rangers. "They were tough and they stopped them, but now the stuff's coming in all the way from Central America, sometimes in a caravan of Mercedes-Benz trucks."

In this borderland, ranchers are caught between nostalgia for the old ways and the need to change them. "The old saying that ranching is a way of life needs to be stomped and buried, because it's destroying farms and ranches," Danny Butler had said. "All the other factories in the United States are having to change. All your other business models, your other industries — Ford, IBM, Microsoft — if they don't change, they won't survive, and neither will we. It's either change or lose the farm." Dan's conviction that ranching is an industry and not a way of life is contradicted, however, by his deep belief that America is still one vast ranching frontier. "We've still got that get-ahead spirit where the harder you work the more you can keep, like Bill Gates," he says, even as he worries about the loss of community among younger generations. "Even on the frontier there was that communal spirit of circle the wagons, right?" His words tumble with moral ambiguity. "Look, we're a new country. We're barely out of Custer's Last Stand. That restaurant in Paris, La Tour d'Argent, is older than the whole of the United States, so we're just getting started. I'm not that far from my ancestors from Scotland or Mexico who came here when land was free and whatever you could fence off and hold was yours. Of course, all of Mexico and Texas originally belonged to the Queen of Spain and of course the Spanish took it away from the Comanches and Apaches up here, and in central Mexico the Spanish just cleaned Montezuma out of everything." Cleaning Montezuma and the Comanches out of everything in the name of that frontier get-ahead and circle-the-wagons spirit is the push-pull embedded in the hearts of these borderland ranchers, whose lives are bonded by family heritage to lands that, down the line, had always belonged to somebody else.

IN EARLY FEBRUARY, the one thing you can count on in the Northeast Kingdom is the cold. But in 2006 this month has been unseasonably warm, and rain has frayed the edges of the usual thick blanket of snow.

As I drive northeast from Burlington toward Mount Manchester, I'm relieved to see large snowflakes falling. I want this corner of northeast Vermont bordering New Hampshire and Quebec to live up to its reputation as one of the coldest spots in New England, a fact not lost on its first settlers in the 1780s. No one from the colonies along the coast seemed to be in a hurry to get to these wild parts, and when they did, they brought sheep, rather than cows. Sheep were far easier to handle in a ruggedly forested land of mountains and streams and rocks that was more like Wales than Devon. When they did bring cattle, they were dairy cattle, good for small pastures and subsistence farming. There was no question of raising cattle as a commodity in this wilderness, and they hardly needed cattle for meat in a woodlands so full of game.

But I'm here to look for beef cattle, on the two-hundred-year-old family farm of Bryan Adams near Passumpsic, a crossroads near Barnet, another crossroads just south of St. Johnsbury. Bryan wasn't easy to find, or even to find out about. While the Vermont Beef Producers Association lists around two hundred members who are raising steers for beef, on what are relatively small farms, I wanted something more. I wanted a farm with a history that went way back, and I wanted a farmer who was using his land and his cattle the way his ancestors had. I wanted an unbroken New England tradition at an ecological extreme. As I turned off Route 5, with snow thick on the ground, past barns weathered like bread loaves, and as my car slipped on the icy road running parallel to Joe's Brook — narrow, rushing, exploding over rocks on its descent from Joe's Pond — I knew I'd found it. Joe, I later learned, was an Indian guide buried in a cemetery in Barnet, where Bryan Adams's sister runs the village deli.

I turn sharp left up the hill from Joe's Brook Road onto Rake Factory Road to Bryan's green trailer with "additions," as he's described it. Someone made wooden rakes up here a century ago, and it's easy to feel time-warped right back there. On the other side of Joe's Road is a cluster of barns and stables, a corral with horses and cows, and a brand-new building with an old board sign, "Deer cut and skinned." This is the new cutting plant Bryan has designed and built, since his business for the past twenty years has been cutting deer. But his night job during this same period was the lobster shift in a factory outside Barnet, which helped to support the four children he had with his ex-wife, and the three more that came with the divorced woman, Sandi, with whom he's lived for the past three years. The first time I called and got Sandi on the phone, she said she had to hang up because she was in the middle of skinning a bear.

In person I see what I'd heard: Sandi is strong, forthright, solid, a blonde with green-blue almond eyes and full lips. She grew up on a farm nearby, the only member of her large family to finish high school. Bryan seems her opposite at first, taciturn and wary until you get him going. He maintains his hippie look of former years with hair that droops long from the bald spot on top, two earrings in the left ear — one a gold ring, the other a silver horse. He wears a Western shirt and a black leather cowboy hat above long ears and puzzled brown eyes. He's not comfortable sitting still and rubs his thick square hands over his face and along his arms. Bryan's new business card says: "Bryan's Custom Cutting, Deer Moose Bear Beef Pork, custom cut, double wrapped, and labeled."

"We're licensed by the state of Vermont to do custom cutting," he says, "but we can't do it for stores. We do it for the individual who's going to put it in his freezer."

Their own beef they raise for friends and family, around a dozen cows at present — three steers, two bulls, and the rest heifers — "more as a savings account than trying to make money." Beef for the family involves a quantity of beef, for together they have eleven siblings: Bryan's father was one of ten, his mother one of fourteen, his grandfather one of eight. But the Adamses are by no means the biggest family in these parts. They're outnumbered by the Bogies, who own their own mountain, and by the Roys, who own a mountain and a croquet factory in East Barnet.

On this New England farm, family comes first, just as it did with my Texas ranchers. But here there's no oil, and hanging on to the land means twenty-four-hour labor under hardship conditions, both economic and ecological. The trailer is wall-to-wall laundry tossed amidst the detritus of four teenage girls and fifteen cats. Another fifteen cats live in the barn. People drop off kittens at the end of the summer because they don't want to buy a cat carrier to take them back to the city, Sandi says. For Sandi and Bryan, every animal is special, with its own name and personality, just like each child. A Persian cat saunters in and studiously ignores us. "Her real name is Jody, but we call her Joe." The many dogs include Casey, half Dalmatian and half Australian dingo. As in Texas, the borders between tame and wild are blurred, but with farm families like the Adamses, who scratch a living in the Northeast Kingdom, hunting is neither a business nor a sport, but a method of survival. Sandi calls coyotes "cotedogs," and she's shot a fair number with her rifle. She is, of course, a crack shot.

City folk would call this a sustainable farm, because it is small-scale and integrated. We go down to the barn to look at the chick house, where they raise broilers because Bryan doesn't like laying hens. I ask about a round plastic barrel with hundreds of brown rubberish fingers inside. It's a plucking machine, Bryan explains, and will hold two to four chickens at a time. Big-eared pigs, white and black, root in a pen next to the chickens, and a small corral holds a couple of boarding horses. In another corral are a few mixed-breed Herefords and Jerseys. They point out a black heifer, Tigger, who'll be a year old in June and kept for breeding. They had a pair of bulls named Hamburger and Cheeseburger, two others they named T-Bone and Porterhouse. "You might as well name them what they're going to be," Sandi says. "Give them a cute name, and the girls are gonna get mad."

Their cows are not strictly grass-fed, because New England winters negate that, Bryan says, and buying hay to supplement what you've grown is too expensive. They're looking into crop silage as "a feeder enrichment" because the calves are coming in mighty thin lately, but so far all they supplement with in winter is cracked corn. He doesn't give it to them every day, but it fills them up, gives them some protein, and calms them down, he says. "Besides, they like you a little better." When Bryan's dad was alive, the family grew their own grains, mostly barley and oats, and had their own granary. "But I don't see me grinding my own flour when I can go get a bag for a buck and half." Still, they're very careful of the grain they buy for livestock. They won't buy medicated grain of any kind for their chicks because "they don't live long enough to get it out of their system."

They've discovered that a lot of people these days want to know what their cows ate. "More and more people don't want grain-fed because that one stupid cow out in Oregon that came from Canada was fed Canadian grain," Sandi says. She's referring to the first cross-border cow discovered in the United States to have mad cow disease. "People want their cows to eat grass, like a moose," Bryan adds. "They don't want growth hormones and antibiotics and genetically altered. Farmers don't use the word 'organic' but 'grass-fed,' because organic scares people away, and besides it can be a racket. City people have got to have it 'organic.' So okay, when I grew up, everything we did was organic — we just didn't know we was doing it. When we could afford to, we bought commercial fertilizer because things do grow faster, but my dad told me to find out how many pounds per acres they said to do it and just do half. Otherwise, it'll bleach the soil and wash away, and you end up wasting your money on a short-term fix."

Their daily farm routine is not so different from what it might have been two centuries ago, when the first Adams came to Barnet. Get up at 5:30 or 6:00, feed the cows, keep an eye on the chickens, feed the pigs. There'll be a lot of fence work in the spring, and haying starts the second week of June, just as school gets out. "You can do it in three weeks if the weather cooperates and the machinery doesn't break." Then as now, weather was the main problem in raising cattle. "There's no way to pasture cattle year round with several inches of snow on the ground through most of the winter," Bryan says. Machinery, on the other hand, is one worry his ancestors didn't have until the first horse-driven McCormick Reaper appeared in 1831 and the first McCormick-Deering Tractor Binder in 1885. "Machinery breakdown is the killer," Bryan says. "Last year the mowing machine died on me along with the tractor, and the front went on the tractor two years in a row." Bryan's got around 60 acres of hay land, and he pastures some of that, with more pasture up the hill. "We need to put some good fencing over there across the brook," Bryan says, "but we got the cows now so that you can shake a bucket at them and they'll follow you."

EXCEPT FOR MACHINERY, Bryan's farmer talk is not so different from what it might have been three and a half centuries ago, when the first English colonies began and when the two key words were *fences* and *dung*. Unlike the Spanish, the English system was based on fences to distinguish plowed land for crops from pasture for animals. But for English colonists, the fence represented much more than a physical boundary that related livestock to planting in an "organic" whole, the word at that time suggesting art rather than nature, since its etymology referred to the parts of the musical instrument called the pipe organ. For colonists, the fence was "the most visible symbol of an 'improved' landscape," writes historian William Cronon, and therefore of an improved mankind. An equivalent symbol was the cow. Governor John Winthrop was only one of many to take for granted that the natives of the place where they'd disembarked had no rights to that place because they "inclose no ground, neither have they cattell to maintayne it." Civil rights came only with proper use, and the sole measure of use was English agriculture, made visible by enclosure and manurance, which in plain English is fences and dung. Dung was a form of capital improvement because it increased the output of crops for trade and for fodder to sustain more livestock. And dung, like seed, was an infinitely renewable source.

As New England towns were laid out with a central commons for grazing livestock surrounded by individual planting fields, on which livestock were loosed after harvest, farmers pooled their labor to build fences for both. The number of animals a farmer owned determined how much fence he had to build: for each cow, 20 feet. Because it took time to create planting fields by cutting down trees and plowing earth, for a while as settlers moved into virgin forests and meadow, they used these as common domain for their livestock. As the colonies became so crowded with people and livestock that they had to expand westward, the habits of free-range husbandry proved useful "agents of empire." Settlers sent their cattle herds ahead of them, in the understandable belief that the one thing they would never run out of was land. When English cattle trampled Indian cornfields, the Indians retaliated, often mutilating the animals as if they were the colonists themselves on whom they sought revenge. According to Governor William Bradford, the Narragansett chiefs promised that they would "lay the English cattle on heaps as high as their houses, and that no Englishman should stir out of his door to piss, but he should be killed." The Indians saw animals, whether wild or tamed, in a relation of reciprocity among equals, an egalitarian creaturehood, rather than in the European hierarchy of creature kinds imaged in the Christian world's Great Chain of Being with God at the top.

Human civilization, defined by God, depended upon Adam's subduing and improving the savagery of nature. But you didn't need God to sustain the Chain. Thomas Jefferson, in a nimbus of secular Enlightenment, envisioned the taming of the land as a progressive evolution from east to west, with the savages of the Rocky Mountains still "living under no law but that of nature, subsisting and covering themselves with the flesh and skins of wild beasts." This in stark contrast to "our pastoral state, raising domestic animals to supply the defects of hunting . . . this march of civilization advancing from the seacoast, passing over us like a cloud of light." As historian Frieda Knobloch points out, "Western agriculture was ultimately about cultivating the nature that was the American West in the minds of the colonists."

In their own definition of animal husbandry, English colonists saw further evidence of their natural superiority to the Spanish, whom they believed treated Indians like cattle rather than civilizing the savages by example. Giving a cow to Indians "will be a step to civilizing them and making them Christians," proclaimed the burgesses of the Virginia Colony in 1656. Roger Williams instructed natives to keep cattle in order to move "from Barbarism to Civilitie," for their new stewardship would instill responsibility toward ownership and property rights. Since cattle were capital, they hastily sought to improve their investment by importing English grass seed, which was generally higher in nutrients. As early as 1672 Joseph Josselyn counted twenty-two European plants which did "spring up since the English Planted and kept Cattle in New-England." (To our misfortune, crabgrass was introduced two centuries later, in 1849, as "crop-grass" for forage.)

Hunting in the home country had been strictly a class matter. In 1605 James I had initiated a Game Act to limit hunting to gentlemen who had an annual income of £40 or more, or goods worth £200 or more. Yeomen could neither hunt nor own hunting weapons or dogs, which made both game and the pursuit of it a mode of private property. Because hunting was only for sport, it symbolized the height of human mastery over nature. Just like Texans with their deer feeders, royal hunters stacked the decks. Queen Elizabeth hunted what were in effect farmed deer within the enclosure of a park, and it was not uncommon to cut off a stag's foot before the animal was released to be chased by bloodhounds.

BRYAN AND SANDI earn their living by cutting meat, whether it's cattle or game. I ask Bryan where he learned to butcher. "We grew up cutting," he says, though his father was a dairy farmer who was "kind of soft" and didn't butcher off any cows until he had to put meat of some kind on the table. "Then my sister bought a store in Barnet — the deli's the only store in town, just across from the post office — and I learned to cut from the guy that owned the store. Just keeping my mouth shut and asking questions and listening. I catch on. I guess you have to have a feel for it."

Usually they kill only one steer for themselves, but this year they cut four cows, which was excessive. "We did one extra we shouldn't have done, a good heifer, barely two, but we didn't think she was going to breed. She'd been running with the bulls and still hadn't calved." It wasn't certain that she was sterile, however, not as if she'd been a twin. Twins are always sterile, he explains, and that's why dairy farmers sell them off. They're called "freemartins," and many say they give the best beef you'll ever have in your life, because they get incredibly fat. Bryan personally prefers the flavor of older beef of two or three years. He has a harder time selling his older beef, however, because as the cow gets bigger people can't afford to buy it. He sells his beef by the half, quarter, or whole car-cass and customers pay by the pound, hanging weight. "The people we do business with, they're just the average Joe. What everybody wants is aged beef. That's the first question — how long will I let it hang?" De-pending on the fat covering, he hangs beef at 34 degrees in his cooler, anywhere from five days to three weeks. Fat keeps the air off and keeps the meat from drying out.

Cutting is the butchering, slaughtering the killing, which Bryan also does but doesn't particularly like to. "I just shoot him in the head with a .22, but I don't do it alone. I need somebody to help me raise him up from the tractor. Then you have to lay him out and skin him." Their son Sean is a fast skinner — his sisters once timed him at five and a half min-utes to skin a deer. Unfortunately, Sean prefers carpentry, and Bryan and Sandi have pinned their skinning hopes on Matt, a kid who began to hang out at their place so much after he lost his driving license that they call him "Little Bryan." They got him into skinning and he really likes it, so they hope he'll be the one to take over.

I follow Sandi and Bryan into their new "processing barn," which they designed and built themselves. The first room holds their office and computers. Running across one screen is "Hey baby, where's the beef?" A sign on the wall says "We Love Vegetarians, More Beef for Us." Back of the office is the aging room, chilled to 34 degrees, and the cutting room, with a concrete ceiling 14 feet high and 10 inches thick, because it has to support heavy steel rails for hanging carcasses. State and federal regula-tions specify that a rail must be 11 feet 8 inches off the floor if you're hanging a half carcass, and 8 feet minimum if you're hanging a quarter. Government regulations drive everybody nuts, Sandi says. First they had to get a variance for the building because the whole town is zoned for agriculture. Sandi filled out twenty-two pages about the environmental impact of the building, which they got approved with twenty-three stip-ulations. "What would be lost agriculturally by putting this building up?" she asks. "About ten bales of hay. It was just a hay piece, and mowing it twice, I don't think we got ten bales." They had to get special flood insur-ance, too, even though an elevation map shows the building at 230 feet above the brook. "Route 5 would flood before this building does." The exterior siding had to be plaque board of white vinyl with a brown roof; the interior of the cutting room had to be VMRP, a textured white plastic board with a washable surface and special trim to cover seams and rivets, because it must be hosed down each night. Customers must sign papers guaranteeing the age of the cow and specifying that the meat is for home consumption.

Bryan puts on his cutting clothes of white jacket, apron, hat. He sharpens his four boning knives and lays them out flat, then puts on stainless-steel chain-mail Whiting & Davis gloves, the same kind that scuba divers wear when diving with sharks. By the end of today he will have cut and wrapped two whole carcasses of 800 pounds each. Equipment is costly — $15,000 for a new electric saw — so they buy as much of it used as they can. They've got a new (used) electric grinder that can turn 65 pounds of meat a minute into hamburger, which is a big deal because many people just want hamburger, Sandi says. "'Oh, my teeth are bad,' they'll say, or 'We don't like steaks and we don't like roasts and we don't eat pork or chicken,' so tenderloin that goes for $15 a pound at the store, they'll say, 'Grind it.'" She adds that she'd never eaten a tenderloin in her life until she met Bryan. Bryan cuts through big bones with the stationary electric saw, but not the spine. "There's rules now about the spine for beef over 30 months. You have to cut it out, but you can't run it through the saw. You notch it out, or I just pull it away. I do cut it with a handsaw but you clean that well. They don't want any meat or bone left together." As for innards, he doesn't like to do heart, liver, or tongue, and he won't do tripe. "My grandmother's always askin' for it," he says, "but she's not gettin' any. I got enough to do without turnin' stomachs." The bones go to a landfill, for which their renderer charges them $30 cash for each load. Bryan remembers when the renderer paid the farmer for the bones.

Sandi, in her own white laboratory costume, is efficient wrapping the cuts as they come from the cutting table. She uses a long roll of heavy plastic. "People ask if we wrap in Cryovac. We're going to go that way, but have to get money ahead. It completely eliminates freezer burn." If she wraps all day, by nightfall her shoulders burn. Today Matt is on hand to help. While they cut and wrap, cut and wrap, there's a lot of family teasing and chitchat, like the small talk of surgeons and nurses around the operating table. "Got a *Vogue* pattern on sale to make a prom dress for Meighan," Sandi says. "With skinny straps, real tight to the knees, then godets at the bottom, so it flares, like a mermaid." She makes all of Bryan's Western shirts.

What they make their living at is not beef, but game. Bryan's posted prices are a reminder of just how much is involved in the process of turning a dead animal into meat and other commodities:

> Cutting prices: Deer $50 plus skinning, bear $65 plus skinning, moose 45 cents a pound, hanging weight, plus skinning. Beef boneless 50 cents a pound, hamburger grind 75 cents a pound.
> Skinning prices for game: Deer $15 we keep the hide, $20 flat you keep. $25 rolled you keep. Moose $40 we keep the hide, $60 you keep, $25 we remove antlers. Bear $25 we keep the hide, $50 you keep, $25 to skin out the head. We reserve the right to refuse any kill. Charge $25 to gut any game.
> Skinning prices domestic: Beef $40 we keep the hide, $50 you keep. Pork $30 no matter who keeps the hide. Sheep $25 we keep the hide, $35 you keep.

They charge five to twenty-five bucks less if Bryan keeps the hide because they can make that amount selling it. Most of the deer hides go to China because tanneries have vanished from the Northeast, along with almost all renderers. There are only two left in the whole area: one in eastern New York, the other in Massachusetts. "We couldn't stay in business if we used them. You can't even compost without a license."

The only trouble with game, Sandi says, "even though we're wicked busy during hunting season," is that it's seasonal. Their principal income comes from doing roadkill moose for the state of Vermont. June is the best month for that because moose who are ready to calve kick out last year's babies. "They're fairly stupid animals," Bryan says, "and they like to lick salt off the road, right in the middle of the road." It's also hot and heavy in September if the doe season's going well, right through Thanksgiving. "It's stupid for me to give up cutting moose when they bring it right to me and there's more money in it," Bryan says. "Last year wasn't a good roadkill year, but this year we've already done four moose." People are allowed up to 100 pounds roadkill meat per household per year, and Bryan churns it into steaks, hamburgers, and sausages. They charge double for their maple breakfast sausage because they use their own maple syrup, getting 100 gallons a year from 1,000 taps.

Of course, there are fewer and fewer small operations like his, but from Bryan's point of view, the bigger the worser. On a small farm, you know what you're getting; on a big one, you don't. Even locally people wonder whether they're getting their own back from an outfit that processes thirty animals a day. Bryan knows that he doesn't want to get so big that he'd end up managing. "I don't want to manage. I want to farm." Although farming is a business, he wants to keep it small and oriented toward the family. "We're just trying to make a living, not trying to be independently wealthy. We just want to pay back what we had to borrow and have time to do things with the kids." His son Sean says that he doesn't want to be like his dad and work all the time. But if you don't, Bryan tells him, you're not going to have anything. "It's working all the time, but it isn't. If I make it, I make it because of me, not because of somebody else doing the job. Few farmers end up with much money, especially starting out. You have to buy your farm, your cattle, your sheep, then the food for them. You handle a lot of money, but you don't keep any of it." The bigger you get, the more you have to deal with the government. "They're not real farmers. All they're looking for is what looks good on paper." He finds America's dependency on foreign oil "absolutely asinine" and finds no reason other than greed for Exxon or Mobil or whoever to make $36 billion dollars profit when he's paying $2.38 a gallon for oil just to heat the house. Bryan and Sandi mostly burn wood, anyway.

In the 1990s Bryan did buy a herd of beef, something like 30 head, but beef prices dropped and he had to sell 28 of them and all the hay in the barn and didn't make a dime on the beef. He sold the cows to a big slaughterhouse down in New York, and the man actually came and wrote a check and they were his. It was the buyer's problem to get them out. "A lot of times a guy will buy and then won't pay until he sells them, so if they die in transit, you're done. I'd rather take less and get my money than have them mysteriously drop dead in transit."

IF EATING IS an act of agriculture, in Wendell Berry's quotable words, agriculture is an act of eating. Man eats land to turn it into something else, an act of mastery suggested in the words "husband" and "husbandry," derived from "master of the house or farm." Up until the sixteenth century, Europeans usually imaged land as feminine, a nourishing Mother Earth in which man planted his seed after deflowering virgin forests to plow virgin land. When they came to America, Europeans discovered an entire continent of virginity, untouched by civilized hands. In America, the raising of crops and animals, whether breaking the sod or breaking a horse, seemed to require an additional masculine violence to transform wild to tame. As land diminished into property, however, it lost its suggestions of nourishing womb or ravished virgin and became a gender-neutral resource, exploitable for the conversion of raw materials to capital. Land and its products were thus de-animated and made mechanical. The ideology of "improvement," whether of land, crops, or animals, by definition employs the dead language of commodity.

When the language of "improvement" became a major banner in the march toward industrialism, once again English fences led the way. In England in the middle of the eighteenth century, country folk began to move to cities in large numbers after enclosure laws — fences — displaced them from the land. As the burgeoning industrial revolution beckoned them to new sorts of work in urban factories, these workers needed food that they no longer raised themselves. This was the immediate impetus for entrepreneurial farmers to start "improving" English breeds of cattle for the sole purpose of producing more meat to feed city workers.

In the midst of New England farms like the Adamses', which seem to have preserved untouched a pocket of early-colonial rural life, it's a shock to discover that the Northeast Kingdom itself was founded on the "improvement" of a mechanical device. In fact, it's a shock to find a town as grand as St. Johnsbury, a city on a hill, founded in 1790 and built by an entrepreneurial invention, the platform scale. Still used in doctor's offices today, the scale was patented by Thaddeus Fairbanks in 1831 and manufactured in partnership with his brother Erastus, after their experience in making cast-iron plows and pitchforks. Like agricultural and livestock improvements, Thaddeus improved an earlier type of platform scales by simplifying the levers and streamlining the whole with polished steel. Success in the media of iron and steel was guaranteed when Erastus became president of the Passumpsic Railroad Company and then governor of the state of Vermont. Four railway lines converged here and a handsome brick station remains today on Railroad Street in memory of the small St. Johnsbury and Lake Champlain Railroad, better known as "St. Jesus and Long Coming." Typical of New England, St. Johnsbury was built by the power of water. The meeting of three rivers — Passumpsic, Sleepers, and Moose — provided power for sawmills, gristmills, hemp processing for textiles, and ironworks, all of which Thaddeus's father had engaged in when he moved to this corner of Vermont from Brimfield, Massachusetts.

One of the quarrels between Founding Fathers Alexander Hamilton and Thomas Jefferson was over Jefferson's exclusive emphasis on agronomy. Hamilton had believed that manufacturing should balance farming. "Since manufacturing and agriculture obeyed different economic cycles, a downturn in one could be offset by an upturn in another." Hamilton, with his self-made career in finance, was urban and progressive in the modern capitalist way. Jefferson was rural and traditional, a Southern plantation owner who looked to a feudal past of serfs and slaves. After the Civil War exploded the pastoral vision of the South, the industrial vision filled the vacuum with a vengeance and fueled the manufactories of the North.

The newly enriched Fairbanks family in St. Johnsbury turned their attention to education, culture, and the arts by founding the St. Johnsbury Academy in 1842, the Fairbanks Museum and Planetarium in 1891, and the St. Johnsbury Athenaeum and Art Gallery in 1871–73. This building was designed by John Davis Hatch to express Victorian grandeur in cathedral ceilings, stained-glass windows, and spiral wooden staircases. Erastus's son, Horace, built the gallery expressly to display the star of his collection of contemporary American painters. It was Albert Bierstadt's supersized rendition of a supersized scene, *The Domes of the Yosemite,* painted just after the Civil War in 1867 to glorify the West. Bierstadt, who'd been raised in New Bedford, Massachusetts, had gone west with a surveying party and took photos with a stereoscopic camera. In translating photos of the Yosemite Domes onto canvas, he evoked the vertical forms of a medieval Gothic nave to suggest the divinity of Nature. One of his traveling companions described Yosemite as Holy Writ: "Never were words so beggared for an abridged translation of any Scripture of Nature."

America's coming of age through industry required the kind of glorification provided by the Centennial International Exposition of 1876 in Philadelphia, which heralded a new era of American culture and art. In the same way that the language of the machine demanded the heroic imagery of the cowboy that machinery had displaced, so the language of a nature demeaned by mechanical "improvement" demanded the heroic imagery of wilderness as sublime. As one modern commentator wrote of Bierstadt: "The paintings celebrate an ideal of the American landscape . . . that the war and rapid industrialization had rendered virtually obsolete." Like the myth of the cowboy, the myth of the American West came into full bloom only after the Machine had taken over the East. A century later, the realities of the machine could be a daily worry. Bryan, scrambling to hang on to his farm in the Northeast Kingdom, took the vicissitudes of nature for granted. His enemy was deadlier. "Machinery breakdown is the killer."

✦ Playing Cowboy ✦

The "Cow Boy" depicted in 1887 by J. R. McFarren (in a lithograph based on a calligraphic design) presents a rider dressed for show in the costume and trappings of a *vaquero*, set against a romantically embellished backdrop. McFarren lived in Gainesville, Texas, near the Chisholm Trail, which supplied him with plenty of cow herders in dirty work clothes if he'd wanted realism.

— From the Popular and Applied Graphic Art Collections,
Prints and Photographs Division, Library of Congress

Buffalo Bill's Wild West
And Congress of Rough Riders of the World.
Actual Scenes — Genuine Characters.
In our Grand Open Arena with Covered Grand Stand
Seating 20,000 people. Twice Daily — 2&8 P.M.
Night as Light as Day.
— Advertisement for Colonel W. F. Cody's show (1883)

The statesman of the past has been merged, I fear for good, into
the cowboy of the present.
— Theodore Roosevelt, in a letter to Henry Cabot (1880s)

——————————————— ◆ ———————————————

O N A GRAY DAY IN JANUARY 2004, a cold north Texas wind
blows right through me. I am waiting with a group of tourists in front of the Spanish colonial arcades of the Fort Worth
Live Stock Exchange and the Cowtown Coliseum, built at the turn of the
century on the main street that ends in the red brick packing plants, hard
by the railroad tracks. We are not waiting for the thousands of fattened
steers that once would have been driven from the holding pens into the
plants, oblivious to the destinations — "Armour" and "Swift" — spelled
out in front in red and white. We are waiting for a bell, which clangs now,
loudly. The longhorns are coming.

There are only forty or fifty of them, and they're being herded by a
group of mounted cowboys, but the bell's warning is real: These big-
boned cattle are armed and potentially dangerous. Colored red and white
and most everything in between, they wear horns of such extreme length
and curvature they look like cartoons or, as James Michener put it, "like
rocking chairs," and they look as if they could turn nasty at the drop of a
handkerchief. Unless you're the type who runs with the bulls at Pam-
plona, you don't want to call attention to yourself, even though it's all for
show. The cattle drive is just part of the daily ceremony for tourists in the

National Historic District, at a moment when the whole of Fort Worth is dressed for show. This January the town is celebrating its 108th annual Texas Fat Stock Show, as it was called back in 1896, which makes this the oldest continuing livestock show in the country.

Fort Worth, founded as a military post in 1849 and named for General William Jenkins Worth after his victory against Mexico, was the first to be called "Cowtown," even though Abilene got there first. But Fort Worth became famous for its Hell's Half Acre of saloons and bawdy houses, a major pit stop for cowboys working the Chisholm Trail north to Abilene. When the Texas and Pacific Railway arrived at Fort Worth in 1876, pens were built and then permanent stockyards, and there was less need to go on to Abilene. With money in their pockets, the town fathers rechristened Cowtown the "Queen City of the Prairie," as if a change in gender might make it more respectable. Today town fathers have reverted to the Fort's earlier attractions and point proudly to the giant saloon called Billy Bob's, "The World's Largest Honky Tonk," with thirty-three bars, half a dozen dance floors, an arena for bull wrestling, and a theater for country singers like Willie Nelson, Johnny Cash, George Strait. It doesn't hurt that *Urban Cowboy* was filmed here and that the mechanical bull Travolta rode awaits imitators seeking to invoke the spirit of Gilley's Bar. For a buck anyone can play cowboy for a day — or night.

When the Fort Worth Stockyards Company bought up the Fort Worth Packing Company in 1893, packers from the north had fierce local competition bidding for herds driven in on the trail, for cattle could now be slaughtered and shipped on the spot. You can find an echo of that bidding in the live cattle auctions today at the Stock Show, even though these days the major action takes place year round, via satellite video. In a small enclosed arena at the end of one of the cattle barns huddled behind the grand art-deco facade of the Will Rogers Memorial Center, men in cowboy hats on wooden bleachers focus on auctioneer Eddy Sims, whose ululating chant drums up interest in a group of calves standing below his platform. These are Red Angus heifer calves, the offspring of dams with names like Foxy Baby and sires like Heaven's Gate, to be sold as breeders. "Ten big ones," auctioneer Eddy calls out, "let's see $1,550 for ten." He coaxes, inveigles, and insults with "Thanks for your help" when the bidding stalls. Five assistants around the arena cajole bidders frantically with hands and arms. The key players are like club members, and the auctioneer calls them by name. "Give me $325, Hank, now give me $350." When a group of calves goes for $800, Eddy moans, "A steal!"

Next up is "Cowtown's Select Sale," which shows off Rose, a champion Hereford heifer. She looks as if she'd been drawn with a ruler, straight down the back to the square angle of the tail, and straight down each leg to the hoof. So exact is the line where hair meets hoof that her legs are like tubes with hooves. The arena has emptied because there will be no bargains here, and when Rose goes for $2,500, nobody notices the man next to me who says, "A steal." Excitement mounts and buyers return when the auctioneer offers semen from Monument Bull, a Hereford who died just before Christmas from "wire in his stomach," so this is the last of a kind. Eddy suggests a starting bid of $225 times five, meaning five straws of semen at $225 each, and gets the price up to $600. Next a girl in a pink sweater tight as her jeans and blond hair straight as a bull's back leads in a live one. "Full bull, full promise, great spread, heavy muscle," Eddy chants. "You're buying one half bull and one half interest in his semen." This bull brings in $20,000 because he's a show animal who'll win prizes before they sell him for breeding.

That the cattle business is a form of show business was apparent from the start. At a time when "men were cheap but cattle cost money," Fat Stock Shows and Cowboy Roundups were double-barreled acts of the same show, in which real work became theater. Cattlemen showed off their bulls and heifers, and cowhands showed off their skills. Cowboy roundups, or "gatherings," began with the need to round up cattle on the range for branding or slaughtering on the ranch, as Mexican cowboys, *vaqueros*, had done for centuries in the West. The skills required by horse and man for roping and tying naturally generated competitions, called "rodeos" from the Spanish verb *rodear*, to encircle or surround. Ranch corrals formed a natural theater in the round, where workers were also spectators to a kind of group theater, in which the taming of a bull or a bronco might stand for the taming of a wilderness. Stockyard corrals provided a larger stage, this time for a mixed audience of cattlemen and investors, in which a cowhand, by guts and ability, could reinvent himself in the American way.

Look at "The Dusky Demon," a Texas ranch hand better known as Bill Pickett. You can see him in bronze wrestling a bucking bull in front of the Cowtown Coliseum. Pickett was a major exception to the rule that banned blacks, Mexicans, and Indians from rodeos — never mind that throughout the period of cattle drives, at least one in five cowhands was "colored." The all-white rule of rodeos stood in glaring contradiction to their origins in Mexican *vaquerías,* when the roundups of wild cattle by mounted cowherders began to be controlled as early as 1574 by Mesta rules to prevent the decimation of cattle herds simply for hides. Although Pickett was not Mexican, he was definitely "colored," being part black, part white, and part Cherokee. He capitalized on this "savage" image by inventing steer wrestling, or bulldogging, sinking his teeth into the lip or nose of the animal to throw it to the ground, an act he performed in 1904 at both the Fort Worth Stock Show and Cheyenne Frontier Days. After he honed his skills in Wild West shows touring South America and Europe, Pickett starred in a 1923 movie called *The Bull-Dogger,* billed as "The Colored Hero of the Mexican Bull Ring."

Dressed like a Spanish matador astride his horse, Pickett conflated two very different Spanish ways of fighting bulls for sport in order to display horsemanship. When the Moors invaded Andalusia in 711 A.D., they introduced a short-stirrup style of horsemanship for fighting and hunting derived from Bedouins on their Arabian steeds. As hunting was the perquisite of royalty, whether Moorish chieftain or Christian knight, fighting the Iberian bull on horseback became a ritualized festival, the first recorded *corrida* in 1133 celebrating the coronation of Alfonso VIII. The mounted aristocratic bullfighter was not replaced by his squire, a plebian matador on foot, until the eighteenth century. Certainly horsemanship was an essential class marker for the Conquistadors in the sixteenth century, when — invading Mexico — they forbade Indians to ride a horse for any purpose. As wild cattle multiplied and the natives died off, however, Mexico's ranching elite, the *hacendados,* faced a severe labor shortage that eventually put Indians and mestizos on horseback to do the dirty work. Mission padres speeded the process by training their new converts in all the arts of handling livestock. Over the next three centuries, the Mexican *vaquero* evolved from an outcast mestizo to a theatrical character of the West, with skills and trappings that were an amalgam of Old and New Spain. As horsemanship democratized in New Spain, landowners reasserted their elite distinction through Spain's *charro* tradition, which had adapted the Moorish style first to medieval jousting and then to cavalry fighting. Performed in New Spain originally as military drills to intimidate the natives, Mexico's *charreadas* continued through the early twentieth century as riding exhibitions designed to show off the skills of upper-class *caballeros* in a form of stylish social-political theater.

As Anglo cowboys in the States proliferated in the cattle drives after the Civil War, they adopted wholesale the skills, costumes, gear, and language of Mexican *vaqueros,* while rejecting wholesale the Mexican race. The American buckaroo (*vaquero*) called his braided halter a hackamore (*jáquima*), his horsehair rope for reins a McCarty (*mecate*), his braided rawhide rope a lariat (*la reata*). From hat to spur he was outfitted in his predecessor's costumery for the same practical reasons. Wide-brimmed hats (*sombreros*) protected him from the sun. Leather chaps (*chaparajos*) protected his legs from thorny brush. Iron spurs (*espuelas*) helped tame wild *broncos.* But the greater his debt to the *vaquero* tradition, the greater his racial contempt.

As always in America, showbiz was a way out for the dispossessed like Pickett and, following him, Will Rogers. Rogers was part Cherokee, born in Indian Territory before it became Oklahoma. As a cowboy on the trail, he developed skills with a triple lariat that brought him in the teens and twenties to Broadway, Hollywood, and the hearts of Americans as "The Ropin' Fool." It was not his ropin' but his down-home folksy chucklin's, without the bite of Twain, that so endeared him to my parents and made him a star with a Memorial Center like Fort Worth's built in his honor. Will made my parents feel that he was one of "us," that he spoke for us country people on a larger stage and thereby enlarged our lives. Nobody in my family ever mentioned he was Indian. I doubt they knew it.

From the start, American cowboy competitions were used to promote something — the ranch, the cattle business, the town, the nation. Rodeos were as natural a fit with Fourth of July celebrations as pie-eating contests and political orations. In fact, the first ranch rodeo on record was held on July 4, 1869, at Deer Trail, Colorado, when the boys from Mill Iron, Camp Stool, and Hash Knife competed on a slick-saddled bronc for a suit of new clothes. On July 4, 1888, a new ranch town like Prescott, Arizona, used a cowboy competition to promote its first Pioneer Days Celebration and charged admission for it. But ranch owners had already recognized the theatrical value of their cowhands and often required them to stage a show for visiting stockholders from the East. In 1868 the same Joseph McCoy who founded Abilene hired cowboys and vaqueros to rope wild buffalo in front of his railroad boxcars painted with the words "McCoy's Cattle." He then loaded up cowboys and buffalo together and shipped them from St. Louis to Chicago's stockyards, where they could perform again.

No one was a better promoter of cowboy competitions as a stage for national identity than William F. Cody, who morphed from all-around frontiersman into our first protoplasmic showbiz cowboy. Hard as it is to believe, in these days of television "reality" shows, Cody was for real what he purported to be in the melodramas of his Wild West Show: a Kansas frontiersman who'd worked cattle, driven a wagon train, trapped for fur, mined for gold, scouted for the Army, hunted buffalo, and fought Indians. He learned early the dramatic values of the cowboy when he teamed up in 1872 with John Burwell Omohundro, Jr., better known as "Texas Jack and His Lasso," to perform in one of Ned Buntline's farces in Chicago. Cody had already been made the hero of four of Buntline's dime novels, which in the 1860s generated the popularity of Western pulp fiction and made millionaires of later scribblers like Zane Grey, that

dentist from New York (89 books at his death in 1939), and the most pro-
lific of them all, Louis L'Amour (101 books, 200 million copies sold, at his
death in 1988). No slacker himself, at his death in 1886, Buntline had
churned out 557 pulps, which primed vaudeville audiences for Cody's
shows, just as Wild West shows lent credibility to the pulp writers, all of
whom claimed historical authenticity.

Remarkably, Cody was what he claimed. He had in real life killed
and scalped the Cheyenne chief, Yellow Hand, after the Battle of Little
Bighorn in 1876; a decade later, the showman staged the action at Madison Square Garden, to the wild enthusiasm of Manhattanites who'd
never seen an Indian. Cody made a star of Sitting Bull when they toured
America and Canada together, with Sitting Bull performing the role of
"The Slayer of General Custer." In 1890, when Cody learned that Chief
Sitting Bull was about to be arrested falsely for stirring up the Sioux, he
hopped a train from Chicago to the Standing Rock Reservation to bring
candy and other gifts to his old costar and pal. Unfortunately, Cody got
drunk en route and Sitting Bull got murdered in his bed.

Easterners lapped up a moralized circus that displayed, as Cody's ads
said, "an exposition of the progress of civilization." This was civilization
without its discontents or ambiguities. In show time, Native Americans
were villains and white men victims, but in real time Sitting Bull was a
celebrity who'd met President Cleveland, carried the flag for the opening
of the Northern Pacific Railroad, and got rich selling his autographs for a
dollar apiece. By basing his melodramas on a manipulation of real life,
Cody invented a new category. As he said of himself, and might have said
of Sitting Bull, "I'm not an actor, I'm a star." Audiences of his Wild West
shows had it both ways: the moral satisfaction of melodrama and the
emotional exhilaration of stardom. As our first Roughneck Celebrity,
Cody toured not just the cities of America for eleven years, but took ship
to entertain Queen Victoria and her countrymen at her 1887 Golden Ju-
bilee. Cody ushered in a new wave of new icons. The Easterner's Yankee
Doodle Dandy in top hat and tails was replaced by the Westerner's Wild
Bill in Stetson and spurs. Buffalo Bill was the first to popularize not only
the idea of the cowboy, but also his clothes. Sears Roebuck began to sell

cowboy boots in their 1897 catalog; $2.95 bought you Western style, but $3.95 made you a Blue Ribbon Cowboy.

WESTERN STYLE, BEGINNING with jeans, is an identity marker for millions of the world's people, from Khartoum to Kyrgystan, who've never been near a cowboy but know every visual sign. Designer-jean fashionistas now advertise "the rodeo look": "High on the saddle . . . it's dusty. It's horsy. It's denim, denim, denim and more denim!" But American cowboys, cattlemen, and civilians alike who truly want to participate in Cowboyana make the pilgrimage each year to one of the annual Stock Shows and Rodeos around the country. The National Western Denver Stock Show, Rodeo and Horse Show, in January, is one of the biggest and flashiest. Never mind the cow barns, where owners shampoo, brush, and blow-dry their cattle until the Angus look like black velvet sofas, the Charolais like buckets of cream, and the Highlands like shag rugs. It's the enormous exhibitors' halls that most people are here for, a super-mall dream kingdom where everyman can fantasize his command of cattle, live horses, and mechanical horsepower.

The cowboy paraphernalia is overwhelming. Silver belt buckles the size of dinner plates, leather belts hanging in rows like skinned snakes that have been tooled, embossed, engraved, covered in rhinestones, studded with silver, filigreed with spangles. Military rows of cowboy boots in brilliant pink, green, yellow, purple from Justin's, Nocona's, Tony Lama's, Lucchese's, Rocketbuster's. Cowboy hats stacked like Greek Revival pillars of felt. You can buy leather armchairs with fur backs and armrests flaming with antlers. You can buy bedsteads made of lacquered tree trunks surmounted by steer horns, or pine cupboards with cowhide insets, or a toilet seat lid inlaid with a replica of *The Dying Indian on His Horse*. There is nothing in this world that can't be Indianized, cowified, or cowboyed.

But clashing with all this decor are large pieces of machinery, which in magnitude and expense demand respect. RTV 900 Utility Vehicles by Kobota threaten a booth of pink cowboy hats and feather boas. A line of bright yellow Suzuki Quadrunner ATVs overwhelms a line of floor lamps crafted from deer antlers. "Only a true cowboy can handle this much horsepower" is the way GMC advertises its Sierra 1500 Crew Cab with a Vortec V8 engine. "Grab life by the horns" commands a banner above a Dodge Heavy Duty Ram 3500 Dually Truck. The really big shows display really big livestock-handling equipment like hydraulic squeeze chutes, dual or single alleyways, head stanchions, alley roll gates, loading ramps, silage and grain bunks, stock trailers, heavy-duty steel cattle fountains, slant-bar round bale feeders. They remind us of all the backstage stuff you need to fatten and sell a cow, which includes tractors, excavators, hayers, tillers, grain augers, fuel pumps, water pumps, fertilizer wagons, and specialized equipment I've never heard of like calf pullers, vaccine guns, ear-tag guns, emasculators. It seems only fitting that one of the most popular installations in the hall is a mechanical horse which teenage girls and boys mount to practice their roping skills on a mechanical cow.

What steak is to beef, rodeos are to stock shows. A century after Cody's Wild West shows, television has brought rodeos an ever-bigger audience, making them as industrialized as beef, and proud of it. "Rodeo — an industry and a way of life" proclaims the banner across the Hall of Fame in the ProRodeo Museum in Colorado Springs. I happened to be there in August 2004, on the twenty-fifth anniversary of its first induction. I found the walls inscribed with names like Jim Shoulders, Dean Oliver, Tom Ferguson, Larry Mahan, Bodacious the bull, Bullet the steer-roping horse, and the biggest name of all — Casey Tibbs. Three times world champion, the young bronc rider swaggered across the cover of *Life* magazine on October 22, 1951, reducing a headline of THE FATEFUL MEETING: CHURCHILL, ROOSEVELT AND STALIN CONFER TOGETHER FOR THE FIRST TIME to a boxed footnote. There have been a lot of champs since Tibbs, but the bull rider Ty Murray beat Tibbs's record in 2002, having won the world championship nine times before retiring at thirty-two. Few bull riders make it into their thirties in this extreme sport, which today brings an audience of 60 million people to watch rodeo on TV and 24 million to attend live rodeos each year. The only sport more heavily attended in America is baseball, where the collateral damage to players' bodies is considerably less.

"There is no greater athlete than the rodeo cowboy," shouts Dave Smith, sports editor of the *Dallas Morning News,* and today's master of ceremonies at the induction. He's applauded by men dressed in identical costumes of white cowboy hats trimmed in black above shirts tucked tight into silver-belted jeans wrinkling over boot tops. Dave introduces today's inductees, who include Alvin Nelson, world champion of saddle-bronc riding. Retired since 1973, Nelson tells us that his grandfather homesteaded in North Dakota, his father died when he was eight, and he entered his first rodeo at sixteen to win seventeen dollars, "more money than I could earn milking cows for a week." The money's been climbing ever since. When Fort Worth held the first indoor rodeo in its Coliseum in 1918, contestants competed for a total purse of $3000, good money at the time. When Ty Murray retired, he'd won $3,000,000. The big money today is for those few contestants who reach the National Finals Rodeo in Las Vegas each year. For the rest, even with corporate sponsors like U.S. Smokeless Tobacco Company, which supplies the cowboys' favorite plug, a rodeo cowboy is lucky to break even. He has to invest heavily in fees, transportation, equipment, and time. Most of his time he spends on the road, recovering from the last bash-up or preparing for the next. Far more than basketball or football, rodeo is a young man's sport.

Women had competed at that first indoor rodeo in the Coliseum in 1918, as they had in Wild West shows and rodeos at the turn of the century, including the tough stuff like bulldogging and bronc busting. But in real life, they could not be working cowboys earning wages. As the frontier pushed west, women were always vital to ranch life and work, but cowboying was strictly for men. Women had to learn to ride and rope and shoot, but "cowgirls" were a showbiz label and creation. Annie Oakley from Ohio (real name Phoebe Ann Moses) set the image of a Western cowgirl in hat, skirt, and spunk, but Cody hired her in 1885 because "Li'l Missie," as he called her, was a sharpshooter, rather than rider or roper. Annie was even the first to appear as a "cowgirl" in a movie Western, with Buffalo Bill and a few Indians, in footage taken by Thomas Edison in New Jersey in 1894. But the cowgirl label was attached first to Lucille Mulhall in 1905, when she performed at age ten the roping skills (learned on her father's Oklahoma ranch) in Madison Square Garden. In the first decades of the twentieth century, many other cowgirls won fame in rodeos — Prairie Rose Henderson for her fancy costumes, Mabel Strickland as "World Champion Ladies' Bronc Buster," Bertha Blankett as "Ladies' Bucking Horse Champion." But in 1936, when rodeo cowboys first organized themselves into the Cowboys Turtle Association ("turtle" because slow to organize but steadfast of purpose), women were shoved out of rodeo's chief events under new rules instigated by president Gene Autry, whose movie fame gave him clout. From then on, women were relegated to the roles of rodeo queen, half-time–show chorus girl, and pseudo-event barrel racer. Despite the efforts of the National Cowgirl Association, the popular culture of the West just can't make room for women. In its ritualizing mode, rodeoing, like cowboying, is a man's world, as movie Westerns from *The Great Train Robbery* to *Brokeback Mountain* have repeatedly affirmed. Women can eat meat, but they can't ride it.

With indoor rodeos, what you notice first is the smell, a combination of dirt, dung, hay, sweat, boredom, excitement, and fear. What you notice second are red, white, and blue flags in every shape and size hung like laundry, crisscrossing the ceiling, draped around the sides. A car speeds around the arena bearing the message "God Bless America." Flagbearers on horseback race in with a giant Stars and Stripes while the audience rises for "The Star Spangled Banner." At the Pike's Peak Rodeo in Colorado Springs in August 2004, an Air Force general opens the show with "Our boys over there are lassoing terrorists, they're riding herd, so let's RODEO!" The audience cheers. The emcee announces that Julia Child died today and that her favorite meal was "Red meat and a bottle of gin." The audience cheers again.

At the end of July 2005, I went to one of our oldest outdoor rodeos staged in the nation's largest outdoor stadium during Cheyenne's Frontier Days, "The Daddy of 'Em All." Cheyenne, Wyoming, was a cowtown quite unlike Fort Worth, even though Cheyenne was founded the same year as Abilene, 1867, and for the same railroad reasons. Cheyenne was built when the Union Pacific Railroad came through the Dakota Territory on its way west, and it attracted not just the usual entrepreneurs but also a clutch of Eastern dudes and English toffs. Cattle barons were literal as well as metaphorical in Wyoming, and they bred and marketed their beef specifically for the European market. The discovery of gold in 1875 fueled the transformation of a tent city along the tracks to one that in 1880 was said to be the richest per capita city in the world. A dozen cattlemen of inherited wealth founded the Cheyenne Club, with tennis courts and wine cellars, no drunkenness, profanity, obscenity, no betting on cards or pipe smoking in public rooms. You could get thrown out for kicking a club steward, but not for the vicious actions that precipitated the infamous Johnson County Wars of 1889, disastrously but magnificently staged for the wide screen by Michael Cimino in *Heaven's Gate*.

By the late 1880s, the buffalo were gone, the Indians demolished, the frontier closed, and the cattle drives done, the cowboys more or less obsolete. The Johnson County Wars marked the tail end of what settlers and cowboys and homesteaders had dreamed of as the open range of the West, but which from the very first Land Ordinance of 1785 had presented a land grab for Eastern speculators. Corporations, not cowboys, had come to dominate the real West through legislation like the Homestead Act of 1862. This long-argued act had promised to provide free land from the public domain (up to 160 acres) for ordinary homesteaders willing to improve it (over five years and for a $10 fee), but in reality it increased speculators' ability by various forms of fraud and connivance to seize the best ranching, farming, and railroad lands for themselves. The Desert Land Act of 1887 continued the job, allowing 95 percent of the land left in the public domain to be "acquired fraudulently by or for corporations." Later, the Taylor Grazing Act of 1934 completed the corporate takeover.

Ironically, the seasonal cattle roundups that had produced the first rodeos also produced the ongoing wars between large-scale ranchers and small nesters, including cowboys who itched to settle down. Cattle traditionally were let loose on the range for the winter and rounded up for branding after calving season in the spring. "Mavericks" was the name cattlemen gave to weaned but unbranded calves, and whoever found one could legally brand it as his own. However, an unscrupulous rancher could slit a calf's tongue to create an "instant" weaned calf, and the "running" branding iron (which made a serpentine squiggle like the "running W" of the King Ranch) made it easy to alter an already-branded calf. Outright rustling by cattle thieves was common, but so was calling a man a rustler and hanging him in order to claim his land. A man — or a woman.

The opening shot of the Johnson Wars between the big guys and the little guys was the hanging in 1889 of Ella Watson, whom Cheyenne newspapers called "Cattle Kate" to suggest she'd been a whore and therefore ripe for lynching. But she was in fact a small homesteader with a pasture on the Sweetwater River next to fellow homesteader Jim Averill, who had himself annoyed large ranchers with complaints, so the pair were hanged side by side. The Wyoming Stock Growers Association had meantime consolidated its power over the local legislature to squeeze out small ranchers with laws like the "Maverick law," which gave the Association legal power to dispose of all unbranded cattle. On the ground, however, disputes over ownership of both land and cattle were frequent and increasingly bloody. By 1892 the Association, in collusion with the Cheyenne Club, hired twenty-two gunmen from Texas to join with a like number of cattlemen in an expeditionary force called the "regulators" to rid Johnson and Converse counties of "rustlers." Their first targets in 1892 were Nate Champion and his men at the KC Ranch, a modest cabin and a herd of only 200 head of cattle. Champion, however, had incurred the wrath of the Association when he formed a rival group of small stockgrowers to protect their interests. The regulators surrounded his cabin and began to chop wood to fire it at night. Inside, Champion noted these events in his diary, where he wrote his final words: "The house is all fired. Goodbye boys, if I never see you again." He didn't, because they shot him and his men when they came out. After a sheriff's posse went after the invaders, the ensuing mini–civil war caused President Benjamin Harrison to send in the Sixth Cavalry to protect the "regulators" and guarantee they got off scot-free. An Eastern writer, Owen Wister, used the events in his novel *The Virginian* in 1902 to make heroes of the Association ranchers and to shape the mythical West in fiction and movies to conform, as in John Wayne's 1970 *Chisum*, to patrician ideals.

But myth takes over when history falters, and as the cowboy left the land, his legend lit up the imagined stage of the West. The sheer scale of Western ranchlands and cattle herds in places like Wyoming must have excited the imaginations of Eastern and European capitalists eager to expand. Space was so vast it required a figure on a human scale to market it. That image became the cowboy, which remains the number-one marketer of macho. I wonder if our cowboy myth didn't first take root in the all-too-human fear of being nothing and nobody in an alien land. As Jefferson's agrarian vision vanished into the Western blue, the yearning to be somebody demanded embodiment. The fact that farmers began to migrate to cities to become wage earners fired the fantasy of an independent loner in the wild. In 1880, a farmworker's average salary was $150 a year, an industrial worker's salary $345 a year, while a cowboy's salary, which included food and housing, might reach as much as $500. Besides, a cowboy got to work outside and on a horse. Those perquisites gave him an edge in an increasingly urban proletarian world. As Clark Gable says in *The Misfits*, "It's better than wages," but cowboys had always worked for wages. Yet as corporate factories took over the ownership of both land and herds and pushed them into the industrial mold, even the ranchers — the men who owned and bred calves — became far less important than the growers who fattened them and the processors who marketed them. It was inevitable that small ranchers, too, would begin to work for wages.

What's surprising is that, a century after this division of labor, we still haven't come to grips with it. Most cattlemen I know, like the men of ProRodeo, find no contradiction in their motto "An industry and a way of life." The dream of a fresh start is part of the iconography of the West, where life is forever pure and innocent. In this brave new world, the corporate chief and the cowboy were alike men of reason, energy, optimism, and courage, with a belief that they controlled their own and other people's destinies. But the more the machinery of industrialism controlled both, the greater the retreat to imagery unsullied by machines. Fort Worth's glory as a railroad center ended with the discovery of Texas oil in the 1930s. In the 1940s, airplane manufacturing replaced the town's meatpacking industry, and in the 1950s trucks replaced railroads. It was inevitable that a business tycoon like Amon G. Carter, who parlayed his success with oil drilling into founding American Airlines, would create a museum in Fort Worth devoted to the romanticized Western art of Frederick Remington and Charles M. Russell.

THE ORGANIZERS OF Cheyenne's first Frontier Days in 1897 had wanted to wipe out the images of violence left by the Johnson County Wars. More than a hundred years later, Cheyenne remains a small Victorian town encircling a proper town square, and Frontier Days is still a big deal, drawing some 400,000 people to nine nights of rodeos interspersed with country music. I went there to see a cooking friend, Beverly Cox, who'd grown up on a ranch near Cheyenne in the 1940s with her glamorous parents, Mark and Betty Ketchum, and who rode with them and her three brothers as a ranch family in the Grand Parade, as all ranch families did.

Beverly asks me to join her on the official Cowgirls of the West wagon in this year's parade. She has laid out my official tricolor Cowgirls costume: a white Ralph Lauren blouse, a deep red broomstick skirt, black and red Tony Lama boots, the official Cowgirl bandana, and a straw cowgirl hat. It's about a fifteen-minute drive to Cheyenne from her Eagle Rock Ranch on the Colorado side of the border, and as we go I have to clamber down from the pickup truck to open cattle gates, teetering on my cowboy heels. Behind the capitol building, we find our parade truck squeezed between a 1931 Ford coupe and the Biblical pageant float of the Assembly of God. Our truck is already loaded with grandmothers, mothers, and babes in arms, everyone flaunting the club colors beneath the Wyoming state flag and Old Glory. We drive slowly through streets jammed with local families sitting on the curb or on folding chairs, the lucky ones in the shade, the unlucky melting in the heat. This is communal theater and we shout "EeeeeeeeeHaws" to get our audience to eeeehaw back. They do. They smile. They wave. They cheer, particularly the women. "There's a little Cowgirl!" we shout at a girl in pigtails holding her mother's hand. Even as the big-city girl I have become, for this moment I'm transformed into a Cowgirl of the West like Prairie Rose Henderson or Bonnie McCarroll, whose death in 1929 after bronco riding at the Pendleton Roundup hastened the end of women in rodeo. Or my favorite, Pearl Hart, a stagecoach robber caught with her boyfriend Boot and imprisoned in 1899. After her release, she started a career in showbiz as "The Arizona Bandit."

After Coors and burgers at the Buckle Up Club, we cowgirls are ready for the afternoon rodeo in the outdoor arena, despite lightning and thunderclouds. Today is the finals, which means ritual events will speed up and performances improve. Steer roping, tie-down roping, senior steer roping, team roping, steer wrestling, bareback bronc, rookie bronc, saddle bronc — events based on the skills and violence built into handling cattle for real, by branding, castrating, dehorning, ear-cropping, tail-bobbing, roping, and prodding. This foreplay is all well and good, but most of us in the audience are here for bull riding. We are out for blood. Nonetheless, we must crown Miss Frontier and her lady-in-waiting, we must sit through the parade of the Dandies Riding Group, pretty young things promoting Wrangler Jeans, Justin Boots, and Bailey Hats. We must endure unfunny clowns doing soft commercials for Coors and Jack Daniel's: a clown popping out of a giant Coors can distracts a bull from a trio of cross-dressers in denim skirts and bobby socks. In the industrialization of rodeo, there's a big gap between the professional skills of the athletes and the amateurism of the vaudeville entertainers killing time. When the bull riding finally does come, it seems that the climax is too quick for such extended foreplay. A few eight-second rides and it's over. Although rodeos begin in the real work of *vaqueros* and cowboys, what is missing is an ending. What is missing is blood.

I had been to the bullrings of Madrid and Sevilla in Spain in the 1950s. I had taken my kids to many improvised rings in small towns in

Provence in the 1960s. Even at these *novillero* bullfights, our hearts were always in our mouths because death was in the air. We prayed that the kid in the suit wouldn't get gored to death before he found out whether he was good enough to be a bullfighter. Death is not lurking at an American rodeo the way it is at a Spanish bullfight, even a sloppy beginner's bullfight. In a rodeo, an injury may be fatal but the death of man or animal is a tragic accident, not part of the script. The rodeo bullrider is always hopeful not only that he'll be able to stick with his bull for the required eight seconds, but that afterward both will walk away on their own power. The matador who escapes death, if he does, does so by inches. There is no escape for the bull. Spaniards anciently took to bullfighting because it's a "ballet dance with death," expressing human mortality as well as mastery. But Americans, as Woody Allen says, believe that death is optional. If Spanish bullfighting is a tragic ballet, American bullriding is a comic hoedown of the kind Agnes de Mille choreographed in *Rodeo*. What excites American rodeo audiences is the explosive energy of the performer courting danger within the confines of a happy ending. We are hopeless optimists who want heroic conflict without tragic resolution. At one rodeo I went to, the bulls seemed notoriously lazy. "I liked that bull that just stopped," said a man next to me. "That was a union bull. 'I've done my eight seconds. That's it.'" We smiled.

AFTER PLAYING COWBOY in Fort Worth and Cheyenne, I was startled to find a real cowboy working longhorns on what had been a real ranch in Texas, but was now mostly a heritage museum designed to show schoolchildren and tourists what a working ranch was like at the end of the nineteenth century. There are a number of show ranches like this around the country — King Ranch in Texas, Alisal in California — but the George Ranch Historical Park in Richmond, about 30 miles southwest of Houston, is impressive in its spread of 23,000 acres and in its history. Here in 1824, Nancy and Henry Jones built a wooden cabin they called "the Homeplace" as part of the colony Stephen F. Austin settled at this bend in the Brazos River. In the course of the century, four generations planted cotton, grazed cattle, discovered oil, and finally established a museum as real history moved on. Today reenactors in Victorian costume work the gardens, cook chuckwagon meals, weave blankets, grind corn, plow fields, brand cattle, and feed the chickens and hogs.

What charmed me most was my cowboy guide, Jim Hodges, a blue-eyed Texan in his forties, who once worked cows and dreamed rodeos. His favorite rodeo is the one in Fort Worth: "It's one of those old-timey cow rodeos and I like to be on the rail, hear the leather popping, the bronc snorting." He wanted to be a bull rider when he was a kid, he said, because that's where the girls hung out, but when he found he wasn't good at it, he took to riding saddle broncs. "I could flat put a whipping on a horse pretty handy, so I did real well in that." When he went to bucking school at Muskeegee, Oklahoma, he learned the difference between real cowboy boots and Western boots. His boots, I noticed, were so battered, they were held together with duct tape. He explained that on a cowboy boot a spur strap keeps the spur from falling on the ground, so you don't have to squat down all day to readjust your spurs. The strap, however, will wear out the arch, so what he favors are Double H boots. "I like them because they match a 1930s Olsen-Stelzer pair that were notorious around here. They've got that buildup across the arch, an extra-thick sole, and they're all bull hide, so they wear better." Even so, duct tape is required. "When you're cowboying," he explains, "you leave your spurs on when you take your boots off. They're part of your body. You only change your spurs if there's a few ladies around." In the old days, they wore a chain underneath that connected to the spur knob on the other side. "We broncbusters wore that chain a little too long so it slapped the ground when we walked, and that way we attracted a lot of attention. Some of the old cowboys put jingle-bobs on their spurs, you know, as in 'I got spurs that jingle, jangle, jingle.'" The pair of boys who work for him favor high-tops in canary-yellow and bright green. "Everybody's a buckaroo nowadays," he says. "But if you're cowboying for real, you order your boots one size too big and double-E wide, so that if you get your spurs hung up in your rigging, you can get your foot out of the boot. If you can't get loose from that saddle, you're a dead man."

Jim says that in the old days, he always wanted to be a cross between Gene Autry and Roy Rogers, but he never could sing too good. Retired from real cowboying, he joined the George Ranch nine years ago and feels lucky that he can still ride all day. "In the old days cowboys were boys, so by the time they were twenty-four, they'd been busted up pretty dang good, so they became carpenters or odd-job men or cooks. The cook was the meanest dude on the ride because he was in charge of everything in the wagon — all your valuables, extra saddles, extra ropes, payroll money, food, rifles, pistols. You might argue with anybody else on the drive, but you don't ever mess with the cook." You also don't mess with a cow. He points to one in the pasture nearby that they call Oreo. She's a Piney Woods, a variety of longhorn, black with a white belt around her middle. "You ride out there and try to get her to herd, she'll come after you and lift you and your horse up and throw you about thirty feet through the air. It's not like a bull. A bull will come up and bump you and run off, and he's got his little macho thing out of the way. But a cow will stand there and finish you off." When a visitor asked him once why you never saw cows in Spanish bullfights, his answer was simple: "You go wherever they fight bulls for real, and they don't fight cows. A cow won't duck her head and run at you. She'll walk right up and skewer you like a shish kebab and then stand there. She's not going to chase a cape and play the game. I would rather fool with about a hundred head of longhorns than that ol' poll Piney Wood cow."

He's also had his share of bulls. "We had a huge Brahman once, about 2200 pounds, big hump, big dewlap, horns straight out and stumped off. Black on front, silver on the back, and the meanest-looking dude you ever saw. He'd go after the biggest horse on a roping operation and jerk it flat because he knew how to work his leverage against a horse, and he loved it, loved to fight. He ate a couple of my guys for lunch. You looked in his eye and saw he was a machine, a killing machine, so we had to get rid of him." Rodeo bulls, on the other hand, are professionals, trained for rodeo. "That big rodeo bull Bodacious, they had to take him off the circuit because he could buck so hard, he could literally turn his butt straight up in the sky and his rider fell straight forward and got it full in the face, caved his whole face in. A handler could walk Bodacious around the ring with a halter and lead him like a dog, but if you put him in the chute he knew what he was supposed to do. Same with saddle broncs and bareback horses. Watch close and you'll see the same horses come back out with different cowboys roping off them. They're professional athletes just like the cowboys. The boys are all taped up, got their vests on, got their tobacco. We chewed Day's Work plug tobacco, looked like an old pancake that somebody found out there in the bush after about a year. Cut a big chunk, stick it in your mouth, takes about thirty minutes to become pliable, and it *does* last all day. My first foreman, he'd be chewing that stuff all morning, come to the wagons at noon, pull the plug out of his mouth and stick it in his pocket, eat his food, and the minute he was done, put it back in."

Turns out that my real cowboy is a professional trainer of horses for rodeos and TV commercials. Jim tells me that before 9/11 changed the imagery of New York, he got a job riding his old cutting horse Curly Bill for a commercial staged by Fox Morning News, in which he and a bunch of cowboys were pictured sitting around a campfire at dawn, watching TV and flicking channels with the remote. One of them says, "Nah, we're not gonna watch that, that looks like it came from New York City," at which point Jim ropes the TV set and drags it through the campfire. "There's not a whole lot of horses on this planet that have roped a TV, and Curly Bill didn't like that too much. He saw those sparks coming after him and that TV flying up in the air and glass smashing when it hit the ground, and boy, he really didn't like that." But Curly Bill had done a lot of photo shoots. "I got him up at three o'clock in the morning and got him all slicked up and clipped and saddled, and he stood next to that fire for three and a half hours and never moved a muscle."

Curly Bill was a pro.

◆ The New Range Wars ◆

"Army Beef Swimming the Occoquan River, Virginia," sketched by Alfred R. Waud, appeared in *Harper's Weekly* July 4, 1863, above "The Battle at Milliken's Bend," sketched by Theodore R. Davis. The demand for beef during the Civil War jump-started the beef industry in America.

— From the FSA-OWI Collection, Prints and Photographs Division, Library of Congress

Oh it's squeak! squeak! squeak!
Close and closer cramps the wire!
There's hardly play to back away
And call a man a liar.
Their house has locks on every door;
Their land is in a crate.
There ain't the plains of God no more,
They're only real estate.

— Charles Badger Clark, Jr., "The Old Cowman"

---◆---

THE SUN IS BEGINNING to redden and disappear behind Hart Mountain National Antelope Refuge by the time I dip into the Catlow Valley. There are green pastures and streams, a few black cows, a cluster of ranch buildings, and — thank god — people. If you've driven hundreds of miles over the high desert of southeastern Oregon and seen nothing but sage and juniper, you're grateful for a glimpse of your own species.

Elaine Davies is a fine specimen of that species. Eyes blue as lakes, blond bangs, a big smile, a cheerleader body, Elaine in her late thirties looks far too young to have bred six boys, the youngest practicing his roping skills on a hobbyhorse in the yellow juniper-paneled living room of Roaring Springs Ranch.

"If we have a good snow pack on the mountains and a couple of warm days," Elaine says of the spring runoff that gave the ranch its name, "you step outside because you hear it, and you look up and these cliffs are roaring, waterfalls all over the place." The runoff lasts no more than forty-eight hours, and villagers from Frenchglen come running up over the mountain to hear the roar. In the arid West, which at the beginning of the nineteenth century was named the Great Desert, water is the key to life, liberty, and property, which are more or less the same thing.

In country like this, the water that brings grass allows grazing, and grazing is the number-one issue for everybody. Overgrazing is what brought the Davieses to Oregon seven years ago, from their ranching job in Florida. The owners of Roaring Springs are a lumber family who live in Portland and Vancouver and bought the ranch as a retreat from city life because they liked to hunt and fish, but they knew little about ranching. The Bureau of Land Management (BLM) told them that their cattle were seriously overgrazing the mountain, giving the Nature Conservancy a good argument for taking over their land. Some sections had been eaten to the ground, while others were left untouched. With a ranch of 500,000 acres, that's a lot of sections to look after, even with the help of helicopters. But it takes this much acreage to support 5000 cows, which makes Roaring Springs one of the area's largest ranches. Of course this is small potatoes in comparison to the Mormon-owned Deseret Ranch near Orlando, where Elaine and her husband, Stacy, worked before this. There, the same amount of acreage supported ten times as many cows. The difference is water. There they had to pump water out of the fields into the ocean, says Elaine. Here they have to irrigate even when it's raining because it's never wet enough.

The owners of Roaring Springs hired Stacy with a mandate to streamline the operation, to manage better not only the land, but the people who worked it. "Before we came there were twelve guys, and now there's only one," says Elaine. "Stacy got rid of the old buckaroo way of sitting around the bunkhouse having coffee all morning or up at the cow camps in the mountains having branding parties all summer." Now the rule is no coffee in the bunkhouse. "Come to work saddled up and ready to go, and if you need a coffee break, have it on your horse."

They're much happier working here than under Deseret's corporate structure. Deseret was so large that it was subdivided into a few mid-sized ranches, which were further divided into fourteen mini-ranches, each with its own manager and crew. When Stacy made suggestions about improving the cattle and the ranch, his bosses would say, "Your job is not to think. Your job is to do what we tell you to." One day Stacy came home from work and said, "Today I stopped breathing because the day I can't think is the day I can't work. We've got to go."

The Deseret experience gave them a lasting understanding of what it's like to be low man on the pole. "Stacy's the first one out and the last one in, and doesn't take a day off and doesn't ask any man to do what he isn't willing to do himself." They work as a family, she says, the boys sharing in the work all the time they're not at school. The younger three go to the one-room schoolhouse in Frenchglen, which has all of thirteen kids. The older three go to high school in Crane, about 60 miles away, at a public boarding school for locals who are so scattered it's the only way a high school could exist. "I'm just trying to make them good citizens and good people," Elaine says. "I have the most perfect life there is. I raise boys, my husband raises cows."

On our way to the Frenchglen School with her littlest boy to pick up his brothers, we pass the airstrip, a mile long, "big enough for Air Force One if the president ever wanted to hide out from anybody." She points out the U-shaped canyons that indent the mountain where homesteaders a hundred years ago built their houses. That's where the water was. But the weather was tough on ranchers and they all starved out. We pass Dry Creek Ranch, where the Davieses used to keep a feedlot, but now they ship their yearlings to a place near Sacramento in November so that they can keep eating grass through the winter. "They run around all winter and they come back in the spring when their growing is done and they've mowed all those people's pastures. Cows are lawn mowers. They keep the grass growing if you manage them right. Instead of a muddy feedlot, they're healthier if they're out, not stepping in each other's poop, out on fresh grass, fresh water, keeping their feet sound." All this is part of the natural-beef program instituted by Doc and Connie Hatfield up in Brothers, Oregon, for whom the Davieses worked as a couple after they'd graduated from Ricks College in Rexford, Idaho, where they'd met. "We were with them for six years and that was the very beginning of Country Natural Beef, when we were twenty-one and twenty-two, and I was the bookkeeper and Stacy did the cattle flow and Doc and Connie did the marketing." It was through the Hatfields that I'd visited the whole chain of member ranches in their co-op scattered over eastern Oregon. The Hatfields, who now sell their product under two brand names, Country Natural Beef and Oregon Country Beef, through the expanded Whole Foods chain, were an important part of the contemporary story of beef.

We drive by the meadow where the Davieses calve heifers. Experienced mommas can calve on their own, way out in the desert, but first-timers have to be watched because they can get confused. On wet meadowlands they can have a calf a year, just like people, and they can go for the usual fourteen to sixteen years, but out in the desert, where they're digging and chewing the dirt to find grass, they don't have any teeth left after eight or nine years, and that's when it's time to send them to the commodities market where old cows are turned into meat.

We drive by Homecreek Canyon, where the Davieses are building a reservoir to help preserve Catlow redband trout. They were glad when it missed the Endangered Species list because they feel they can make the trout population explode if only the government would stop interfering. The issue that threatens them all, says Elaine, is the hidden agenda of control. In the seven years they've been at the ranch, the owners have spent six-figure sums to benefit wildlife, fish, ducks, the land itself. The mountains abound with wildlife like bighorn sheep, antelope, golden eagles, and wild horses. After spring runoff, the pasture itself is a wetland for migratory birds, and the streams jump with those trout. The owners had consulted with the Wildlife Refuge people on how to help the fish population, and had spent $10,000 to install a screen that would channel fish swimming upstream through a central trough. There was a 1 percent chance that a fish might die if it missed the trough, but without the screen, a trout's chances of dying were total. USDA regulators, however, denounced the screen as illegal and demanded they install a modernized computer system with motion sensors that cost close to $60,000, plus the cost of a maintenance person equipped to contact a computerized fish center at the U.S. Department of Fish and Wildlife. Elaine tells me the owners are now in litigation with the USDA to avoid installing that

$60,000 system on every stream and creek on their ranch, which is, Elaine says firmly, "entirely private land."

Basically, they're in court over who owns the water. All ranchers are in a fight over water, Elaine says, because the state has claimed ownership of all water rights not previously claimed. Her distrust of government deepened after Stacy had driven over to Salem at 3:00 in the morning to hand-deliver their claim to the agency and six weeks later got a letter that said their claim had been denied. She suspects old-fashioned claim jumping because documents show that the state filed just a week before the Davieses did. "Kind of fishy and kind of sad," she says. She is certain the state lied to them and is covering up the lie by means of a "predated stamp pass." Earlier personal experience confirms that distrust. Her dad was locked out of his job when the government shut down the timber industry in the early 1980s. "My dad went from a middle-class job managing logging equipment to working-class poverty in six weeks." She blames pressure from environmentalists for getting logging outlawed where the family lived, near Yellowstone Park, and believes that the Endangered Species Act is now being manipulated by the same agenda of control.

The issue became acute, Elaine says, when President Clinton claimed Steens Mountain, which rears up a mile high just behind Frenchglen, for a national monument in 2000. The federal government had said ranching could continue, but that was what they'd said when they made a monument of the Grand Staircase–Escalante in Utah. "They lied to them," says Elaine — in three years, all the ranchers were gone. So Stacy was prepared. He helped initiate the Steens Mountain Cooperative Management and Protection Act of 2000, which put Steens Mountain in the category of National Conservation Area rather than Monument. He wanted the name of the place to be so long that no tourist would ever come visit and create another Yosemite, Elaine explained. "We created a co-op board of twelve different groups, representing government agencies, environmentalists, recreationists, ranchers. Our neighbors felt we were selling out, but they didn't realize it was their homes Stacy was saving."

Later Stacy tells me, "When you're on the outside, you can look at ne-gotiating as betrayal, but when you're on the inside and the gun's pointed at you, you either fight and die or negotiate the best deal you can."

IN FRONT OF a small white frame building with a flagpole is a sign that reads Frenchglen School, and across the street is a white frame building labeled Frenchglen Hotel, and down the block is a white frame building labeled Frenchglen Mercantile. Not surprisingly, the town was founded by John W. "Pete" French, who arrived from California in the 1850s with a herd of 1000 head. As the herd grew to over 40,000, French fenced in the Donner and Blitzen River Valley, named thus by German homestead-ers. So many cattle and so much fencing earned the resentment of his neighbors, and in 1897 one of them shot French in the back, burned the body, and got off scot-free. Range wars between homesteaders and ranch-ers, sheepherders, and cattlemen, evoked by movies like *Shane*, are as inte-gral to the continuing history of the West as conflicting visions of the land itself.

To a child's question "What is the grass?" Walt Whitman answered with a metaphor, "a uniform hieroglyphic." When Whitman finally vis-ited the West for the first time in 1879 and saw prairie grasslands with his own eyes, he wrote how delighted he was that the landscape conformed to his vision of it: "The greatest thing to me in this Western country is the realization of my 'Leaves of Grass.' . . . How my poems have defined them. I have really had their spirit in every page without knowing." His vision came first, and it shaped what he saw. What he saw was not the land but an idea of "landscape" that conformed to European ideas, trans-posed from feudalism to capitalism and in the process applying value to land as private property with exchange value. This commodification of space turned even poets into tourists, so it is small wonder that poets could also be capitalists. To Whitman, the boundless space of these grass seas mirrored the boundless enterprise of American genius, unifying na-ture and commerce. Of the West, Whitman wrote: "It seems to me that our work at present is to lay the foundations of a great nation in products, in agriculture, in commerce, in networks of intercommunication, and in all that relates to the comforts of vast masses of men and families."

Whitman was echoing the vision of Thomas Jefferson a century before him. Jefferson saw the prairie as a blank slate, Locke's *tabula rasa,* on which he would lay down the template of individual freedom and natural rights. Thus Jefferson called the West he never saw the "Great Empty," a void waiting to be filled by an agrarian Utopia. The perfection of geometry was Jefferson's way of ordering the chaos of emptiness. When he unscrolled a mechanical grid across its vast space in his Land Ordinance of 1785, he not only put into practice the Eastern colonizers' idea of the West but set in motion most of the national controversies to come. The 160 acres decreed by the BLM for Steens Mountain are the same 160 acres prescribed by this Ordinance, based as it was on the amount of land an English yeoman would need, in theory, to sustain his farm.

Presidents are mythmakers just as poets are, and the results of Jefferson's attempt to mold the American West by England's agrarian mythology was but the first of many national policies driven by fictions mistaken for facts. No matter that European pastoralists were mountain and forest people, whose modern descendants were not grass lovers but "tree huggers." No matter that America's native grassland people were nomads, not settlers, since aridity requires extensive coverage, which the introduction of the horse aided. No matter that the vastness of American space required a culture of mobility directly at odds with England's cottage sensibility. When Spanish horses spread to the American plains in the sixteenth century and increased the mobility of native nomadic tribes, they were returning to their origins. Horses had first evolved in the grasslands of the New World sixty million years ago, before they migrated across the land bridge of the Bering Straits to the Siberian steppes. Grasslands, where movement between drought and regrowth is constant, have always produced their own mobile culture. "For the nomad," Bruce Chatwin writes, "movement is morality," but he adds that nomads have also always required settlements for markets and tools.

Jefferson believed that America's geographic space would supply a new moral and political vernacular, but one based on cultivating individual space. In Jefferson's mind, "American virtue was linked with space," George F. Will explains, "meaning room enough for Americans to develop the virtues that undergird personal independence." In America accumulated individual destinies would create the foundation for Manifest Destiny. Thus Frederick Jackson Turner saw the frontier as a private realm from which governance would emerge by voluntary cooperation among individuals. But, as George Will points out, Turner delivered his famous paper "The Significance of the Frontier in American History" in 1893 at the Chicago Exposition, which celebrated the industrial Machine. And it was in the aptly named Gallery of Machines at that exposition that Henry Adams said that he felt "his historical neck broken by the sudden eruption of forces totally new." Although political talk at the turn of the century took the traditional form of Individualists versus Progressivists, the real question was twofold: Who owned the land, and who ran the machines?

Land ownership and machine ownership went hand in hand. Abraham Lincoln's Homestead Act of 1862 extended Jefferson's Land Ordinance to cover 270 million acres. At the same time, the Pacific Railway Act gave 90 million of those acres to the railroads as an incentive to move forward, to speed the "progress" of the Machine. In 1869 the Central Pacific–Union Railroad was granted alternate 10-mile sections of a belt of land 40 miles wide from Omaha to San Francisco. That same year, Lincoln dispensed many million more acres under the Morrill Land Grant, which gave to each state 30,000 acres of public land to establish a state agricultural college. A century later, this would provide the USDA with a pool of scientific agricultural Progressivists who would cement the links between government, agriculture, and business, and promulgate the industrialization of all three.

The Eastern equation of democracy with 160 acres was repudiated by the geopolitics of the West. But Major John Wesley Powell was a lone heroic voice in contradicting Jefferson's Platonic ideal with empirical observation. The loss of an arm in the Civil War did nothing to deter this extraordinary explorer and ethnologist, whose credo in *Report on the Lands of the Arid Regions of the United States* in 1878 was in the context of progressivism a rebel cry: "knowledge and custom are particular to place." To report that the West was arid was to say that the Emperor has no clothes. Powell saw, as Wallace Stegner writes in *Beyond the Hundredth Meridian,* that "Water is the true wealth in a dry land . . . if you control the water, you control the land that depends on it." But the "riparian rights" of English common law, on which American law was based, did not work for land that needed to be irrigated. (Riparian rights stated that a farmer had the right to use water on his land, the way a gristmill might use it, provided that he returned the water to the stream when finished.) Powell suggested that the West would require irrigation in 80-acre plots where that was suitable and the rest should be grazing land. Pasture farms would require not 160 acres, but sixteen times as much — 2560 acres. He proposed topographical surveys to indicate water frontage and prevent water monopolies. Settlement should follow rivers, not grids, and should be modeled on communal villages like the Mexican *ejido,* which had evolved from fort to mission, built on a system of settling a village near water with shared lands surrounding it for grazing. He warned government agencies that a wet country must not impose its habits on a dry one. For his trouble, the government tucked Powell safely away as director of the obscure Bureau of Ethnology.

The progress of machines in commodifying land by Eastern ideas speeded the transformation of prairie grasslands to commercial corn crops. As Richard Manning suggests in *Against the Grain,* technology redefined freedom as the motion of capital from East to West. Railroads, as the prime mover, helped rid the prairies of buffalo by shipping quantities of "green hides" to satisfy Europe's lust for buffalo robes. The British Army "went soled and saddled into Crimea on American bison." With buffalo out of the way, John Deere's cast-steel plow of 1837 was able to cut the thick mass of prairie sod and allow farmers to plant corn. For a time, longhorn cattle still grazing on native grasses replaced buffalo in the commodities market, but corn increasingly became food for fatter breeds of cattle like Hereford and Angus. Cattlemen followed the corn, just as they followed the railroad tracks, to market, where the coming together of cows, trains, and corn happened so fast that beef became a full-blown industry almost overnight. As early as 1876, 3 million pounds of beef had been transported by train and shipped to England in refrigerated ships. Five years later that amount had increased to 100 million pounds a year. In competition with plowmen, cattlemen began to use Joseph Glidden's new improved fences made of barbed wire to claim public-domain acreage for their own use. The war between ranchers and farmers was fueled by the conflict between Spanish law, which required farmers to fence in their crops to give animals free range, and English law, which required livestock owners to fence in their animals to protect crops. Branding, along with fencing, became a mechanism for enforcing corporate monopoly, and freedom was no longer equated with individual freeholds, but with corporate size.

Plowed land required water, and the Desert Land Act of 1887 at last recognized the vital fact that the West was arid and would require irrigation to be farmed. The act increased allotments to 640 acres for anyone willing to pay $1.25 per acre with a down payment of two bits per acre, but it hardly increased individual property, because 95 percent of the titles granted were fraudulent. In the same year, the now-infamous Dawes Act gave away or "sold" to white settlers 90 million of the 140 million acres of tribal lands granted for Indian reservation, under the moral canopy of turning nomads into farmers and directing savages toward what Charles Dawes called "the civilizing power of private property." Companies were not slow to take advantage of the myth of the open range. The right to public rangeland was assumed to be God-given, and the right to graze without interference or regulation was part of the package of the individual rights of man in a country founded on independence. The result was disastrous overgrazing. The chief regulator was nature, which produced the droughts and blizzards of the late 1880s that reduced some herds by 70 percent.

Individual range rights included control of water, which was expanded by fencing. The government did not step in until the Forest Service was created in 1906, under the Department of Agriculture. Set up to manage water and timber on 191 million acres, the Service decided to require a permit and a fee for livestock grazing. The monthly fee was five cents per animal unit (AUM), an animal unit being one cow or horse, or five sheep or goats. Ranchers resisted in and out of court, and as a result the Supreme Court ruled that national forests are government property and that "The U.S. can prohibit absolutely or fix the terms on which its property may be used." Ranchers made an end run around valuable forest land by pressuring for marginal lands. The Stock Raising Homestead Act of 1916 granted 640 acres of public land "deemed of no value except for livestock raising and forage" to any rancher who needed it for grazing. That the prairies would turn into a Dust Bowl a mere decade later would not have surprised Major Powell, but the fact that two decades later more than half the carrying capacity of the range was found to be "depleted" and 16 percent "extremely depleted" finally forced the government to act.

The Taylor Grazing Act of 1934 purported to regulate grazing allotments on public land, but under a new leasing system with token fees, it transferred millions of acres of public land to private ownership. As the Act did not apply to wild animals of any kind, including horses, 80 million acres of federal grazing land served livestock interests only. Clearly there were other legitimate uses of public land, but who was going to define what they were and how they would be apportioned? Enter the Bureau of Land Management, created in 1948 by merging the Grazing Service with the General Land Office under the Department of the Interior. Although the new BLM nominally controlled 262 million acres, it was from the beginning "understaffed, underfunded, and underpowered." While the Bureau was supposed to regulate uses and resources as conflicting as livestock, energy, mineral, timber, wild horses, fish habitat, and wilderness, in fact it favored stockmen. Hampered by a couple of centuries of contradictory laws involving public land, the BLM had no systematic legal guidelines until the Federal Land Policy Management Act (FLPMA) of 1976. By this time, 84 percent of the lands under BLM control were determined to be in poor or deteriorated condition. As the BLM struggled to get its house in order by requiring a reduction in livestock, ranchers responded with the Sagebrush Rebellion, demanding that BLM sell its lands to them outright. Environmentalists responded with charges of a "Great Terrain Robbery." The problem is chronic: Only 2 percent of livestock producers in the U.S. graze on public land, but this constitutes 258 million acres of Western rangeland, or one acre out of five. Critics of the system claim that the producers are federally subsidized because the fee charged the rancher is absurdly small in relation to the current value of the land. Today the number of animal units on BLM land is about the same as it was in 1936, around 13.5 million. Although the monthly fee had risen to $1.97 by 1991, the true lease value would have been $8.70. Taxpayers were paying for the difference, as they continue to. This form of subsidy stoked the fires of environmentalists like Edward Abbey, who proclaimed the land "cow-burnt."

When the Forest Service began, there was a need for tree huggers as a way to preserve wilderness, and one of the first huggers was the notable Forest Service agent Aldo Leopold. Although born in 1887 in Iowa into a family of manufacturers who sold barbed wire, he was Eastern educated at Lawrenceville School in New Jersey and Yale's School of Forestry, where he specialized in wildlife management. Today he stands as one of our first radical ecologists in daring to state that land, its health and value, cannot be measured simply by increased yields. In *A Sand County Almanac,* he demanded no less than a new land ethic: "Quit thinking about decent land-use as solely an economic problem." He began to enunciate a credo of sustainability in farming and the preservation of wildlife. As a good Forest Service agent, he believed in multiple uses for the forest, including timber and grazing rights. His real fight was against the encroachment of the automobile and its takeover of national parks to supply it with roads. His antipathy to recreational tourism was car-driven at a time when merely to own a car was a sign of wealth for the new leisured classes. He excoriated "The Great God Motor" as a monster of modernity from which wilderness needed to be protected and preserved for the benefit of all. By the 1940s his tone was elegiac: "It is increasingly clear that there is a basic antagonism between the philosophy of the industrial age and the philosophy of the conservationist." He died in 1948, but not until he'd written that our tools are better than we are, that they may crack the atom, "But they do not suffice for the oldest task in human history: to live on a piece of land without spoiling it."

Until the formation of the National Park Service in 1916 to preserve "pristine areas," forest lands had served as an improvised commons to accommodate varying uses, but the notion that such uses might include natural scenery and tourists mobilized to look at it was new. A split between preservationists and conservationists revealed differing ideas of what wilderness was. Leopold worried about the erosion of watercourses from grazing and argued that some portions of park and forest should maintain "wilderness as a minority right" free of rules and regulations, free of recreational development, free of hated automobiles and roads. Today a wilderness free of rules is as inconceivable as a wilderness free of motorcycles, snowmobiles, and dune buggies. How astonished Jefferson would be to learn that the U.S. Department of the Interior is the biggest landholder in the country.

LONG AFTER ELAINE fed me and the boys supper, Stacy finally gets home. He is a small, solid-boned man, intense, fiercely competent, someone who clearly is happiest when he is working — and overworking. He is articulate and precise about every variety of land-use issue. He is particularly vociferous on the subject of environmentalists who, in his view, manipulate, overextend, and pervert laws passed in the late 1960s and early 1970s — the Endangered Species Act, the Water Act, the FLPMA, the Wilderness Act. "Since the environmental community found ways to litigate using those laws, the BLM office doesn't have time to manage the land, it just does its best to stay clear of lawsuits." He points out that the first major victory for the "enviros," the spotted owl, shut down the timber industry, which was 30 percent of the economy in the Pacific Northwest — and failed to stem the owl's decline.

Stacy finds the Forest Service more paralyzed even than the BLM, with no funds for people to manage grazing or monitoring, and heavy pressure from environmentalist groups who want no grazing at all.

"Their image of the land is about 1800," says Stacy, "when you had griz-zly bears and wolves roaming free."

There's also the war between federal and state agencies. When the Forest Service tried to declare Catlow Valley streams "wild and scenic rivers," they were abrogating states' rights, Stacy believes. "Historically, water on *public* lands belongs to the state, which is supposed to be sover-eign, but the federal government has simply taken more and more con-trol." The irrigation structures for most of the ranchers begin in the watershed, which is on federal grounds, and many of these were put in place before the Forest Service even existed. But the head of the environ-mental group Western Watershed Project, says Stacy, "hates cattle on public land, period." Water is key. "If you take away my irrigation water for my meadows and hay fields, I can't graze public lands because I don't have a ranch to come home to."

"Without public land, grazing in the West isn't much," Stacy says. In Oregon 60 to 70 percent of the land is public, in California 75 percent, in Nevada 94 percent. Ranchers have been losing since the beginning of the Forest Service, Stacy believes, portion by portion, cow by cow. If they lose the use of public land, they'll have to sell, but it's not the government who'll buy. Most of the land will go to developers. In the early 1970s, Oregon enacted some of the toughest land-use laws in the nation to pro-tect open spaces, but when there is pressure to develop, land-use laws tend to go out the window.

Ranchers don't have time or money to fight back in court. It took four years to hammer out the legislation to pass the Steens Mountain Act, which succeeded in broadening the definition of "protection" to include people who earn their living from the land, not just those who seek recre-ation on it. The land in question was typical of ranchland in the West: 40 percent private intermingled with hundreds of thousands of acres of public land. The problem arose with the Homestead Act, when the best land was grabbed and fenced by homesteaders: the creek bottoms, the meadows, the deep soil. Marginal land, like the rocky ridges, was given to the BLM. Before fencing came in big, wildlife, ranchers, and recreational-ists had no need to distinguish public from private. If Steens Mountain had become a national monument, landowners would have been forced to break up the present wide-open range with fencing. The best land — the land with water — would be used by wildlife and domestic animals and be heavily grazed; the rocky ridges of public land would go ungrazed. Ranchers knew that lack of grazing would destroy the mountain. Mile after mile of fences along the streams would keep wildlife and recreationalists alike from migrating.

The most recent battle is over access not to water, but to ranchers' own land — what Elaine had called road rights, or the right to cross public land to get to your land. Landowners never had an official right of way, but their access had long been allowed by the agencies. Now it is being denied. "The agencies are going to pick off landowners one by one. Divide and conquer. The BLM offered one landowner $250 an acre for land he'd paid $1,000 an acre for. They're going to make that land worth only $250 an acre before they're done."

There were other obstacles, too, like unreasonable time limits on trail permits for moving cattle to public lands, and then little for them to eat when they arrive because of BLM's failure to manage the population of wild horses on its land. But the environmentalists' legal manipulations — often courtesy of pro bono assistance — are the worst, especially given that when the ranchers lose, they levy "humungous legal bills" that the loser must pay. "This means that your tax dollars are paying the attorneys that are fighting you." No wonder so many ranchers finally get tired and quit, Stacy says. There's also the misuse of settlements; a settlement sets up case law just as if the case had gone to trial, so enviros may sue in order to settle. A judge's settlement of a suit against ranchers under the Wild Snake River Bill concluded that grazing did not "conserve, protect, and enhance the natural and scenic wild values" of the river, so cows are no longer allowed on the river.

To Stacy, the enviros are like absentee landlords who want to exert control over property they never see. He tells the story of a woman from Boston who flew to Boise to complain to the BLM Office that they'd allowed all the Douglas fir trees to be cut down. The agent tried to explain that since this part of Oregon never got rain, it never had Douglas fir, but she wouldn't believe him. When I talked to him in Boise, the agent, Roy Kay, found conflict inevitable between all the groups because "each constitutes a wholly different culture."

"A lot of people who've never been to the West don't understand it at all," Stacy says. Their vision of control is to turn land into biological reserves for wildlife alone. "If they could move us to town and retrain us, all this land could be returned to the wild and then nature could take its course." A descendant of Basque sheepherders on Stacy's committee sees in this a new version of Manifest Destiny: "When settlers came West they got rid of the Indians by killing off the buffalo and taking away their food," he says. "Now *we* are the Indians."

◆ Circling the Wagons ◆

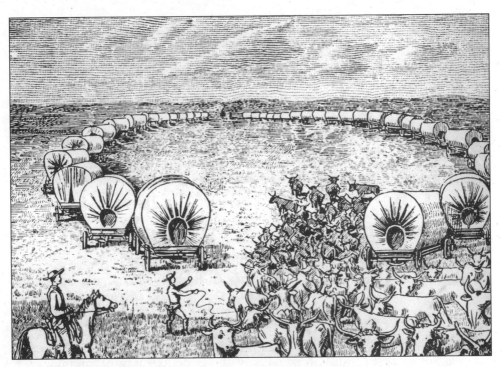

A nineteenth-century drawing shows a wagon train drawn into a circle to make a temporary corral in which to herd their cattle.

— *Courtesy Picture Collection, New York Public Library*

The whole idea was to get our cows to harvest the grass which the sun and rain and soil grew, not what somebody made with a big machine.

— Doc Hatfield, Brothers, Oregon

———————————◆———————————

TO RE-CREATE THE WEST is to begin at the literal grassroots. Almost every rancher I ran into in that part of the country asked me if I knew about Allan Savory and his "holistic grazing–type thinking," as one of them put it. Allan Savory is the guru of grass, an innovative thinker whose interest in why grasslands become deserts began in Zimbabwe, where he was born in 1935. Trained as a wildlife biologist, Savory was inspired by his experience managing a game-and-livestock farm in the grasslands of South Africa and by the thinking of Jan Smuts, the South African statesman who coined the word *holism* in 1926, from Greek *holos,* with its double way of meaning "whole": seeing a whole world before you inspect its parts, and seeing wholeness as a mark of health.

Savory's aim is both ambitious and business oriented: "Healthy land means healthy profits." His key word is management, and his goal is to change the way we look at the environment in relation to ourselves. In order to sustain any part of the environment, we must first view the ecosystem of each particular place as an organic whole, which includes not just air, earth, water, plants, and animals, but also the people who live and work there. We must study the dynamic interactions between all these elements, social structures as well as biologic and chemical ones. His aim was to provide a framework that would be universal in concept but local in application, and when he applied his method to livestock grazing in America, he recommended practices that even in the 1980s were considered radical by ranchers and farmers.

Conventional environmentalist thinking had assumed that cows on rangeland damaged the range, and therefore that the best way to recover it was to remove the cows. But Savory had found in the work of André Voisin, a French farmer-chemist whose *Soil, Grass and Cancer* (1959) linked both human and animal health to the health of the soil, a missing key: "Time, said Voisin, not the number of animals, controls overgrazing." How much time and in what season plants were exposed to animals was complicated by the fact that different kinds of plants grow at different rates in different kinds of of environments. He divided environments between brittle and nonbrittle and found a major difference in plant growth in each. A brittle environment meant dry country with sporadic rainfall, like the American West, where dead vegetation dries out and breaks down slowly. Nonbrittle meant wet country with seasonal rainfall, like America's East, where dead vegetation breaks down quickly. The conventional way of resting the land by removing livestock (rotational grazing) works well in wet country, he concluded, but not in dry. In brittle environments, large numbers of herding animals are needed to help keep the land healthy: their hooves pound dead plants into the earth, and their dung helps to compost and reseed it. While two-thirds of the earth's land environments can be described as brittle, Savory's immediate experience was with southern Africa, where buffalo and elephant herds were disappearing, along with the grass. When he came to the United States in 1979, in political exile from the Ian Smith government, he realized that America's herds of nomadic buffalo had once maintained a natural symbiosis on the High Plains, but when they were replaced by fenced cattle, the entire ecosystem changed and desertification began to create an American Sahara. With his wife, Jody Butterfield, Savory in 1984 founded the Center for Holistic Management in Albuquerque, New Mexico, and marketed his program so successfully that the Center changed its name in 2006 to Holistic Management International.

In fairness, Savory's ideas weren't entirely new to the States. As early as the 1920s, range scientists in the Forest Service had proposed some kind of rotational grazing to maintain the productivity of the range, but this countered the aims of range managers, who under the BLM aimed for productivity of the livestock, not of the land. In any case, most rangeland was outside the jurisdiction of the Forest Service, and most government agencies continued to treat land as an infinitely renewable commodity. The deterioration of the Plains into a giant Dust Bowl in the 1930s had demonstrated the dangers of that thinking, but not until after the Second World War, which had heroized America's industrial might, did those who lived on the land as ranchers or farmers take alarm at the destruction of our common ground.

In the 1950s and 1960s, when viewing any environment holistically was revolutionary because it countered our progressive view of mechanics, the voices of counterculturists began to be heard. Rachel Carson's *The Sea Around Us* in 1951 was as shocking as *Mother Earth News* in 1970. While ranchers at large were hostile to movements they accredited to urban hippies, they did not wholly ignore Midwestern spokesmen like Wes Jackson, a farmer-scientist who in 1976 founded the Land Institute in Salina, Kansas, and focused on restoring the health of the wild prairie by planting the perennial polyculture of vegetation that monocropping had destroyed. (Our current loss of topsoil to erosion is 2 billion tons each year.) But, as always, the underlying issue was the use of public lands, and Jackson had little use for cattle or buffalo in his goal to restore the prairie. In this either/or context, ranchers welcomed Savory's solution of saving livestock and prairies together by a minutely plotted system of "high-intensive short-duration grazing," marketed as HRM's SDG. While the gospel of green — "organic, natural, and sustainable" — was being spread by a wide range of environmentalists in the 1980s, ranchers were attracted by Savory's businessman "progressive scientific" style, which has created skeptics as well as converts.

One early advocate of holistic sustainability in the 1970s was farmer/
rancher Fred Kirschenmann, who keeps 113 brood cows on 3500 certified
organic acres in North Dakota and in 1979 founded the Northern Plains
Sustainable Agriculture Society. A man of wide interests, Kirschenmann,
who has taught religion and written on the relation of ethics to agriculture, was the first director of the Leopold Center of Sustainable Agriculture set up in 2000 at Iowa State University (where Henry Wallace earlier
"invented" industrial corn). Kirschenmann began to make changes in his
own operation in the late 1970s, when he asked himself, "Why are we
raising corn and bringing it in to the cows when we've got all this prairie
here that they could eat themselves?" Now he uses 1000 acres of mixed-
grass prairie for grazing his livestock, and the rest for rotating eight or
nine crops a year of diversified grains and forage.

Going to grass changes the rhythm of life on a ranch. "Grass-fed is almost a different species," says Bill Niman, "and the beauty of it is that
you're using photosynthesis to produce flesh." Niman made his name
in the 1990s by branding "Niman Ranch Meats" as a guarantor of animals "humanely and naturally raised" in sustainable environments. Today
Niman's operation embraces 500 ranches, most of which raise hogs for
good-tasting pork, but 50 of which supply cattle. "The beauty of beef,"
he says, "is that cows convert grass and naturally occurring florage
to muscle and bone. In the West there are huge tracts of land where
nothing but florage and grasses grow, and that's where mother cows and
calves should grow." Niman himself came west to Marin County from
Minneapolis in the 1960s, built his own ranch house on 11 acres of land
near Bodega Bay, and first raised hogs there with Orville Schell, a fellow
counterculturalist who put "back to the land" words into action. When
Niman began to raise beef, he discovered that there were two natural
calving periods in the United States, spring and fall, dictated by the
growth of grass. In the coldest part of the country, like Montana, calving
is in early spring, February or March. Since a cow will produce only as
much milk as her calf can use, she doesn't need much grass when her calf
is very small. As the grass season peaks in late summer and her calf has
grown big as a pig, she needs to produce as much as five to eight gallons a

day. The following fall, the calf should be ready for slaughter. In milder climates like California, calving season is in the fall because the mothers are able to feed on winter grass, so that the slaughtering season is in the spring of the following year.

Kirschenmann in Dakota, however, has altered his breeding season so that cows will calve in midsummer, when their calves can be weaned and go to grass quickly. From a calf's point of view, he says, harsh March is the worst possible time of year to be born. Now Kirschenmann does the calving in July and finds that he's eliminated most calf diseases, because by the time the calf is a few days old, it can fend for itself on summer grass. He breeds Angus with Tarantaise crosses for their strong mothering instincts. "Just a little Tarantaise breeding in those animals, and those cows are right on that coyote." But he's also experimenting with a "low-line" bull from Australia — "looks like an Angus dachshund with little short legs" — because they are a grass breed with a good live weight-to-carcass ratio.

Slaughtering is often the weakest segment in the circle of holistic husbandry. Kirschenmann is lucky because he can do his slaughtering at a local locker plant, where "they still look at slaughtering as an art" and where they make "an out-of-this-world" beef jerky but can't sell it because the spic-and-span processing room doesn't have the sixteen-foot ceilings required for USDA inspection-site certification. "We've got to put together community processing plants that not only meet the requirements but are efficient," Kirschenmann says, "like some of the multispecies processing plants in Europe." His hope is that the state of North Dakota can get the USDA to approve a state inspection service that would be equivalent to national inspection. When I ask if he's looking for a niche market for his grass-fed beef, he corrects me. Instead of an economic definition of "niche" to mean small, he says that the word more properly means "adapted to its place, uniquely adapted to its place," and such localism can bring a major shift in our thinking.

Kirschenmann believes that we're at the end of the industrial model of farming and ranching, in which we attempt to make narrow "machine applications" solve specific problems — all too often creating new problems. Instead of recognizing that "farms are not factories," our national research still goes toward technologies to keep the old industrial system going. Sustainability, he believes, requires holistic solutions rooted in particular ecologies, each of which requires its particulars to maintain the dynamics of the whole. He agrees with Savory that decision making must be decentralized and particularized: "Holistic management provides a framework that recognizes the uniqueness of each situation."

WHILE RANCHERS FAVOR the idea of uniqueness, they are temperamentally disinclined to focus on interdependence. They tend to pride themselves on the kind of rugged autonomy they imagine their homesteading ancestors to have had when they fled from the corruption of cities to be redeemed by nature in the West. When activists started to boycott cattle on public lands, some ranchers were motivated to work with environmental groups in order to preserve their grazing rights and prevent expensive lawsuits. Eventually one group drew up a set of "Graze Well" principles to make ranchers themselves better environmentalists by placing grazing uses in the context of watersheds, wildlife, and people. This led to bumper stickers like "Ranchers — the Original Environmentalists."

But it was a far simpler impulse that brought Doc and Connie Hatfield in 1976 to a 25,000-acre ranch in the high desert plain of black sage and bitterbrush in eastern Oregon, just outside Brothers (one gas station, a one-room school, and a nearby village called Sisters). They'd been going broke. In Montana's Bitterroot Valley, where Doc had worked as a vet for commodity cattle and Connie was a mother of two who ran a small herd, the price of steer calves dropped and the costs of fertilizer, labor, and energy rose. As the grandchildren of pioneering homesteaders, the Hatfields felt there had to be a better way to live and work with what they knew best, which was cattle. So, like their forefathers, they moved West.

Two-thirds of their acreage was public land, but it came with a permit for grazing issued by an unusually flexible BLM agent named Earl McKinney, who was responsive to the wild ideas of men like Allan Savory.

They found they needed such an ally, Connie says, because Oregon in the 1970s was overrun with enviro groups like Earth First! and the Oregon Natural Resources Council, among the many groups who wanted to rid public lands of any vestige of moo. Although the Hatfields are reform minded, they are also, by temperament, mediators. In 1986 they founded Oregon Country Beef, a group of ranchers in the region who shared the quest to get away from commodity thinking and to get back to a sustainable enterprise that included the customer. Those aims may seem like common sense now, but to mainstream ranchers in the beef industry even twenty years ago, they seemed dangerous.

In bucking the individualist tendency so beloved in Western lore, the Hatfields were acknowledging a truth that had been ignored for half a century: Every rancher is dependent on the economics of the cattle market run by the modern cattle industry, which began officially in 1883 in Chicago, with the first meeting of the National Cattle Growers Association. Every rancher tied into the industrial system today is dependent on the city markets and commodity processes by which live animals appear as meat in supermarket counters, a complex and conflicted reality that the mythos of the cowboy and the machine covers up rather than addresses. Despite a powerful selling voice proclaiming that the beef industry is driven by "what consumers want," the industry is driven not by consumers but by a process designed to supply a mass market with cheap food for maximum profit. The majority of ranchers have no contact with the consumer market as such. "Traditionally in agriculture we don't market," says Doc, "we sell."

The Hatfields decided to start with genuine demand and then supply it, for a reasonable profit based on their actual costs. Connie started talking to Oregonians in stores, in restaurants, on the street, in little places like Bend and big cities like Portland. Meat eaters told her they were concerned about health, hormones, antibiotics, too much fat. When she found out that meat eaters in neighboring Bend were trying to get "natural" beef from Argentina, the lightbulb went on. Connie called up the ranchers she knew in her area and invited them to a meeting. Thirty-six of them came, sat in a circle, and talked. "We're all going out of business," said Doc. "What can we do?" Addressing that fact and asking the right questions set a new model for ranching. They were like settlers under siege, circling the wagons to stay alive.

They had a forerunner to look to, as both inspiration and cautionary tale. Mel Coleman was a fourth-generation rancher in the high desert of San Luis Valley southwest of Denver, who in 1979 was also going broke on his 240,000 acres with commodified cows when he hit upon the notion that there might be a market for meat free of hormones and antibiotics. He located a small feedlot in La Junta that would do the job right for him and slaughtered his first ten head of cattle in 1981. During the year and a half it took to get the USDA to approve a "natural" label for his Coleman Natural Beef, he sold it out of an old fridge in the back of his pickup truck to natural-food stores in Colorado. When the USDA approval came through, Coleman Natural Beef became a brand name and a media hit. The company grew rapidly, and by 1985 the Grand Union supermarket chain contracted with Coleman for 500 cattle a week. Quickly he formed a group of ranchers to meet the new demand, took on heavy loans, and became a popular television and radio spokesman for sustainable agriculture. Only two years later, however, Grand Union suddenly slashed its order in half and the Federal Land Bank foreclosed, forcing Coleman to sell out to a business consortium and relinquish control over his business. Today Mel Coleman, Jr., is still a successful spokesman for the brand, and Coleman is still one of the bestsellers in the "natural beef" niche, but the company is actually owned by Booth Creek Management, one of whose partners, George Gillett, is chairman of Swift & Company.

Coleman's fast rise and fall as an independent company could only have supported the Hatfields' belief that they needed an unconventional structure to pursue unconventional aims. Their first major innovation was getting ranchers to work together as a community in which each man and woman had an equal voice and an equal vote. (It didn't hurt that when they started they were on an eleven-party phone line.) But putting a bunch of ranchers together in those days, as one of them said, was "like a gunnysack filled with a bunch of tomcats." In addition, it was important to Connie that ranchers' wives spoke out as ranchers in their own right. She had found her own voice at the age of forty, while attending an Allan Savory seminar, where one of the teachers gave her the liberating insight that she was dyslexic — not stupid, as she'd always thought. In fact, Savory viewed the participation of ranching women like herself as essential. "When he first came over from South Africa, he was obnoxious," Connie recalls. "He couldn't understand how ranchers would come to his meetings and go home and not make any changes. He said, 'We've got to have women come to these meetings because they'll ask questions.'"

Doc agreed that it was easier for women to think about consumer needs, whereas men tended to be stuck in the industry formula of quantifying profits at the producing end. "We were all scrunched around in our living room trying to sit in a circle, and that's when the men and the women all started talking together." The consortium turned out to be a family affair. "Oregon Beef is not just about bringing money back into cattle, but about bringing young people back to do the work," Connie says. "And now we have to have babysitters because young mothers come. The little babies that were being held at our first meeting have gone off to college. We're growing our replacements."

At first a lot of ranchers had trouble with the idea of a group making decisions by consensus. "One person flat out wouldn't do it," says Doc. "He was a successful businessperson with a small ranch and he wanted somebody to be in charge. He asked me once, 'Do you know what a hierarchy is?' And I said, 'Yeah, that's what we're trying to avoid.'" One woman who was a part-time rancher with a lumber business left the group because she hated the lack of structure, the lack of rules. The group has what business types call a "flat structure." Each ranch family elects a director and the directors elect a chairman, but at meetings they must find common ground for consensus or they can't proceed. "That's slow and sometimes painful," Connie says, "but it builds a lot of trust."

With her newly won confidence, Connie believed she would be good at marketing, so she donned her jeans skirt and headed for the big city to talk to supermarkets. "We sent her," Doc says now, "because we men knew it wouldn't work."

"And because I didn't know that, I just went," Connie adds. "I said, 'We have 10,000 mother cows, how can we serve you?'"

Inside two years, Connie had found a feeder, a packer, and ten retailers who would buy 8 to 10 of their cattle a week — a start, but not enough to survive. They were saved by Hiroshi Tanaka, head of the Japanese restaurant chain Kyotaru, who wanted 50 head a week for his 800 restaurants. Tanaka had seen a Western TV show called *From Oregon with Love* and was determined to get his beef from Oregon. One of the older ranchers of the group, Ken Bentz from nearby Drewsey, came up with a pricing model that would cover the costs of production, bring a return on investment, provide a reasonable profit, and be sustainable. That was it. They had cut out all the middlemen. They owned the cattle from pasture to market. They didn't have to raise any capital because they had no overhead, no offices, no equipment, and they had no stockholders but themselves.

Raising a cow is a long-term investment, and being dependent on the vagaries of the daily market made no sense to Connie. "It's just silly to work real hard and have the right kind of cattle and the right kind of grazing and then one day you sell them and the price of the day is what you get." What seemed silly to Connie was standard for the industry. "OCB is the only company that doesn't buy cattle," says Dan Probert, a ranching member who with his wife Suzy is on the financial team. "We can actually budget what we're going to make, and that's a huge thing in agriculture. OCB had a chance to control their own destiny." The cowboys could run their own machine.

Only they learned to use other metaphors. From Mr. Tanaka they learned the principle of *shen rai*, Connie explains, traditional in Japan but not in the United States, where two companies work together intimately to share benefits and costs. Unfortunately, the Kyotaru company did not survive the crash of the Japanese economy in the 1990s, but the Hatfields were able to replace their Japanese customers with America's fast-growing natural-food market in health stores and at Whole Foods. On the *shen rai* principle, Oregon Beef has no signed contracts with anyone, but instead has "working partners," which have increased exponentially since I first interviewed members of the OCB in 2004.

The traditional industrial beef chain moves in sequence: The cow-calf person sells to a backgrounder (or yearling operator) who sells to a feedlot who sells to a packer who sells to a wholesaler who sells to a retailer. But Oregon Beef owns the whole process, assuming responsibility and as much control as possible over what happens to its cows, from conception to consumption. Direct contact with end consumers — the people who actually eat the cow — has a strong impact on ranchers and consumers alike. To foster that contact, the Hatfields arranged for every rancher to do in-store demonstrations. North Pacific Whole Foods alone has twenty-two stores, so OCB families go together and spend the weekend in Portland. "We set up a little table in the store and demo our hot dogs and talk to people." Even reluctant ranchers became sold on the idea once they found out that people were really interested in what they did, how they lived, how their cattle lived. OCB also has a Customer Appreciation Day when all their working partners — the feedlot owners, the meat cutters, the store owners, the chefs, and their families — get together on one of the members' ranches for a giant barbecue.

The Hatfields want ranchers to control every aspect of the cows they own in order to be accountable to their consumers at the end of the line. For some ranchers, the idea of continuity and accountability is a big draw. "Here's a way to have control of the whole process," says one. "We can trace an individual steak right back to where it was processed, fed, raised, and born, and even tell you its genetic ancestry and why it's like it is." Creating good seed stock, where genetic data is kept on every animal, is part of this accountability. "We're still trying to find out why, with two blood-related animals raised the same way, one may be a lot tougher to chew than the other."

But there's many a slip between pasture and plate, as outside players and processes put ranchers' principles to the test. The Hatfields discovered that there was a big difference between being in the cattle business and in the meat business. "Seventeen years ago, we didn't know what was under the hide," Connie says. They did know that in the meat business, grade depends upon fat, and that a carcass that yields 30 percent waste fat is standard in the industry. "But that's not acceptable," says Connie.

"These animals have been overfattened. Feedlots started during the '40s, when we needed fat for tallow for the war, but our industry's forgotten that the war's over."

The chief difficulty for any group marketing its own beef is to produce a year-round supply. Beef that is entirely grass-fed, for example, is usually not ready for slaughter until it's around 3 years old, instead of the 12 to 15 months for grain-finished calves. OCB would like to produce a healthy grass-fed animal year-round, but in their region they may be under snow four or five months of the year. "We have to work together to get the year-round supplies, but a rancher has to figure out whether it's worth the freight cost of getting his cattle to our central feeding point," Probert explains. A lot of their cattle come from ranches in Hawaii like the Parker Ranch, where cattle raising has always been big, but the slaughterhouses are long gone. The Parker cattle are shipped live to Seattle, then trucked to the slaughterhouse.

There are only a few areas in the country that provide a proper locale for slaughterhouses in conjunction with feedlots, often euphemized as "facilities" or "bivouacs" (Bill Niman calls them "bivos"). For a bivo you need a very dry climate to prevent disease, Niman explains, and you need to be right next to a slaughterhouse because slaughtering is also about seasonality. Animals have an internal clock in sync with the plant cycles, because they need to store as much fat as they can getting ready for winter. During that period they'll feast on everything, on whatever crop is taking energy out of the soil — wheat, wild grasses, barley, corn. This is also the period when they're ready to feed on a high-energy grain ration because their stomachs have been callused, the linings transformed from smooth to honeycombed, as in honeycomb tripe. "The transformation allows them to churn huge amounts of cellulose and roughage and convert that to starch and nutrition," Niman says, "so their digestive tract goes through this metamorphosis between weaning and finishing." Niman was not an advocate of 100 percent grass-fed and grass-finished beef when I interviewed him at his California ranch and Idaho bivo in 2004. From him and from the Hatfields, I learned not to demonize feedlots or grain fodder abstractly, but to look holistically at the particulars of each enterprise in the framework of humanely raised livestock in sustainable environments.

On his own ranch in Bolinas, Niman weans his calves just after "this season of plenty," when the grass turns brown in June. At this point the calves are nice and fat — "greasy," they call it — from so much mother's milk. If these were dairy cattle, this is the point where you'd slaughter them for veal, because dairy cattle are selected to produce milk, not flesh. The males of dairy cattle are useless for any purpose other than veal. With beef breeds, this is the point where you can take a 900-pound steer at 13 to 14 months and finish him at about 7 pounds of grain per pound of meat to reach the desired 1200 to 1400 pounds for slaughter within four to five months. "They can eat about a ton of grain in the finishing period," Niman says, "because they like to eat."

One of OCB's working partners is John Wilson, owner of Beef Northwest Feeders, a sizable company of diverse interests, including three feedlots in Oregon. Wilson is a five-generation rancher, young-looking at fifty, and full of energy. His great-grandfather came over the Oregon Trail and in 1878 homesteaded his allotted 160 acres near Boardman, now the site of Wilson's major feedlot. With 40,000 head, it's considered midsized. Wilson zips around his territory in a helicopter on a fast-track schedule, so he was taken aback by the OCB setup, which required him to demo hot dogs in a little grocery store in Portland. To his surprise, he discovered he liked it. He also likes cooperatives like OCB and companies like Niman's, which offer opportunities for young people to return to ranching. "Because ranchers are so traditional, they're unwilling to change their model," he says, "but OCB has demonstrated one way to grow within a mature industry." In the six years he has been an OCB partner, the cooperative has grown from 60 to 900 head of finished cattle per week. While the price for sustainable beef has to be higher because costs are higher, the reasons for it require education for both producer and consumer. "But not everyone has to get on board," he says. Ninety to 95 percent of the population will continue to buy commodity beef, he believes, because it's cheaper.

Wilson makes room for both kinds of beef within his feedlots, keeping OCB beef separate from the commodity herds. His Boardman feedlot has the advantage of not being near anything but alfalfa fields. It is undetectable by sight or smell until you're immediately upon it. I'd read a lot of good prose about the horrors of supersized feedlots, but after visiting a dozen small to midsized ones in different parts of the country, I found that feedlots in the right location and on the right scale can be run humanely and soundly. If they are not an ideal way to fatten cows, neither are they in themselves the devil's work. The details matter. Only 7000 out of the 23,000 head of cattle at the Boardman lot are OCB's; the rest belong to commodity producers. The OCB herd remains on the lot for 95 to 100 days, coming in at around 800 pounds and leaving at 1100 pounds. Bill Gover, who has been at Boardman for eleven years, runs the lot, along with a mostly Hispanic crew of forty, many of them second-generation Oregonians. "It's not technology that makes a good feedlot," Gover says, "it's people."

Gover says that this is good country for a feedlot because it's dry, with annual rainfall of no more than 8 inches. In the pens, the animals are given around 400 square feet per cow, more in winter when storms come. Each animal is provided feed three times a day and 9 to 10 inches of headroom at the trough, but the cattle eat in their own pecking order: The alpha ones eat breakfast at 6:00, others arrive for lunch at 9:00, the slowpokes for lunch at 11:30. What I notice most is the smell, not of cow dung but of corn. Here are mountains of high-moisture corn fermenting for silage, mountains of flaked corn milled on the site, mountains of alfalfa hay, and another mountain of potato slurry, which Boardman gets from a local Borden's processing plant that supplies McDonald's with fries. While the plant mashes waste fries into potato patties for feed, OCB eschews them because "we can't guarantee the kind of fat they've been cooked in." I ask Gover whether cows prefer corn or potatoes. "What do you say about brandy?" he replies. "You have to develop a taste for it." By using such by-products, the feedlot has managed to cut grain use by half and thereby lessen costs. Gover finds that cows are creatures of habit that will eat because food is there, not because they're hungry for a particular feed. His job is to maintain the edge of their appetites, and their job is to eat.

Maintaining cows' appetites means keeping them healthy. With the feedlot's head doctor, Dr. Min, I check out the hospital compound, which consists of twelve outdoor pens and additional space indoors for more severe cases, usually respiratory ones like pneumonia. Because OCB disallows antibiotics, they use vitamins, sulfa drugs, and lots of TLC. ("Amazing what you can do with TLC," says Dr. Min.) You have to watch out for "bloaters," he says, cattle whose belching gets restricted by something, because if they aren't able to belch, they basically explode. If a steer's sick enough to require antibiotics, he's pulled out of the OCB program and sold to the generic groups.

I found another feedlot that bore evidence of TLC in Caldwell, Idaho, just over the border from eastern Oregon. This is one of the feedlots Bill Niman uses, and the locale is as different from his Bolinas ranch as coast fog from desert sun. "The challenge in raising beef," says Rob Stokes, who with his wife, Michelle, runs the Purple Sage Feedlot, "is to utilize the entire gastrointestinal tract, not just the stomach. The two common feeds we use for that are feather meal, which is a bypass protein, and distiller grains." "Feather meal" is hydrolyzed chicken feathers, in common use because their protein content degrades slowly in the rumen. The Stokeses pride themselves on having developed a number of refinements in their feeding methods. They bring in hay at the beginning of the season and carefully control its moisture. They steamroller their grain, flattening the corn kernels to make them easier to digest. They use an 80/20 grain-and-molasses mix with whey and lactose, then add sugar to provide energy and keep dust down in the ration.

Speed of fattening depends on breed, Stokes says, and in the West they stick with Herefords and Angus because of their consistency in putting on weight. The mega-feedlots in the Midwest tend to use bigger cattle, the Continental breeds, because they'll feed up to 1,500 or 1,600 pounds in the same amount of time. Rob shows me what to look for to determine if a steer is ready for slaughter. They get little pom-poms or fat balls around their tail; they get a lot of fat around their "cod" (penis), where their testicles would be if they had any. They get "ties" of fat in the middle of the back on both sides. When some steers get really wide in the front, they call it "clapping"; when they're "clapped," they're ready.

Most cooperative groups of ranchers come to grief over where and how to handle slaughtering and processing. Although an average of 30 million cows are "harvested" each year in America, all but a very small percentage of them are turned into meat by only three major packers. The industrial cliché that economy of scale breeds efficiency has also bred monopoly, and what many see as a cattle cartel. From the Hatfields' point of view, packers are just one part of the process and should not be calling the shots for both producers *and* consumers. "We're pulling our product through the packing plant on its way to our customers" is the way Doc explains it.

One of OCB's working partners is the packer/processing company Washington Beef in Toppenish, where I first met up with Doc and Connie, because they wanted to show me the plant. Washington Beef is located in a small town that calls itself "Where the West Still Lives," a town where every building displays a mural. You can take a walking tour or hop into a covered wagon to view the more than sixty-five murals that paint the town's public buildings with such historic events as "The Prairie Chicken Dance," "Trading with the Yakama," "From Horse to Horseless Carriage."

The plant is owned by Agrabeef, which is an animal-pharmaceutical company, and their major production is commodity beef. But Washington is happy to work with OCB because the group can guarantee a steady supply of cattle each week, for which the packers receive a processing fee without the risk of buying cattle from feedlots and speculating on their market value. At Washington, OCB cattle go through first and are kept separate throughout the cutting and packaging process. All their cattle are identified with ear tags and can be traced backward and forward to the supermarket. On Sunday night, the cattle are delivered and held in pens overnight. Next morning two animals at a time enter the back chute, and since they've been in chutes before, they're not frightened. Each is shot with a bolt-action stun gun in the forehead. Then it slides down to a pit where a man takes one back hind leg, shackles it to a chain, levers it up to the rail, and slits the animal's throat so that it will bleed out immediately. It takes no more than two or three minutes from chute to rail. "The cows can't see ahead of them, so they're not wild-eyed or scared. They don't smell any blood." Remember, Doc is a vet, and his standard answer to customers' questions about the killing part is that the animals are not frightened. "I certainly hope that when my time comes, it's that gentle." "Quick" might have been a better word.

Because of the size of Washington Beef, which processes about 1000 head *a day* in contrast to OCB's 900 head a week, OCB was able to save nearly $100 per animal killed. Washington buys its cattle for the processing at a fixed price and then sells OCB back the boxed beef. Anything OCB can't use, like the hides and other waste parts, Washington sells. When the Hatfields discovered that only 12 percent of a carcass goes for top cuts like steaks, they realized that nobody can sell an animal for steaks alone. They located a regional chain called Burgerville with thirty-nine outlets and were able to turn their trim meat — up to 16 tons a week — into gourmet hamburgers.

They also have less "shrink" now, Connie explains. "We used to get paid on the basis of how much water is in the animal when you walk him to the scales. A buyer will look at your cattle, and if they think they've just had a drink, they'll pay you less because they don't want to pay for water. That's one kind of shrink. Another is when the seller weighs them when they go on the truck, but they may have a lot of manure in them, and you don't get paid for that when they go to the scales at the packer's. There's still a different kind of shrink in the grocery store if the butcher cuts steaks and nobody buys them until they begin to turn black and have to be ground into hamburger or given to an employee to take home. There's shrink all the way through." The Hatfields now hedge against shrink by rewarding quality. "We set up a target and a bull's-eye. If the rancher hits the target weight, he gets a bonus, and if he hits the bull's-eye, he gets more."

WHEN THEY SUCCEED in staving off the hostile forces of the industrial marketplace, wagon circles beget wagon circles. In Paonia, Colorado, population 1,497, under the name Colorado Homestead Ranches, a smaller group of six ranchers has banded together to provide the meat for their own local slaughterhouse to be sold in their own village market. "The Hatfields were our inspiration," says Sue Ayer of Ayer & Ayer Ranch. "They came here to give a talk eight years ago and one of our friends said, 'Why don't we just do this?'"

Sue's husband, Jim, explains, "We got tired of the cow market going up and down and we figured if we could retail our own meat, then we could streamline so we'd have a steady flow. Before, there was always somebody in the middle somewhere who sold your calves to a feedlot or, if you finished 'em out, you still had to deal with a packer, and most times he had his thumb on you, too."

They helped organize the original group of five and now run Homestead Market on the main street of Paonia, misleadingly called Grand Avenue. Whatever "local" means in the rugged country of North Fork Valley, Homestead is it. OCB had to drop "Oregon" from its name to become "Country Natural Beef," once they'd expanded the number of their ranchers to keep up with the demands of a vastly expanded chain like Whole Foods. But Homestead raises and sells its meats within a relatively small region, or locale. The Market is next door to the offices of *High Country News*, one of the best environmental nonprofit magazines in the country, devoted "to inform and inspire people to act on behalf of the West's land, air, water and inhabitants" and to create "a society to match the scenery." Paonia is the kind of Colorado crossroads where enviros and ranchers live literally cheek by jowl. Ed Marston, former publisher of the *News* and a 1970s émigré from Manhattan, reflects that groups like the Homestead and the Hatfields are mending the divisions between old hippies and old ranchers, "building a foundation for a self-supporting economy that can create a middle class, the source of all progress and the way to move the ball politically in a progressive way."

In a street of a dozen storefronts, it's not hard to find Homestead Market. I'm drawn there by the smell of hamburgers, turned by an elderly man on an iron grill set up on the sidewalk in front of the shop. Inside, the shelves are stocked with rows and rows of local wines labeled cherry, fire-mountain red, pear-apple, produced by Carlson Vineyards and Orchard Valley Farms, and a large, glass-doored freezer is full of meat. The market is also a café, and Sue Ayer runs both. In the kitchen she turns the meat of Homestead ranchers into meat loaf, beef Stroganoff, beef tips in wine sauce, oriental beef in soy sauce, chuck-wagon barbecue, sloppy joes. Homestead also sells its meat at farmers markets and to restaurants throughout North Fork. In back of the store they've set up a processing room for custom-cutting game, and here I find rancher-member Steve Kossler, preparing the place for a dozen elk coming in tomorrow.

A local friend of his, he says, herds domesticated elk for hunters to shoot, which Homestead butchers for the hunters. The man used to raise elk for meat until the bottom fell out of the elk market, Kossler tells me, so now he just arranges "no-kill, no-pay" hunting parties. "The hunters didn't want the skins," Kossler says, "so we'll keep them, but I'm sure Willy will want the antlers." There's an international market for their velvet, which is full of glucosamine and chondroitin for the arthritic, and aphrodisiacal properties assigned to them by elderly Chinese. And there's always a market for dried antlers for decor. "One of our fellows does leatherwork and his daughter beadwork," Sue says, "so they mount the antlers in different ways and they're absolutely beautiful and sell well in Aspen — worth more than the meat." The thing about elk meat is that it's low in fat but expensive, like buffalo, Sue explains. Nowadays there's not enough land for elk to graze, so you have to feed them supplements. "Wild" game takes on new meaning when I learn that they are even feeding buffalo now in feedlots. "Ted Turner's got many thousand bison in ranches in New Mexico and Wyoming," says Jim Ayer. "He's one of the largest landowners in the United States — you should see his feedlots."

According to Turner's Web site, he owns 2 million acres and plans to return some of his feedlot bison to grass so they can be marketed for a higher price as "Turner Reserve Grassfed Bison."

Homestead sends its cattle for butchering to a small plant nearby, in an even smaller village than Paonia — Cedaredge, northwest of Hotchkiss. The plant is a low wooden building with a corral out back, next to the home of the owners, who've run the plant for the past twenty-seven years but are ready to sell to the Homestead group. Signs announce "Beef bones for dogs @ 25 cents a pound," and "Vegetarian is an Indian word for lousy hunter." In comparison to the Washington Beef plant, this one is a doll's house, with a total of nine workers and just two or three of them doing all the butchering by hand. Homestead supplies about one-third of the total beef they butcher annually, maybe 700 head, in addition to lamb and pork and custom butchering for individuals.

Even though their ranch herds are small — the Ayers run about 300 head on 4500 private acres plus public lands for grazing — Homestead still needs to sell most of its calves elsewhere. Homestead grain-finishes its cattle on corn and silage for the last 30 to 90 days, but they prohibit any hormones or antibiotics. "The hardest thing is trying to get everything done because we're already busy with ranching," Jim says. "Processing is a whole 'nother full-time job." Homestead hopes to double its output from 200 carcasses to 450 in a year and a half and to jump up the custom part of it. They've also been using another processing plant in Pierce, Colorado, because they're doing so many value-added products now. They had so much hamburger left, Sue says, that they decided to make Polish sausage, summer sausage, bratwurst, and jerky sticks. "We take our butchered meat to where we can get a good-quality product made, and World Meats in Grand Junction makes a lot of them for us." They also want to expand their precooked entrees, and set up a USDA kitchen so that they can sell entrees in places other than the store and farmers markets and rent out to organizations like the Elks. "Some friends think we're nuts," Sue says, "but we've got to keep growing."

"The demand is there," Jim says. "People want to know where the product comes from, want to know that it hasn't sat on a dock for a week." While they looked at other places in the area, Cedaredge was an established business with a clientele, so when they take it over, they won't be pulling clientele away from someone else. Sue shows me with some excitement how she's going to put a new store all across the front, so they'll have a full market and processing plant combined. "Because Cedaredge is a retirement area, there's a lot of people with a lot of money." The locale is also right for natural and organic products. Jim says it looks as if about one-third of the natural and organic companies in the United States are in Colorado. Homestead gets good word of mouth at farmers markets, they've gotten good media coverage, and they get good help from Colorado State University. "We vowed when we started this that we would try to educate any way we can," Sue says. "And when CSU people like John Scanga of the Meat Department have helped us with grants, we've put part of that grant money back to helping ag kids through college. We figure we'll help anybody get started. The neat part is we found five ranches to work together, and you know how darned independent agriculture people are."

Jim's great-grandfather had come over from Meeker in the late 1800s, after the infamous massacre there. He'd been an Indian agent in Utah with the Utes, and when the trouble began in Meeker, he came over the hill to Paonia. Jim's grandfather had run a livery stable across the street from where the Homestead Market is today and homesteaded in nearby Crawford, planting orchards and potatoes, raising Percheron horses and trained teams. His maternal grandparents from Ireland had been home-steaders here, too, and Jim and Sue now rent out their cabin to hunters and tourists. "That's one of the things that helps keep us alive. You have to be real enterprising. Sometimes you wish you could just focus on ranching, but we know that we have to change and grow."

Jim and Sue's three children and five grandchildren all live in the Crawford area. Their daughter has married a rancher, one son works with Jim on the ranch, and their other son is training in Bell Mountain in the Castle Rock area to become a paramedic and firefighter. The ranch can't pay for three families, but with a good part-time job elsewhere, their firefighter son could help with the ranch, too.

I hop in the Ayers' truck with a refrigerated trailer of beef carcasses to help them deliver meat to their regulars on Friday, pickup and delivery day. We stop to deliver at Grandma's Kitchen opposite a sign reading "Antelope Hill Orchards. Turn Here. Pies, Cherries, and Peaches." Some of their customers order a whole animal to be custom-cut to put in their freezer. In the fall they sell a lot of roasts because out here a lot of people still cook. "We sell oxtail, soup bones, marrowbones we call 'soup steaks.'" They've also been doing custom game butchering for four years now and have learned the hard way. "The first year was a hell year," says Sue. "We were having our butts chewed out. People think there's just one big tenderloin and you cut it into steaks. Or they'll bring in some game full of bullet holes and blow up if they get less meat than they'd planned." The second year, Sue was ready for them. "We'd ask how many bullet holes and where are they? Then tell them they could expect such and such meat loss. Now we even make them sign for it. It's been a real learning experience, but this fourth year is going to be great. We started with the hope that all of us could have a little more time and a little more money to live on."

On the drive home, listening to the local radio station play "Lord have mercy, Baby's got her blue jeans on," talk turns to the mountain lion Jim killed recently, so big it made the record book. "We're getting him mounted — a full mount — eight and a half feet," Jim says. Sue worries about where to put it because their house is small. "Move the couch out or something," she muses. "If I wouldn't have been with a bunch of men, I would have just wanted to look at the lion — that animal was so clean, just gorgeous — but they are killing the sheep, and I wonder how many elk does it take a week to keep a lion fed? They have the most incredible eyes, even in death, and the meat is wonderful. Tastes like pork. Seemed a little bit dry, but I didn't know how long to cook lion because I'd never cooked it before." Sue and Jim took some of the meat to her aunt's in Palm Springs for Thanksgiving. "I cut the meat into chunks and put some in freezer bags and some in a Crock-Pot and cooked it a long time. If I did it again, I would cook it slower. I think I cooked it a little too fast. Just real nice meat, no gaminess, no fat."

◆ Buffalo Commons ◆

"North American Bison" was drawn and engraved by Messrs. Sly and Wilson as a woodcut for *The Penny Magazine*. The magazine was published every Saturday from 1832 to 1845 by the Society for the Diffusion of Useful Knowledge to enlighten the working classes of Great Britain, few of whom would have seen a bison live unless they emigrated to America. This one appeared in 1835 in a collection of "one hundred and fifty wood cuts, selected from *The Penny Magazine:* worked, by the printing-machine from the original blocks."

— *Courtesy Picture Collection, New York Public Library*

Now the buffs, they evolved on the plains with the plants — the two grew up together, they *belong* together in this place, this landscape . . . Your cow is out a place here and that's why they are so much work.

— Annie Proulx, *That Old Ace in the Hole*

◆

KIOWA, COLORADO, is only forty-five minutes south of Denver, but after speeding through miles of metastasizing urban development, it's a shock to slow down for a one-street village tucked along the edge of prairie that unrolls like a rug east of the Rockies. From here it's less than eight miles to the Groves Ranch sign, featuring cowboy boots and a lariat, and only a mile and a half more to the Log House. In this strangely corrugated land of ridges, ravines, prairie, and ponderosa pines, I'm not surprised to walk into a double-storied log palace studded with buffalo skulls, antelope heads, at least one large fox, and a wall-sized buffalo robe hung over the balcony. An old wagon outside holds a dozen white skulls bleaching in the sun and in the distance beyond are unmistakable humped silhouettes. This is the buffalo ranch of Dave and Marlene Groves, who grew up together in Southern California, married as teenagers thirty-five years ago, went into business together, and eventually decided to ranch together. They thought about cows, but they didn't want to lose money, and they wanted to be independent. Cattle didn't fit that equation. Buffalo did.

Bison is, in fact, the scientifically proper name for the huge bovine that migrated to North America during the Pleistocene era, 1.8 million years ago, to evolve into subspecies named wood bison and Plains bison (taxonomically known as *Bison bison*). Europeans knew the wild ox and had given Latin names to Asian water buffalo (*Bubalus bubalis*) and African Cape buffalo (*Syncerus caffer*). To them this New World beast looked more like water buffalo than cow. One of the first of them to describe it was the seventeenth-century Spaniard Antonio de Solís y Rivadeneyra: "It has a Bunch on its Back like a Camel: its Flanks dry, its Tail large, and its Neck covered with Hair like a Lion." At the beginning of the last century, there were no "bison buffalo" on ranches anywhere in the world. America's native herd had dropped from over 35 million (some say 60 million) in the sixteenth century to as few as 500 at the beginning of the twentieth, although possibly only the 23 buffalo left in the preserve of Yellowstone Park could still be called purebred.

Along with the buffalo went the prairie grass that had once covered 40 percent of the United States; now only 1 percent that can be called "native" remains. The name itself is a clue to how this came about: *Prairie* comes from the French for "meadows," as if the aboriginal grasslands of the Great Plains were pasture for sheep and cows. As our settlers moved east to west from the Mississippi to the Rockies, the sequence of tall grass to mixed grass to short grass charted the ecology from wet to dry, but prairie grasses were alike conditioned by buffalo, fire, and drought, their natural companions for survival. The strategy of the grasses was to grow long taproots; 60 percent of their tangled mass crept underground in search of water. Buffalo grazed the tops and moved on, their hooves trampling the earth, their manure fertilizing it, to encourage regrowth. This had been the message in the 1980s of Allan Savory. Fire and drought, claimed a couple of Eastern geographers from Rutgers University, Deborah and Frank Popper, were similarly needed for good maintenance, as were prairie dogs for the support of wildlife like ferrets and hawks.

We've had a full century to experience what happens to the land when you slaughter prairie grass to grow corn and slaughter buffalo to raise cows. LaVon, the endearing prairie prophetess in Annie Proulx's *That Old Ace in the Hole*, is eloquent on the subject: "Buffs don't graze like cows — cows are selective. They'll eat all the creampuff grasses and plants so you have to keep moving them after a few days to another pasture unless you like to see bare dirt. . . . The bison and the native plant species have a *relationship*." Comparisons between buffs and cows are inevitable because they are now in serious competition both for actual land and for the imaginary land in our heads fought over in the war of ideas.

In the 1980s, the Poppers had to be protected by the police when they spoke to townsfolk across the Great Plains, telling them what might be done to revive towns long abandoned. Their ideas seemed not only suspiciously leftist but overtly Eastern. But what had happened to them was visible to all. Since the 1920s, the Great Plains had lost one-third of their population, and the land was dotted with ghost towns collecting nothing but memories and dust. To revitalize the Plains, the Poppers suggested creating a "Buffalo Commons," a metaphor they employed to describe both an actual place and a larger method, where opposing interests might coexist without clashing in order to restore the prairie and reinvigorate its communities. They originally suggested a preserve about the size of Montana and used the word *commons* to connote "the need to treat land more as a common property resource, much as we do with air or water." As geographers, they wanted to show that cycles of boom and bust in the Plains were part of the cycle of rain and drought specific to that region, and this cycle did not fit the intellectual prediction of an inexorable drive toward either progress or decline. Despite initial hostility from all hands, the metaphor took hold, as opposing groups began to see the possibilities of a Great Plains Partnership, from the Nature Conservancy and Forest Service to the North American Bison Cooperative to the Plains Indians InterTribal Bison Cooperative.

The buffalo took hold, too, and in a sharp reversal, domesticated buffalo at the beginning of the twenty-first century are beginning to impact the meat business. In 2006 the National Bison Association — upgraded from "National Buffalo Association" no doubt in an attempt to elevate the imagery of buffalo nickels to bison green bills — listed 4000 private ranches raising a total of 270,000 buffalo in the United States, plus

150,000 in Canada, most of them in the Great Plains, where they belong. In addition there are around 20,000 in public herds, like those of Yellowstone Park, and 7000 on Indian reservations.

DAVE AND MARLENE haven't always been ranchers. After years of working separately in Los Angeles, they teamed up in the 1980s to manufacture stainless-steel kitchen equipment for the likes of Wal-Mart and Costco. They picked their land in 1995, Marlene says, when the buffalo business that had begun slowly in the 1980s exploded after the success of the film *Dances with Wolves*. Once Dave got the fencing up on the 400 acres of their homesite, they bought their first herd and now run about 100 "buffs," as Marlene calls them, on 2000 acres.

"We make a good team," says Marlene. "I like the number crunching and he's the hands-on guy." Dave makes the woven-metal fencing of their pens and corrals. A fence at least 5½ feet tall was crucial, Dave explains, because buffalo can spring like deer. They can also splinter wood like kindling. Other evidence of Dave's handiwork is everywhere, from the stripped and varnished tree trunks that support the cathedral ceiling of their home to the skulls, mounted heads, and robes that he prepares from their animals. Meanwhile, Marlene's marketing eye has emblazoned buffalos on quilts, pillows, coasters, rugs, trunks, pipes, tiles, shaped them in porcelain, cast them in iron, engraved them on glass, painted them on wood, carved them in quartz, sculpted them into jewelry. Over time the entire family, which includes two married children and four grandchildren, joined the buffalo team.

I first ran into Marlene's organizational talents at the national conference of the American Grasslands Association in the Wabash Methodist Campground near Clay City, Indiana. Marlene had thoroughly investigated the ranching world of cattle and buffalo and was gung-ho for grass, even though 90 percent of buffalo producers today do grain finishing. She's also adamant about truth in advertising. "If you call it grass-fed, that should mean 100 percent and no antibiotics. If not, call it 'grass-fed with minimal grain.' Just don't lie about it." It's that kind of vigor that has

helped the AGA create standards for a rapidly growing grass-fed population of livestock of all kinds. Marlene — strong sturdy body, square chin,
striking green eyes, straight blond hair parted in the middle — is a
straight shooter who believes that what she wants to happen, will. Witness the old red dump truck she found, which now provides monthly
tours for visitors and school kids who want to see buffalo on the ranch.
When somebody else began to bid on it, Marlene told him, "I want this,
and no matter what you bid, I'll bid higher because I'm going to have it."
The man stopped bidding.

Their grow-out pasture is around 1,600 acres, and Marlene drives me
out in an SUV to pay obeisance to the herd patriarch, Noah, 2,800
pounds, 11½ feet long nose to rump, 6 feet tall ground to hump. He's just
made the cover of *Bison World* (Fall 2002), but he's used to being a
celebrity, and the other animals give him space. Feeding peaceably on
prairie sand reed, western wheatgrass, big bluestem, prairie cane flower,
yucca, elk sedge, buffalo grass, the scattered herd looks as cinematic, or as
real, as the herd that stampedes in *Dances with Wolves*. Buffalos like to
"slounge," Marlene says, in a word that combines "lounge around" and
"slough off." They like being prairie lounge lizards, but what they don't
like is stress. A sudden charge of adrenaline can be fatal. We approach
one pasture that has mostly mothers, equipped genetically with very tiny
udders so that they can maintain running speed when needed. They're
usually good producers and can birth calves for twenty years. They're
also fiercely protective, says Marlene. "You don't mess with Mom's kid."
What I like about being up close to beasts "as big as parked cars," as
someone described them, is that they are not mowing machines, not predictable, not cuddly. They command their own space.

I'm forcibly reminded of this next morning when I rise at 6:00 A.M. to
watch Dave and his son, Robert, "harvest" half a dozen young buffalo
which are ready at 1,000 pounds or so for the slaughterhouse in Colorado Springs. The men have already sequestered their chosen ones in
the maze of sorting pens designed by Dave to maximize control while
minimizing stress. It's a matter of fooling the buffs into entering the
chute in the back of the loading truck without frightening them. Dave

uses a long-handled paddle with a blue flag on the end to herd three steers at a time into the labyrinth with shouts and flag waves, while his son works the truck portcullis and drops it behind each group of three so they won't crowd each other inside. The slatted vents don't allow them to see out, so although they shake the truck as they move about, they are not stressed by a change of scene. The process is not without fear for the herders or the watcher. To be this close to an animal so damn big is to acknowledge its power; a single thrust of a horn, and you're dead.

THE GROVES'S BUFFALO are slaughtered at G&C Packing Company. A ramshackle cluster of buildings on the outskirts of Colorado Springs, G&C is the largest buffalo slaughter and packinghouse in the country, and therefore the world. Since it was founded in 1868, it is also the oldest continuously operating slaughterhouse in the country. Frances Grindinger and her brother, Frank, started in on buffalo when they began to be raised here locally in the 1980s. These days they slaughter 1100 to 1400 carcasses per month, 95 percent of them buffalo.

The buffalo G&C slaughter have usually been fed on grass until the last ninety days, then finished on grain — not corn, but "a secret formula." The buffalo come from all over — the Dakotas, Montana, Wyoming, Texas, Oklahoma. Agents buy the animals and then distribute the meat, so the packing company doesn't deal directly with customers. "There's not a lot of places that actually process the live animal because these animals are strong," says Frank. "We had to totally remodel the pens." To Frank, the buffalo is "a magnificent animal that demands respect all the way along the line." The reason the animal is so quick is that it can pivot on either its front or back feet, and when it moves, it dashes rather than saunters. "The wildness has not been bred out of bison, America's original natural meat," Frank says.

G&C was the U.S. plant where the owners of the patent for the rinse-and-chill method of blood removal first set up their apparatus on a trial basis, in the summer of 2000. The live animals come through the "drive

valley" into the kill floor, where the room is kept at 40 degrees F. The buffalo are killed the same way cattle are: shot with a stun gun, then hung on
the rail, where an incision is made in the neck. But instead of a "deep
thoracic," better known as a "heart stick," to sever veins and arteries, only
the jugulars are slashed, to keep the cardiovascular system intact. The
common carotid artery is stripped out and a cannula is inserted into it so
that a chilled isotonic liquid — extrapurified water mixed with organic
glycerin and then irradiated to sterilize it — is forced through the cardiovascular system to push out the blood. This process is the most thorough
way to remove blood there is, says Frank, and it lowers internal temperature immediately. "We get a pH drop in five minutes that normally takes
thirty-six hours in the cooler." The results, he finds, are longer shelf life, a
fresher product, and a cleaner taste. Yet only two other plants in the
country use this method, because it takes an additional three to six minutes, and in a high-speed production plant where they're running a carcass every nine seconds, three minutes is huge. But for Frank's plant, the
investment of $500,000 has changed them from a small local business to
a national one.

The government calls buffalo "bison" and exempts them from federal
meat inspection because bison are "exotic," government lingo for wild
game like elk. Inspection is "voluntary" and must be paid for by the
bison producer or packer on a carcass-by-carcass basis. Regulations differ
state by state, and those differences make clear how existing laws evolved
higgledy-piggledy for cattle raised in industrial volume by industrial
means.

G&C's best customer is Rocky Mountain Natural Meats, which has
developed a one-pound pack of ground buffalo distributed nationally,
from Wegman's in New York to Vaughn's in California. Now they're
doing a buffalo hot dog and a buffalo steak-pack at prices competitive
with beef. There are other products, too. Like his Indian predecessors,
Frank tries to utilize every bit of the animal. Bones are ground for bone
meal. Hides are slipped off the carcass like a glove and rolled up on a
drum. Later they are cleaned and shaved. The leather is used for boots

and shoes. The hair is of two kinds: a coarse guard hair which weighs about 3 pounds per animal, and a soft underdown which a buffalo grows in winter, finer than cashmere and no more than 1¼ inches long. This is now being marketed for wool, and a designer named Ruth Huffman has created a company in Oklahoma, American Buffalo Designs, to sell knitted garments made from the underdown, which she guarantees keeps you very warm.

Marlene and Dave follow a similar "use everything" philosophy. Behind the exercise machines in their basement, buffalo robes are spread out on the floor to dry. Jawbones — some plain, some painted — are lined up for display next to scented bars of buffalo tallow soap. Styrofoam packaging contains everything from ground meat and ribs to steaks and roasts, including the hump, which is not the tenderest of roasts because of the muscle required to hold up that giant head. It takes 1000 pounds of buffalo to produce 10 pounds of filet, Marlene says, so they're always eager to utilize other cuts. The orders are delivered free in the area and shipped around the country. One order goes to a federal-prison chaplain in Texas, who first ordered a skull for Indian ceremonies and now orders buffalo-meat packs weekly.

Because there's no fat layer on the outside of their purely grass-fed meat, it can't hang longer than ten to fourteen days without deteriorating. Like other grass-fed meat, buffalo roasts favor slow, moist cooking to tenderize them. For dinner, Marlene had cooked a 2½-pound pot roast all day in a Crock-Pot. "If you can operate a knife and fork, you can have a good experience with buffalo meat," she says, "but meat is not porridge." After she found many potential customers were afraid of not knowing how to cook buffalo, she compiled a family cookbook with tips on how to cook meat that is so lean. For example, if you are cooking buffalo burgers, Marlene advises, "When you flip 'em, don't squish 'em." Now every order goes out with a booklet of recipes and a thank-you note.

Marlene believes that people choose buffalo meat first for taste and second for health. Twenty years ago, when the fat scare arose, beefalo

(⅜ bison and ⅝ domestic cattle) reared its hybrid head for a while. In my memory, it tasted more like a tough cow than a flavorful grass-fed buffalo, and while there are around fifty small producers still listed with the American Beefalo Association, the market for it is small potatoes compared to buffalo. There's no controversy over the superior nutritional value, bite per bite, of buffalo to beef as a protein. One retailer calls it "the healthiest meat in North America," which reveals the lengths to which we have gone in turning our meat unhealthy: Commodity beef has four times the fat and therefore almost twice the calories. Because it takes at least a year and a half of grass feeding to develop its full weight, buffalo meat will have more beta carotene, more omega 3s to balance the omega 6s, and more conjugated linoleic acid (CLA). Even with a grain finish, however, buffalo flesh doesn't marble the way beef does, so its flavor is sweeter and its color is redder (although, as with beef, a grain finish helps change the color of the fat from yellow to white). Marlene remains committed to pure grass feeding for any livestock. "Dave's cholesterol was way high when we were changing our lifestyle and the doctors wanted to put him on drugs," she says. "But he stopped eating any red meat but grass-fed buffalo and stopped drinking sodas, and in a couple of months the problem was solved."

She sells twice a week at the Cherry Creek Farmers Market in Elizabeth and is a tireless promoter of local products. Everything we eat at dinner is branded "Colorado Proud." She gives me a menu with the name of the farm and its location for every single item served, from the cucumbers (Monroe Organic Farms in Kersey) and pattypan squash (Full Circle Farms in Longmont) to the Mojo Nuevo Sauce produced commercially by a local friend in Littleton under the label "Aspen Leaf Gourmet." The rye bread is baked by Styria Bakery in Aurora. The cobbler is made with peaches from the Forte Farms in Palisade and honey from the Colorado Honey Company in Fort Collins. (The honey she serves at breakfast is from bees that have fed on knapweed, an enemy to other grasses but very good for honey.) Even the wine, Lemberger, is a Colorado red from Trail Ridge Winery in Loveland. When I leave, she sends me off with a large packet of postcards, brochures, buffalo patches, and decals of a buffalo head with sunglasses and the motto "Eat Buff."

DOWN THE ROAD from Denver and up the road from Colorado Springs on a hogback near Morrison, with a fine view over the Denver valley, I get to eat buffalo with my favorite purveyor of the product and its lore. Forty-some years ago, Samuel P. Arnold was a young business-man from the East who saw an 1830s drawing of the trading center on the Santa Fe Trail known as Bent's Fort and decided to build one for him-self and live in it. He installed a restaurant on the ground floor, had adobe bricks made on the site, laid down historically accurate floors of earth and oxblood, began to study cooking with James Beard and other professionals, and opened in 1963, quickly becoming famous for his his-torical buffalo dinners. Certainly his was the only restaurant in the coun-try forty years ago that regularly served buffalo hump, tongue, sausage, and testicles ("Rocky Mountain oysters").

Since its beginnings, the Fort has been a kind of Buffalo Commons, a gathering place honoring the history, traditions, and peoples of the Southwest. In mid-May every year, the nonprofit Tesoro Foundation, which Sam and his wife began, sponsors the largest Native American powwow competition in the country, with workshops, arts and crafts, storytellers, tribal dances. "This little valley was sacred ground," Sam ex-plains. "They never fought each other here, only in the flatland."

Now Sam is thin and gray and carries his oxygen tank with him, but his eyes are bright and his puns as sharp as always. "What do you say when a herd of buffalo get on an airplane? There goes the herd shot 'round the world." In front of a roaring fire, I'm served a plate of grilled buffalo marrowbones the size of a man's thighbone, split in two. Pioneer diaries noted them as a great delicacy, called "prairie butter," and indeed you spoon up the marrow like butter. In his *Fort Cookbook* (1997), Sam instructs the homemaker: "Ask your butcher to obtain buffalo femurs and cut off the knobs with a saw, then split the bones lengthwise in two, being careful to wipe away any bone dust." The marrowbone was Julia Child's favorite when she came to the Fort, Sam recalls. "She'd always order two or three of them."

Sam went to their suppliers and found they were throwing the bones out, so he said, "'If you'll saw them in half, I'll buy them.' We would take them, broil them to get a crust, and serve them as an appetizer like 'Lincoln Logs' with some toasted crostini, and people just spooned it up," Sam says. "When President Clinton brought the Summit of Eight here for dinner in 1997, they returned night after night to order marrowbone." While local butchers are as endangered a species as buffalo once were, the Internet has rescued us partway. You can order buffalo marrowbones online, usually advertised as dog food.

The Fort gets some of its buffalo meat from Alberta, near the Canadian Rockies, says Sam's daughter Holly, a dark-haired beauty who has been running the show for a while now. The grass grows big there, the animals are bigger, and the herds are as vast as the range. Sam tells me that a buffalo has "fin" bones, five of them that grow up out of the spine like a dorsal fin on top of the shoulders. They're about 1½ to 2 inches wide and "go up yea high of the backbone," encased in the big blob which is the hump meat. Usually that meat is ground for burgers, but Sam likes to roast it whole, "slow, slow, slow" so it won't toughen up. Most people when they come have an appetizer platter of assorted buffalo parts or the game plate entree, a sampler of quail, buffalo, and elk.

Buffalo liver's also good, Sam says, but for a long time none of his customers would try it. After Sam told a group of his friends, who called themselves "Mountain Men," that Native Americans used to eat it raw as a symbol of bravery, the men began to eat it cooked and found the dish "very tasty." When he cooks it, Sam heats the butter really hot, dredges the liver in a little flour, sears it very briefly until no more than medium rare, then deglazes the pan with crème de cassis and a little crème fraîche. Real Mountain Men don't eat crème fraîche, but when they gather at the Fort, they repeat the toast: "Here's to the childs what's come afore, and here's to the pilgrims what's come arter. May yer trails be free of grizzlies, yer packs

filled with plews [pelts], and may you have fat buffler in yer pot." And
Sam roars his unreproducible roar: "WAAAUUUUGGGHHHH!"

TODAY, SO RAPIDLY has the market for buffalo meat grown (20,000
animals slaughtered each year, 1 million pounds of meat sold each
month) that vertical integration for rich entrepreneurs like Ted Turner
has been easy to accomplish. Today Turner has the largest buffalo herd
(40,000) in the world and the largest acreage devoted to them (as of 2001,
1.8 million acres on thirteen ranches in the Western states, plus ranches
in Patagonia and Tierra del Fuego). His buffalo kingdom, though smaller
than Connecticut, is bigger than Delaware. It seems that wherever I went
in Colorado, Montana, New Mexico, or elsewhere, someone would mention that Turner had buffalo nearby, particularly after he'd bought the
580,000-acre Vermigo Park Ranch near Raton, Nevada. To control the
process from grass blade to tabletop, Turner started his own restaurant
chain of Ted's Montana Grill in 2002 and has now extended it to urban
spots like Manhattan. While Turner grain-finishes most of his buffalo,
it's rumored that he's going to go 100 percent grass-fed with some in
order to market them as "Ted's Premium Reserve."

Today there are so many buffalo at large that the National Park Service has organized buffalo hunts on public lands such as Yellowstone. As
a symbol of the wild, buffalo are caught in the crossfire between the
usual antagonists for control of public land. Environmentalists like Earth
First! complain that the Park Service has no business organizing hunts or
entrapping buffalo and penning them in areas like Horse Butte Trap in
an attempt to domesticate their wildness. Cattlemen complain that wild
buffalo pass brucellosis to cattle, but when both animals are on the open
range there is little evidence that they do. Buffalo advocates complain
that cattlemen simply want to eliminate competition for forage. While
hunters are not supposed to shoot buffalo from a moving vehicle, there
are no state or federal regulators to prevent it. The Humane Society USA
complains that these planned hunts afford "trophy hunters the opportunity to shoot what are effectively parked cars."

Native Americans in the InterTribal Bison Cooperative (ITBC) have not been fighting each other, but they have been fighting the U.S. government and the North American Bison Cooperative (NABC) over what a buffalo is, a wild or domesticated animal. This is an important battle because it hinges on whether an animal has any value other than meat and exposes the bizarre system whereby the government subsidizes a billionaire buffalo rancher like Ted Turner to dump his surplus "bison trim" (excess fat), through the North American Feeding Program, on "poor Indians." The InterTribal group has taken offense at that, particularly since one reason for the surplus is the NABC's requirement that its members feed their bison grain for at least 100 days. Grain finishing enables the USDA to classify buffalo as domestic livestock, rather than wildlife, and treat it simply as a commodity. But the InterTribal group argues that in their culture the buffalo is sacred and should be free to roam and graze on grass as the Great Spirit intended. They have, as they say, a "spiritual relationship with the animal and you can't separate the spiritual aspect from the economic." That is a language as alien to the USDA and the NABC as Choctaw or Arapaho. Maybe we need more metaphors than money when we seek common ground.

✦ Greening Beef ✦

"View of Kingsbridge Road Near Dyckman's Farm" in New York in 1866 reveals the elements of an iconic American pastoral, where a man tends cows by his farmhouse while a horse and carriage pass beneath green trees.

— Courtesy Picture Collection, New York Public Library

To make a prairie it takes a clover and one bee,
One clover, and a bee,
And revery.
The revery alone will do,
If bees are few.

— Emily Dickinson

◆

IF VANDANA SHIVA had mated with Thomas Jefferson, their progeny might be Joel Salatin. "Soil is the earth's stomach" is one of the maxims of a wordsmith who delights in turning industry rhetoric upside down. A favorite device is to compare the indestructibility of "industrial pseudo-food" with what happens to real food. You know that "Archer-Daniels-Midland amalgamated, reconstituted, chlorinated, extruded, extracted, adulterated, irradiated, genetically prostituted, inhumane, globally transported, disrespected protoplasmic pseudo-food" is not real, because "real food rots." In the Will Rogers tradition of folksy comedy, this Utopian of the chicken coop talks like a chicken farmer because he is one. Traveling the country on lecture tours, he's become a grass-and-manure evangelist, a self-described "Christian libertarian environmentalist capitalist" keen on provoking a one-on-one shoot-out with the machine.

In his prime at forty-eight, Salatin is a sturdy man with black horn-rimmed glasses that emphasize his square chin, his close-cropped hair mitigating the first signs of baldness. Raised on a family farm that dates to 1750 and educated at Bob Jones University, Salatin trained as a journalist

with the *News Leader* in Staunton. He combined his agricultural and ver-
bal skills to make Polyface Farm, in Virginia's Shenandoah Valley, into
what Michael Pollan calls "one of the most productive, sustainable, and
influential family farms in America." He's done so by spreading the word,
challenging factory farms not just by setting up a working model based on
the holism of nature, but by employing the language of the Machine even
as he ridicules it.

He deconstructs animal manufactories into low-tech contraptions
he calls "eggmobiles" and "gobbledygos" — mobile chicken houses and
turkey houses. "We need to extract ourselves from the entire industrial
loop," Salatin says, and rediscover the farm-friendly seasonal loop, where
compost feeds grass, grass feeds cows, cows feed chickens, chickens feed
pigs, and mountains of winter manure feed grass in the spring. He protects his 10,000 chickens in portable hooped huts, the eggmobiles, and
combines these with electric fencing so that the chickens can follow
where cows have grazed and dine on their patties. Meanwhile, as the
birds peck grubs and worms from the cow patties, they sanitize the pasture of unwanted fly larvae and similar pests. The by-product of the
birds' chemical-free land management is 30,000 dozen totally natural
eggs. The seasonal loop makes the ultimate connection between sunlight
and shit.

As the name Polyface suggests, and its Virginia location affirms, his
farm is a return to the multiuse agriculture of Jefferson's day, combining
woodlands and pasture in its 550 acres, combining planting with husbandry, combining producing with direct marketing and promoting.
Even Salatin's libertarianism reflects Jefferson's animus toward federal-
ism, for Salatin's chief enemy is the federal government, specifically the
government regulations in the 1970s that all but wiped out small farms
and small producers of meat and poultry. "I'm a libertarian, I want
choice," he says, in defiance of industry spokesmen like his neighbor
Dennis Avery, director of the Center for Global Food Issues for the Hudson Institute, who wrote without irony a book titled *Saving the Planet
with Pesticides and Plastics*.

Salatin's form of radicalism maintains a deeply conservative base and a return to spiritual values that have, at one extreme, been taken hostage by America's evangelical right. As a libertarian, however, Salatin believes the Western world needs an injection of Eastern thinking to counterbalance "the quintessential soulless Western food system." In addition, he is temperamentally opposed to extremes. "Don't go bankrupt being pure," he advises. "You don't have to be a nudist Buddhist." Instead, he prefers to stay in the "middle-muddle" of making connections between healthy soils and healthy souls, between local families and local communities.

There's a strong evangelistic component in the best of our grass preachers who would restore to food a face and a soul. Many are latter-day environmental versions of the messianic health gurus of the nineteenth century, beginning with Jethro Tull and Alma White and evolving into Sylvester Graham and the Kellogg brothers. They share that American conflation of physical with moral purity in their search for utopia through oral intake, and are apt to quote messianic nutritionists like Adelle Davis and Weston A. Price.

Price was the Cleveland dentist turned nutritionist who in the 1930s saw the dangers of industrialized foods first in relation to teeth, jaws, and other bones and then traveled the world to find preindustrial cultures untouched by processed foods. His was a form of romantic primitivism like Gauguin's or Melville's, only under the aegis of science rather than art, by which he believed he could prove that whole foods, excluding soy and including animal fats, might achieve not just health but lasting bodily and spiritual perfection. This strand of the tradition continues in the work of Sally Fallon, head of the Weston A. Price Foundation, which continues to spread Price's maverick message that red meat, saturated fats, eggs, dietary cholesterol, polyunsaturates, and salt are not evil, but necessary to human health. The enemy for the Price Foundation, and its newsletter *Acres*, is industrial processing; their consistent preachment is to avoid processed foods and instead go organic, go whole, natural, unrefined, nonpasteurized, real. Their ultimate admonitions are to think positive and practice forgiveness, for in this paradigm physical nutrition feeds spiritual health.

For environmental messiahs today who focus on what feeds the earth's stomach, the health of land, man, and beast depends upon grass — pasture in the East and prairie in the West. It has given new meaning to Wes Jackson's work at the Land Institute in Kansas. When thirty years ago, he proposed that man's original sin was farming and that the prairie should be our model of how to mimic nature instead of dominate it, he aimed to meld ecology with agronomy into "a natural systems agriculture." This spoke to a new generation of greenies, who were calculating the long-term ecological and sociopolitical costs of our oil-based agriculture. Like Savory, Jackson explained that over eons the prairies had evolved a web of hundreds of different wild grasses that worked together to hold and fructify the soil. To nature, bare ground is anathema. Seeds want to stay there, to hold the ground, and if the land is managed well, seeds that have been buried there for decades and even for centuries will come back. Jackson's aim is to restore polyculture perennials to land made sick by oil-dependent monoculture annuals like corn and soy.

Once the health of human bodies and the earth's body are connected, the logic of reconnecting cows to grass is inevitable. The only wonder is the speed with which this has happened, at least in the media and increasingly on the ground. Even cattle have learned how to greenspeak on cue: "I come from good stewards of the land," say the cows in media ads for the TallGrass Beef Company, "independent ranchers and farmers who raise cattle in a time-honored manner that sustains and enriches the environment." TallGrass beef comes from Red Buffalo Ranch, owned by CBS newsman Bill Kurtis, down in Sedan, Kansas. Elsewhere in Kansas, government agencies have gotten into the act. The National Park Service has established a prairie preserve in the Flint Hills near Emporia, where the soil was too flinty for the plow, but not for the cows who graze there. The Nature Conservancy has established pockets like the Tallgrass Prairie National Preserve between Topeka and Wichita in the very heart of the cattle industry and has reintroduced buffalo to graze it. Far to the north, in Malta, Montana, the Conservancy has created a grass bank at the historic 60,000-acre Matador Ranch specifically for cattle to graze, and at reduced fees. Once grazing can be seen as a way to protect prairie habitat, land conservationists can join with independent ranchers in a new Cattle Commons.

One of the earliest ranchers to equate healthy grasslands with good beef was Dale Lasater, scion of Lasater's Grasslands Beef and a fifth-generation rancher with an Ivy League pedigree. Dale has worked for industrial feedlots in Kansas and for the Peace Corps in Colombia, has been a student in Buenos Aires and a schoolteacher in Mexico. When he took over the family ranch in 1986, he was determined to put Wes Jackson's theory into practice: Treat the range as if it were wild and treat cattle like buffalo.

I meet up with Dale at his ranch outside Matheson, Colorado, one of those typical abandoned prairie outposts that is no more than a false-fronted post office, a gimcrack store, and a prim white church on a hill. A stretch of green dotted with horses drinking at a trough under a windmill abuts a yard full of rusting farm machinery, a common prairie cenotaph. "This is the way Americans farm," Dale says when I remark on these strange juxtapositions. "We don't connect the two ends." Dale is a thoughtful rancher, slender, sincere, and soft-spoken, who connects to the prairie. "This is marginal farmland," he explains as we drive across prairie looking for some of his cattle, "but great ranching land." He names the plants as if they were pals: blue gamma, hairy gamma, western wheatgrass, switchgrass, sand grass. The weather is also personal. In a June without rain, the grass looked like August, but in late July the rains came, he said, and in August the prairies were spring green with a robin's egg blue sky. "Tallgrass prairie" means waist-high plants, he explains. "Mixed" means thigh-high, "short" means knee-high — not a couple of inches, like turf or a lawn. The prairie is a living thing. "For you and me, this all looks the same when you look out across it," he says, "but for the plants it's not at all the same; each one likes a certain thing, a little more clay or little less sand. We understand just a small piece of this whole miraculous system. Even though I know six or seven thousand names of grasses and forbs [herbs], I still don't know them all. We call ourselves ranchers and cattle people, but we're sun farmers. We simply promote the harvesting of the sun via these green plants."

We stop to walk through a field toward a few of Dale's cinnamon-colored bulls. "They won't charge," he says, "they're not Jerseys or Holsteins — dairy breeds that are notoriously mean." These are Beefmasters, a crossbreed created by Dale's grandfather Ed, down in Falfurrias, Texas, and one of only two genuinely new breeds of cattle to have originated in the United States. In 1908, Ed imported Brahman bulls to mate with two English breeds, Hereford and Shorthorn, in order to improve his dairy production. But when Dale's father, Tom, took over the breeding, Tom selected for superior beef. In 1948 Tom moved from Texas to the 30,000-acre ranch in Matheson and bred, in addition to cattle, a family of seven boys and a girl. All of his siblings love the land, Dale says, as the French version of their surname suggests: *La-sa-terre* means literally "there-his-land."

It was Dale's businessman son, named for his grandfather, who persuaded Dale to get into the retail-business end of beef production. "If I'd known what lay ahead, I wouldn't have done it," Dale says now, because it requires so much money, time, and energy to market your own beef. But the family already had a fifty-year history of raising beef sustainably without antibiotics, pesticides, or fertilizers. They'd studied Savory on rotational grazing and the timing of grass growth. Today, as the market for natural beef and sustainable grazing grows exponentially, Dale points to his father's motto as prophetic: "Nature does all of the thinking and most of the work."

This new-old way of thinking of Nature as a partner instead of an object led Dale to found three years ago, with Marlene Groves and others, the American Grasslands Association. Their annual meeting drew me to Clay City, Indiana, twenty miles southeast of Terre Haute, along the Wabash River in the flat prairie land of Indiana. Renowned as the home of Clabber Girl Baking Powder, Clay City also boasts that it is "The Mayberry of the Midwest." Driving through bleached fields spotted with cows on a March afternoon to get to the Methodist camp-meeting site did nothing to dispel the Mayberry claim. The camp was in Wabash Park, a communal summer camping grounds with screened meetinghouses under the pines. The main building had a large painted mural with the command in English, "Go Into the World," repeated in Spanish and Korean. A wooden cross behind the podium embraced a cutout of the state of Indiana and a flame.

The attendees included agents from Range Management, vets from the USDA, representatives from Consumers Union and Slow Food, cooks from the Chefs Collaborative, activists from the American Livestock Breeds Conservancy, and promoters of organic soil enrichers like Turf-Pro, along with livestock growers of many kinds, all of them drawn to the idea of a Commons. The keynote speaker was Allan Nation, another pastoral evangelist, who edits one of the country's oldest farming newsletters, *The Stockman Grass Farmer.* His way of spreading the gospel of grass is to link unorthodox farming to hard-core economics. "Ranching is a business, not a lifestyle," he likes to say. Raised on a cattle ranch in Greenville, Mississippi, Nation has traveled the world looking at other countries' ways of managing grass and livestock. His converts are men like Steve Hittel, who testifies that he'd been a grain farmer running a typical cow-calf operation in Kansas, with 70 percent of the world's feed-lot cattle within 100 miles of his home, until he saw the green light that "turned his brain inside out."

Nation's appearance — short and rather crumpled in khakis and cardigan — belies the emotive power of his voice and hardheaded ideas. I don't know anyone who takes a sharper view of the global beef industry and America's precarious place in it, nor anyone who sees more clearly the gap between cowboy romance and capitalist logic. Typically Nation quotes economist Louis Rukeyser to detail the romance: "According to something called the *Western Wrangler Index,* 60% of USA men and 50% of USA women yearn to be a cowboy . . . at least for a day." He does not quote Sam Shepard, "If you ain't a cowboy, you ain't shit." Instead, Nation talks the talk of capitalism and believes that the only people who can afford to be cowboys — even for a day — are those who don't expect to make money at it. "If you can buy a deed-land ranch, you have enough money to not work," says Nation. "Most ranchers are the working rich."

Nation's newsletter column, "Allan's Observations," and his many published books subvert the romance with the realpolitik of a money man, colored by the self-help optimism of a Dale Carnegie. His own family farm went broke in the 1950s because he and others in the region didn't understand that "land ownership and cattle are two separate businesses" and that ranchers should be grass producers, not cattle owners. Once his family lost their cattle, his dad had to pay mowers to cut the grass on the Mississippi levees. What he should have done instead, Nation says, was to charge the levee board for "forage control service." The levee grass had "negative value" until the cows added value to it and solved the grass problem. "Grass without grazing animals is a cost to someone."

Ranchers, in Nation's view, should eliminate land and cattle ownership altogether to become "custom grazers": running other people's cattle on leased land. He quotes Forrest Gump: "Don't own nothin', even rent your shoes if you can." Ranchers should model their business on "services," he says, not manufacturing. Custom grazers need do no more than market grass, whereas cattle owners are stuck not only with the fluctuations of the stock market, but with the immutable fact that a cow is an animal, not a machine. The investor who is a cattle owner lacks control of both natural and economic forces, which combine in what industry calls "the cattle cycle." That cycle is like the ocean, Nation says: slow tidal changes are caused by the reproductive cycle, but surface chop is caused by short-term disturbances: the price of grain, feedlot capacity, the volume of fed cattle. The rancher has to gamble on so many variables: the future price of livestock, the price of corn, the weather, government taxes and subsidies, the nonfarm economy, the price of oil. "Until an animal has been sold and replaced," he warns the cattleman, "the only profit that exists is in your mind."

The only "real" price in the cattle market is the fed-cattle price: the price the cow sells for at the moment of slaughter. A rancher-owner profits only when he produces beef for less than he sells it *and* when he captures inventory price increases. But to capture those, he has to estimate accurately each of the four segments of the cattle cycle: cow-calf, stocker-grower, finisher, and processor. Inventory prices are controlled by investors' expectations about the future, so that even the cow-calf producer is dealing in a futures market. What complicates bets on the future is that a current price creates its opposite: "Anything that creates a high price sets in motion a chain of events that eventually results in low prices." Ranchers want to raise more cows when the price is high, but an increased supply will lower the price for the next cycle. Fifty-some years ago, when prices were less volatile than now, most cattle feeders owned the cattle they fed because there was no futures market. A rancher's best road to profit was to buy heifers at the bottom of the cycle when they were cheap and sell them as grown cows at the top of the cycle. Feeders were priced against each day's fat-cattle price, so that profit and loss could be calculated before the animal was fed. The price difference in the feedlot between incoming "feeder" cattle and outgoing "fat" cattle is still called the "swap." When grain is cheap, the supply of feeder cattle will expand and necessarily lower the price of fat cattle. Producers have to decide how to make a profitable "swap": Should they buy back those calves when they are cheap and grow them another few months, hoping for the fat-cattle price to rise?

Advances in cattle genetics have also muddled calculation. The industry has increased beef volume in recent years without increasing cow numbers. Cattle are now bred to stay in the feedlot for a longer time, where they can increase their slaughter weight without getting overly fat. In the northern states, that weight is close to 1400 pounds and in the southern, 1200. In 2003 America produced 637 pounds of beef per cow per year, an increase of more than 50 pounds over five years. That means that beef poundage is increasing without any quantifiable warning in terms of increased cow numbers.

Despite the rancher's romance of owning a herd, profit is no longer in ownership, but in trading. "The big money in the last five years has been in trading cows," Stockman says, "rather than owning cows to produce calves." Yet even the trading game is an investor's bet on futures. "Buy and hold" works only in a rising market. You must always be willing to sell, Nation warns. When you're at the top, go to cash; when at the bottom, invest, but keep the cash and cattle moving because what you're really in is the "vegetation control" business. That is a new context for ranchers. "Most organic beef and dairy producers have taken the industrial grain-based production model and just changed the source of the inputs," Nation says. "Certified Organic" products sell for more, but organic inputs, whether grain or grass, cost more, so the "swap" isn't better. Even though economically profit lies in the pasture and not the animal, culturally the idea is alien to us. "We don't trust pasture." We trust the plow; we trust the crops we plant — like corn.

Not anymore. The reign of corn as cattle feed may be finished, Nation told his audience at the Grasslands Association gathering. Corn eats up the profits because it's no longer cheap. Over 90 percent of the total energy needed to produce a pound of edible beef goes merely into keeping the cow alive. In order to make a profit, the feed a cow eats can have only negative value, which means if the cow weren't there, you wouldn't have to spend any money to control the vegetation. Over 70 percent of the world's beef cattle are located in the tropics and subtropics, where grass has negative value: There it's abundant and of poor quality.

Corn also kills the soil. Industrial monoculture has produced the most traumatized, battered, abused, and "boring" landscape on the globe, is the way Nation puts it. "Modern row cropping is the soil's equivalent of having been on the receiving end of a mugging by Jack the Ripper. . . . Your soil is in a state of shock." Commodity agriculture in the developed world is finished, he believes. In 2003 the United States was the world's number-three beef exporter; today it's not even in the top ten. While our country has increased its cow herd by 194,000 head, Canada increased its numbers by 300,000, Brazil by 1,400,000, and China by 2,500,000 in a global increase of 4,600,000 cows in a single year. Despite the projection of $77 billion of American agricultural exports in 2007, Nation believes that for America, "export agriculture is O-V-E-R." Every farm program, including the new Farm Bill of 2007, is another nail in the coffin because it is geared robotically to increasing production. Fueled by our religious belief in endless growth, America's economic machine dictates that all industries eventually become overcapitalized and overproduce.

At Polyface Farm, Joel Salatin puts into practice Nation's precepts about livestock without giving up the romance of owning the cows as well as the farm. Salatin prides himself on being able to make a profit by trusting pasture. He eschews the organic — "I'm beyond organic" — because the word has already been co-opted by industrialism and is as dependent on oil for transport as it is on chemical fertilizers for production. He celebrates grass. His small herd of 100 cattle shelters in open-sided barns, protected by portable shade mobiles as they are moved from one day's pasture to the next, which he measures by "cowdays" per acre. What one cow will eat in one day determines how many cows you can put on one acre. He can put as many as 400 because he supplies them with "salad bars." As he explains in *Salad Bar Beef*, what goes into the salad bar is the key to the happiness of his pastures and his cows. "An animal always eats dessert first," he explains. For a cow, the choice between clover and ragweed is like the choice for a human between ice cream and liver. The cow will always choose ice cream. I remembered grass rancher Ernest Phinney telling me what was wrong with corn-saturated diets for cows in feedlots. "It would be like me locking you in a room for several months and forcing you to eat nothing but vanilla ice cream. You'd get really fat, but also really sick."

Salatin's solution to the ice-cream diet is a trick he calls "pulsing the pasture." His variety of rotational grazing, based on Virginia's pastureland and seasons, is to follow "the blaze of growth" in a plant's growth cycle. This charts the relation of root growth to top growth in an "S curve" and can be helped by letting a plant grow several inches before it's lightly grazed, then by letting it regrow to the same length before it's grazed again. In winter the entire farm, including the soil, hibernates. Soil needs rest because the organisms within it go to sleep. He makes a winter bedding of straw for his cattle and has devised a pulley-raised trough of hay which can be raised as the bedding grows higher with manure and urine, 3 pounds a day, covered each day with fresh straw. Wood chips and sawdust are mixed into the bedding as it grows, then whole corn kernels, so that the entire mass will ferment and generate heat. Cows do the mixing with their hooves and stay sweet and dry. In the spring, he sends in the pigs to aerate the mixture as the animals root around for the corn. These are his "pig-aerators," his "living machines." This ready-mix compost is then spread on the fields to grow vegetables, hay, and new grasses for the salad bar.

Turn your liabilities into assets, says the preacher. Instead of thinking of soil and manure as "dirt" and "waste," we should turn them into "resources" and our animals into wage earners. Be crafty and "use animals as landscape managers," not as prisoners in "fecal factory inhumane concentration camps." "We must romance the next generation," says Salatin, urging libertarian rebellion. "Everything I want to do is illegal."

◆ Good Breeding ◆

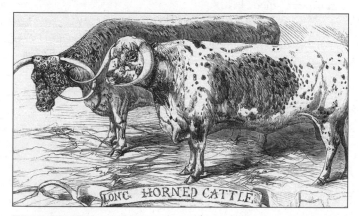

"Long horned cattle," drawn by Harrison Weir and printed in the *Illustrated London News* July 23, 1859, were exotic imports among the "Prize cattle from the Royal Agricultural Society's show at Warwick." Texas Longhorns, descended from Spanish cattle in the sixteenth century, adapted well to the rough country of the American West. The Shorthorn breed, developed in England in the eighteenth century, was bred to fatten rapidly; Americans crossbred these two types in the nineteenth century to create industrial beef.

— *Courtesy Picture Collection, New York Public Library*

It is astonishing, as well as highly encouraging, to note the marked improvement in color, form, and weight, arising from a cross of Texan cows with Durham bulls . . . the ordinary observer will scarce believe, or recognize that the cross, or half breed, has any Texan blood in it.

— Joseph G. McCoy, *Historic Sketches of the Cattle Trade of the West and Southwest* (1874)

◆

WHEN COWS CROSSED THE ATLANTIC half a millennium ago, European breeds had to adapt to a significantly different locale. In Europe, at 45 to 60 degrees latitude, cattle breeds had adapted to cold weather, which produces grass that is high in protein and low in fiber and produces cattle that put on protective fat. But most of the United States is at a lower latitude, where our landmass creates extremely hot summers. Low-latitude grasses grow quickly on acid soil, which results in grass low in protein but high in energy. Cattle that have adapted to heat tend to be long legged and high in body area, with a large head and nose and an ability to shed their hair rapidly. These characteristics belong to all the breeds that developed in America after the first Spanish imports, which adapted in various locations to strong heat and scrub grass.

Names confuse, but partly because names, too, are regional. From Mexico south to Argentina, Criollo is the term generally used to describe the descendants of Spanish cattle, which spread throughout the New World. In the States and along the Mexican border, they're called Corriente, which means "common cattle," or "the cattle of the country." What you call them depends on where you come from. In Baja California, the same cattle are called Chinampo, in Texas their descendants are called Longhorn, and in Florida and the South their slightly smaller cousins are called Scrub, Swamp, Cracker, or Pineywoods. Today all of these are raised largely for rodeos, for team roping and steer wrestling, because they are wily and tough, fast on their feet, and far smaller than commercial beef breeds. Other qualities account for their usefulness in crossbreeding: They're fertile at less than a year and may produce a calf a year into their late twenties. They're excellent mothers and good milkers. They're disease and parasite resistant, as well as heat resistant, and in the acidic soils of the southeastern United States will eat forage that other breeds scorn. That low-protein diet makes them slow growers, but master survivors. However, their individual breeds were nearly eliminated in the 1920s by excessive crossbreeding with standard commercial European breeds.

THOSE BREEDS GOT their start in the mid-eighteenth century, in England, under the spur of needing bigger animals to provide more meat for the new urban markets. Farmers began to breed the ancient Celtic stock of Shorthorns selectively, for their large frame and ability to put on fat. In the 1780s, deliberate inbreeding produced the Durham ox, shown around the country as a monster cow of 3400 pounds. When the first Shorthorn was brought over to Virginia in 1783, it was called the Durham and touted as a good all-purpose breed that could furnish meat and milk, plow a field, and pull a wagon. Farmers quickly bred it with Spanish Longhorns to add tractability to its virtues. By the mid-nineteenth century, Midwestern farmers began to import Shorthorns in quantity for the expanding meat industry, and in 1846 they became the first beef breed to be registered in the United States in a Herd Book.

Anglo settlers in America had condemned the Texas Longhorns they encountered as barbaric. "They are indeed nothing else than Spanish cattle, direct descendants of the unseemly, rough, lanky, long-horned animals reared for so long and in such large herds by the Moors on the plains of Andalusia." An employee of the USDA in the next century described them more mildly as "semi-barbarians" that needed to be crossed with English stock for "self reliance and initiative." A second breed, the Hereford, had been developed in England around the same time as the Shorthorn and for much the same reasons. Like the Shorthorn, Herefords were bred to be much larger than they are today, but mere size became valued less than their early maturity, hardiness, and high yield of meat. By 1840, a major breeding herd was established in upstate New York, and after the Civil War, Herefords became known as "the great improver" when they were bred with Texas Longhorns, prized by that time only for their ability to survive both the cattle drives and transport by rail. The wide popularity of Herefords as improvers was strengthened after the 1883 Chicago Fat Show, when C. M. Culbertson won the grand championship for his Hereford steer Roan Boy and began the popularity for younger steers of 2 rather than 4 years. The Herefords' early maturity and "finishing ability" (the ability to fatten well on forage) helped revolutionize beef production in America at the turn of the century. But that same trait caused the breed to lose favor in the 1960s, when the beef market wanted a leaner, more muscled animal.

In comparison to these breeds, the Angus was a latecomer to America. The first were imported from Scotland to Kansas in 1873, by Scotsman George Grant. These, too, were crossbred with Texas Longhorns. The breed got a considerable boost when it was crossbred with the Aberdeen into the Aberdeen-Angus and won first prize at the International Exposition in Paris in 1878, after which it was imported into the Midwest in large numbers. Within a century, the Angus breed or crossbreeds had gone far to eliminate most other breeds in America.

Not surprisingly, the first alarms at the prospect of heritage breeds disappearing altogether were sounded among livestock farmers in Vermont and Massachusetts, when preservationists who had helped to organize Old Sturbridge Village in Massachusetts in the 1940s went in search of historical livestock to fill it. Eventually, in 1977, the American Minor Breeds Conservancy (AMBC) was founded, bringing together beef and sheep farmers, agronomists, veterinarians, and ecologists. Before long, they added poultry to their livestock concerns, and by 1993 they morphed into a national American Livestock Breeds Conservancy (ALBC) and published an album listing seventy rare and endangered breeds. Their annual directory today includes a "critical" list and numbers hundreds of heritage breeders from every state in the union, with the possible exception of Alaska. The critical list also numbers several descendant breeds from those first Spanish Criollos.

FLORIDA SEEMED THE right place for the Spanish in 1521 to land 300 head, on Ponce de León's second expedition to Florida. When he was killed by Caloosa Indians, the livestock was left to shift for itself. Accustomed to the Caribbean, the cattle adapted well to the subtropic climate and prairies of Florida. Their numbers were enlarged by a herd Don Diego Maldonado landed at Pensacola Bay in 1540 to supply de Soto, whose expedition also came to naught. Not until 1565, after Pedro Menéndez de Avilés founded the garrison of St. Augustine, were herds raised in the settlement for meat. "When the Pilgrims landed, St. Petersburg was up for urban renewal," jokes a Southern historian who maintains that the first cattle drives began in Florida when herds were driven to the coasts for trade. Jesuit missionaries established ranches in the thirty-eight missions they built in this part of New Spain and supplied each with abundant livestock herded by Indians, whom they taught to ride horses, contrary to the Spanish prohibition against it in Mexico. The cattle industry in Florida took off as trade with Cuba flourished for the next three centuries, especially as ranchers could avoid paying a cattle tax to Spain by this dodge. Land-grant ranches also increased, as did tension between enslaved Indian workers and Criollo *vaqueros*. Matters came to a head in the Indian revolt of 1647, which can be said to have sowed the seeds of future cowboy-and-Indian movies in the prairies of Florida. As France and Britain warred with Spain over control of the peninsula, all sides benefited from the abundance of local cattle and horses. By the time of America's Civil War, Florida, not Texas, was America's leading producer of cattle.

Until around fifty years ago, Cracker cattle — the name is said to come from the crack of a whip — could still be found roaming wild in

Florida. But fence laws in the late 1940s, combined with crossbreeding with Brahman, Hereford, and Angus, came close to killing off the breed. Today there are fewer than 500 "purebred" Crackers alive, according to the Florida Cracker Cattle Association. Somewhat smaller in body and horn length than Texas Longhorns, the cows average 600 to 800 pounds and the bulls 800 to 1200 pounds. What they call "Guinea" cattle are even smaller. The small size and musculature of all these cattle prevent them from being used for commodity beef, but they are sold for roping cattle and for breeding, often with Charolais. Often they are bred simply for "color," because they come in so many varieties with names to match: broken-brindled, roan-sided, linebacked, pied, speckled.

The difference between Cracker and Pineywoods cattle is location, rather than genetics. Pineywoods are mostly from Georgia, Alabama, and Mississippi. At a cattle auction at an annual meeting of the ALBC in Florida, I met a man named Justin Pitts, who told me that President Jefferson Davis had had Pineywoods on his Mississippi plantation. Oxen had been used for pulling cotton and corn wagons and for clearing the Deep South of the yellow pines for which they are named. Justin had come over from Mississippi to plead the cause of Pineywoods, perhaps the most endangered breed of all. A farmer demonstrated the skills of a pair of his Pineywoods oxen. "Watching those oxen I near teared up. Nobody here's in their teens. I'm thirty-seven and the youngest one in our Pineywoods group," said Justin. "All the big herds are going, going, gone. When they're gone, heaven and earth can't bring 'em back."

Others were a touch more sanguine. "This year we're being discovered," said one member, "a little bit like cowboy poetry, in high-gloss places."

COWS ARE A good model of how organisms of all kinds, including people, adapt to specific environments. Preserving that local specificity and diversity is what we now call taking a "bioregional" approach — as opposed to industrial "mono-breeding" and other practices that ignore local conditions and in the process not only wipe out diversity but create a host of unintended consequences. For example, since the early nineteenth century, grazing practices based on Eastern climates, where rainfall averages 2 inches a month, were imported into New Mexico. Over the past half-century, 50 percent of forest grasslands in the northern part of the state have disappeared, thanks to those practices, which are disastrous to Western deserts.

The best bioregionalist I know is Gary Nabhan — poet, nature writer, ethnobotanist, traveler, and creator of the Center for Sustainable Environments at Northern Arizona University in Flagstaff. Gary is himself a product of genetic and cultural diversity, his blue eyes and black curly hair and beard the product of Irish, Lithuanian, and Lebanese ancestry. A plant troubadour who's been on the move since age sixteen, backpacking into Utah's Canyonlands, through Papagos territory, through the Sonora and Chihuahua deserts, through the mountains of Lebanon, Nabhan has now created a RAFT (Renewing America's Food Traditions) program that aims to preserve hundreds of foods specific not just to the Southwest — Chapalote corn, Tepary beans, Navajo Churro sheep — but to other regions of the country, where we are in danger of losing Pineywoods cattle, Iroquois corn, Moon & Stars watermelon, eulachon smelt, the Native American sunflower.

Gary drove me to see a Corriente herd in a place the opposite of Florida's wet palmetto land — the sandstone desert of northeastern New Mexico. The Cates Ranch at Wagon Mound is a nearly invisible adobe built in a gully deep enough to shelter it from the wind. A five-year drought in the region has finally uncovered some giant prehistoric clamshells in the dried-up mud flats. Hard to imagine that this land they call "the highlands," now covered by buffalo and gama grass, piñon and juniper, was once covered by the sea. Ginny Cates comes out to greet us, the sunlight setting her red hair on fire. Her husband, Jack, is a hunter with a patch over one eye and an accent that makes you believe him when he tells you his dad came here from Texas in 1916 to ranch, farm, mine, and kill a couple of guys.

The Cateses are prime movers in the Corriente Association and its registry, which began in 1981 when there were only 170 registerable

Corriente in the whole Southwest. They started their own herd first with eight Chinampo bulls and some "Indian cows" resembling Corrientes, but with tighter horns, little wild cows that were all around the mountains here. But the Association didn't form until people realized they couldn't find any more Corriente for the sport of team roping, which began in Arizona about twenty years ago and spread rapidly after movies like *Urban Cowboy* gave the cowboy itch not just to people living on the edge of Phoenix, but to guys in the middle of Chicago. Team ropers are a different culture, Ginny says. "They aren't interested in heritage breeding. They've never heard of the American Livestock Breeders Conservancy, and they don't want to." Still, "All kinds of things came together for the Corriente business."

We drive out to a group of handsome bulls scattered in a field and there is Juan, Jack's prize, "a beauty." Jack tells me what to look for: tightly sheathed testicles, the way the horns curve and where they begin, the tight, slim hips. Ropers will watch how they run, the shape of their withers, how they lift their back legs. Their horns don't set until they're a year old, so they're usually 14 to 16 months old and weigh 400 pounds before they're ready for roping.

Now the Association numbers 3500 cattle. Still, a good Corriente is hard to find even across the border, because they've been "mixed up so horribly," says Ginny. The value of cattle that have adapted to areas like southern Baja is that they seem able to live off the brackish water in the region and are good browsers, even where forage is only bitter acacia and bitter mesquite. They've evolved different-shaped tongues to cope with these plants. They also carry their weight differently: Their legs are finer, their horns tighter. Once the Papagos on both sides of the border kept Corrientes and would have continued, but the U.S. Bureau of Indian Affairs told them, "Switch to Herefords" and then sold them out. "It's ironic because a lot of Indians are good team ropers," Ginny says. "I get a lot of calls from Indians looking for steers, and they could have had their own."

I learn more about Corriente from an extraordinary cattle researcher named Ed Frederickson, at his Jornada Experimental Range near Las Cruces. Ed rises tall and lean, with a short beard and mustache and a notably soft voice that loves to explain, clarify, persuade, ask questions. Originally from Oregon, "a recovering logger," he's ended up with two degrees in range ecology and a fierce enthusiasm for his work. "I love to bring in these cattle because not only do you bring the genetics, but that learned part of their behavior," he says, "and after all, these animals have evolved in the Sonora desert for over four hundred years. Cattle from northern environments carry their fat differently. A cow from Montana will put its fat up against the skin to keep warm. Down here they put fat in the muscle and in the kidney-pelvic-heart area because they don't need to conserve heat."

Around 1915, breeders started crossing Corriente with Hereford bulls, under the auspices of "improving" the breed — never mind that it had survived self-sufficiently for four hundred years. The real motivation, Ed says, was for fatter cattle because the fat from cattle was needed for bullets in World War I. The nitrogen surplus and corn surplus from World War II continued to push the system that way, with packers and fertilizer companies completely redirecting consumer tastes via commercials like Betty Crocker's pushing corn-fed beef on the radio. Now a rancher's biggest cost is all the supplements he has to buy to feed his calves. If you could knock those off, profit margins would increase by 2 or 3 percent, Ed says.

"When these guys talk about the consumer," Gary adds, "they mean the packer."

Ed is more like an engineer than a botanist in his 179,000-acre laboratory, where he observes the interactions between livestock, wild animals, insects, and plants. Technically, he's a range manager, working for the Federal Government and New Mexico State University, but he's also an inventor who's devised a system for tracking cattle with a wireless chip embedded in the cow to send signals by way of a minisatellite. In his range lab, he can examine the physiology of cattle in relation to diet and metabolism, depending upon individual breeds. He can see how animals move through a landscape, how they use it; how the shape of a cow's head, how its energy requirements will direct what it eats. Here he can look at "postingestive feedback," at liver enzymes and mechanisms for detoxification. He can look for the kind of food and gene interactions in animals that they've been looking at in humans, where they've found that the "gut biode" (microbes in the intestinal tract) of different cultures varies dramatically. Gary contributes a human example: "When we bring Papago Indians to stay with us in Flagstaff, in three days they've got turista, from the abruptness of the change." With animals, Ed says, he's looking at breed differences and behavioral differences in their ability to recycle nitrogen: finding the percentages at which microbes in the rumen can break down roughages. His hypothesis is that these native cattle have been eking out a meager living for so long that they're better able to recycle nitrogen and detoxify plants, plants like protein-rich yucca that cows will eat right down to the ground.

Ed has invented a monitor, a cattle collar that works like a Global Positioning System, which allows him to monitor heart rate and movement. Right now he's measuring bite rates on different kinds of forage by what he calls "jaw wags." What wags a cow's jaw depends on the particular site. "You can't generalize," says Ed, generalizing. "Rules of thumb are always wrong. You can't beat the person who just knows how to read the land, and hopefully science helps those people get better at what they already do."

Reading the land has become crucial. "Here the mesquite spreads, from overgrazing. Cattle eat the pods and scatter them everywhere. Comes a drought, knocks out all the small mammals, rain comes and the mesquite grows up so thick that small mammals can't eat them down. You need prairie dogs because they're a keystone species, an 'ecological engineer' that modifies the environment and provides for a whole suite of other species like the ferret, burrowing owl, Swainson's hawk." He theorizes that the first expansion of mesquite came with the Europeans who brought in foreign plants and the next expansion came in the 1880s with the spread of livestock. Ed points to Russian thistle, a non-native plant. "You see all these old Western movies with tumbleweed blowing across the screen. That's not tumbleweed, which is a cowboy myth, but Russian thistle." The seed that came from Mongolia got Westernized after the song "Tumbling Tumbleweeds," a trademark of the Sons of the Pioneers since 1932, spread through the airwaves thicker than mesquite by the nostalgic twang of Gene Autry and Roy Rogers and Tumbleweed Smith, broadcasting today out of Tumbleweed, Texas.

Leaving Las Cruces, Gary and I run straight along the border from New Mexico to Arizona on Highway 10, listening to Petey Mesquitey on KXCI Tucson, who celebrates in harmonica, song, and story the flora and fauna of the Sonora desert. All the fauna but humans know that the presumed border is no more than an imaginary line on a map paralleling a real highway of trucks and Winnebagos. Everywhere you spot the blue-and-white of border-patrol trucks, waiting. Everywhere you hear tales of coyotes tricking their load of wetbacks by telling them that Tucson is just an hour away if they walk due north. You can track the main migrant trails by a baseball hat caught on a mesquite bush or a blue plastic bottle by a rock. We're headed for Bisbee, just north of the Arizona-Mexico border and just south of Tombstone, to get to the "47 Ranch" of Dennis and Deborah Maroney.

For miles the landscape has been remorselessly flat against a backdrop of literally rocky mountains, the typical "basin and range" of rocks and sand in the Malpai Borderlands, where a wild jaguar was spotted just ten years ago. Malpai, sometimes spelled Malapai, names a type of volcanic rock that covers these desert badlands, an area without borders at the juncture of Arizona, New Mexico, Chihuahua, and Sonora. It's an ecological unit, not a political one. But it has also given its name to the Malpai Borderlands Group, a nonprofit organization begun over ten years ago when a group of ranchers created their own version of Buffalo Commons by rounding up the usual suspects of government agencies, Nature Conservancies, and university scientists in the common cause of restoring a viable ecosystem. On the U.S. side of the border with Mexico, they manage about 1 million acres of land that is half private, half public, with the unified goal "to support a diverse, flourishing community of human, plant, and animal life in the borderlands region." Among other innovations, they've established a "grassbank" preserve on the 300,000-acre Gray Ranch, so that in a prolonged drought, a rancher can recover his cattle there. In return, member ranchers donate land of equal value to the group, which puts the land into easement to prevent subdivisions. "Even if a ranchland is overgrazed, it can recover, but not from subdivision," a rancher explains. "Then it's gone for good."

Dennis Maroney is a red-faced Irishman with a handlebar mustache, small-boned, wiry, quick-witted, who raises quarter horses and mixed-breed cattle. His famous horse, Old Whistle, is hanging out in the yard, perhaps remembering Tony Norris's cowboy song that sang him into fame. Dennis's wife, Deborah, is round-faced, dimpled, full of fun. She works in a public-health clinic with Papago Indians, but also runs a convenience store that sells gas, a few vegetables, and their own meat — beef quarters, mostly. The Maroneys are gradually restoring a century-old adobe house, which fortunately escaped the plans of the former owner of the property to bulldoze everything and put in big roads. A couple of wooden sawhorses with horned cow-heads are set up in the yard for the Maroney kids, a boy and a girl, to practice their roping skills.

Living on the border, Dennis sees crossers all the time. Most of his workers are Mexicans, who transmit the *vaquero* tradition of the ranch. "All our ways of training horses and working cattle come from the Spanish," he says. "We 'dally' when we rope. You just wrap your rope round the saddle horn and use the friction of the rope against the horn to hold the animal. Old-time gringo cowboys, they tie hard and fast." Dallying is important to the *vaquero* way of teaching horses to yield to pressure, gently, to work with you because it's the easiest path. "If you press, they move away. If you don't, they move toward you." Dennis uses reins of plaited horsehair that prickle the horse's neck slightly. After a while you can go to a bridle or bit and, with just fingertip pressure, ride them all day. This method takes time — sometimes as long as six years — but he claims that a horse trained this way will live another twelve or fourteen years. A horse "broken" the other way, he thinks, is almost like a broken-spirited person. "We make the right things easy for the horse and the wrong things difficult so the horse can make the choice."

We pile into Dennis's battered four-wheeler to bump over rocks up hill and down through an ocotillo cactus forest, varied by nopales, agave, yucca, buffalo grass, and oak. The ranch is about 25,000 acres, of which

5,000 are deeded, 16,000 are state, and 2,400 are BLM, on which he runs around 400 cows. The ocotillo that look like sticks now are incredible in May, he says, when they green up and the hummingbirds come. Summer rains, however, may not come until July. Dennis has installed solar panels on the wells so that they can pump water all over the ranch and help out the wildlife, which includes not only the usual mountain lions, bears, cats, coyotes, and javelinas, but the threatened two-striped skunk, lesser long-nosed bat, and Chiricahua leopard frog. His crew does one big drive in the summer to get the cows into the mountains, and then they're on their own until winter. Once in a while he'll find a cow dead from eating a shrub called mountain mahogany, ordinarily palatable and nutritious, but not if a hard freeze in October concentrates the plant's cyanic acid to toxic levels. A more significant threat is ingesting the plastic from water bottles left by the migrants from Mexico. "I wish they'd just meet these people at the border and drive them to their jobs," he says. "If there was honesty on all sides, we'd all have a better life."

Up a small canyon, an isolated group of cattle seems to have a pretty good life grazing near a water hole. Another group clusters around a molasses lick, made of syrup boiled down to a thick block so the cows have to lick it rather than just gobble it down. Dennis's multicolored mixed breeds are well camouflaged in the desert, and their mixture spells survival — Brahman for withstanding heat, Longhorn for good calving, some Hereford, Charbray, Charolais, but not much Angus because their black hides get too hot in summer. "We try to get gentle cattle and keep them gentle by handling them that way," he says. "When we start with them, I just go out to a place like this and lean against a juniper tree and let them come up and smell me." He shows me how to tell a cow's age by its horns. At the base of each horn is a series of rings, like tree rings. Since they grow no rings for the first three years, the first ring represents four years, and you calculate from there. He points to a cow who's fourteen and still breeding. When she's too old for that, they'll feed her up and put her to slaughter. Hamburger completes the biotic cycle.

"What I see down the road are sort of biotic communities, a mix of animal agriculture, education, ecotourism," Dennis says. "We need to teach kids that using the landscape doesn't have to mean destroying the landscape, and for that you need a lot of witnesses."

I am still thinking of his words when my plane takes off from Phoenix airport a few days later. What I witness is land the color of flesh, looking soft and rubberoid, with mesas in the distance like gray hair and canyons like jagged pink wounds in the flesh. What I witness after we cross the convoluted peaks of the Rockies is a flat plain, once prairie, now beaded with millions of silver dots — identical houses in symmetrical patterns stretching as far as the eye can see.

AS I HOLD the white-hot iron with both hands and press firmly, a voice shouts, "Don't move except to move it up." I freeze, not so much because of the voice as because of the smell of burning hair. Then I move the iron up slowly, to complete the top of the letter *W*. Wally hands me a new hot iron to burn a *C* just below it. The long, thick auburn hair catches fire the same way and smells just as bad. Still, I step backward into the foot-deep mud with satisfaction. At Wally Congdon's annual Branding and Barbecue on his Garr Canyon Ranch in Dell, Montana, I've just branded my first cow, and the fact that it is a shaggy Scottish Highland has made the moment theatrical.

Of all cattle breeds, this is the showiest, but it's also one of the hardiest for cold weather, because of its weatherproof double coat, an outer coarse layer and a soft inner woolly layer, not unlike a buffalo's. Plus bangs called "dossan," a tuft of long hair over the eyes that makes a Highland look like an oversize shaggy dog and helps to prevent pinkeye and similar ailments. One might expect a breed that has survived since the sixth century in the fierce climate of the Scottish Highlands to learn how to grow a coat like this. The ones that didn't, died. Those that lived became especially good calvers and easy handlers, because they lived with their keepers: in winter, they stabled on the ground floor to keep the family warm in the room upstairs.

Wally's ranch is the kind of place you imagine when you hear the words "Big Sky" — valleys of intense green against deep blue skies and

mountains blindingly white with snow. It's the middle of May and spring
is springing and lambs are cavorting and mama Highlanders are calving,
105 purebred ones. I've just been to the calving pasture with Wally's wife,
Ann, and their eleven-year-old daughter, Ona, who shows me a newborn
from one of *her* cows, still wet, with its umbilical cord dangling and its
mama eating the afterbirth. Calves are littered all over the place, looking
like spaniel puppies colored yellow, silver, dun, white, black, red. They
show me a "bum" calf, rejected by its mother but adopted by their heritage Welsh sheep and now thinks it's a sheep. A large white llama takes
care of the sheep. The next morning I see nine-year-old Sam driving a
pickup truck across a field while his sister pitches out bales of hay from
the back. On this ranch everybody takes care of everybody.

The Congdons typify a new breed of pastoralists in a part of the
country old with history. When Lewis and Clark struggled through here
at the beginning of the 1800s, Sacajawea guided them by recognizing
Beaverhead Rock. The discovery of gold in 1863 at Grasshopper Creek
near Bannack brought in crooked sheriffs and thieving "road agents" and
hanging vigilantes. It also brought cattle ranchers to feed the miners and
the crooks. In the 1870s the last of the Nez Perce won the Battles of Little
Bighorn and Big Hole Basin and lost the Indian war. In the 1880s the
Utah and Northern Railroad linked Montana to the Union Pacific and
enabled the territory to become a state. While Beaverhead County self-
consciously preserves its history in a cluster of re-created mining towns
like Virginia City and Nevada City, which stage events for tourists like
"The Hanging of George Ives," ranching has changed.

This part of Montana is the heart of greening and good breeding,
partly because Montana has the kind of space that attracts big money (a
Rockefeller neighbors the Congdons on one side, Ted Turner on the
other); partly because, unlike the southwestern desert, the northern plains
get rain; and partly because consumer demand for organic beef has taken
off. In Livingston, Montana, outside Bozeman, I'd visited Rob Forsten-
zer, a former landscape architect from the Hamptons, and his gynecolo-
gist wife, who are raising Belted Galloways organically, on a small ranch
of 560 acres. For their niche breed, which shares with the Highland the

virtues of a thick double coat (black, encircled by a dramatic broad white "belt"), winter hardiness, and calving ability, they found a ready market. Four organic-beef companies were lined up to buy their calves, big boys like Dakota Beef and Organic Valley. "It's the Starbucks syndrome," Rob says. "Start small and go global. Big companies are now developing organic markets and brands either directly or by buying smaller existing companies."

Rob sells most of his steers to a local slaughterhouse named Big Timber, which handles "certified organic" but can't sell meat outside Montana. Fortunately, the Bozeman area is booming. I met another family, the Toroks, who breed both Highlands and Galloways on a small sustainable organic farm about half an hour's drive southwest of Bozeman, along with Morgan horses, a few goats, sheep, and quite a few chickens. Like the Congdons and the Forstenzers, the Toroks are originally city people. Mike is still a pilot for American Airlines, but hopes to take early retirement so he can ranch full time. Janie homeschools the three teenage boys, who prepare our lunch and clean up and share the farm chores in a startlingly uncitified way. Everyone the Toroks know in this area is into sustainable living, alternative energy, and alternative education. On the western horizon they can see the outlines of "Turner Mountain" on the Flying D Ranch, where any hunter with $4000 can pay Cowboy Heaven Consulting for a one-day Trophy Bull Bison Hunt on the ranch's 113,600 acres. That, too, is an integral part of the new pastoralism.

Wally and Ann Congdon are newcomers to Dell. He maintains a law practice in Missoula that helps pay for the ranch. "Most ranchers live in poverty," he says, "but they've got the land." The question is how to use the land you own, not how to become one of Allan Nation's "custom grazers." Wally began with a commercial herd of Red Angus, then switched to Highlands after studying the relation of wildlife and livestock to this particular land. He and Ann are people of independent mind for whom the Highland is a symbol of quality. Wally's mission is to restore the breed, not just for its hardiness, but for the flavor of its meat. In comparison to a modern Black or Red Angus, which has been bred to fatten up fast, a Highland puts on flesh slowly. When they had Angus, Wally slaughtered them at 1248 pounds when they were 13 months old, he says, just before full maturity. Their Highlands don't reach slaughter weight (1050 pounds) until 32 months, almost three times as long as an Angus. "We learned that when we bred animals to grow faster, we were breeding the girls and boys we hated in high school, the girls who gave up their training bras at age twelve and the boys who grew a beard at age thirteen because of early physiologic maturity." Wally advocates Slow Beef. The slow maturity of the Highland allows flavor to develop within the meat, not just from the fat. Highland beef is much closer to the way beef used to taste, Wally believes; an average steer in Montana in 1945 was killed at 40 to 48 months of age. Quality makes you think differently, he says. "It's not about pounds of gain, which is the agenda of the beef magazines and the agriculture colleges and the research funded by packers.

"The focus of the beef industry has not been on the dinner plate," he says, "but on fast growth and carcass cutability per pound." That's industry-speak for tenderness, which he decodes with lawyerlike thoroughness. Increasingly the industry adds water to hamburger meat to increase both "tenderness" and weight. A lot of hamburger meat imported from Australia and New Zealand is made from bull beef that has a longer protein fiber than steer meat and is able to hold together even when you mix water in. A McDonald's or a Wendy's quarter-pounder will lose significant water and fat during cooking. "Water is free for the producer, but not the consumer." The industry is now at work to locate a "tenderness gene," he says, which may measure density but can't measure palatability.

Palatability is not simply a matter of what cattle are fed, nor even for how long, but also of how much work they had to go to get the feed and at what time of year. "In the fall, when we trail our cows off the mountain and turn them loose on the hay meadow, the first things they eat are the seed heads of the grass because they're building fat for the winter." In the autumn, Wally gives his cows a bit of grain in the field to put enough fat on the outside of the animals so that he can hang their meat for twenty-eight days. Four weeks is a long time. The beef industry can't afford that kind of time or precooking weight loss — dry-aging reduces an animal's body weight by about 8 percent — and does no dry-aging at all.

Instead, it substitutes "wet aging," which is the term for its system of vacuum-packing individual cuts in heavy plastic like Cryovac at the processing plant. The function of the vacuum pack is to prolong shelf life, or preserve without change, which is the very opposite of natural aging, in which enzymes break down muscle fibers and develop flavor.

For Wally, thinking outside the industrial box keeps him outside greening orthodoxies as well. To him, Allan Nation stays inside the grass-fed box and Joel Salatin stays inside the rapid-weight-gain box. "They go partway, and they're clever missionaries about it, but they haven't changed the traditional target in agriculture from quantity to quality." It's not simply grass instead of grain that makes the difference. "Some days dealing with the grass-fed coalition is like dealing with the Christian right — it's a zealous thing." On the other hand, he disapproves of anyone who "uses a feedlot, but implies that it ain't one." A feedlot is based on a fixed rate of pounds of production, which is very different from turning a cow loose in the pasture to grow its growth in its own sweet time.

Hard-core environmentalists fare no better in Wally's book. "They're all from the East. You want to rehabilitate the wolves? Fine, I'll send you a pack to live in Central Park." When conservationists returned wolves to Yellowstone, he says, they put nine packs in a place that could hold only five. The result? The wolves killed the elk and then left the park for the surrounding countryside to find food like cattle, deer, and sheep. The real agenda of the park agents, he believes, was to get rid of the cows.

After the branding, it's time for a barbecue, in a yard full of families that Wally feeds from his smoking grill — platters of hot dogs for the kids, slices of Highland salami, firm, lean, good-flavored steaks — while the grownups drink Wally's homemade mead. It's like a church supper — everybody's brought something: macaroni salads and baked beans and fruit pies and double-chocolate brownies and a white-chocolate cheesecake. A couple of chefs are in attendance: Eric Stenberg, who now heads Chefs Collaborative, and B. M. Troxler, who heads the kitchen at Lone Mountain Ranch in nearby Big Sky. Chef Troxler likes the fact that he knows where all his beef and produce comes from, knows who raises it and how, tries to buy everything organic and local. He's also trying to use lower-end cuts like pot roast and what Wally calls "steamship roast," a whole haunch of beef — hip, rump, flank, sirloin in one piece — weighing somewhere between 50 and 80 pounds and cooked with the bone in for 24 hours. "The last one went down with the *Titanic*," Wally says, but he's got his processor to cut a lot of them because there's a new call for them.

One of Wally's new neighbors in Beaverhead County is William Kriegel, whose contribution to the new pastoralism and "natural ranching" is to combine raising "natural beef" with practicing "natural horsemanship." The 88,000 acres of what he has named La Cense Ranch cover alfalfa-rich valleys and grassy mountains bubbling with hot springs and trout streams. This is one of the oldest continuous cattle ranches in Montana, built just six years after the discovery of gold in Grasshopper Creek in 1863, but William, who discovered billions as an entrepreneur in the field of independent energy, has owned it for only the past seven. His passion is horses, specifically a special method of training that he developed in France but that derives more from the *vaquero* tradition of the American West than from the classic dressage of Europe. Kriegel has institutionalized his method in a unique four-year program at the University of Montana–Western in Dillon.

Greening horses in Montana led William to greening beef. Although he began his ranch with a cow-calf operation to sell to feedlots in the conventional industrial way, he soon became passionate about grass. He learned about the science of grass feeding from Voisin's classic text, then learned from his veteran ranch-manager Bud Griffith, who's been in the area for fifty years, what's important for cows. He learned how best to balance grass growth with the cow's muscle growth, relating nutrition to fiber to grass length to time of grazing and to exercise. La Cense cattle feed on grass 10 inches tall, so they eat only the nutrient-packed tops. When the tops are gone, the cattle are moved to a different pasture. After twenty days, when the grasses have grown back to the same height, the cattle return to eat more tops. In this way, the same pastures of bluebunch, wheatgrass, and alfalfa can be grazed four times a season. Valley pasture provides for winter grazing because this part of Montana gets relatively little snow. For summer grazing, the cattle move into the Black-tail Mountains, green with grasses and juniper trees.

What affects beef flavor most, according to Bud, is what's in the soil and how it got there. Old ranchers know that we are what the cow eats, and the cow is what the grass eats. As a Frenchman, Kriegel would call this *terroir,* and find it logical that the ripening of cattle for beef in a specific place can be as exact and exacting as the ripening of grapes for wine. While Kriegel favors Black Angus as a breed, he feeds and finishes his cattle on grass until they're ripe for slaughter at about 18 months. He dry-ages the cut meat for nineteen days and then sells direct to locals and on the Internet under the brand name La Cense Beef. By keeping full control from pasture to plate, he can promise that his prairie beef all comes from the same place, the same *terroir.*

Perhaps as more and more beef is raised artisanally, as Slow Beef in the international Slow Food movement, we'll learn to think of a breed of cattle as a meat varietal, which is only the beginning of the long and arduous process of turning cattle into meat. Once quality is the goal, instead of quantity, the whole world changes. Just as we value the subtle shades of difference that we experience in a fine wine because each bottle speaks of a local place, so, perhaps, we'll learn to taste and value steak the same way. We'll speak of a "flight" of rib eyes, each of them grass-fed and -finished, each from the same breed but from a different *terroir,* or each from a different breed and a similar *terroir.* We'll do blind tastings of a Charolais from the Dordogne and from the Sand Hills of Nebraska, or an Aberdeen Angus from the Argentine pampas and a Hereford from Iowa grassland. Just as jug wine has its place, so does commodity beef, but there's no point in comparing an industrial production to an artisanal one. We just haven't begun to explore the possibilities in creating vintage beef.

IN NAPA, CALIFORNIA — where else? — Tom Gamble and his partner, Bill Davies, have already made the artisan wine-beef connection. The pair jointly own Napa Free-Range Beef and Source–Napa Winery, the latter an appellation that covers a number of vineyards where they produce boutique brands like "Origin-Napa" and "Mount St. Helena." Exemplary of the new pastoralists, Tom and Bill know ranching and winemaking from the ground — this particular ground — up. They met in an area nursery school in 1965, the year Bill's parents, Jack and Jamie Davies, bought a derelict house and vineyard above St. Helena and turned it into Schramsberg Winery. Tom's parents had been raising cattle east of Napa in the Berryessa Valley of the Vaca Mountains since 1916. Tom escaped south for a while to produce movies in Hollywood, but part of him never left the ranch. In 2000 the childhood pals teamed up to practice sustainability in farming and ranching, from pasture to plate and vineyard to glass.

Their motto, "Great wine speaks of place," applies also to great beef. Tom finds that raising all-grass beef in Napa today is where winemaking was in the 1960s. "In Napa they knew they could make good wine. The artisans were there. But they hadn't proved it to the world and they weren't doing it consistently." He describes the increasing shift from corn-fed to grass-fed beef in wine terms: "It's like going from insipid hearty burgundy to a Cab that maybe needs more age but has more complexity." And just as mobile bottling lines have helped small independent producers of boutique wines, so the potential of mobile slaughtering units may help liberate boutique beef producers from the control of big packers.

Tom admits to an unfair advantage in their location, with a local retail and restaurant market in the Bay Area that gives "place" a different resonance than anywhere else in the country. "Bill and I have tried to learn from the wine industry, which has marketed itself well over the past generation and a half to show how a good-quality product is associated with a quality lifestyle and with health and environmental benefits. We're trying now to show the same for beef." The state helps, by giving economic breaks to endeavors such as theirs that qualify as a "progressive green business." So do local regulations that set minimum parcel sizes at 160 acres in the hills, 40 acres in the flatlands, designed to prevent the process that turned the farmland of Santa Clara Valley into one massive sprawl. The concern is economic as well as environmental: urban sprawl creates an immense burden in social services.

Tom's grandfather raised beef as a commodity product to be slapped into tins, but he lost 3000 acres of his farmland after World War II, when the government put in a dam. Tom's father carried on with a cow-calf commodity program until the big processors got too big and prices fell. Now Tom and Bill keep a small herd of around 100 animals, Angus pure and crossbred, which they've built from a herd of 30. Tom thinks Short-horns would also do well here, though feedlots dislike the breed: "They get too fat in the feedyards, but that's a quality we like because we don't have enough feed for them to get fat." They slaughter their steers at around 1200 pounds when they're two years old and have just enough fat cover to age well. They'd like to become certified organic, but have too many problems still with invasive weeds like star thistle, medusa head, and two kinds of goat grasses, which they can't yet control without pesti-cides. In the future, they hope to do the job with sheep and goats and with better "fire ecology," which they're working at with the University of California at Davis and the California Department of Forestry. This year they seeded a large area with rye because it creates a fuel that burns very hot. "I respect weeds," Tom says, holding up a seed head of medusa. "I fear weeds. They're like cockroaches. They're survivors."

As part of their collaboration with the university, they're building a database that allows grass samples to be correlated with what old-timers say, as in "That place over there, that's where the cows always get really fat." In the extremities of winter or summer, they supplement grass feeding with hay. "When it's really hot, the cattle just don't want to eat. And when it's really cold, they can get pneumonia." From their new rotational-grazing practices, they've seen a massive sprouting of grass and oaks. They move cattle before they can start nibbling on the oaks, which they don't really like, Tom says, but eat out of boredom. I ask how he knows they get bored. "You watch them," he replies. By watching, you also learn which are the leaders and which the followers. "One will finally get curious and cut out of the herd and come over and see what you're doing. If you're fixing a fence, they'll start chewing on it because a cow's eyesight is not great and they get to understand something by touching, especially with their tongue."

Tom was the first rancher to tell me about the American Grassland Association and how they'd been working to define standards because the USDA was being pushed by the big guys. How do you define big? "We were processing less than sixty animals a year, and the big guys do an animal every sixty seconds." The big guys wanted to claim their cattle was grass-fed as long as they weren't in a feedlot more than three months. But they didn't make it with that one because the green ranchers were able to generate 10,000 protests by e-mail and got a lot of congressmen involved. "You know, in America we've had the luxury of turning the entire Midwest into a part of our feedlot system, and there's got to be a better way that's less energy intensive. People are getting fed up. If we can be smart about what we're creating, we can hit the triple-E in sustainability: economics, social equity, and environment. I get kind of passionate about it because I think we're doing something important even though, I don't know, it's just cows."

❖ The Smell of Greeley ❖

"Panoramic View of Kansas City" in 1895 shows the railroad stockyards and packing-houses of the "West Bottoms" in Kansas City, as drawn by Augustus Koch and published in 1895. Here cattle are packed so closely into the gridded feedlots that they look like sheep. Contemporary with Chicago's stockyards, Kansas's yards brought fame to Kansas City strip steaks and Kansas City barbecue, as in Arthur Bryant's. The CAFOs (Confined Animal Feeding Operations) of Kansas City had the jump on Greeley, famed for its clean air and pure morals.

— From the FSA-OWI Collections, Prints & Photographs Division, Library of Congress

The whole American West stinks of cattle.

— Edward Abbey

◆

I'M SITTING ON A STOOL in the Greeley Hat Works, where Trent Johnson is fitting a local guy who's there with his friend. Neither are cowboys, but both are cowboy shirted, booted, and jeaned. The guy has already bought one cowboy hat from Trent, a hat for the friend he's with, a hat apiece for two ex-girlfriends. He stands in front of the mirror and looks, adjusts the angle, looks again. "I want it a little more square on the crown." Trent blasts the crown with steam, makes a crease down the middle, and puts a dent on either side. Our Greeley man tries it on again. "Okay, now I want the sides up more on the brim." Trent blasts the brim with steam and carefully pushes each side up for symmetry. Another look in the mirror. "Can we get it a little more square in front?" Trent blasts and reshapes the front. Greeley guy looks, turns, looks, readjusts. "I want something, don't know what it is. Maybe if the top is a little squarer now . . ."

"You want a couple of indentations in front of the crown?"

"No . . ."

"What if I smooth out the side dents?"

"Let's try that."

"I'll scoop out one side, just a little."

Another blast, another adjustment, another pose before the mirror. "That's it, that's it!" The curtain falls on the end of the Cowboy Hat Dance, an entertainment that will set our guy back $170. "Good buddy," he says as he struts out the door, ready to hit the bars because he is a looker and has just broken up with his latest girlfriend and all the pretty gals will be waiting for him.

It's not easy being a cowboy-hat maker, and Trent Johnson is the best cowboy-hat maker in the country. I was delighted to find him in Greeley because I have a personal connection to that town, where both sets of my grandparents lived, and my parents, too. Greeley was started by Nathan Meeker, agricultural editor for Horace Greeley's *New York Tribune*, who shared Greeley's moral compass — "Go West, young man, and grow up with the country." In a *Tribune* ad in 1870, Meeker solicited members for a colony founded for Union Army veterans by touting a climate of pure air and pure morals in which a utopian community could flourish by means of temperance, agriculture, and irrigation. Of the three thousand readers who responded, seven hundred were chosen, and a fee of $155 was collected from each.

Greeley was laid out on a grid, a construct of rational order. It was also the nation's first "gated" community, surrounded by two ditches and a high fence around Colony land. Cowboys complained that the fence was meant to separate "Greeley Saints" not just from "bovine blight," but from the rest of the world. Sainthood, as always, had a price. Having borrowed heavily from the Greeley family for the fence as well as the *Tribune*, at Horace's death Meeker was obliged to sell all he owned and go to work as an Indian agent at the White River Indian Agency. His hardnosed insistence that the Utes become farmers sparked a rebellion in 1879, which ended with Meeker's death and the capture of his wife and daughter, who were rescued peaceably a week later.

My grandparents, on all sides strict teetotalers, farmers, and colonic irrigationists, would have been drawn to the Union Colony at Greeley as if to Bethlehem. Here the colonists had put together the first large-scale farming-irrigation system in the United States, developing small ditch companies and appropriating rivers, including the Colorado. Irrigation was meant to transform the Great American Desert into the Garden Spot of the West, a garden of commodity crops. At first colonists grew their famous "Greeley spuds," but by the time my father's parents came to town to Iowa, in 1911, sugar beets had taken over from spuds. Livestock was a major business, but it concentrated on sheep, not cows. My grandfather and his wife set up an osteopathic practice in Greeley and bought a small farm in nearby Gilcrest to raise a few chickens and grow sugar beets. My mother's parents moved there from Nebraska to run a boardinghouse for college girls of "high ideals and refinement" near Colorado State Teachers College. My mother taught music at the college when my father met her, and once he'd gotten his teaching degree, they married.

The Hat Works began as the Greeley Shining Parlors in 1909. Twenty years later, and not long after the shoeshine parlor became a hat shop as well, both sets of my grandparents left for Southern California, where my mother birthed me and died two years later. After her death, my father took my brother and me to stay for a while with our grandparents on the Gilcrest farm. I was too young to remember anything, but family snapshots of me in a baby's sunbonnet remind me I was once a farm girl.

"I was going to be this cowboy guy," Trent says of his youth, when he worked on the ranch of Susie Orr, who bought the Hat Works in 1985 and ran the business out of her barn. But even as a boy, Trent had been fixated on hats, which he collected. "You know, a fedora, a Keystone Cop helmet, a fez, a pith — I've always been a hat guy." At age twenty-four he got a loan from his uncle, bought the Greeley Hat Works, and was off and running in the world of custom hats. When the president of the NCBA wanted to do something special for the nation's president at his arrival in Denver in 2005, he asked Trent to build him a hat. With the help of Red Steagall, cowboy poet of Texas and a Bush pal, Trent decided on a champagne color with a "traditional rancher-style crease" and a "3M-I" brim. "The presentation of the hat to President Bush was on television, and when he holds the hat up and I could see my name inside it, I almost vomit," Trent says. "And when he gets on Air Force One, he's wearing my hat, and when he gets off for the Winter Olympics in Salt Lake City, he's wearing my hat, and when he gives a speech in front of the

Olympic flame, he's wearing my hat. And the president sends me a hand-written thank-you note."

Trent makes a big distinction between traditional cowboy and Western hats. "Western is a crossover style that you can wear with jeans and tennis shoes. But cowboy has a bigger brim, rolled up with a cattleman's crease down the center and a crease in each side." The definitive shape is credited to an Easterner, John B. Stetson, in 1865. After he'd contracted tuberculosis in New Jersey, where his father was a hatmaker, Stetson went west in hopes of recovery. The story goes that on an expedition to Pike's Peak, he and fellow campers needed a shelter when bad weather set in. They'd shot some game and, because Stetson knew how to make felt, he improvised enough felted fur to make both a tent and a hat. He modeled the hat on a sombrero, with a high creased crown and upturned brim. His friends laughed until a Mexican bushwhacker gave him a five-dollar gold piece for it. When John returned east, he set up a hat factory in Philadelphia and called his Anglicized sombrero "the Boss of the Plains." He died in 1906 and, while the Stetson brand is now owned by a con-glomerate, the Stetson model has survived for a century and a half, with slight variations.

The creases in the crown, or "pinches," Trent says, originated in guys grabbing their hats to remove them or tip them to a lady. Today each rodeo specialty has its own crease: bull riders' creases differ from those of ropers, cutting-horse riders' from quarter-horse riders, Arabian horse riders' from those who ride paints. Then there's the hatband. Whether it's got a buckle, knot, or feather, it's always on the left side. Trent explains that when a knight went into battle and put his maiden's token on his helmet, he put it on the left because most knights, like most people, were right-handed.

The base material is felt, the cheapest being wool, then rabbit, then European hare. Beaver felt, the most costly, is light, weather-resistant, durable, and warm. It takes the hair of six to eight beavers to make a pure beaver hat. "The felt is so valuable because beaver hair has lots of little barbs on it, like God's Velcro. You skin the beaver, shave off the long guard hairs to get at the fine underbelly hair, then boil and mash it and those barbs will mush together and lock tight." Most of the hair comes from beaver farms in Europe, where it is initially processed, then sent to a felter. Trent's felter, who's in Tennessee, ships him the raw hat bodies, "a woolly thing that looks like a fuzzy bell and is called a 'hood.'" The hair is bleached with mercury, even today, to produce different shades, which gives meaning to the phrase "mad as a hatter." After the hair is boiled, it goes into a centrifuge like a huge cotton-candy machine. Trent shapes the raw hood with a pressing machine from 1920, which steams the crown and stretches the brim flat. He sands the crown with a special paper and then oils it. A vintage Singer sewing machine chain-stitches the sweat-band in place to cover the seam inside. The outside is covered by the hatband.

Trent details 360 handmade custom hats a year, but he also has a workshop around the corner where eight employees turn out a line of production hats, a dozen a day. All of his hatmakers were customers first. "You have to have the passion," Trent says. Since I visited, he's combined store and workshop into a single space just outside Greeley in Garden City. But his plan has always been "to grow smart and not fast." The Greeley Hat Works has been doing quality work for a century, he says, and he doesn't want to get up to heaven and have Mr. Martin point a fin-ger and say, "You're a bad hat man." When he asked his twenty-one-year-old assistant, Jared, what his long-term goals were, Jared replied, "I'm going to be you and I'm going to buy Greeley Hat Works from you." Meantime, Trent has built a second and a third style hat for President Bush. The last one the president will give to visitors to his ranch in Craw-ford, Texas; the first he keeps in the Oval Office. Trent shows me a photo of the president and himself, with his "I'm-just-about-to-vomit" smile. When we step outside to say good-bye, I ask him, "What's that awful smell?"

"The smell of money," he says, and he doesn't mean from cowboy hats.

I'd tried to locate the source of that smell when I first came to town, a smell as inescapable as the smell of beer in Milwaukee, Wisconsin, or of chocolate in Hershey, Pennsylvania. As another visitor said, "At first I thought everyone must have a horse in his backyard. Then I found out that the lots were to the east and the wind was coming from the east." The lots! Greeley has the largest concentration of cattle feedlots (CAFOs — Confined Animal Feeding Operations) in the country, which has put the town on the map in a way it never expected.

That Greeley is home to both the best cowboy hats and the most concentrated feedlots in the country puts teeth in the paradox of the Cowboy and the Machine. But what struck me most was that while the symbolism of cowboying is ever more visible — modeled by the president himself — the reality of cowdom is ever more hidden. East of Greeley, ConAgra's feedlots run for a couple of miles on the north side of Highway 34, completely screened around the perimeter by tall hedges and fences. At the entrance a sign reads, "No public tours." Rising from the midst of what has been called a "concentration camp for cows" are the tall gray metal towers of the original silos, with the faded name "Monfort Feedlots" barely legible on the tallest tower. Cornfields abut the feedlots on either side, visibly enforcing the industrial equation of commodity cows with commodity corn. The cornfields are there for everyone to see, but the only way you can really see the cows in their concentrated encampment is from a helicopter or airplane.

It's easy for me to see William D. Farr, however. Better known as W. D., Farr is the best-known and most-beloved elder in Greeley. At ninety-six he's just been inducted into the Hall of Great Westerners at the National Cowboy & Western Heritage Museum in Oklahoma City. I find him at his desk in his office at Bank One, courtly in suspenders and an impeccably white shirt, bent nearly double in front of his large-type computer, his blue eyes red-rimmed, but his mind sharp as an old-fashioned letter opener. Now that his wife is gone, he says, he gets tired of sitting around home alone, so he comes down to the office from ten in the morning until three in the afternoon, not to make too long a day of it.

W. D.'s grandfather came to Greeley in 1878, attracted by the Union Colony and its ranching-farming possibilities. His grandfather and father had fed sheep on prairie grass and finished them on a little imported corn, when fields were beginning to be planted with sugar beets and spuds. As teenagers, W. D. and his friend Warren Monfort loaded their sheep on Denver-Pacific Railroad cars headed for Cheyenne, and then on to Chicago for the Eastern markets. W. D. got his nickname "Cowboy" from summers spent tending cattle in the high country, and both boys felt that the future belonged to cattle, not sheep. As the demand for lamb and wool dropped, they asked themselves why they couldn't do for cattle what they'd done for lambs: fatten their livestock on the spot rather than ship them to be fattened by big-city packers in railroad centers. That way they could spread out the market for beef instead of selling them only in the fall, after they'd come off summer grass. The budding entrepreneurs decided to hold and feed their cattle until the market rose. Together they formed the T-Bone Club, which became the Colorado Cattle Feeders and grew to a thousand members.

In this water-rich region, crop wastage — beet tops and old potatoes, for example — had long been fed to cattle. "The South Platte River was the lifeblood of this whole valley," says Jim Miller of Miller Feed Lots in LaSalle, near Gilcrest, an enterprise advertised with signs along Route 85 that read "Beef, Beans, and Beets." A ruddy-faced man with white hair, standing tall against a backdrop of silver silos, Jim explains to me that Gilcrest was one of the first areas in the country to raise commercially potatoes, pinto beans, and sugar beets. In the spirit of the Union Colonists, farmers in the 1930s developed co-ops like the Early Potato Association. "Early because at Gilcrest and LaSalle the sandy soil heated up real fast," Jim says, "so they could get their potatoes out before anybody else." The same cooperative spirit produced the Farmers' Independent Ditch Company, which brought families together on managing irrigation and sold shares in the water that went with the farm, he says. "I'm sure you know that the only reason cattle feeding is here is because of irrigation — it's a wonderful place to grow crops."

In 1930 Warren Monfort devised a system to feed crop surpluses to his first 30 head of cattle, and by the end of World War II he was ready for the huge explosion of crop yields that would soon make corn cheaper than grass for feed. Ammunition plants that had geared up during the war to produce ammonium nitrate for gunpowder were converted after the war to high-nitrogen fertilizer factories. As early as 1946, farmers began to spread this fertilizer on cornfields throughout the Midwest, which tripled the harvest for that year and the next and the next. "We were at the right time in the right place, when World War II was over and everybody came home, everybody had money in their pockets, times were good," W. D. says. "It was a wonderful time to get started."

Yield would grow from 20 bushels per acre in 1900 to 138 in the 1990s. Excess corn from excess nitrogen was encouraged and maintained by federal price supports, a circular logic that feeds corn to cows today. "It was a way of getting over a hump that became a way of life," says Ernest Phinney, who runs the Western Grassland Beef Company in California. The logic of commodified corn for commodified cows was impeccable because now ranchers, through genetic selection, could breed cows that would fatten quickly on corn rather than grass. "Besides which," Phinney explains, "corn feeding forgives a lot of sins. An animal that doesn't do well on grass can still get fat on corn, and that's all you need for the USDA grading system."

Jim Miller remembers that when Monfort's cattle-feeding operation started, they'd put the feed bunks in the middle of the pens. A team of horses swept the corn into a heap there; they'd shake some soybeans on top. Then they got the bright idea of putting feed bunks at the end of the pens, so they could use trucks. In the 1950s they used "those old John Deeres with boxes that would rachet — *chk, chk, chk, chk* — like manure spreaders, only we put them on backward and filled them with corn and silage and a little extra protein, and when the truck went forward, the feed would mix itself up."

After bringing a feeding operation to the cows in the field, Monfort's second major innovation was to bring a packing plant there. W. D. and Jim Miller remember this development differently. W. D. attributes the innovation of the packing plant to Ken's father, in 1960. "He wanted my father and me to be partners in the packinghouse, but we chose to stick to feeding, and he brought in a big marketing man from New York who taught them how to market beef. While Monfort envisioned a new integration that combined processing with marketing, W. D. stuck to the old ways. He went on to become president of National Cattlemen, which preceded the NCBA, and consisted of range-cattle producers "most of whom had never seen a beef carcass." But the Corn Belt feeders running the feedlots weren't cattlemen, they were corn growers, W. D. says. They'd fatten up the cattle until their corn ran out, and when they slaughtered the animals, they might have 4 inches of fat on them. "My job was to gradually decrease the fat because we learned that what counted was the fat on the inside, not the outside."

Jim Miller gives credit for the packing plant to Monfort's son Kenny, who eventually took over his father's company. As Jim remembers it, a packing company in Denver came to Kenny and proposed building a plant near the feedlots. People thought, "Oh boy, they'll take Kenny to the cleaners, those guys know what they're doing," says Jim. But "Kenny was a very driven guy, extremely bright, and in about five years they were out and Kenny owned it all." His company was a model for feeders like Jim, who got a group together and built a packing plant over in Sterling. But in the 1970s, they lost out to the huge conglomerates like IBP and Excel. "We were trying to manage it like farmers and not business people. Kenny managed his like a business person."

The Monfort operation was the first modern large-scale feedlot, a pioneer in a movement that was shifting slaughterhouses and packinghouses from cities like New York and Chicago to cornfields in Kansas and Nebraska. The Monfort plant killed 7 head the first day it opened; seventeen years later, it was killing 2300 a day; by the 1960s, the feedlot accommodated 100,000 head. Monfort's annual revenues were over $85 million, and the company was Greeley's largest employer. In 1970 Kenny built another giant feedlot at Gilcrest. Four years later, he built a third one near Kersey and closed the original site because of chronic complaints about the smell. For a while, that smell seemed to be the only fly in the ointment of industrial progress.

With this kind of volume, Kenny turned next to the marketing tool of "boxed beef," which had been initiated by the men who started Iowa Beef Packers, A. D. Anderson and Currier Holman. In 1961 IBP had streamlined meat processing by increasing the automation of slaughtering and "fabricating." Aiming to "take the skill out of every step" of butchering, as Anderson said, they could now take "boys right off the farm" and put them on the disassembly line. The new automation of breaking down a carcass into 44 primal cuts, stripped largely of bone and fat, packaging them in Cryovac and shipping them in boxes, lowered shipping costs radically and cut out middlemen.

What *Forbes* praised as "a triumph of logic," however, the Amalgamated Meat Cutters Union, along with local butchers in retail stores, deplored as a triumph of job cutting. Extreme mechanization had an immediate impact on meat workers, and in 1965 IBP experienced what would be the first of an increasingly violent series of union strikes until finally, in 1982, the National Guard had to be called in. Monfort's Greeley plant had been hit by a lengthy and violent strike in 1980. Ken Monfort's response was to close the plant and transfer processing to a Nebraska plant he'd just bought. When he reopened the Greeley plant two years later, he hired fewer workers at a lower wage. At the same time, he continued to expand his company by adding another giant feedlot at Yuma, in eastern Colorado, and by acquiring Swift Independent Packing Company. But the 1980s were a period of massive consolidation among the big boys in the meat industry. As one of his peers told me, "Ken saw the handwriting on the wall and decided to get out because as an independent he didn't have the financial clout to compete with the bigger corporations." In 1987–88, he sold kit and caboodle to ConAgra, the food giant based in Omaha, which kept the Monfort name on the Greeley part of its operation until 1999. The entrepreneur who brought the spirit of the independent cattleman to the process of feeding, slaughtering, and processing beef cattle retired to Florida a rich man. But the logic of integration that drove his company so dominated the beef industry as a whole, at the turn of the new century, that it put a stranglehold on independence.

In 2002 ConAgra was forced to recall 19 million pounds of beef tainted by *E. coli,* after the death of one woman and the illness of forty-five other people in sixteen states were traced to beef at the Greeley plant. ConAgra's form of damage control was to sell its meat company to

Swift & Company but retain 46 percent ownership in Swift, so that the change was largely semantic. In 2004 Swift kept the packing plant but returned control of the feedlots to ConAgra, which then sold them to Smithfield, the world's largest hog producer and pork processor. The very next year, these same feedlots were regrouped under a corporate umbrella called Five Rivers Ranch Cattle Feeding L.L.C., which sounds a lot better than CAFOs, and which merged Smithfield with ContiBeef (a division of ContiGroup Companies, which were originally grain suppliers) to gain a feeding capacity of 813,000 head of cattle concentrated in ten sites in five states.

What the growth of railroads after the Civil War had brought together, the growth of highways after World War II had only seemed to disperse. Packers were once again in control of the vertical integration of feeding/processing/marketing, and while neither intensive feeding nor its integration into processing was unique to this country, the epic scale and its consequences were. In the mid-1960s, there were 200,000 feedlots around the country. In 2005 the trade directory *Beef Spotter, the Feedlot Atlas* listed a mere 800 feedlots covering twenty-four states, most of them located between the Mississippi and the Rockies, with the largest (over 100,000 head) concentrated in only four states: Texas, Kansas, Nebraska, and Colorado. Five Rivers, with its bucolic name, boasts that it is the world's largest cattle feeder, with the Greeley lots (now called M. F. Cattle Feeding) providing a mere 305,000 of its grand total. Cactus Feeders of Amarillo, Texas, created in 1975, boasts that its 520,000 cattle make it the world's largest *privately owned* feeding company. These are numbers games. The number that counts is that only 2 percent of these feedlots market 85 percent of the 34 million cattle slaughtered each year from a total of 97 million live ones to make 26 billion pounds of beef.

And now, of course, that integration is global. In 2007 Swift sold its processing plant to the largest beef processor in Latin America, JBS S.A., with headquarters in Brazil. With the name change, the company can sidestep Asia's ban on Brazilian meat because of foot-and-mouth disease, but despite all the convoluted name juggling, this is, in fact, the largest meat conglomerate in the world.

Greeley, which for my grandfather and the elderly men I met there had stood for good old American small-town git-go, eventually came to stand for everything that went wrong with the beef business. A prescient few could see the fall from grace coming. *Meat,* a black-and-white documentary shot by Frederick Wiseman in 1976, at the very crest of Monfort success and just after the end of the Vietnam War, shows without commentary the machinery of feeding and processing cattle at Monfort. The excesses of America's glorification of the Machine that had once produced the slapstick comedy of Charlie Chaplin's *Modern Times* now evoked darker images of commodified death. In *Meat,* as we watch live cattle move silently and inexorably toward death and disassembly, it's hard not to associate human meat moving toward the "cleansing rooms." Although the mechanization of cattle-into-meat had been building for twenty years, however, most people were unaware of how radical it was in scale, and very few people saw Wiseman's film. It took another twenty-five years before Eric Schlosser published *Fast Food Nation,* echoing Upton Sinclair's *The Jungle* of 1906, nearly a century earlier. The following year, PBS provided another shocker on the scale and secretiveness of the beef industry, in "Modern Meat," its 2002 *Frontline* segment.

The hunger for bigger and bigger numbers is both symptom and cause of the disease of industrial concentration. Both the concentration of cattle in one spot and the concentration of what we feed them have for the past decades put our cows on drugs. Drugs begin with the perversion of feeding cows too much grain. Michael Pollan points to the illogic of feeding corn intensively to a ruminant that has "the most highly evolved organ on the planet, the rumen, designed specifically to do something we can't — transform grass into protein." Ironically, the natural digestive system of a cow is a model of industrial efficiency, if only the cow is given the chance to do its job of chewing cud every waking minute of its day and night. A cow's rumen is "a 45-gallon fermentation tank," which takes in the crude raw material for refinement. Bacteria in the rumen breaks it down in a repetitive process of burping, chewing, and reswallowing, until the mass is refined enough to go through "the hardware stomach" (reticulum) where the honeycomb lining acts as a kind of sieve, into the round "third stomach" (omasum) where all the liquid is squeezed out, and on into the "true stomach" (abomasum), where digestive juices finish the job. When they give up mother's milk, that's what cows do for the rest of their lives: become chewing machines.

Cows like grain because it's tasty, but if you gorge them with grain and little else, bad things happen, like bloat and acidosis. Corn is mostly starch, and with too much starch, rumination shuts down and a layer of slime in the rumen traps gas the cow would normally burp. The result is bloat, where the rumen blows up like a balloon and, if untended, suffocates the cow. Corn also turns the normal pH of a rumen acidic, giving the cow acidosis, which can abscess the liver, produce ulcers, and weaken the entire immune system. Recent innovations in cattle's diets haven't alleviated the problem. When food-processing plants followed meatpacking plants into rural areas, feeders began to supplement corn with by-products from ethanol plants, breweries, and other food factories. "We started out feeding junk — potatoes, carrots, beet tops, sugar beets — then we went to feeding corn, hay, and silage, and now we're back to feeding junk again," Jim Miller comments wryly. Since I spoke to him, cows' junk diet has expanded to include chocolate bars, popcorn, pretzels, potato chips, and Tater Tots, all from food factories located near feedlots.

Such a diet necessitates heavy "subtherapeutic" reliance on antibiotics like rumensin (against bloat), tylosin (against acidosis), chlortetracycline, oxytetracyline, sulfamethazine. Apart from diet, crowding large numbers together results in bovine respiratory disease, better known as "shipping fever," or BRD, which can run through a herd like flu through a kindergarten. BRD can account for 75 percent of feedlot cattle illness. Industry magazines are packed with brand-name pharmaceutical ads: "Excede (Ceftiofur Cystalline-Free Acid) for extended BRD therapy"; Micotil (Tilmicosin injection) "Easy on your cattle. Tough on BRD"; "Got Scours? Get First Defense" from ImmuCell.

Besides antibiotic injections, cattle are routinely given growth-hormone implants, like the estrogen Revlar, which puts cattle on steroids; 92 percent of feedlot managers implant these routinely during the initial processing at the lot, half that percentage a second time, and 10 percent a third time. The hormones have only one function: to fatten up those cattle fast. The European Union has banned both drugs for the very good reason that Europe is concerned about the health of its meat eaters. The increasing concern among American eaters finally drove the National Research Council in 1999 to study "the potential risk to human health directly associated with the use of antibiotic drugs in food animal production" and to conclude that, yes, "there is a link between the use of antibiotics in food animals, the development of bacterial resistance to these drugs, and human disease." Common sense had told us as much long ago.

The most recent alarm bells, however, come from yet one more unintended consequence. The feedlot cow's rumen has become a breeding tank for *Escherichia coli* 0157. This is a monster of our own making. Formerly, the germs in a cow's manure that might pollute water or earth and the food growing near it would be killed off by the acid in our stomachs when we ate that food. But our mutant *E. coli* is resistant to acid, and even a microscopic amount of it can create a national crisis when spinach or any other crop grown industrially borders an industrial feedlot. *E. coli* has replaced salmonella as the frightening germ of choice.

No one has better detailed the sci-fi unreality of what happens to an industrial steer start to finish than Michael Pollan in "Power Steer," first in the *New York Times* in 2002 and then *The Omnivore's Dilemma* in 2006. Pollan's steer #534 was fattened at Poky Feeders in Garden City, Kansas, which he says you'll nose out by "an aroma whose Proustian echoes are more bus-station-men's-room than cow-in-the-country." The feedlot, so large that it is a city of cows, reminds him of a medieval city awash in sewage and threats of plague, with the feedlot in the center rising like a Satanic cathedral. And no one has better traced the sickness of these cow cities back to their source in an oil-sick society.

I SAW SUCH mega-lots only at a distance, well-fortressed by ranks of electrified wire and bureaucracy meant to keep me there. But what I saw more intimately was the history of these feedmills and how they grew from innocence to monstrousness. And I saw that through Western eyes, tuned to the prairie landscapes of my ancestors and the Western landscapes of my birth. While no one has better calibrated than Pollan the ominous logic of the cow-corn-oil connection, I believe he brings an Easterner's view to the West. What I saw from Texas to Idaho in small-to-middling feedlots, and even some sizable ones, was not simply the carbon footprint of industrialism but the human face of men who'd grown up with cows and cared about them, men for whom cows were a way of life even when they were confined to a lot instead of roaming the range, men who acted more like old-fashioned cattlemen in small towns than serfs in medieval cow cities. I saw them set in a human scale, and I felt their pride, the pride of men who sensed the winds of change, yet believed that they were engaged in useful, honorable work.

Jim Miller remembers hauling fattened cattle to Denver, where packers from twenty-six different companies "would come right out to the feedlots and buy them there." Today the cattle don't have to travel as far. Feeders in the area just haul them in to Swift and base their price on whatever the first feeder got. Young people think that any dickering about prices is a conflict, Jim says, but he still maintains the old ways. "I bought cattle this morning in Idaho and we came to a price over the phone, trading a million dollars' worth of cattle by phone, without even a handshake or even seeing them. I love that — that's the best part, everybody does it on trust. I love that business of saying, 'You want $1.05 and I can't do that. I'll give you $1.03,' and eventually we arrive at $1.04. That's the way our industry has run for years and years.

"I would love to see my children and grandchildren involved in agriculture in some way, but I don't see the future of it being that great," he says over coffee in his feedlot office. "This is going to sound crazy to you, but for my grandchildren, I don't see how you can beat working for the government. You get lots of time off, wonderful benefits. I'm one of those old people who likes to see dirt under my fingernails, but to be really honest, four or five years ago I lost millions and millions of dollars because the market was so bad, and we couldn't turn it around. Too many cattle and too much bad press. I'm afraid that what we're going to do is drive agriculture, as we know it, out of the United States, and going to import our food from Mexico, South America, Asia. If the environmentalists think our food is dirty now, wait until they get all their food from foreign countries."

The walls of his office were covered by paintings of cowboys and photographs of elk and a log cabin; on his desk was a signed photo of George and Laura Bush. "People like to eat, but they don't like to be around the packinghouse industry. They don't want to put up with the smell. It used to be a kind of neat thing to say you were in the cattle business, but today when somebody asks me what business I'm in, I say 'agriculture,' because I'm ashamed of it."

I came to feel that if you must single out any single element of the contemporary beef industry in order to condemn it, it should not be corn or feedlots per se, it should be industrial scale. I even learned that it was possible to defend, when it came to scale, the smell of dung. I'd heard that the smell of a particular feedlot in California's Central Valley, near Fresno, had set Pollan on the road to writing "Power Steer," and I wanted to check it out for myself. What I found when I turned at the sign for Coalinga off Highway 5, which cuts the Valley from L.A. to Sacramento, was a startling oasis of pink adobe walls and tiled roofs in Cal-Spanish hacienda style, with fountains and swimming pools hidden by massive palms and orange trees, oleanders, and geraniums. This was the Harris Ranch Inn and Restaurant and it was just down the road apiece from the Harris Ranch Feedlot. You might think it risky to integrate a lush upscale restaurant and inn with a farm and feedlot, but this is the place John Harris grew up in and he wants to preserve it.

John Harris is a farmer-rancher-entrepreneur who has somehow managed to create an unusually integrated empire and keep it within the family. A tall, handsome man in his late fifties, he has gray hair that matches his eyes, a low voice, an easy laugh — a man in jeans at ease in his surroundings. The first thing he shows me is the clapboard house where he was born. The second thing is the feedlot, no longer small. This is a big lot of 100,000 head, but unlike the cows at the ConAgra lot in

Greeley, these cows are not only visible from the highway but accessible. Harris showed me around and encouraged me to talk to his superintendent, Bob Martin, who'd once worked for John's father. Right off, Martin defended the smell: "People just don't understand agriculture because they didn't grow up with it."

Their aim at the lot, Martin says, is to not underfeed or overfeed the cattle, but just to keep the diet steady. "It's kind of like Thanksgiving dinner. The cows are no smarter than we are, so if they eat too much they'll get sick and not eat the next day." Even so, they get most of their weight from what grows in the hills: wild bunchgrass like the native purple needlegrass, wild oats, and a native legume that grows wild all over the West. "This is country not otherwise good for anything but lookin' at," he says. And it's this kind of country that gives the cattle their first 800 pounds. They add the last 300 (nearly one-third of the total) in the lot. "Grain may not be natural," he admits, "but we get them accustomed to it gradually, and the only way you're going to get well-marbled beef is a concentrated ration."

Like Niman, Harris turned his name into a brand that guaranteed quality beef, hormone and antibiotic free, long before the current greening movement. Unlike Niman, Harris is a Californian whose connection to regional history is up close and personal. In 1916 his grandfather, J. A. Harris, came to California from Texas to establish a cotton gin in the Imperial Valley; in the 1920s he began to farm in the San Joaquin and Sacramento valleys; in 1937 his son Jack, with wife Teresa, founded their own ranch near Coalinga. Just as irrigation brought spuds and sugar beets to Greeley, to Coalinga it brought first cotton and grain, then nut and citrus orchards, fields of garlic, lettuce, melons, tomatoes, and grapes. But what brought this part of the valley to full flower, Harris says, was the invention of the centrifugal pump, the first deep-turbine drill, which was able to tap into the aquifer.

In the 1960s Harris's father, like Warren Monfort, added a processing plant to his feedlot, and this farsightedness enabled the Harris Ranch to survive as a family-owned company when the big boys concentrated on the Midwest and Texas Panhandle. In the same decade, the Harris family began to breed and train Thoroughbred racehorses and establish the Harris Farms Horse Division. In the 1970s they founded the inn and restaurant to showcase their beef, along with their farm produce. I don't know anybody else who's put a feedlot within sniffing distance of a restaurant, but Harris completed his farm-to-fork chain by integrating diversified farming (thirty-three crops of nuts, fruits, and vegetables) with cattle raising and processing (800 head a day), with manufacturing cooked products (meat dishes, sauces, marinades), with direct marketing (to restaurants, supermarkets, mail and Internet orders). While Harris Ranch restaurants feed over 2000 people a day, they also sell takeout foods like roasts and stews.

In a way, John Harris is living Doc and Connie Hatfield's vision of total control and Salatin's vision of total integration, the one specific to western desertland and the other to eastern pastures. Maybe it can happen only in a place as unreal as artificially irrigated California, but I liked eating and sleeping in the midst of all this agricultural activity, including a feedlot, as if horses and cattle and tomatoes and garlic were all part of the day's work and the night's pleasure. It was almost enough to make me believe that to smell the roses without a whiff of cow dung is to diminish that act of agriculture we call eating. Yet, when I later sat down in The Steakhouse to eat a cedar-planked Harris Ranch rib-eye steak and drink a Harris Reserve wine, the only aroma was grilled steak among the oleanders.

✦ Slaughterhouse Blues ✦

"Heads of Beef Cattle," in a packing plant in Austin, Minnesota, was photographed by John Vachon in 1941. Behind the skinned heads, the eviscerated innards hang like rags.

— From the FSA-OWI Collection, Prints & Photographs Division,
Library of Congress

People want their steak, but they don't want to know how it's butchered. There's a lot of things it's better people don't know.

— A soldier in the 82nd Airborne Division in Iraq, speaking in the 2005 documentary *Operation: Dreamland*

AFTER ALL THE CLASSROOM STUFF, it feels really good to run our hands along the bristly black-and-white hide of our steer, alive and chewing in the paddock — all six of us, running twelve hands along his brisket, over his rib cage, just in front of his flank, and (carefully) along the base of his tail. He is ours, in every sense: Steer #4, a white-faced Simmental with white eyelashes and white socks on his back legs. But we aren't giving him love pats. The job of our Yellow Team is to "read" his musculature and the size of his fat depots in order to estimate when he is alive what he will be worth dead. We've been told that a steer begins to fatten from front to hind and from bottom to top. We've examined the size of his muscles over forearm and shoulders, the roundness of his rear, and especially the roundness on the inside of his thighs — the degree to which that roundness has pushed his legs apart. Roundness spells money. Tongue to tail, it is all about the money.

I'm in the biggest meat department of the biggest agricultural college in the country, Texas A&M, one of thirty attendees who have come from all over the country to take Davey Griffin's three-day workshop, Beef 101. I'd run into Professor Griffin at the NCBA's annual convention in San Antonio in January, and I couldn't wait to get here in May. Davey's a

Texas boy, born fifty miles out of Dallas, and a Texas A&M man from student all the way through to professor of meat science. A large, genial man, he invented this program seventeen years ago as a service to public education. "It's like two funnels you put together — all these producers over here and all these consumers over there, and we're the guys in the middle."

My fellow team members are all connected in one way or another to the beef industry, usually on the marketing end for packers, food companies, supermarkets, food services, hotel and restaurant chains. Definitely white-collar and accustomed to encountering their science and economics spread thin over sheets and charts, not live in the paddock. We bond as we compare our steer to five others, each fed the same food but each of a different breed and therefore producing a different frame and weight. We've been told that genetics is the key to the growth ratio of bone, muscle, fat — and especially of marbling. We've been told that a feeder can manage growth by slowing it down or speeding it up, but that he can't change the ratio. We're told that beef cattle are the true factory and feedlots merely the hotels where the manager's job is to turn out consistent occupants for the "harvester." We're told that each stage of the fragmented beef industry adds value and needs profit, from the seed-stock breeders to cow-calf producers to background feeders to feedlot feeders to slaughter/processors to retailers — it's a very long chain strung together by complex mathematical equations that calculate profit and loss. It's about the money.

At lunch we feast on brisket and ribs, coleslaw and chocolate pudding, no longer exactly innocent, but still lulled by euphemisms for the harvest to come. In industry slang, when a steer is ready for the slaughterhouse, it's ready "to go to town." We are assumed to be ready for a spectator tour of the Teaching/Cutting Lab of the Rosenthal Meat Science and Technology Center, from Harvest Room to Chill Room, where well-trained graduate students will do the work at academic — not industrial — speed. Whereas a large industrial plant will process 300 to 400 animals an hour, which means harvesting 6 steers a minute, or about 10 seconds per steer, our pace will be leisurely, a film in slow motion.

In the Harvest Room, our steer, along with the others one by one, enters the kill chute, which opens into a tight black enclosure with a rectangular peephole in front so that for a moment we can see the steer's nose and eyes. Then his face drops from view when a man with a stun gun reaches down and shoots the top of his head. Immediately the steer reappears upside down, hoisted by its left leg onto the track, and immediately its throat is slit vertically with a thin, sharp knife wielded by a young gum-chewing guy who avoids the blood spurting out in a red gush. Another guy hoses the blood down the drain. We know that the man has used a Cash-Knocker (nonpenetrating concussion produced by a bolt) rather than a Schermer Stunner (which penetrates). We know that the bleeding should take no more than 6 to 8 minutes, and that a 1000-pound animal contains around 30 to 35 pounds of blood. We know that in an industrial plant this blood will be saved and processed into feed for calves.

A third guy cuts off the front and rear hooves while a fourth begins to skin the head, from the back of the neck forward. Off go the ears, the hide crawls forward over the skull, then the nose, and is discarded. The head is severed and saved, along with the tongue, in a macabre row of heads lined up and bound for Mexico for barbecue. A special cutting device of air knives helps remove the hide from the body, beginning with the back legs, so that the hide zips off impressively in one piece. In a large plant, there are specialists for each stage of hide removal: header, foreshanker, hindshanker, rumper, rimmer, sider, hide puller. An older man slits open the belly from neck to tail to release the emerging balloons of stomachs, the coils of intestines, all those innards officially termed offal: "abdominal viscera" and "thoracic cavity pluck." He wraps a plastic bag around both ends of the intestines to prevent any contents from oozing out. (The cattle have fasted for a day before slaughter to make this job cleaner and easier; the two critical moments of potential contamination are skinning and eviscerating.) He next removes the long red tube of the esophagus and the thin ovoid of the spleen. Then he takes out the liver, heart, and lungs, but leaves the squiggly lumps of fatted kidneys attached. (The kidney area is another significant fat depot and will help estimate worth.) With a large electric saw, he cuts the carcass in two straight down the backbone. A USDA inspector examines the offal, like an ancient Greek priest looking for omens. The inspector also examines the teeth in the skull to guarantee that the steer is younger than 30 months, a precaution taken since the scare of bovine spongiform encephalopathy (BSE), or mad cow disease. If the steer proves to be older than 30 months, the bones of the carcass are marked with blue stripes to indicate that all spine marrow must be removed by hand before the carcass goes into the processing chain.

Next day we suit up like astronauts for "Fabrication," or butchering, in the properly named Cutting Room. First a sweatshirt for warmth — the Cutting Room is kept in the low 40s. Over that, a white cotton coat like a surgeon's whites, then an armor-plated apron made like chain mail to protect us from our own knives, then a white cloth butcher's apron. On the head, a plastic shower cap, topped by a hard hat — mine yellow, for my team. I don a glove for the noncutting hand and over that a pair of thick gloves for each hand and over that a pair of green surgical gloves, then a plastic arm guard for the noncutting arm, and finally a thin boning knife that fits into a metal holster hanging from a chain around my waist. I swagger like a cowboy into the Cutting Room, ready to draw first.

Beside the big cutting table the half-carcass of our steer is hanging, already cut horizontally between the twelfth and thirteenth ribs. In the meat industry, the fat of the twelfth rib is used as a yardstick for the worth of the whole steer. The rib, which looks like a potential rib-eye steak, is graded for two vital categories, standardized by the USDA: yield and quality. Yield, on a descending scale of 1 to 5, refers to the degree of salable meat, meaning the amount of edible muscle in relation to exterior fat and bone, a relation the industry calls "cutability." Quality, on a scale from Prime to Utility, means the amount of marbled fat within the muscle, or "palatability." Secondary considerations for quality are "maturity," which screens out any older cattle that might have slipped through, and "color," to lower the boom on any "dark cutters," meat that has darkened from age or undue stress. Together, the two grades of Yield and Quality (with "Yield 1 Prime Quality" being the optimum) are the coordinates of the baroque money formulas that determine each step in the mechanized chain from pasture to plate.

The width of the external fat on the twelfth rib is a quick clue to Yield, and we are pleased that Steer #4 comes in at a solid 1.8. Now we do the Quality test on the rib, measuring its degree of marbling by means of a transparent sheet called a "dot grid." The marbling of our steer is not so good and is calculated to be a disappointing "Small" (on a scale of Moderately Abundant, Slightly Abundant, Moderate, Modest, Small, Slight). That means our boy can be graded only High Select, a step below Prime and Choice. We press the top three cartilaginous tips of his thoracic vertebrae, where ribs attach to sternum, known as the "chine buttons" which harden with age, and discover they are soft enough to garner our steer an "A" in maturity (meaning somewhere between 9 to 30 months, with the average at 12 to 18). His color is a good bright red.

We've been told that packers don't usually bother making retail cuts of cattle that grade below 3 on Yield or below Select on Quality. (Grades descend rapidly from Standard, Commercial, Utility, Cutter to Canner, the upper grades of which might go to a discount steakhouse chain, the lower bound for a "grinding program.") Most industrial beef that is cut instead of ground achieves Select with a Grade 3 Yield, although producers will shoot for Choice with a Grade 2 Yield, because it's worth more. As an eater, I can see that none of the grading systems were designed for me. They came out of an industrial need to standardize a product from a source as variable as live cattle.

As far back as 1916, the USDA began to develop a system that would distinguish carcass weight from live weight and the amount of excess fat in the carcass. The need to supply troops in World War I and again in World War II boosted the grading system into a kind of federal imprimatur, but such grading remains entirely voluntary on the part of the packers. It is they who pay for the USDA inspectors to stamp carcasses in the plant. Any carcass a packer decides not to grade, he calls a "no roll" and the meat goes to the grinder. Grading remains a baseline marketing tool for the producer, extended now into "Certification" stamps to promote special standards of breed, like Certified Black Angus, or marketed brand names, like Nolan Ryan Beef and Creekstone Farms Premium Beef. Safety inspection, on the other hand, is mandatory for any packer selling retail. Here the USDA inspector's stamp is paid for by us, the taxpayers. In practice, beef that is not USDA inspected cannot legally be sold in a retail market. In practice, any beef you buy in a commodity retail market, except for hamburger, will be graded either Choice or Select because those — not Prime — give the industry the highest profit.

I sharpen my knife. All that external fat that has been put on by corn must now be sliced away as we attack the forequarter, a primal cut that we will turn into subprimals like chuck and blade, brisket, skirt steak, back ribs, and rib-eye roll. I try to remember our lengthy anatomy lesson as our grad-student instructors indicate a carnal lump of red and white and ask if we know where the skirt steak is. Struggling to relate my vertical body to a cow's horizontal one, I find it easier to imagine a cow standing upright than to imagine myself on all fours. Removing the bone from big pieces like the chuck is a lot more fun than the tedious job of trimming muscle of membranes, connective tissue, and all but a rim of fat. This requires patience, knowledge, skill, but all we have is patience. In the shoulder clod we look for the "flatiron," a new cut the industry has devised to utilize the more tender parts of the clod. The flatiron is tucked into the blade bone and you slice it lengthwise like a fish fillet and cut out the center connective tissue. On the back of the clod are some lean strips now called "petite tenders" or "Texas grillers." Behind the blade is a chunk now called "chuck roll."

Beneath our table are bins in which we dump fat for the renderer, bones for the bone mill, and trim to be ground or turned into stew cubes and kebabs. We work slowly, for no muscle meat is to be wasted. You have to be stronger than I am to use the handsaw that cuts through the large dorsal bones and nervier than I am to use the electric saw that removes the backbone. After a lunch break, we attack the simpler hindquarter and try to distinguish tenderloin from strip loin, top from bottom sirloin, top round from bottom round. By now I've lost all sense of connection to my own body and can think only of fragmented cow. By now the floor is slippery with spilled fat and liquid from the beef joints. I worry about slipping and falling with a knife in my hand. Which team member would I take down with me?

Our final job at the end of the day is to weigh all the cuts separately, then the fat, bones, and trim. When each item is weighed, we begin to see the disparities between weight and value. In the forequarter the shoulder clod weighs the most (21.4 pounds), but its value is only half that of the rib-eye roll ($30), which weighs half as much as the clod (12.7 pounds). In the hindquarter, the top round weighs the most (23.5 pounds) but its price per pound is $1.70 rather than the $6.86 per pound of tenderloin. As for waste and trimmings, we learn that we've trimmed with a heavy hand, reducing the profit on our subprimal cuts. Our regular trim comes in at a whopping 73.9 pounds and will earn only $1.45 per pound. Our fat, which weighs 62.3 pounds, earns only 13 cents a pound. Our bones weigh about the same — 67.7 pounds — but they earn only 4 cents a pound. Total trim and waste weigh just over 207 pounds, in a total half-carcass weight of 388.5. All our work has yielded up less than 50 percent of meat that can count as subprimal cuts. And of that, only 10 to 12 percent goes to the top cuts, which come from the part of the animal we're willing to pay the most for because it's the most tender — the middle. No wonder the margin of profit in turning a live steer into meat is so small. The live weight of our steer was 1210 pounds, its total carcass weight was 777 pounds, and its total value was $1,169.79. But the price paid for our animal at the feedlot was $1,089. That brings a net gain to the owner of $80.79, and *our* labor was free.

As a reward for that labor, we are treated by Davey to an outdoor barbecue in a green park with a little pond beside a rustic wooden cabin. It's a hot night, and we guzzle beer. Davey is feasting us with a prime boneless rib eye, rolled, rubbed with a pepper rub, and smoked for eight hours. One bite and all memory of gory carcasses and butchering is gone. The flavor is magnificent and for once the meat is medium rare, pink as a baby's bottom and juicy. It's a tongue-on introduction to tomorrow's final morning of lectures, on "palatability factors," where we will sample in a blind test nine different kinds of meat, none of them graded prime, rating each for juiciness, tenderness, and flavor.

Cooked to 158 degrees, however, all the samples are too dry, okay on tenderness, but depressingly bland to my tongue. The sample with the most intense flavor turns out to be grass-fed and dry-aged. On our charts, "grassy," as a flavor adjective, is not a plus; fattiness in the form of "mouthfeel" is. Grassy is linked to other disparaging terms labeled "off flavors," like "serumy, livery, gamy." I ask about the difference in flavor between dry and wet aging and am told that dry aging has a different flavor, "more like putrefaction," and that "less than one percent would want this flavor." I think of the Noël Coward song that spoofs the disparagement of delicacies like caviar, truffles, and such as "Too Good for the Average Man." The beef industry is based entirely on providing food for the average man, as fictional a critter as the consumer in the mantra "What the Consumer Wants." What the industry attributes to consumer wants is what the industry wants to produce: cheap beef. When one of our lecturers explains different methods of meat identification, so that a consumer might trace a piece of bad meat to its source, he claims that consumers don't really want "traceability." "They say they do but they don't," he says. "People really don't want to know where their meat comes from. They don't want to think about it."

IN BEEF 101 we reenacted the classic moves that butchers have made for the last couple of hundred years in killing, skinning, halving, quartering, and cutting the carcass of a cow into manageable pieces. In contrast to modern plant workers, we had all the time in the world. Our tempo, our hands, our eyes, were artisanal. It was not common sense that had changed all that in the real world of the late nineteenth century, but romance — the romance of the Machine that fit size USA XXX-large. The explosion of industrialism that roared across America after the Civil War was fueled by our permanent love affair with both scale and speed. Americans like Big, Americans love Fast, and the romance of the Machine overlaid the romance of the West that was grounded in both those elements. The vision that drove adventurers across the continent at the beginning of the century — endless space, crossed by men galloping on horses and protecting their rights by drawing guns fast — that same vision drove adventurers toward the end of the century to mine coal and iron and hammer them into steel on a scale and at a pace that boggled the minds of the progenitors of industrialism in England. America longed to fulfill its destiny as the biggest industrial empire in the world as fast and as heroically as possible. Vertiginous skyscraping buildings were one expression of empire; vertically integrated and horizontally mechanized meat-scraping buildings were another.

European tourists like the French writer Paul Bourget, visiting the Chicago stockyards in 1893, saw the capitalist businessmen creating this empire as "new conquistadors" who had tamed the wild and erected monumental cities in one generation, an extraordinary feat. He saw the Meat Kings of Chicago — Gustavus Swift and Philip Armour — as warriors, the way we would see "top guns," or battling cowboys. Swift and Armour were in fact both farm-boy Easterners who had arrived in Chicago less than twenty years before, Swift as a young country butcher and Armour as a gold miner and grain dealer. They were both drawn to the synergy of transporting butchered meat instead of livestock by railroad and therefore cutting down on shipping costs, as 60 percent of the animal was waste. All they needed were refrigerated cars, for which Swift constructed a system by harvesting ice in Wisconsin and establishing ice stations along railroad routes to the east. Armour followed suit, and opened up trade to Europe. Both devised a coordinated overhead trolley system so that a side of beef could arrive at the wholesaler's in New York City on the very same hook it was hung on after it was killed in a Chicago plant. Although Americans had developed a taste for preserved pork products like bacon and ham and other forms of salt and pickled pork, they always wanted their beef fresh.

It was less invention than organization that built the Meat Kings' empire of fresh beef. The buzz word "efficiency" was defined as volume and speed, and both men created companies to maximize control by owning all the elements in the process of production and distribution, from the calf on the ground to the steak in the shop. But both men were faced with the problem that their imitator Henry Ford was spared when he adopted their method of disassembling carcasses to assembling metal cars. The Meat Kings were stuck with the obdurate reality of organic creatures. Mechanization can never take full control of a natural product like a cow or a pig by standardizing its shape or eliminating its decay, as historian Roger Horowitz notes: "The meat industry remains tethered to a natural product." As the machine couldn't turn cow flesh into metal parts, the industrialists turned slaughterhouses into "machines made up almost entirely of human parts." To make the system work, workers themselves had to become machines.

The Founding Fathers' ideal of property had not changed, it had merely intensified as ownership of machines and industrial serfs replaced ownership of land and agricultural serfs. What was slaughtered in Chicago's Union Stockyards was only the agrarian part of the Jeffersonian ideal. Just as savage creatures like Indians and buffalo had been slaughtered in the name of the plow, now foreign workers and domesticated cattle were subjugated alike to the "technology and progress" represented by the machine. There were skeptics, of course. Upton Sinclair's depiction of the horrors of the new urban jungle of the stockyards was echoed by journalists from abroad, reporting on what they found in Packingtown: a branch of the Chicago River turned into "Bubbly Creek," reeking of animal blood, grease, entrails, feces, carbolic acid; workers so stiffened by blood and grease that they walked like zombies and, as Italian journalist Giuseppe Giacosa wrote, had "neither the body nor the face of humans."

At the turn of the century, "modern efficiencies" demanded more and more concentrated ownership of the entire rationalized process, from breeders to retailers, and that remains the model of the beef industry today. Just as four major packers in the United States control over 83 percent of the slaughtering/processing segment, in 2004 five major retailers — Wal-Mart, Kroger, Safeway, Albertsons, Ahold USA — controlled 46 percent of the marketing segment. But the tighter the integration at the meat end of the industry, the more the cattle end of the industry has put on protective blinders to flee reality. Fragmentation allows ranchers to concentrate on calving and weaning and shut their eyes to what happens to their babes once they've left the ranch. Unlike the meat end, the ranching end is not about the money. Despite their endless business talk and cowboy costumes, the majority of the 800,000 ranchers today who raise cattle cannot make a living out of cattle alone. The breaking point for profit is 500 head, but the average herd size in the United States is only 43 head, and 90 percent of U.S. cattle owners have herds under 100 head. That may account for the fact that the average age of a rancher today is sixty. That may also account for the fact that the imagery of ranching today is pasteurized nostalgia — cowboys far distant from machines, revealed in racks of cowboy magazines named *American Cowboy, Cowboys and Indians, Range, Cowboy,* and *Shoot!* (yes, it's all about cowboy guns). Only big-time feedlots in conjunction with packers in conjunction with retailers — in other words, the industrial beef chain, supported by government agencies — make big-time money.

But once in a while, a genuine cowboy gets mad. Enter a Wild Bill Hickok fighter, bull rider, inventor, marketer, entrepreneur, provocateur — Mike Callicrate, of No-Bull Enterprises in St. Francis, Kansas. When I met Mike in his retail store, Ranch Foods Direct, in Colorado Springs, I found a guy who's never sung anything but "My Way." He flies his Piper Comanche back and forth across the border between his feedlots in Kansas and his markets and restaurants in Colorado. For ten years he was a professional bull rider on the rodeo circuit, and made enough money to put himself through college. He'd been raised on a ranch outside Denver, but married a girl he met in rodeo, whose folks had a ranch in St. Francis. It was soon clear to him that he couldn't make money ranching, so he built a feedlot and discovered then what "captive supplies" meant. At fifty-five, he's stocky, balding, nothing out of the ordinary except for his eyes, which sparkle with a moral passion that makes you pay attention when he fires at you, "It's *wrong!*"

I'd first heard of Callicrate when he and five others, including Alabama rancher Lee Pickett, took on IBP in a class-action suit filed on behalf of 30,000 cattlemen who had sold cattle to IBP between 1994 and 2002. The suit dragged on for eight years before the case even got to court, by which time it was renamed *Pickett v. Tyson,* since IBP had been bought up by Tyson in 2001, not long after President Clinton had pardoned Tyson executive Archibald L. Shaffer III, convicted of bribing Secretary of Agriculture Mike Espy. The charge essentially was price-fixing, a violation of the Packers and Stockyards Act of 1921, when Senator John Kendrick of Wyoming had told the Senate: "[The big packers] have their fingers on the pulse of both the producing and consuming markets and are in such a position of strategic advantage they have unrestrained power to manipulate both markets to their own advantage and to the disadvantage of over 99 percent of the people of the country." The plaintiffs charged that seventy-five years later the big packers were abusing power in just the same way, fixing prices by the device of "captive supplies" or "forward contracts," by which they locked in prices before the cattle were ready to be delivered to the slaughterhouse. In other words, the plaintiffs claimed, Tyson Fresh Meats, as one of the Big Four, acted as a monopoly to the disadvantage of producers and consumers. As a result, cattle producers and feeders lost billions of dollars in sales and consumers paid ever higher prices. In addition, to keep their plants busy, packers continued to import large numbers of live cattle from abroad, especially Canada and Mexico. Although the United States is both the biggest producer and the biggest consumer of beef in the world, we nevertheless import 20 percent of the beef we consume in a market controlled by packers, not producers. In such a market, "It's *wrong* that American producers are going bankrupt," Callicrate says. "The packers are putting them out of business."

What Callicrate is really taking on is the industrial model, which he believes is continually rationalized by the NCBA's being interlocked with the USDA: "I'm saying the efficiency and economies of scale arguments are a lie, and that the corporate-controlled industrial model is not mutually beneficial. It is not sustainable and is not inevitable." For a brief moment in February 2004, Callicrate was exhilarated when the District Court jury not only found for Pickett et al., but awarded them $1.28 billion, a sum based on the estimated amount of money the ranchers would have earned during the specified years if the market had been truly open. But the verdict was overturned on appeal, a district judge stating that the "use of captive supply arrangements is supported by the legitimate business justification of competing in the industry." The appeal was upheld, and in April 2006 the Supreme Court declined to hear the case. After ten years, Tyson the Goliath, with its captive inventory of big money, won.

In 2004, however, Callicrate won a settlement against Farmland National Beef Packing Company (later merged with Swift/ConAgra), which Callicrate sued for boycotting his feedyards after he'd publicly criticized Farmland for having too much power. And during its decade of litigation, the Pickett group won the support of an unlikely assortment of organizations. In addition to the usual suspects — the National Family Farm Coalition, National Farmers Union, American Corn Growers Association, Organic Consumers Association, Organization for Competitive Markets — the Pickett group was joined by the Catholic Bishops of the United States, who went on record against the "monopsony" (a market situation in which one buyer exerts a disproportionate influence on the market) of the beef industry: "Food sustains life itself; it is not just another product . . . [Agriculture] is not just another economic activity." When one of Tyson's lawyers demanded a public retraction from Callicrate for having said, "These guys are nothing but old-time gangsters, thugs and thieves," Callicrate responded with a five-page letter that was eloquent on the definition and applicability of each adjective, citing the company's indictment for bribing Espy, its guilty pleas to twenty felony violations of the Clean Water Act, its fines by the Department of Labor for violating U.S. child-labor laws and cheating workers of wages, its support of Cactus Feeders in its lawsuit against Oprah Winfrey and other critics, and topping all these with Bruce Babbitt's characterization of IBP as a "corporate outlaw."

The Tyson case brought public attention to the general problem of agricultural concentration: fewer independent farmers and ranchers, more illegal immigrants, suppression of labor unions, greater violation of safety laws, and galloping secrecy and silencing of critics by "defamation laws." A spate of academic articles sustained the attention, including a 2004 *Harvard Law Review* study that examined the issue of concentration in the meat industry and concluded that the federal government has the laws it needs to avoid abuses like price-fixing, if only it would enforce them. It cited the "unique risks" posed by modern meat processing because of its scale and speed — large volume of animals, high injury rate of workers, contamination — but pointed out that it is the largest processors' market share and the deference paid them by regulators that allow them to deal with these risks as they choose, away from inquiring eyes. "The isolation of the modern meat industry from the general public has allowed the industry to hide harmful practices from public scrutiny."

About three years after the Tyson suit began, Callicrate helped to found Rancher-Cattlemen's Action Legal Fund United Stockgrowers of America (R-CALF USA), which broke away from the NCBA. The group, which consisted entirely of lifelong NCBA members, believed that the organization had been hijacked by the big packers since 1996, when the beef industry's lobbying group, the National Cattlemen's Association, merged with the Cattlemen's Beef Board (made up of the National Live Stock and Meat Board's Beef Industry Council). Since 1986 the Beef Board had run a fund "for promotion and research," based on an obligatory member assessment called the "beef checkoff program," in which the Board was prohibited by law from political activity. With the now-overtly-partisan NCBA (with seventeen lobbyists in its D.C. office and an endorsement of Bush in 2004), which gets 85 percent of its revenues from the checkoff fund, many objected to the "incestuous relationship" between the Beef Board and its contractor, which put big feeders and packers on its board. In 1998 R-CALF brought the war against the packers to a head when they filed three trade cases on behalf of the U.S. cattle industry against the practice by Canada and Mexico of "dumping cattle" across the border. These imports, they charged, filled the packers' inventories and depressed domestic cattle prices.

I first heard of R-CALF in January 2005, at the Denver Stock Show rodeo. R-CALF was holding its annual convention just down the road from my hotel and its president, Leo McDonnell, invited me to attend. It was as if I'd walked into the middle of the French Revolution. A small fierce woman in the large convention room was addressing Bill Hawkes,

Under Secretary of the USDA: "I think we should disband the USDA. We don't need you. You've been very successful in getting rid of the small farmer and rancher." This was exciting. This was unlike anything I'd heard at an NCBA convention. A lawyer named David Domina gave an update on *Pickett v. Tyson* (many R-CALF members had been witnesses for the plaintiffs) and finished with a passionate declaration: "The most efficient system is monolithic — one producer, one processor, one product — but this country was built on diversity, not efficiency. This nation cannot exist as a monolith. No system of free enterprise ever existed for efficiency, but for fairness. Freedom begins with economic freedom."

The discussion moved on to other issues, including mandatory identification, the relation of beef safety to BSE testing, and the relation of BSE to trade issues. Bill Fielding of Creekstone Farms, an independent rancher/packer firm specializing in Black Angus beef, one line of which is "naturally raised," complained that the U.S. government would not allow his company to test its own beef, or even buy the test kit for BSE, so that they could sell to a Japanese market that had closed its borders to American beef. Why wouldn't the USDA allow them to voluntarily test their own cattle for BSE, he asked, after Japan's ban had caused Creekstone to lose a third of its sales? He railed against Hawkes, who'd said "we must educate Japan about science," and decried the USDA's "shibboleth of 'science-based.'" He warned that the real problem was *E. coli* and that "we must go beyond the current minimal standards for food safety."

"The USDA has been captured by Tyson," someone shouted, "with the NCBA right behind!"

"I love being a thorn in the side of big packers," said a soft-voiced, gray-haired rancher.

Another rancher quoted Callicrate: "I have nothing against packers. I just wish there were five hundred of them."

Among the group was chef Victor Matthews of the Black Bear Restaurant, near Colorado Springs. When a rancher asked him if he used natural beef in his restaurant, he replied, "No, I *like* the flavor of pesticides and hormones — hey, I'm kidding." Matthews does blind meat tastings for his customers like wine tastings, offering different breeds, producers, aging methods. "What the customer wants has changed," he says. "They used to ask for a cut and a grade, now they want to know, is it natural, organic?" As with wine, now they don't just ask for a Cabernet but for the place, the producer, the brand. "They are beginning to understand the dangers of not knowing." Steve Sands, CEO of Premium Protein Products, said, "There's a major sea-change in the industry. There's no one customer, but lots of special niches. We want to be the thirty-five flavors of beef. We want multiple brands with different prices."

I talked to Leo McDonnell — why is it that ranchers always have sky-blue eyes? — who with his wife, Debra, operates one of the largest sales in North America of purebred bull stock. He told me about the case that had sparked the founding of R-CALF in 1998. A number of U.S. producers believed that the Canadian Wheat Board was suppressing grain prices, which allowed Canada's fed cattle to be more competitive than U.S. cattle and which drove down prices for U.S. producers. When the group brought this violation before the International Trade Commission, the NCBA refused to help U.S. producers and instead "sat with the Canadian packers." The ITC threw out the case. Nevertheless, in the years since, membership in R-CALF has grown from 3000 members to 18,000, while membership in the NCBA has dropped from 38,000 to 24,000. After BSE was discovered in a cow in Alberta in 2003, R-CALF filed an injunction with the USDA to stop bringing in edible beef products from countries known to have BSE. The big packers don't take this kind of interference lying down. When Governor Brian Schweitzer of Montana, a rancher himself, spoke up for the protesting ranchers, the feds closed down a Butte packing company in retaliation. Schweitzer, in response, called USDA officials "a bunch of stooges" in bed with the Big Four. The owner of the Montana plant, reopened after pressure in high places, and the governor said, "We circled the wagons here."

R-CALF has also got a Country of Origin Label (COOL) law passed, which the USDA was "still fighting tooth and nail" and had not yet implemented. "They came out with newfangled rules a week or so ago and we filed against them again," McDonnell says. "But we're going to win again, I guarantee you. Everybody that eats beef is part of our business. If you eat, you're part of agriculture."

In America, if you eat, you're part of agribusiness. When I talked to Callicrate later about the relation of big packers to consumers, he saw red. "All their talk about 'the consumer is king' is baloney. 'Sell them what we want and deliver them what we've got' — that's the big packer. No consumer ever asked for hormones." A big packer, he claims, "makes private secret deals, goes to the feedlot and says, 'Listen, you've got some Angus here that we can get a premium out of, and we'll pay you a little more, but you've got to agree not to tell anyone.' The cattle they buy are of lesser quality than in a cash market, but they pay premiums so they can depress prices for everyone else." Callicrate believes that an alliance of this sort between packers and feedlots is anticompetitive. "When two thieves have their hands so deep in each other's pockets, they can't separately plunder a third," he asserts. "Mandatory ID was forced on us by the government to punish us for asking for COOL. Many of us are already doing individual ID, have been tracking our animals all the way for seven or eight years. But what good does it do to ID animals with the border wide open and they're all being blended right in? It's not about the consumer at all."

What concerns Callicrate is not just price but meat quality and its concomitant: safety. "I'm concerned about what is in our food that we don't know is there." Imported cattle are a safety issue, as only about 1 percent of the 20 percent imported beef that the big packers slaughter is inspected. So are techniques like Advanced Meat Recovery (AMR), a process invented and patented in 1995 by Eldin Ross of Beef Processors, Inc. in Sioux City, Iowa, to salvage meat from bone crannies. Ross's machine takes small bones — backbones, rib bones, and so on, throws them into a super grinder, and extrudes a bright red paste. Because the paste spoils quickly, it is frozen in pellet form and added to beef trim while grinding. "That's the stuff that's in your hot dogs, bratwursts, hamburger," says Callicrate. "USDA analysis shows that 35 percent of sample food-service hamburger patties contain brain and spinal tissue."

Callicrate explains that he has nothing against people who invent devices, but sometimes the way they are used makes meat unsafe. In Beef 101 we learned about the general use of electrical stimulation, used for two reasons. First: to counter the toughness in the muscle caused by hormone implants. In 1970 Henry "Bud" Ross, an ex–fighter pilot and aerospace engineer, had invented the Ross 501 Tenderizer, which inserts thousands of little needles into the flesh (thirty-two surgical incisions per square inch) to tenderize it. Second: to counter the muscle contractions induced by "cold shortening," or rapid chilling of meat, which helps to prevent pathogens. The electric shock treatment in effect speeds up the conversion of glycogen to lactic acid in the muscle and hastens the tenderizing action of enzymes. All of this is a substitute for dry aging, which, because it causes meat to lose up to 30 percent of its weight, is not "cost effective." Nowadays tenderizers are also used to inject brine solutions. But needles insert into the interior what's on the surface, and so increase the possibility of *E. coli* contamination. That in turn requires "antimicrobial intervention" like hot-water washings.

Hormone implants are usually applied when male calves are castrated, typically at 200 pounds, but if castration is delayed, natural testosterone can help the calf put on weight. That's why Callicrate invented and patented his Callicrate Smart Bander, a sturdy ¼-inch band of rubber that tightens around the scrotum until the testicles eventually dry up and fall off, no surgery required. His latest patented device is the Velvet Antler Bander, which deadens the nerves of deer antlers so they can be removed painlessly. There's a large Asian market, in particular, for the glucosamine and chondroitin in antlers, reputed to speed healing, reduce arthritis, and boost the immune system. "These are the inventions that have given me the income to tell the packers how I feel about them."

Callicrate is appalled by the wholesale use of Modified Atmosphere Packaging (MAP). "It's nasty awful stuff that the consumer shouldn't be forced to buy," but it's now standard industry procedure for prolonging shelf life by removing oxygen in a sealed package and replacing it with nitrogen or minute quantities of carbon monoxide. This helps retain the red color of meat and delays the darkening associated with age, so that a consumer can't tell by looking how long a steak has been on a supermarket shelf.

He took me through the construction site of his own market-restaurant, to be called the Ranch House American Grill and Market, in the Garden of the Gods just north of Colorado Springs where a beloved landmark, the Hungry Farmer, once stood. He envisions dining rooms and patios to be filled with butcher-block tables, local produce, Colorado wines, photographs of local ranches, a wraparound mural of the Grand Canyon. "We're going to tell the story about these ranchers," Mike adds, "not some wealthy-looking dudes but a guy with duct tape on his boots. There's a lot of fourth- or fifth-generation families with a lot of history. These are people where the leading cause of death is suicide because they're losing their whole family history when they lose the ranch."

THE SLEEK MODERN headquarters of Beef USA in Centennial City, a glittering silvered glass tower in an industrial park just south of Denver, isn't far from Callicrate's rebel outpost geographically, but it's light-years away ideologically. I make my way through an atrium that's like a resort hotel, with white umbrellas and tables and chairs around a serpentine fountain spouting water, past conference rooms named "Rib Eye" and "Sirloin," to find the office of Bucky Gwartney, Executive Director of Research and Knowledge Management, which is connected to the offices of Public Relations and Promotion. Bucky is tall, with a small head, tiny ears, sparse blond hair, and intense blue eyes. He greets me as if I'd been waiting all my life to learn the secrets of Bovine Myology and Muscle Profiling.

Bucky started in medical technology at Oklahoma State and switched to animal science after he got involved in meat judging. He has worked for Tyson, for a global genetics company called Pig Improvement, a meat plant, and an R&D food lab. He loves his job with NCBA for its constant variety and excitement. "I get to publish, I get to be on the cutting edge of research, I get exposed to a lot of different things." He is an excellent industry spokesman. "Beef is one of the top five nutrient-dense foods known to man — we call it 'naturally nutrient-rich.'" Okay, I'll go with that. Bucky is part of a team of meat scientists, including researchers from the Universities of Nebraska and Florida, who have just won an international prize for the most extensive study ever made of beef muscles — 5500 individual muscles of the beef chuck and round. In 1996 the Beef Board began the Beef Value Cuts program, bought and paid for with checkoff dollars, to add value to these particular subprimals, which had been in decline, by locating muscles that might be fabricated differently on the basis of tenderness and taste. As Bucky puts it: "The overall goal is to increase demand for underutilized cuts, for new cuts, and take the pressure off middle meats (loin and rib)."

In every way, the new myology project is a work of art. There's a print manual, a CD, and an interactive Web site (http://bovine.unl.edu, also reachable through www.beefresearch.org) that is spectacular in its multiple modes of imagery. You can manipulate each side of the photographed carcass to get cross sections that unfurl like red banners of flesh and bone. You can rotate the carcass like an architect's CAD so that it looks like a missile turning in space. You can clothe and unclothe with flesh each part of the skeleton; you can digitally extricate and rotate any muscle you choose.

Bucky's team "sought a wholly different way of capturing a muscle" to provide an encyclopedic guide to the traits of each. "If you can take this low-priced large piece of meat and bring it down to these single-muscle applications, you get a much better price." The study was designed on the assumption that a muscle had to weigh at least half a pound to count. In the chuck alone, there are twenty-seven muscles of that size. Once the muscles were distinguished, they were ranked on a scale of quality traits like tenderness, so that the industry could focus on the ones that came out best: flatiron, petite tender, ranch steak. With cuts like these, Bucky explains, you can fill a void in the product line between ground beef on one end and premium steaks on the other.

The results of the study promise to increase the value of the beef chuck more than 5 percent, according to the chairman of the joint group, who is a Florida beef producer. To the beef industry, such an increase is

major, because the chuck and round account for 69 percent of total carcass weight. The success of the study has demonstrated the power of
"collective industry effort and cattle producers helping themselves." So
says *Cattle Today* in railing against "a vocal minority" — they mean
R-CALF — that has put the future of the checkoff program in doubt by
bringing suit against it. This is the kind of research that has resulted in all
those "heat-and-eat convenience products" and that has "led the charge
of turning consumer demand around." So much for giving customers
what they want.

And yet Bucky is more sophisticated than most about consumers and
what they want. From tenderness you "get a halo effect," Bucky says, "an
increased perception of overall palatability." That's why they're redoing
their National Beef Tenderness Survey this year, "a genomic study dealing with tenderness markers," because you've also got to have good
mouthfeel, good texture. If you give customers a choice, visually they'll
pick a lean cut, but if you give them a blind tasting, they'll pick a fat one.
While fat plays a role in the perception of flavor and tenderness, "Fat is
not the key," says Bucky, "not the most significant component by far." He
was the first meat scientist I'd met who admitted that. "Even though we
preach that we want more consistency, more uniformity, the last thing in
the world we need is for everything to be Grade-1 Yield, Prime. That's
not going to fill the desire of the consumer. The consumer wants choice."

IN WICHITA, KANSAS, I meet another eminent meat scientist who'd
also got his start in intercollegiate meat judging. Dr. Dell Allen retired in
2003 from Cargill Meat Solutions, after teaching animal science at Kansas
State for more than twenty years. At Cargill, one of the Big Four, with a
daily slaughter capacity of 6,000 head, or about 1.5 million per year, Dell
had been involved in the redesign of the slaughter floors to incorporate
food-safety features. "Unless you've seen a modern facility, you have not
truly seen current-day practices and facilities," he'd written me. I accepted his offer of a Cargill tour with alacrity.

I arrive at the plant looking for a scientist, but find a thick-torsoed man in cowboy belt and jeans, ruddy skin framed by a halo of white hair, radiating energy. Dell's brought along his older brother Coy, a gentle, bespectacled man who is a farm analyst for the County Extension Agency, trying to find "solutions" for the many farmers in the area who are having trouble staying afloat. The brothers know all about that, having grown up on a small farm in southeast Kansas, where their grandparents were hardscrabble folk who'd come in covered wagons from Tennessee. On their mother's side, there's Indian blood, Cherokee and Osage, in Grandmother Lett, who signed her name with an "X," but knew all the wild plants in springtime.

The brothers are proud that Kansas has the largest concentration of beef slaughterhouses in the United States in the triangle of Dodge City, Garden City, and Liberal, with a capacity for 20,000 at each plant. Add Emporia, between Wichita and Topeka, which has an even larger plant of 25,000, and Kansas represents 25 percent of the country's total slaughtering capacity. As we speed like an arrow through thousands of acres of ripe corn, Dell explains that the state is now second in the country in the number of tillable acres, thanks to the Oglalla aquifer, although it is losing population because the average farm size is now 2000 acres. The cattle industry took off here, Dell says, because of the climate of the Plains — more temperate than the Corn Belt, cooler evenings, less severe winters, less moisture — so the packers moved here. Since the state controls the water, the state, in effect, controls the packinghouses and what is grown to feed the cattle. "In animal processing, nobody is as efficient as we are," says Dell.

"Nor as concentrated," I add. I learn later that 80 percent of the nation's cattle are fed on feedlots within a 100-mile radius from misnamed Garden City (just to the west of Dodge) to Amarillo, Texas.

Their pride of place is undimmed by the fact that just outside Garden City is the little town of Holcomb, where the Clutter family was murdered, as Truman Capote told us, *In Cold Blood*. At the moment, a similar happening clouds the sunny image of Wichita, three-time winner of the title "All-American City," and also home of the serial killer Dennis Rader, better known as BTK for "bind, torture, kill." In court he described his hits dispassionately as "projects," as in "Project Susie" or "Project Lights Out." He was disappointed, he told the court, when he'd had to use a gun on one of his victims because "shooting isn't my core competence, strangling is my forte."

The Cargill/Excel plant lies low like an extended concrete bunker opposite a mountain of black cows at Fort Dodge, three miles from Dodge City, once the destination of gunslingers and now of tourist buses, which steer clear of what has become a shantytown of migrant workers to visit the Disneyesque false fronts along the railroad tracks. "Cargill is a people company," Dell says as we turn into the security gate of the plant, sign in, and get our name tags to show to the guards. This global giant is the second-largest privately owned company in the world (Koch Industries is first) — "there are still family members in the company" — and the scale and diversity of its operations are impressive. They include grain, cotton, sugar, petroleum, financial trading, food processing, animal feed, and fertilizer production. As the country's biggest grain producer, Cargill Inc. has had "a presence" in Kansas for a long time, first with grain, then as a salt business (the underground vaults of the Hutchison Salt Mine provide the world's largest storage for movie and television films). Cargill Meat Solutions — an alternate word for "projects"? — is but one small part of Cargill Inc., whose headquarters are in Minneapolis, and Excel is but one small part of Meat Solutions, with headquarters in Wichita. Excel now covers pork and turkey (it is the largest turkey processor in the United States), as well as beef, processed meats, case-ready meats, and food-distribution centers. This is the largest of the company's six meat plants, which include two new ones in Brazil.

I'm assigned tour guide Gene Albert, who's been with Cargill for thirty-six years. He rattles off statistics: the plant occupies 800,000 square feet, or about 21 acres. They usually process about 5800 cattle a day, to produce 46,000 boxes of beef. Using two shifts, one from 6:00 A.M. to 2:30 P.M., the second from 3:15 P.M. to 11:45 P.M., allows the third shift about five and a half hours to clean thoroughly every day, with chemicals and hot water. We meet Inspector Michele, who explains that the industry has developed its own pre-op safety standards since the USDA has none. While the usual industry goal is to have fewer than 7.75 percent coliform units, Cargill averages fewer than 3 percent, "less than a clean dinner plate in a good household," Michele says. Dell was a food-safety pioneer during his time at Cargill, promoting HACCP (Hazard Analysis and Critical Control Point, a federal control system designed to identify potential food-safety hazards) long before its widespread adoption in 1994, and making Excel the first packer to test for *E. coli* 0157.H7 in all its ground meat. He also helped adopt digital technology to help Excel grade carcasses more accurately, after finding that 19 percent of carcasses in the industry had been mislabeled.

I meet Dan, the plant manager, a second-generation meat packer. Cargill wants to be known for its differences from other packers, he tells me. They want to be a model for the industry on safety issues, worker relations, worker injuries. The most frequent injury used to be carpal tunnel syndrome, but they now have better equipment, more shifts, a workout room for employees, English-language training (85 percent of the workers are Hispanic, and some are Asian). Excel pays twice the minimum wage, $10.95 an hour. They've led the industry in cutting worker-turnover rate from 60 to 30 percent. The company encourages entrepreneurship and tolerance. Dan acknowledges that there were a lot of union problems in the early 1990s, but believes they've solved most of them. There are thirteen USDA inspectors on the floor, and inspection capacity drives the "chain speed"; 290 head an hour seems to be the breaking point.

Dan gives me a general prepping on trade issues. Nowadays they export first to Mexico, which wants cheaper cuts and offal. Egypt is their biggest liver market. While avian flu is a worry, nobody seems worried about BSE — "the biggest flap over nothing that I've ever seen." People don't understand that the U.S. system of production is totally different from England's, he explains. We have no need to feed animal protein to our cattle because 90 percent of them are fed in the Feed Belt of the High Plains — from the Dakotas to Texas on the eastern side of the Rockies, which includes the western half of Nebraska, Kansas, Texas.

Before we enter the plant, we have to get fitted with hairnets, tiny earplugs, hard hats, white lab jackets, white gloves, tall rubber boots, and clear spectacles for eye protection. The spectacles won't fit over my glasses, so I leave them off. Then we make our way through the giant mechanical perpetual-motion food chain, up and down stairways, above and below catwalks, in and out of doorways, in and out of red-fleshed carcasses and white-coated workers. But we don't proceed in a narrative order, from receiving pen to boxed Cryovac packs, so that I'm never sure how one unit fits into the others. The entire experience is less linear than simultaneous. It brings to mind Arnold Hauser's definition of modern art as "the spatialization of the temporal."

We begin with fabrication, in the hide-on side of the slaughter floor, where carcasses are washed in a high-pressure cabinet, a method Dell devised for Excel. As in Beef 101, air knives loosen the hide from the body, but here there's a specially designed "down puller" that strips off the hide like ripping off a shirt. Hooves are clipped with giant clippers, heads are skinned with tongues hanging, lined upright on poles like a scene from the Reign of Terror. The carcasses enter a pre-evisceration rinse, then there's a lot of scrubbing and vacuuming around the anal area before carcasses enter the hide-off side of the slaughterhouse. Here they are eviscerated and split, washed in a hot-water rinse cabinet, inspected by a USDA man, blasted again by steam. My glasses and camera lens fog up constantly as we move between freezing-cold chill rooms and boiling-hot steam, and even with the earplugs, the noise of the machinery is deafening. Underfoot, floors are slippery with fat and we have to be careful walking. The scale both dazzles and numbs as I try to take in the long rows of half carcasses replicated endlessly, at a fixed rate of speed, each with an identical thirteenth-rib cut. Tiers of workers are replicated behind them, each repeating a single task, each equipped with knives and a stone to sharpen them as they go. Their motions are rapid and precise as they trim and debone, trim and debone. Every so often they leave a knife on a tray to be honed on the electric sharpener. As we pass through, many workers look up and smile. Are they glad for the distraction, or have they been told to smile when visitors come through?

In the new grinding plant, a machine separates trim meat into lean and fat. The fat is then liquefied, dried to powder, remixed with lean, and shaped into room-length pinkish rolls. Some of the rolls are cut into patties, the rest extruded into squiggles, as if from a giant toothpaste tube. And that is as far as I'm allowed to go. Beyond lies the integrated rendering plant, which I can smell but not see. Rendering has been called "the invisible industry" for a reason.

Renderers now like to be called "recyclers," and because they render 40,000 metric tons of "animal by-product" each week, we might as well call them "environmental protectionists." While there are about 250 rendering plants in the country, only 36 are certified users of the HACCP plan, which is voluntary; most of these are attached to a slaughter/ processor so that the "source material" will be fresh. Dell tells me that Excel brine-cures the hides to preserve them before exporting to China and Korea for processing into leather. Blood they dry to sell as feed for dairy cattle. Bones and fat go into the maw of the giant raw material grinder and then into a continuous cooker, heated to 280 degrees, which frees fat from protein and bone and dehydrates the mass into a slurry. Liquid fat is separated from solids, now called "tankage," which is sent to the screw press, then to the pressed-cake conveyor; it will be sold for bone meal for pets and livestock feed. Edible fat will be also be used in pet and livestock feed, but inedible fat like tallow or grease will go into a wide, wide world of paints, lubricants, soaps, tires, fabrics, cement, polish ink, lipsticks, face creams, medicines, crayons. Like processed corn, processed animal fat is everywhere about us and on us.

Afterward, what stayed with me most was the softness of both human and bovine flesh set against the hard metal of the machines. I couldn't help but respond to the beauty of machinery that so neatly fit form to function: the enormous electric saws that slice each carcass vertically with surgical precision, the mechanical lifters that elevate pallets of stacked boxes and place them ten stories high on grids that look like giant Tinkertoy skyscrapers. I was dazzled by the opposition of verticals and horizontals, by the Rube Goldberg intricacy of conveyor belts, stamping machines, boxing machines, the octopus-armed domes of Cryovac machines sucking air out plastic seals, the stacks of boxes forklifted into refrigerated trucks backed precisely into the bays. Everywhere I saw symmetry and pattern, the exact repetition of curved spine and ribs in carcass interiors mirroring the exact repetition of hand movements, of machine parts. Instead of horror, I saw art, scale and speed the coordinates of this abstraction, airbrushed by the joy of men in sheer technology. In *The Work of Art in the Age of Mechanical Reproduction*, Walter Benjamin based the machine aesthetics of the early twentieth century on the movies, which had speeded up the process of pictorial reproduction until it matched speech. As the movies freed painting and photography from *nature morte*, from "still" life, so they freed consciousness from the stasis of the written word, releasing James Joyce's "riverrun" of language into the currents of our contemporary digital data stream. In the slaughterhouse, the real world of the machine meets the reel world of cowboys.

◆ Riding Point for the Industry ◆

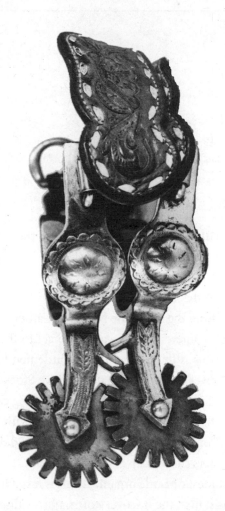

"Cowboy Spurs" made by Oscar Crockett ca. 1930, part
of the "Huff Collection" in Fort Worth. Photographed
by Jane Pattie of Aledo, Texas.

◆

FROM THE BALCONY of the atrium of the Adams Mark Hotel in downtown Denver in August 2004, I look down on a sea of white shellacked cowboy hats, each with a rolled brim and three eyelet holes on the left side of the crown, packed together like cattle in a feedlot. This is the Big Club, the National Cattlemen's Beef Association, at its summer conference. If I wanted to get to the beating heart of the beef industry, this is the place. In 1898 cattlemen met in the Brown Palace Hotel in Denver to form the National Live Stock Association, and from then and until now displayed their prizewinning cattle in the lobby. Prophetically, the first Denver convention closed with "The Last Great Buffalo Barbecue" of beef, game, and beer to feed 20,000, but unfortunately 30,000 ranchers showed up and a riot ensued.

This year this oldest of cattle organizations is faced not with riots, but with a double crisis: first, the discovery of mad cow disease in December 2003 in that Canadian cow on our side of the border; and second, rebellion within the membership against the mandatory-checkoff system, the club's major source of funds. The stated aim of the organization, "working to increase profit opportunities for cattle and beef producers by enhancing the business climate and building consumer demand," boils down to "Get people to buy more beef." But the strategies it employs reveal what has birthed R-CALF and other dissenters, and they are amply displayed in the schedule of speakers at the conference — John Clifford of the USDA, Dan McChesney of the FDA, Kathleen Clarke of the BLM, Rod Bowling of Smithfield Beef, Dale Grotelveschen of Pfizer Chemical — the entwined elements of agribusiness, the chemical industry, and government agencies that had sent Mike Callicrate howling into the night.

There's no reason that the beef industry shouldn't be as full of contradictions as any other American industry that has grown up with the country for the last century and a half, but where agribusiness has more or less exterminated small farmers, the beef industry still has a large herd of small ranchers who cling to a vision of rugged independence utterly at variance with twenty-first-century realities. This is a group that perceives Big Government as Public Enemy #1. "The harder you work, the more the government comes around and trips you up," says a rancher listening to a panel on the Federal Lands Committee and the National Research Council. Yet this same club broke its own nonpartisan tradition in 2004 to endorse President Bush for re-election. In part, the endorsement was payback for the FDA's slowdown in imposing the restrictions on animal feed that it had introduced in response to the new outbreak of BSE. Beyond political pragmatism, the group felt that Bush shared its identity. "I can't think of a better compliment for our president than to call him a cowboy," says Kathleen Clarke, appointed by Bush to the directorship of the BLM. "They're always on the side of right, they're against bad people, they have integrity, they're respected, and they always *win*." She gets a standing ovation.

The rest of Clarke's speech reveals further contradictions on cowboy issues. While her rallying cry is for "sustainable range lands and sustainable ranching" to "sustain the health, diversity, and productivity of public lands, now and for the future," the group she addresses has long ago put the EPA and almost all environmental groups on its hate list. At a meeting of the Committee on Property Rights and Environmental Management, a feedlot owner complains that the EPA is trying to apply the

Clean Air Act to CAFO emissions, even though they are "fugitive" and "naturally occurring." He asks, "How much more of this regulation can we take without forcing our kind of business out of the country?"

The February winter conference is called the Cattle Industry Annual Convention and NCBA Trade Show, held in 2005 in San Antonio, Texas. "Riding Point for the Industry" was the theme for the entire year, and when President Jan Lyons addresses the ranchers as "point riders," she tells them to "look at the lay of the land, use past experience, use landmarks for a trail to the next camp, then sweep the herd in that direction, get your bearings for the trail ahead." While Lyons, a handsome woman with red hair and dimples in black leather cowboy boots and a black slit skirt, is only the second woman president in the history of the club, she also typifies its membership. She speaks with the slow, calm, deliberate voice of reason and common sense. "We're very conservative," she says of the organization and herself. "We pride ourselves on that." Born into several generations of farmer/ranchers in Ohio and Kansas, she breeds a midsized herd of 350 Angus in the Flint Hills, with the help of her extended family of thirteen, when you count daughters, sons-in-law, and grandchildren. But economically she is cushioned by the profession of her husband, who is "engaged off the ranch" as a physician in Manhattan, Kansas.

When I talk to Lyons privately, her delivery is still in public mode. "One of the best things that has happened for our industry is to be able to send back a president who understands the need for ownership society in agriculture, a sustainable ownership society not burdened by undue regulations, not burdened by undue taxes." As she talks, all difficulties, all contradictions are smoothed by rhetoric as polished as saddle leather. Of course it's sad that small farms are endangered and, yes, there's a lot of consolidation and, yes, conservation and stewardship are critical because "there are many of us ranchers who still feel a tremendous tie to the land, who have a commitment to stewardship." Stewardship of the land should be left to committed individuals, but selling beef requires a group. Since BSE has put the industry in crisis mode, the big job of the NCBA is to get the message out that our "consumers are 100 percent safe. The key to our survival depends on increasing demand for products so that more people can enjoy this lifestyle and be profitable at it." In short, the job of the beef industry in general and of the NCBA in particular is marketing. As always, the key word is "more."

A half century ago, president Arthur A. Smith of the National Cattlemen's Association had declared 1949 to be "The Year of Public Relations," because those were "of more importance than any other single item today to our industry." To turn thousands of small ranchers into marketers united in the Big Sell, however, has been an extraordinarily difficult job for an organization that started out as a bunch of stock growers who, even as a group, defined themselves as rugged individuals. "Let it be understood here and now," said John W. Springer, the first president of the National Live Stock Association when it convened in 1898, "that the American stockman proposes to take care of himself, and that he is not supplicant at the doors of the Federal Congress for any subsidy, for any bonus or for any policy which seeks 'forty acres and a mule.'"

The job of marketing has been sold to the ranchers themselves as a mission of "consumer education," which disguises promotion as objective information. Managing language is crucial to managing thought, and one of the club's most important committees is Public Opinion and Issues Management. The hot topic these days, says Bob Rolston, who chairs the committee, is youth education, and he offers a simple syllabus: "We want consumers to understand that beef is good for you. Nutritionists say that our diet should consist of plant-based food, and meat is plant-based." Children have to understand that there are no evil foods, he explains, but at the same time consumers don't have to understand everything. "You don't do anything like ever take them to a feedyard or a harvest facility or something like that. There are some things people just don't need to know."

Funded by beef-checkoff dollars, the club's education programs have become increasingly sophisticated. Its *Beef Training Camp Manual,* a how-to guide that manages to skew beef terminology and merchandising toward commodity beef, won a 2005 IACP Award of Excellence in the category of Consumer Education. The NCBA *Food Safety Playbook,* an auxiliary to *Beef Training*, is similarly designed to reassure consumers, through hundreds of charts and consumer-friendly photos, that American beef is not only good for you but 100 percent safe, when it comes to scary issues like BSE, salmonella, listeria, irradiation, antibiotics, hormones, and other feed additives. In explaining the economics of the business, the *Playbook* extols increased consumption through "value-added products" (Bucky Gwartney's single-muscle profiling shows up nicely on these pages) and outlines the advantages of consolidation. While the charts suggest a blitzkrieg of scientific data, all information is directed toward proffering the beef industry as a model of coordination through "functional integration," "vertical coordination," and "vertical alignment."

An additional source of funds is Pfizer Animal Health, which in 2004 gave the NCBA a $3 million grant to "enhance educational programming." Pfizer, one of the original sponsors of the convention's all-day educational sessions they've called, since 1993, Cattlemen's College, has now established a Cattle Learning Center so that all cattle producers may engage in an "industry-wide educational effort in the future" in partnership with packers, retailers, restaurants, and nutrition associations. Ranchers, it seems, need to be inoculated with the virtues of partnership and alliance because their instinct is for rugged independence.

One sixth-generation rancher, Trent Loos of Loos Cattle Company in Norris, South Dakota, had written earlier of that "dynamic beast of alliance," acknowledging its dangers but also rationalizing its virtues. In 2001 he'd tried to reassure beef ranchers that alliance with packers didn't necessarily mean total loss of control, which he admitted had happened in the vertical integration of the poultry and pork industries. But at the same time, Loos argued, those industries had figured out "how to harness the capital beneath a single production and marketing umbrella." In the name of efficiency, it behooved beef producers to also become part of the full "gene-to-retail supply chain." They should give up a little control in order to guarantee a certain percentage of the profits. Loos cheerily predicted that in five years the industry would be full of players who were not animal-husbandry people at all, but money people.

Some would say that animal husbandry was already long gone in an industry crowded with money people clamoring to sell beef. At the San Antonio convention, Dave Zino of the NCBA's Culinary Center in Chicago waxes enthusiastic over new categories of microwavable "convenience beef." People "don't want to come home from work and spend two and a half hours romancing a beef stew," he explains. His group recently produced a cookbook called *Creating Crave . . . the Beef Factor* that pairs beef with ingredients like mushrooms, blue cheese, and red wine, all ingredients that exponentially intensify the fifth taste the Japanese call *umami* because they contain the key protein compounds (glutamates and nucleotides) that are naturally present in beef itself. Creating crave, sanctified by science, is assumed to be the way to get every man, woman, and child to eat beef because no one is exempt from crave. "We need to insert beef into the family experience," says David Coronna, a fellow marketer who speaks on how to invade, once the Kid Market has been caught, the Aging Baby Boomer Market of elder boomers — "Every seven seconds a boomer hits fifty."

My head reels when I try to join this snappy marketing lingo with rancher talk straight out of a time warp. A tall, slim Sam Shepard type on the NCBA's Production Research Committee tells me his ancestors fought in the American Revolution, and independence was for him the flag of God, country, and cattlemen. "That's why I'm a rancher, nobody tells me what to do." For him, the two enemies were big government and socialism, as espoused by Franklin Delano Roosevelt and Henry Wallace. He didn't vote for Bush, he said, he always voted for the Independent candidate, whoever he was.

My beet-farmer grandfather, turned osteopathic doctor, would have clapped that man on the back while adding a third enemy — established medicine — as yet one more foppery of the East. But Grandpa had been born in Kansas in 1863, and for a United Presbyterian like him, independence meant no popery, no Eastern establishment, but allegiance to a two-fisted Calvinist God backed by inductive science in the open horizon of the West. Hatred of the East as a hotbed of immigrant aliens, for which read Catholics and Jews, and of hoity-toity snobs with "English" accents, for which read FDR and medical doctors, fueled his ever-westering migration. This was the world of stock growers when they first began to form an alliance and held their First National Convention of Cattlemen in St. Louis in 1884, drawing 1300 delegates from thirty-four states and territories.

The battle lines between East and West were already entrenched on every issue of land use, government regulation, and public domain. When the NCBA came to write its official history for its centenary, *Building the Beef Industry*, they began not with England but with the arrival of Spanish cattle in 1493 and the influence of the *mesta* in Mexico City in 1529. These were the first "cattlemen in concert," they said, who drew up rules about brands and ownership. Theirs was never the history of sustainable farming and a village commons, which had evolved in the Colonies, but of raising cattle in large numbers as commodities for the market. For them, the timeline of the industry began with the Western cattle boom in the mid-nineteenth-century matrix of railroads, stockyards, and packing plants, with a maximum of boosterism and a minimum of control. While they condemned federal interference, they also found themselves lobbying Washington heavily to regulate railroads and pass the Federal Meat Inspection Act of 1906, after the bad publicity of *The Jungle*. But the permanent fault line that divided East from West was the idea of what private ownership was and meant. "Federal ownership or control of land is a form of Communism," declared J. Elmer Brock as late as 1947, when he was president of the American National Live Stock Association. "The effete East argues that these public lands belong to all of us. They do not!" In 1950 and again in 1965, the association linked private ownership to the ideal of free and competitive enterprise and to the defeat of "the fallacious philosophies that are beguiling our country into socialism." The issue is still hot, even though only 3 percent of U.S. cattle graze on public lands and fewer than 24,000 ranchers use federal grazing permits.

But even livestock made for too broad an alliance. It was Western cattlemen against Eastern dairymen, and in this war cattlemen felt they always got the short end of the stick. After Eastern dairymen argued that Western stock growers' use of public lands was a form of government subsidy, the dairymen won from the government a "butter subsidy" in 1886, by means of the Federal Margarine Act, which slapped a two-cent tax and license fees on margarine. Cattlemen eventually bolted from the National Live Stock Association to form their own group, calling it in 1905 the American Stock Growers Association, meaning beef only. But eighty years later, cattlemen again felt shafted when the Agricultural Act of 1986 initiated a buyout program of dairy cattle to reduce the surplus that had grown alarmingly during the government's long-maintained price-support system for milk. Cattle producers filed a lawsuit claiming that the USDA, in slaughtering 1.5 million dairy animals, had caused a market loss to cattlemen of $25 million and cost U.S. taxpayers $2 billion.

THE WEST HAD its own take on the granola mix of God and Science that my grandfather served up for breakfast every morning and that fed most of America in the late nineteenth century when we yoked evangelism to scientific progress and teleology to scientific "law." In 1882 beef was so plentiful and cheap it was promoted as the breakfast of choice in *What To Eat For Breakfast* (1882) by a man named Tarbox, who cited God and Science in lauding the virtues of beef: "This Bible and chemically sanctioned food, purposefully designed for man, is very satisfying to the stomach and possesses great strengthening powers." Beef sanctified by God and chemistry was a powerful double whammy, and it reinforced the beef industry's belief in both the sanctity of the individual in determining moral choice and the sanctity of science as God's "natural law." The first belief is embodied in the cowboy. "Thank God for John Wayne, at least for what he symbolized with the American cowboy," wrote editor Troy Marshall in "Cow-Calf Weekly" in 2006. "The cowboy ethos inspires all of us to be better people, and it's largely responsible for us prevailing against our financially and numerically superior opponents." The second is embodied in the industrial machine engineered by science. Over a century ago "rationalism" was co-opted by scientific fundamentalism to make technology a new evangelism, now supercharged by electronics. Instead of a man-made coercive force, market-driven technology is viewed as "natural law." What was once scorned as a Marxist doctrine of determinism is now praised as Margaret Thatcher's doctrine of TINA: "There Is No Alternative."

The NCBA has embraced the TINA principle as an article of faith on which they've erected their elephantine structure of research and promotion. Their marketing information unit called Cattle-Fax (it boasts that it has "the largest private database in the country") produces an eponymous publication of economic charts and graphs, which serves as the industry Bible to spell out the gospel of corn. At a Cattle-Fax Outlook Seminar at the NCBA convention, Randy Blach, executive vice-president of the unit, focused on how weather in the Pacific, specifically El Niño, would affect the corn outlook for 2005. The cattle cycle, which moves inexorably as a natural law of supply and demand, depends on the grain cycle, which is jiggled by the whims of Mother Nature — and sometimes of man. With corn production the largest in U.S. history at 11.8 million bushels, the *Cattle-Fax* handbook predicted an ominous rise in corn prices because of the new demand for ethanol. This was as close as the NCBA got to spelling out the relation of corn to oil. *Cattle-Fax* also outlined the largest import/export imbalance of beef in U.S. history, a difference of 3.2 billion pounds, because of the loss of exports to Japan and South Korea from the BSE scare. This was as close as they got to spelling out the relation of food safety to global trade. The NCBA is not set up to deal with basic issues, only with economic laws of supply and demand. "Keep up the growth in demand," Blach urged.

The manipulation of information has long been a given. The question is: Who's doing the manipulating and toward what end? In 1922, to reconcile the opposing forces of packers and producers, the NCBA created a new marketing committee, the National Live Stock and Meat Board, and set up a campaign to counter propaganda that claimed beef was harmful to health. "Scientific data to correct adverse propaganda should be collected, compiled and disseminated . . . among dieticians, physicians, hospitals, teachers, home demonstrators, household editors, agricultural colleges and others." While they skirmished from time to time, packers and cattlemen were united in viewing any critique of beef or the beef industry as the propaganda of Bad Guys threatening the Good Guys locked together on the Gibraltar of "sound science." I learn at a conference session on Issues and Activism that today the Bad Guys are so numerous they are organized into categories like Negative Advocacy Groups, Anti-Checkoff Groups, Opportunists, Competitors, Key Players, Greening Groupies. The first include Consumers Union, Center for Media & Democracy, Center for Food Safety, Earth First!, Farm Sanctuary, Humane Society USA, Land Institute, PETA, Sierra Club, Organic Consumers, Chefs Collaborative, and GRACE. Anti-Checkoff Groups include the Libertarian Party, Institute for Justice, Campaign for Family Farms, Land Stewardship Project, Washington Legal Foundation. Opportunists are all the alternate-health practitioners and chiropractors. Competitors are Whole Foods, Wild Oats, Working Assets, Organic Valley. Key Players are Consumers Union, Public Citizen, Consumer Federation of America, and a host of acronyms — IATP, CIC, OCA, HSUSA, PIRG, ELF — that cover "environmental philanthropists and food/farmer agricultural groups" — just about anyone and everyone who "used their money to influence consumers and regulators" toward ends other than selling beef. Greening Groupies are condemned for "global warming hysteria," in the words of Steven J. Milloy of JunkScience.com, which "aims to debunk faulty scientific data used to further special agendas," including the prion theory of BSE. All opposition to "factory farming," the senior editor of *Beef Magazine* proclaimed in 2005, comes from environmentalists, animal rightists, "Marxists and other social radicals." Since the publication of *Fast Food Nation*, Eric Schlosser has been a favorite whipping boy, but now there's Michael Pollan, who "wants to make Americans fear their food," Marion Nestle, "one of the country's most hysterical anti-food-industry fanatics," and organic proponent Joan Gussow, queen of the "Nanny Culture."

An editorial in *Beef* magazine warns that all such environmentalists, animal rightists, and Marxists may be agents of bioterrorism, as "foreign terrorists may seek collaboration with these radical, domestic elements." Agro-terrorist attack strategies include causing "consumers to lose confidence in the safety of the food supply." Dan Murphy, whose column "The Vocal Point" appears regularly at Meatingplace.com, took the equation of beef-industry criticism with agro-terrorism a step further in 2005. The real agenda of organizations like the Center for a Livable Future (part of Johns Hopkins University's Bloomberg School of Public Health), PETA, and the Physicians' Committee on Responsible Medicine is "to destroy the evil meat industry — by any means necessary." Murphy, editing his own prose, concludes that if you substitute for "meat industry" the phrase "godless infidels," the agenda fits the mission of "terrorists out to destroy Western civilization." Murphy's language heats up further a year later, in "Cow-Calf Weekly," when he portrays the beef industry as a sacrificial victim of the propaganda tactics "used by propagators of hate throughout history." Now dissenters are identified with Nazi storm troopers and Roman Caesars: "The hate and divisive rhetoric aimed at feeders, packers and the like is the same as that employed against blacks, Jews, women and a host of other groups singled out for persecution throughout time."

In the past couple of years, industry-funded lobbying groups linked to the NCBA have proliferated like tumbleweeds, all aimed to "increase consumer awareness and confidence in the safety, efficiency, and value of modern agriculture." Check out the sponsors for the Center for Food Integrity, Grow America Project (GAP), the Center for Consumer Freedom, and Animal Agriculture Alliance (AAA), designed to tell "the positive story of animal agriculture" by producing educational materials for primary and secondary schools, along with the deliberately youth-oriented Web site www.bestfoodnation.com, sponsored by corporate livestock groups.

I began to understand something that had puzzled me at my first NCBA conference. At an Animal ID session, Allen Bright stated that their first priority was the need for total confidentiality. We must protect producers' privacy, he said, and insist that all information remain in private hands, since "we are surrounded by our enemies." I was so untutored that when he asked for questions, I asked what "confidential" meant. Ranchers turned in their seats to look at an outsider who had dared to ask what any ordinary consumer might have asked. Later, the reasons for not sharing information were clarified when I saw a letter from the executive director of the Kansas Beef Councils addressed to the head of KCARE at Kansas State University regarding the appearance of Marion Nestle at a conference on sustainable agriculture there. The director wanted to thank KCARE for supporting the beef industry in its aim to give consumers "credible, scientific facts" about the role of beef in a "healthy diet and lifestyle." The director continued: "Thank you for visiting with Dr. Nestle to ensure she was not going to criticize beef production. . . . With so many health professionals speaking at events daily, the beef industry feels it is important to work closely with sponsoring groups to ensure information shared about beef is based on sound science." Her remarks were known to be based more often on personal philosophy, the director said, than on sound scientific research.

Finally I could begin to make sense of the battle over the Beef Check-off program. The proposal to set up a mandatory checkoff for beef had begun as early as 1973, but any national requirement had been sturdily resisted by any number of groups, including the American Farm Bureau Federation and the National Farmers Union. In 1985 Jo Ann Smith, a skilled Washington lobbyist and the first woman president of the National Cattlemen's Association, got Congress to enact the Beef Promotion and Research Act as part of the Farm Bill. The act authorized the collection of $1 per head for all cattle sold in the United States or imported into the United States. It had taken more than a decade to persuade 300,000 independent voters in cattle industry organizations to get together long enough to ask Congress to impose a mandatory fee on their own members, with the sole aim of selling more beef. Persuasion was aided by the success in 1984 of Wendy's "Where's the beef?" advertising campaign, which made a star of eighty-two-year-old Clara Peller, awarded an honorary membership in the NCBA for asking the right question at the right time.

In 1986 the fund brought in $4 million; today it's $80 million. Half goes to the state beef councils, where the money is collected, and half goes to the Cattlemen's Beef Board (CBB) for national programs. The structure of the Board is complicated for political reasons. It has 104 members, half of whom are appointed by the Secretary of Agriculture (from people nominated in the 37 state and 3 regional organizations); their job is to qualify the State Beef Councils (QSBC) and oversee the collection of funds. Key players are a dozen members of the Board's Executive Committee, who ultimately approve and allot funding for the projects. What complicates all this parallel structuring is that while the NCBA receives funds from the Board for national programs, by law the Board must keep its distance from the NCBA. No funds may be used to promote specific cattle breeds or to influence government policy or government action by lobbying. Lobbying is the function of the NCBA, which contracts with the Board for specific programs, and is paid by the Board only on a cost-recovery basis. In this way, the NCBA can assure everyone that no checkoff time or money has been used to influence policy. Such a firewall, however, is paper thin, as the stated aim of the Board — "to stimulate others to sell more beef and stimulate consumers to buy more beef" — is identical with that of the NCBA, except that the latter might add "to stimulate ourselves and others." While there are no packer seats as such on the Board, any packer who owns cattle more than ten days before slaughter must pay the checkoff fee, and it's impossible to believe that those who pay the piper never call the tune.

This is the background for the suit brought in 2002 by the Livestock Marketing Association (LMA), the Western Organization of Resource Councils, and five individuals against the USDA, the Cattlemen's Beef Board, and the Nebraska Cattlemen's Association, on the grounds that a mandatory fee violated their rights to free speech and was therefore unconstitutional. Around the same time, the pork, mushroom, and dairy industries were engaged in similar suits over their checkoff programs, with varying results. In June 2002 the South Dakota Federal District Court ruled for the plaintiffs in the beef checkoff suit. A year later, the Eighth Circuit Court of Appeals agreed. In May 2004 the U.S. Supreme Court agreed to hear the case, wherein lawyer Laurence Tribe argued for the plaintiffs that the checkoff program was unconstitutional because it violated the First Amendment, and many ranchers had been forced to pay for speech they didn't support. The message "beef is good," for example, implied that all beef was the same and failed to differentiate between high-quality (grain-fed) U.S. beef and foreign (grass-fed) beef sold in the United States. This was a producer-versus-packer issue, as packers import large numbers of live cattle from countries like Argentina, Australia, and Mexico for processing in American plants.

On May 23, 2005, the Supreme Court overturned the lower-court decisions by a vote of 6 to 3 in favor of the defendants. The majority ruled that since half the members of the Board's Operating Committee were appointed by the Secretary of Agriculture and since all were subject to removal by him, the Secretary had the final approval over every word in every promotional campaign. QED: The message "beef is good," as controlled by the federal government, cannot violate the First Amendment because it constitutes "government speech."

Cowboys saved by the Feds on the grounds that the talk they talked was government talk! That was a new one for the cowboys of yesteryear. But of course it wasn't rancher cowboys, but corporate packers who were bailed out by a government they lobbied and sought to control. The words of the dissenting minority — Justices Souter, Stevens, and Kennedy — were as revealing as the rationale of the majority. Souter wrote that the error of the majority opinion was that a compelled subsidy could not be justified by speech unless the government claimed that speech was its own. Otherwise, there was no check on the government's power to compel special speech subsidies. The government must instead "make itself politically accountable by indicating that the content actually is a government message." Here the advertising scheme was not subject to effective democratic checks: Here "the ads are not required to show any sign of being speech by the government"; here experience "demonstrates how effectively the government has masked its role in producing the ads." Souter calls the ads deliberately "misleading": "No one hearing a commercial for Pepsi or Levi's thinks Uncle Sam is the man talking behind the curtain. Why would a person reading a beef ad think Uncle Sam was trying to make him eat more steak?" Why indeed? Souter deplored the use of concealment to avoid political accountability and accused the officials who did have control of using it deliberately "to conceal their role from the voters with the power to hold them accountable." He concluded that "the First Amendment cannot be implemented by sanctioning government depiction by omission." This was the most damning form of government subsidy ever noted, but it went unremarked by the NCBA.

Before the Supreme Court decision, lawyer Tribe, an expert in constitutional law at Harvard, had been slammed in "Cow-Calf Weekly" for having criticized the government for its indifference to live cattle. "The government program sees every herd of cattle as just so much pre-slaughtered beef," Tribe had said in his arguments to the Court, but the checkoff opponents "don't want to see their animals treated as nothing but meat. . . . Because this program does that, and associates them with it, it is a fundamental insult to their humanity." The battle between producers and packers was being lost by those traditional producers who valued something other than money. Judge Souter didn't get into the distinctions between cattle and meat, but the government speech that won the day was certainly not about anything other than pre-slaughtered beef.

THE ANIMAL SCIENCES Building at Colorado State University in Fort Collins, 55 miles north of Denver, is hard to miss. Unlike most of the surrounding buildings of functional concrete, this one has a bright turquoise mural animated by galloping horses and horned sheep and black-and-white pigs and brown-and-white cows. Leading up to it is a cast-iron fence of animal shapes. Downstairs is a cabinet brimming with ribbons and brass cups won by CSU's Meat Judging Teams. Pinned to a bulletin board is an article by nine department professors titled "Effectiveness of the SmartMV prototype BeefCam System to sort beef carcasses into expected palatability groups," which appeared in the *Journal of Animal Science* in 2003. The board is plastered with "career opportunities" for Animal Science majors, help-wanted ads for Research Management System, Sunnyside Meats, Livestock Identifications, Horizon Dairy Herd Manager, Get Vet in New Zealand, Assistant Cattle Manager at

Kunis Kunaya Feedlot, Tyson, ConAgra, Excel, Easy Goin' Ranch, Steamboat Veterinary Hospital, Genentech, Jobbers Meat-Packing Co., Michigan Cattlemen's Association, Colorado Cattle Feeders Association, Webster Feedlots, Arabian Horse Association, Purina Mills, National Cattlemen's Beef Association. A coffee table is heaped with industry magazines titled *Food Quality, Food Safety, Journal of Food Protection.*

Meat Science and Food Safety is just one of seven programs within the Department of Animal Sciences and the evolution of the department over the last century mirrors the evolution of agriculture from farm to industry. Organized sometime before 1900, the Department changed its name from Agriculture to Animal Agriculture to Animal Husbandry to Animal Science and now Animal Sciences, with an increasing focus on technology and a nod to animal care and environmental impact in its mission to serve "Colorado's large and diverse livestock industries." I'm here to talk to a diverse trio of professors in the Meat Science Department. I begin with John Scanga, who is short, round-faced, and buzz-cut, and who talks a mile a minute. John's specialty is tenderness, the subject of his thesis and of sheaves of scholarly publications he's written since. He's just returned from Japan, and speaks enthusiastically about a Wagyu beef dinner there that cost $875 a person. "It was a white steak with little flecks of red in it," he says, with the highest Japanese ranking of A-5. (Instead of our basic three, the Japanese grading system distinguishes five degrees of fatness.) "It was juicy and tender and had a really nice mild beef flavor." The Wagyu get a high-concentrate grain diet, mostly corn and some soy; it's a myth that in the Kobe region they massage their cattle and feed them beer. While the largest farmer in the country probably has no more than 500 head of cattle, it's still a feedlot environment, but you don't raise Wagyu in 14 months, more like 36. "You look at them and say 'Wow, they are fat — hugely obese.'"

For Scanga, sound science is a matter of getting the facts and putting them in order. To define tenderness, for example, meat scientists set up consumer panels in major cities to sample and evaluate the product, and pay them for their time. That's the best data, Scanga says, but it's also very expensive. And people are schizophrenic. They say they don't want marbling, not a speck of fat. "That's what their eyes tell them, but their mouths tell them a different story." The flavor is in the fat, says Scanga, pure and simple. He admits, however, that there's a lot of argument now about the effect of marbling on tenderness, and he himself believes it accounts for only "a very small proportion."

If fat is not the key to tenderness, what is? The industry's answer is palatability. "Palatability is the three-headed monster: tenderness, juiciness, flavor, and they all interact. When we grain-feed cattle, we mellow the flavor with the fat and we put more juiciness in there with the fat, and that attacks the center in your brain like a drug that makes you happy, makes you satisfied." If you bite into a steak that's juicy and flavorful and you have to chew it a couple more times, you don't mind, because your whole mouth is disposed to like whatever's been going in. Provided it doesn't have too much flavor. Grass-fed beef, he says, has more intense beef flavor because it carries some of the flavors of the forages. "And as a society U.S. consumers hate flavor, they are flavor-averse. They do not like exotic flavors. They like bland."

Science has trouble with something as psychologically complex as palatability, I suggest, because science can measure and predict only when it can fragment and quantify the parts. Scanga is good-natured when I question the assumptions of his science, but he sticks to his guns. They can measure tenderness through the Warner-Bratzler shear-force test, which simulates chewing in order to measure how many units of force, in kilograms, would be needed to shear a cubic centimeter of a given piece of meat (4½ kilograms is the line between tender and tough). In the next step, pieces of beef of varying tenderness are fed to a consumer, who is asked what he would pay for one piece compared to another. These studies are called "Will Pay" or "Vickery Auction" studies, the latter for the economist who devised them, and they are important to companies marketing beef labeled "guaranteed tender."

There have been a number of national beef-tenderness surveys, including some analyzing the effects of hormone implants and other growth promotants, whose aggressive use tends to produce tougher meat. The studies' conclusion was not to stop using them, but to devise a strategy that balances growth advantage with meat quality. As for "natural and organic," these are not programs developed to provide safety and wholesomeness, he says, but simply address production practices, ecology, geography, lifestyle. "As a scientist, if I analyze a meat product produced in a fully organic system versus one produced in a fully conventional system, I will not find a difference chemically." But consumers don't understand that, Scanga says, and if you imply that some beef is safer than others, the consumer will go out and buy chicken.

"Natural" for John is defined legally as "minimally processed," which means "no added ingredients" like water and salt. Any meat in a supermarket that has not been injected with water and salt is "natural." If your beef label reads, as Coleman's does, "natural, no antibiotics, no growth promotants," you have to substantiate that claim, which costs the producer more and therefore the consumer more. "Consumers that buy Wal-Mart beef won't buy Coleman because one, they can't afford it, and two, they may have seen through the smoke and mirrors because chemically the meat is the same." When I ask him to tell me more about added ingredients, he tells me that Wal-Mart's beef is pumped up with a solution of up to 15 percent salt water and phosphate to make it more consistently tender, juicy, and flavorful. The pork industry has done it for centuries, says Scanga. It's right there on the label, and if the customer doesn't read the label, it's his own fault.

I ask about the role of muscle fibers on palatability because I'd read a brief summary by Gary C. Smith, one of his well-known colleagues, detailing how red muscle fibers store more fat than white ones do, a distinction well understood by human bodybuilders. An increase in white fibers in domestic animals, however, may lead to a decrease in quality in relation to tenderness. Here's where genetics comes in. As a breed, Wagyu have a high proportion of red muscle, as do Longhorns, from their Corriente heritage. Yet Belgian Blues — white-muscle-fiber types notorious for not depositing marbling in their heavy muscles — are also very tender, because they have a gene that affects the way their calpain enzymes work. Every time you have a muscle contraction, protein is broken down, Scanga explains, and the calpain enzymes work to restore it. These breeds turn their protein over very rapidly, so it remains "young" protein, which we find more tender.

The fact that tenderness is probably related to hundreds of genes does not diminish Scanga's enthusiastic embrace of a technology that now aims to isolate "the tenderness gene" within the bovine genome. Meta-Morphix, partnered with Cargill, is working on that very thing, along with GeneStar, Merial, Bovigen Solutions, and other companies marketing genetic tests for beef. The ultimate aim is to create customized breeding lines that will help predict which cattle will produce Prime and which won't, so you can vary feed and feeding times accordingly. "The answer is there," Scanga says. "As full sequencing becomes more available, we'll perfect the technology and will end up with genetic lines of cattle targeted for particular markets."

THE FIRST TIME I meet Temple Grandin at CSU, she is commanding an amphitheater full of students. She is dressed 1940s Western style, in a turquoise cotton shirt embroidered with horses on either side of a black kerchief worn like a tie, blue jeans, a silver-buckled belt. She has short wavy hair, bright blue eyes, a prominent chin, a very small mouth, tiny teeth — and dimples. She reminds me of Julia Child in cowboy gear.

A large screen projects a slide show of dozens of diagrams and photographs of her designs. "Half the cattle in the United States are in plants that I designed," she says. A self-described "pragmatic reformer," she is the world's best-known authority on animal care and behavior and the author of the extremely influential books *Thinking in Pictures* and *Animals in Translation*. Her words resonate with authority because, as she wrote in *Thinking in Pictures*, her autism has given her "a cow's-eye view. . . . When I put myself in a cow's place, I really have to be that cow and not a person in a cow costume. I can put myself into a twelve-hundred-pound steer's body and feel the equipment. When I see somebody squeeze an animal too hard in a squeeze chute, it makes me hurt all over." In the world of ordinary animal scientists, she's like an alien from Mars, who's dropped down on Earth to look around and tell us what she sees, with jolting clarity. "Animals are in the details, details, details," she tells her students. "Get down in the chute and see what the animal sees. Look for the little things. Animals 'watch' with their ears. You can gauge fear by an 'ear rating.' Eyes are threatening. Look away and make yourself smaller. Grazing animals have eyes on the side of their heads to scan for danger." She can have a cow's-eye view, she says, because she thinks in pictures. She sees individual pictures, like slides in a slideshow: cows in a field, cows on a truck, cows in a feedlot. Visual thinking is "specific-to-general," she explained in a Harvard interview. "You go from a whole lot of specific examples, and make a theory, rather than making a theory and trying to shove all the data into it." It sounds like the inductive method that I was once taught in school was the basis of scientific thinking, which is not at all the same as "sound science."

She talks fast, in short, quick sentences, often repeating phrases verbatim, and later tells me that sometimes students complain, but she has to build up detail after detail to create a whole. In class, she makes direct eye contact with an entire roomful of students, but in private she looks away when another person speaks. It's not talk she wants, but to get out in the field and do things. "I really like solving problems. I really like building things." She likes writing, too, but that's "more like downloading computer files." Her practicality has far-reaching consequences and is the reason she's upset by a younger generation "who are into far-out stuff like ESP with their animals because they've never had to do anything practical." She worries about young people. "They don't ride the bike more than one block from the house, they've never built a tree house, they don't build snow forts, they don't collect butterflies and insects." She believes that people who've done practical things tend to be more pragmatic and have a more realistic view. When things get all abstract, you get a radical right and a radical left. She instances hard-core animal rightists who don't like her because they want to get rid of beef altogether rather than fix the system. "There are reformists and there are abolitionists," she says. "I want to reform the industry, not get rid of it." She feels that vegetarian eaters put up blinders. "Anyone who drinks milk or eats cheese should know that a cow has to have a calf every year to keep producing milk, and those calves are raised for beef." Ranchers, on the other hand, are very practical. She's been talking to ranchers for thirty years and has found that they quickly pick up her designed equipment for handling cattle because they know that low-stress handling pays. It affects the meat.

She takes a pragmatic view of feedlots. "I think cattle in a feedlot have a pretty good life as long as it's not muddy. If the feedlot's dry, they just sort of lay around and get fat. I'm a lot more concerned about some of these hoity-toity horses locked up in a supermax jail, getting all these stable vices, than I am about feedlot cattle." She thinks Michael Pollan's "Power Steer" was "a little biased" because most of the time feedyards on the High Plains are not muddy, as he described them. "If he had gone there to that feedyard in Kansas another time of year, it would have been dry." The most important thing in building a feedyard is sloping and draining your site, what they call the "dirt work": "You want a 3 to 5 percent slope on your pens, put the feed trough high, and slope your pens with two drover alleys for getting cattle in and out of the pens, and then a 75-foot lane between the two for drainage. That's like a mud alley, and no cattle or people go there. Then the pens need to be scraped regularly because you need a smooth surface for the rain to run off."

She draws me a map of the United States on a telephone book, dividing the country into High Plains, Pasture, and Desert. High Plains are southern Idaho, eastern Colorado, western Kansas, western Nebraska, the Texas Panhandle. Pasture is the East, north to south. Desert is eastern Oregon and Washington, eastern California, Arizona, New Mexico. Seventy-five percent of the feedlots are in the High Plains because it's dry. The Midwest is not. So as feedlots got bigger they had to move to dry country or else just have a giant mud hole. To say that the big-chain feedlots are bad, that's just wrong, she says. She had started in the industry in the early 1970s at the Red River Feedlot in Arizona. In feedlots, you don't find cattle stuffed into little tiny cages like chickens. Feedlots are concentrated, but they're still outside, where the issues are mud and heat stress. Another difference is time: It takes two years for a calf from a cow to grow and have a calf of its own. "A ranch has never been a factory farm, ever. Never has been, never will be."

In comparison to the chicken or pig industry, the cattle industry is extremely heterogeneous, she explains. There are so many ways for ranchers to sell calves, and because there are so many small herds all around the country, the majority of ranchers remain independent. The old method was mostly "farmer feeding," where a farmer would buy cattle at a local auction, feed them in small farmer lots, then send them to the plant. Now, a rancher may sell them at auction to an "order buyer," who sells to a feedyard, where they're fed before they go to the plant. Or an order buyer, who is called a "country buyer," may come to the ranch and buy cattle for a "stocker," who puts the cattle to pasture until they're ready for the feedlot. She takes exception to the statement that at the feedlot it takes 7 pounds of grain to grow a pound of beef, because the steer is on grain for only half his life, so it's only 3½ pounds of grain. Sometimes a rancher will retain ownership all the way through and will pay the feedyard for "hotel and restaurant" before his cattle go to the plant. Sometimes a company retains ownership all the way through, contracting with rancher, stocker, feedyard, and plant in a vertically integrated chain of supply. This is the way the niche market of brands works, choosing cattle that fit the specs for the brand, and these are called "dedicated." The big boys are getting into the niche market on a very big scale, she says, and since "vertically integrated" has become a dirty word, the industry calls it a "dedicated supply chain."

Sometimes the best changes come through the marketplace, she says. Money talks. It used to be that ranchers would take calves to the auction and dump them off. But now the marketplace is demanding ID because supermarkets and restaurants want "trace-back." They want to know where those cattle are coming from. Instead of pushing cattle through the supply chain, she says, it's better to pull them. She is perhaps the only reformer who's been able to effect major change within the industry because she is respected by all sides of the industry. Around 1996 she'd made a survey of major meat plants for the U.S. Department of Agriculture and found that most plants killed animals brutally, but she couldn't get any of the execs to listen until they visited a plant for themselves. McDonald's had brushed off animal-rights activists for years until a couple of deaths forced Jack in the Box in 1999 to recall meat tainted with *E. coli.* Finally a McDonald's executive named Bob Langert agreed to talk to Grandin. Langert said that until he met her, it was just a lot of rhetoric about animal cruelty, but she had figured out how to measure brutality so they could figure out how to fix it. He claims that her inspection system brought "exact science" to the slaughterhouse. Her words are simpler: "Their eyes got opened," she says. "Most had never been near a farm." She took eighteen executives through twenty-six plants. Burger King and Wendy's joined later. "You don't know what's outside the box," she says, "until you get outside the box." Grandin now keeps a scorecard on beef slaughterhouses that measures, among other things, what percentage of the cattle are vocalizing. The more she listened to cattle, she says, the more she realized their moos tell you how they feel. The scorecard winkles out the plants with big problems. The best plants do their own internal scoring, motivated by the possibility that they'll be removed from the supplier list if they don't comply.

Her position on implants is pragmatic. She's found no scientific evidence that growth implants are dangerous to humans, she explains: The implant is a pellet put under the skin of the ear, and when the animal is slaughtered, the ear is discarded — "We're not eating ears." Antibiotics are another matter, they affect environment. And then there are genetic problems when we breed animals like dairy cattle, pigs, and chickens so big they get lame. As for BSE, "it's such a creepy disease," but there's science, and then there's what customers want. These are two different things. "If customers want every animal tested and want to pay for it, then we'll do it. The Japanese want them all tested. Okay, we'll be happy to do it, but we have to charge them for it and they have to pay for it." There's also a difference between spontaneous and genetic mad cows. BSE in a three-year-old steer might be spontaneous, but BSE in a twelve-year-old cow induces concern about feeding beef five parts poultry residue. "I think eventually we're going to have to figure out how to feed this stuff to automobiles."

If anyone speaks within the industry for the animal — and its welfare, as opposed to its meat — it's Grandin. A good stockman is one who recognizes that the animal is a conscious being that has feeling, she says. "It is not a machine or just an economic entity." Temple cites her design for a center track, or double-rail conveyor restrainer, for handling cattle on their entrance to a slaughter plant. It's modeled on the Squeeze Machine she made for herself as a teenager after watching cattle in a squeeze chute on her aunt's ranch. Pressed gently between side panels, the animal relaxed. But at the same time, no one has been more instrumental in connecting the quality of animal welfare to the quality of that animal's meat. "We've got to get rid of the cowboy-rodeo stuff, the yelling and screaming at animals," Grandin said in an NPR broadcast. "One of the things I've worked on is getting people to keep their mouths shut when they're moving cattle. It's very stressful, and stress affects the quality of the meat. Yelling and screaming will raise the heart rate more than just the sound of metal clanging and clanging."

Working with cattle raised questions for her ultimately about death and what comes after. "I hated the second law of thermodynamics," she says, "because I believed that the universe should be orderly." Evidently, it was not. When she worked at the Swift feedlots, she began to realize that people believe in an afterlife because the idea that once cattle walk into the slaughterhouse it's over for them forever is too horrible to conceive. "Like the concept of infinity, it is too ego-shattering for people to endure." But she also saw that for cattle the slaughter plant provided a much gentler death than nature did. At first, at the Swift plant, she couldn't bring herself to say that she had actually killed a live steer herself. She had designed a new kind of ramp and restrainer for them and called it "Stairway to Heaven." "I greatly matured after the construction of the Stairway to Heaven because it was real. It was not just a symbolic door that had private meaning to me, it was a reality many people refuse to face." She realized that most people never observe the birth-death cycle of living animals. "They do not realize that for one living thing to survive, another living thing must die." That's why for her slaughter is always a ritual function and that's why the place where an animal dies is a sacred place. As she told one interviewer, "None of these cattle would have existed, if we hadn't bred them. We owe them a decent life — and a painless death. They're living, feeling things. They're not posts or machines." We also owe it to ourselves, she believes. People who have no problems doing atrocious things to animals at a slaughterhouse probably have no problem torturing people. She quotes Thomas Aquinas: One of the reasons we should treat animals humanely is so that people themselves don't get corrupted.

Many have pointed out that she has put the lie to science's easy assumptions about autistic people and also about animals. Just because animals think differently from the way most people think doesn't mean animals don't think at all, she says. "Animals are much smarter and more sensitive than we assume." Some regard her rescuing an entire category of creaturehood from the cruelty of indifference and contempt as something close to heroic. When we say good-bye, she says, "I had pleasure talking to you." I know not to shake her hand. I admire the way she recreated herself, inventing the machinery she needed to release herself from animal fears and become more human and humane. I like the way she walks tall and free in her long-legged jeans back to her car, embodying in a totally unexpected way the cowboy as one set apart: the Outsider.

ANOTHER OUTSIDER AT CSU with unusual impact on animal science is Bernard Rollin, a big burly fellow in an orange Harley-Davidson motorcycle shirt, a huge bushy beard, and a face that says to the West, "Hey, I'm from New York." If Temple Grandin talks like Hemingway, Rollin talks like Pete Hamill. After studying Scottish philosophy during a Fulbright in Edinburgh and taking a Ph.D. at Columbia in the 1960s, when the streets were so dangerous that he had to guard-train a 160-pound Great Dane to protect his wife from muggings and worse, he decided, "This wasn't a very healthy way to live." He applied only to places he'd never heard of because he figured they weren't like New York, which is how he ended up at CSU. At thirty-five he found himself a full professor in the midst of a midlife crisis: "It didn't seem to me fitting for a grown person to be constantly prowling around the ideas of long-dead people."

He got to talking to one of the vets at CSU who had a gym locker next to his. "I discovered that most serious innovation comes in the locker room because you're bare-ass naked and you end up on equal ground and thus have good conversations." This guy knew that Rollin had been one of the first in the country to teach medical ethics to premeds. The vet wanted his own students to get a handle on how to think in ethical terms and asked Rollin to create a course, so Rollin taught the world's first course in veterinary-medicine ethics in 1978. He also published his first book on the subject, in 1982: *Animal Rights and Human Morality.*

As early as 1976, he'd helped write federal laws for laboratory animals with a couple of CSU vets and eventually got them passed, against the opposition of the entire medical community, he says. On the other hand, the guy in the local Harley shop was on his side. This guy had grown up on a farm and understood that you can't hurt research by demanding that scientists treat animals humanely. There'd been an enormous public outcry after someone had released films of scientists at the University of Pennsylvania jokingly abusing rhesus monkeys while studying brain trauma from simulated car crashes. "There was some very bad stuff," Rollin says, and it was the birth of PETA as a force. All he did was to ride the crest of the social wave. "I'm probably the only person in the country who is credible to both sides, but liked by neither," he says, "because I always give the same message, whether talking to researchers or antivivisectionists": Society is changing, and behavior that was once acceptable is no longer acceptable — whether we're talking about genetic engineering or cattle production — for ethical reasons. People are beginning to demand that the animals we use get the best shake possible.

Traditional agriculture, he explains, was based on animal husbandry, which meant in Old Norse (*husbondi*) "bonded to your household." Because animals were part of your household, you knew that the better you treated your cows, the more milk they produced; your chickens, the more eggs; your pigs, the more piglets. To pig farmers, Rollin likes to quote the

Biblical sanction for good husbandry in the Twenty-third Psalm. "The Lord is my shepherd; I shall not want. He maketh me to lie down in green pastures; He leadeth me beside the still waters; He restoreth my soul." The Bible does not say, "The Lord is my shepherd: He sticks me in a two-by-seven-by-three pen for my working life, rolling on concrete in my own excrement." It's this kind of talk that made him the keynote speaker for the Presbyterian Synod at a four-day conference, despite his assertion that he is not religious. Nonetheless, he has become an unusual missionary for the message of animal welfare within the industry, which has not written him off as an animal activist. He points out that human history has long validated an exchange between animals and husbandry as a kind of contract: We take care of the animals, and they take care of us.

That contract was broken after World War II, he says, when animal husbandry was supplanted by animal sciences, defined not as animal care, but as "the application of industrial methods to the production of animals to increase efficiency and productivity." As a moderate reformer, Rollin points out that this fundamental change was not made by cruel, insensitive, or evil men, but out of a concern to supply the public with cheap and plentiful food, and that mission was accomplished. After World War II, agricultural productivity increased fivefold in thirty years, while the proportion of income spent on food dropped 30 percent. But however decent the motives, this evolution inflicted new kinds of suffering: liver abscesses from high-concentrate feed, physical and psychological deprivation for animals in confinement, lack of individual attention to animals in herds of thousands, use of technological "sanders" such as antibiotics and vaccines to force square pegs into round holes for the sake of productivity — not well-being. Historically, the loss of land, loss of farm labor, increase of technologies, and a "burgeoning belief in technology-based economics of scale" all contributed to the takeover of traditional values by industrial ones. When productivity was made the sole value, welfare was made irrelevant.

Rollin finds ethical husbandry well articulated among the Western ranchers he talks to, but they don't visit the slaughterhouse. "The average rancher has never been to a slaughterhouse and doesn't want to go. They say that their job is to give the animals their life, and they don't want to think about the ending of it." Eighty percent of feedlot people have ranch backgrounds, but feel they're good husbandmen because they're better at confinement with cattle than the chicken or pig people are. They all admit that there are certain practices in the industry that could be made better. "But the point is, they don't see a way out," he says. "Yet at the same time they know there are alternatives." Rollin, like Callicrate, is keen on alternatives. He's been working with a colleague for the past seventeen years on an ID device, now patented, that takes a photo of the retina in a cow's eye, as a noninvasive substitute for either branding or the current ID system that inserts a microchip into the ear.

Europe is way ahead in seeking alternatives, he says. He mentions Europe's rejection of genetic engineering for reasons of ethics, and the Bill of Rights for farm animals brought into being by Astrid Lindgren of *Pippi Longstocking* fame and adopted by Sweden in 1988, outlawing CAFOs for pigs. "In this country, maybe one out of a hundred animal scientists will even have heard of this law," he says. "But Sweden is not Mars." He believes that the last significant group of husbandry people in this country are the Western ranchers, but they won't be around for long. Not one ranch can support three kids, he says. "This generation is the last, and I think it's a terrible tragedy."

Rollin has been cited for being at "the leading edge of quite literally changing the subject of animal ethics," changing the way people think about human interaction with animals. In a 2004 article in the *Journal of Animal Science*, he summoned animal agriculture to explore ways to replace the animal husbandry lost to industrialization. To oppose animal use that tries to force square pegs into round holes, leading to friction and suffering, is not a radical move, but a conservative one, he says. Consumers are not motivated solely by the desire for cheap food, nor is the animal-rights movement based solely on an "ethic of abolition," but on the humane desire for a new contract. He ends with a cowboy image: "It is not too late for agriculturalists to emerge as the 'good guys.'"

Mad Cows and Ethanol

"A Cowboy Boot with Oil Derrick" made by Olsen-Stelzer in the 1940s was photographed by Jim Arndt from the boot collection of Harry Hudson. For more boots, see *The Cowboy Boot Book* by Tyler Beard and Jim Arndt (Gibbs Smith, 1992).

Since horses don't run on oil, I think it's more reasonable that the "windshield" cowboy is afraid everyone's going to switch to cornfed horses and his profits will decline.

— blog entry on *Corrente* (September 21, 2007)

———————————————————◆———————————————————

IN 1997 JANET SKARBEK was twenty-nine, a solid Republican businesswoman, married to her college sweetheart, and living in Cinnaminson, on the New Jersey side of the Delaware River opposite Philadelphia, such an ordinary town that the most unusual thing about it is its name, a Lenni-Lenape Indian word for "stone island." She'd never heard of the FDA feed reform, which was implemented that year and for the first time in the history of America's meat industry placed a few — very few — restrictions on feeding animal-waste parts, including sick or diseased animals, to live animals. Nor had she heard of the nineteen-year-old boy in England who'd died four years earlier from a mysterious new disease named "variant Creutzfeldt-Jakob Disease" (vCJD). This was the first human death linked to the mad cow disease (bovine spongiform encephalopathy or BSE) that had overtaken Great Britain in 1987. What did any of that have to do with her carefully programmed life? "I was never an activist, never a vegetarian, I believed in corporate America."

In February 2000 Carrie Mahan, a family friend who had worked for Janet's mother, a controller for the restaurants and concession stands at the Garden State Race Track near Cherry Hill, died at twenty-nine after suffering the grotesque symptoms of dementia, whose cause puzzled her doctors at the University of Pennsylvania Medical Center until they saw the autopsy of her brain. "She had holes all over the place," one doctor reported. "Her brain was just gone." Her doctors decided it must have been a prion disease of the form called "sporadic CJD," because sporadic medically means "no direct cause."

A prion is a renegade protein crystal that invades normal proteins and makes them duplicate the shape of the invader, in a kind of refolding and unraveling. Prions were discovered by Dr. Stanley Prusiner in 1997 as "an infectious agent unrelated to genetic material," a development so revolutionary it won him a Nobel Prize. Statistically such a case was very rare, one in a million, which meant at the most 250 to 300 cases a year in the United States.

In June 2003 Janet learned that another female employee from the racetrack had just died of sporadic CJD. That made two deaths out of one hundred, rather than one in a million. "It was like my 9/11," Janet told me. "Everything changed." She began to look up local obituaries online and found that a man in the next town over had also died of CJD. Although he was not an employee at the racetrack, she learned that he was a season-pass holder and ate there at least once a week. Concerned for the health of her mother, Janet called the Center for Disease Control and the New Jersey Department of Health to alert them to this statistical anomaly. Their response was immediate and identical: "Little woman, you're not a scientist, forget it." Her eyes darken with the memory. "I'd never felt so dismissed in my whole life." She found a fourth case linked to the track, then a fifth and a sixth. "When I got to seven, I started to call the media." She called local guys and big guys like CNN, but the Texas cattlemen's suit against Oprah Winfrey in 1998 was still fresh in their minds. "Everybody was willing to listen, but nobody was willing to cover it." Oprah had won that suit in 2002, but it cost her over $1 million, and by that time thirteen states had adopted what's popularly called the Veggie-Libel Law against "food disparagement" of any kind, from apples to hamburgers.

So instead, Janet wrote an article for her local newspaper, and people from all over began calling her to report someone they knew who'd died of CJD. In December the first mad cow was discovered in America, in Washington state, and suddenly all the media she'd called were now calling her. The first reaction of government agencies was denial. Someone in Canada told her, "You know the policy — if you have a cow die, shoot, shovel, and shut up." Dave Louthan, who'd slaughtered the affected cow, had said it was walking — which is significant because walking cows usually aren't tested, only downers (sick cows that are unable to walk). Louthan claimed that government men with guns in their holsters came and put pressure on him to sign a document saying the cow had been a downer. He refused and went out and told the story and got fired. Dave had testified to this effect in Seattle before the California State Senate in February 2004. "Everyone has believed corporate America for so long," Janet says, "has believed when we were told that we can't have it here, that we've got firewalls in place, all our processes are fine. But it's not true."

Janet has been working on mad cow full time ever since and has discovered that CJD is just one expression of a frighteningly widespread and amorphous disease. She mobilized some New Jersey senators to ask the CDC and New Jersey's Department of Health to reinvestigate, but they refused even to look at tissue samples. Meantime, she'd found another cluster of CJD victims in Kingston, NY. She also found that Dr. Clarence "Joe" Gibbs, a specialist in diseases of the nervous system and particularly of prion diseases at the National Institutes of Health, had collected tissue samples of CJD victims for a study of transmissible spongiform encephalopathy (TSE) — the umbrella for prion diseases in animals and men. Despite the study's importance, when Dr. Gibbs died in 2001, the NIH closed down the entire project and planned to destroy the collected tissue samples until the families of the victims protested.

Meantime Janet was able to pinpoint at which establishment among the three restaurants and twenty-four concession stands at the Garden State Race Track all the victims ate regularly and half ate exclusively — the ill-named "Phoenix." She was even able to locate the distributor who supplied its meat, but for her the distributor was not the point. "It's not a matter of a single distributor, but of the government covering up for large corporations," she says. "Coming from the corporate side, I never believed these things really happen. I thought corporate America had high moral values and those people who are activists out there picketing were strange."

Janet remembers a lot of strange things happening after that — her "Deep Throat" at the USDA had his windshield broken, her computer was mysteriously wiped clean of files and possibly swapped for a look-alike, she was followed by a green minivan (not unlike the one Dave Louthan claimed had followed him) — although the police dismissed her accounts. She also continued her investigations into TSE diseases and found that they were infectious, that a group of hunters in Michigan had all died of sporadic CJD after eating game at the same meal, that Dr. Richard Marsh at the Animal Sciences Department of the University of Wisconsin had discovered minks dying of TSE after they'd been fed downer meat. Marsh had gone to the USDA with his discovery that TSE was in American cattle in 1985, even before mad cow disease had been discovered in England. Marsh's work was crucial because it provided evidence that chronic wasting disease (CWD) could cross species of livestock through animal feed. Unfortunately, he died in 1997, shortly before the USDA's first step at feed reform through the FDA.

By 2006 Janet had discovered twenty-seven people who had eaten at the Phoenix Restaurant between 1988 and 1992 and who had CJD as the cause of death written on their death certificates. Brain samples from half of those victims have been available to American scientists, but currently the most significant research is being done abroad. Dr. John Collinge of University College London is part of a group that as early as 1996 found evidence that BSE prions could affect humans and that the disease was transmissible by blood. In Italy in 2004, Dr. Salvatore Monaco, a neurologist at the G. B. Rossi Polyclinic in Verona, named a new strain of mad cow disease BASE (bovine amyloidotic spongiform encephalopathy), after his group discovered it in a pair of older Italian cows that appeared to be perfectly healthy. Monaco found this new strain similar to "a subtype that causes sporadic CJD in humans," and raised the possibility that such cases are not "spontaneous," but come from eating animals.

Today Janet is a repository of information for and about families who've had a member die of CJD and want to know why they can't get real information. Other disease clusters have emerged in Texas, Florida, Kentucky, and Michigan. "It's not like a chemical spill," says Janet. "It's more like tobacco." What frustrates the families is continued official denial, which has been the pattern first in the United Kingdom, then the European Union, then Canada, then the United States as cases of BSE and CJD have spread, despite the knowledge that because the incubation period for mad-cow strains may be as long as thirty years, no one is predictably safe. There have now been 158 mad cow–related deaths in the United Kingdom.

An international report to the USDA in February 2004, after America's first BSE cow was found to have been born in Canada, reads: "It is probable that other infected animals have been imported from Canada and possibly also from Europe. These animals have not been detected and, therefore, infected material has likely been rendered, fed to cattle, and amplified within the cattle population so that the cattle in the USA have also been indigenously infected. The administration needs to quickly expand its testing program and further tighten regulations to prevent certain special risk materials from being added to cattle feed." Three years later, cattle are still being fed cattle blood and fat, along with downer cattle, and no agency tests for prohibited material in cattle feed.

"Worse than that, they've made it illegal in the United States to test your own cows for mad cow disease," Janet says, citing Creekstone Farms, the small family-owned packing company that the USDA had prevented from testing its own cattle. After Creekstone was denied permission from the USDA in 2004, the company brought suit against the agency in March 2006; a year later, the U.S. District Judge for the District of Columbia ruled that the USDA's prohibition was unlawful; two months later, the USDA appealed and has continued to ban any private company from buying the test kits that would allow them to test their own herds. "There is no scientific reason to require universal testing," said the industry, and to do so would endanger consumer confidence. Increased testing might uncover here, as it had in E.U. countries — after they'd agreed to impose new BSE testing in 1999 — the disquieting fact that cattle declared to be BSE free were not. Don Stull, an anthropology professor at Kansas University, observes: "If Creekstone Farms tested every one of its animals, that would create pressure for the big boys to do the same, and they don't want that."

The government believes that denial is the best policy. In 1991 a USDA report titled "Bovine Public Relations" had speculated on how best to handle mad cow if it showed up in the States. The report said that the British Ministry of Health had initiated a registry for CJD, which "appeared to legitimize the concern about the link between CJD and human health." But a registry would be reportable, and in the United States even today, CJD is not a federally reportable disease. In the meantime, evidence that new prion strains are at work has continued to accumulate. In 2001 a university researcher at the Howard Hughes Medical Institute suggested that the industry's heat treatment of animal parts in the process of rendering them may have created the more virulent prion that we now call mad cow disease. In 2003 Dr. Prusiner himself reported: "The strain type associated with sporadic CJD and previously undescribed bovine prion shows convergent molecular signatures." Translated, that means prions continue to mutate and to couple "promiscuously."

Richard Rhodes's *Deadly Feasts: Tracking the Secrets of a Terrifying New Plague* was written in 1997, six years before BSE was uncovered in the United States. It explained to the general public a new family of mysterious infectious diseases linked by prions. When you smell the roses, Rhodes warns, remember that rosebushes are fertilized with bone meal from dead cattle, the suspected source of BSE. Dr. Murray Waldman, a Toronto coroner, picked up the plague theme when he linked Alzheimer's disease to the prion disease family in 2004, in a book written with Marjorie Lamb, *Dying for a Hamburger. How Modern Meat-Packing Led to an Epidemic of Alzheimer's Disease*. Waldman describes studies in which researchers have injected cells from the diseased brains of Alzheimer victims into animals, which then developed effects indistinguishable from those of CJD. This was the link Dr. Prusiner had predicted twenty years earlier. As of today, 5 million Americans have Alzheimer's, a 10 percent increase within the last five years, which means that 13 percent of people over sixty-five and 42 percent of those over eighty-five will contract it.

Meanwhile, internal government memos continue to state that the best public gambit is to say that "more research is necessary before any conclusions can be drawn about any possible link between CJD and Alzheimer's." And while there are signs of a more proactive approach — McDonald's, for example, has taken the lead in criticizing the USDA for its lack of precautions against mad cow disease and has been joined by Pfizer and Land O' Lakes in demanding stronger regulations from the FDA — it appears nonetheless that China, Japan, and Korea are in the process of lifting their ban against American beef while testing remains minimal, at 1 percent of cattle slaughtered.

I INTERVIEWED JANET in June 2005, just before the first mad cow to have been born and bred in the United States was discovered. It didn't make big headlines, but it did pose a major PR problem for those who claimed they'd erected an impermeable "firewall" to ensure that American cows were 100 percent safe. The feed reform bill of 1997 — which banned the use of "high risk mammalian protein," meaning the remains of cattle aged 30 months and over (except for their blood and fat), as food for cows, limited testing to live cows older than 30 months, and failed to set up a tracking or labeling system or even to require compliance — had proved to be as illusory a defense as the Maginot Line. "BSE is the Chernobyl of food safety," journalist Nicols Fox had warned in 1998 when she exposed the prevalence of *E. coli* in her book *Spoiled: Why Our Food Is Making Us Sick*. Yet America continued to fiddle while Britain burned. What mad cow did for the world was to expose the interconnectedness of the industrial food chain and its pathogens, and the inevitable pattern of denial that surfaced wherever that truth did.

Eventually Britain had to kill thousands of cows and institute an effective testing and tracking system. Europe followed, then Japan, but Canada and the United States did not. The FDA's feeble reform bill for cattle feed lulled the industry into a deep-sleep belief that mad cow was for foreigners, not for us, even after our homegrown mad cows were discovered. Despite the accumulating numbers of mad cows here and abroad, the industry has swaggered through a wilderness of denial as boundless as that of the war in Iraq. "The key to understanding this administration's approach to regulation comes in three words: cost-benefit-analysis," sacred words to the spokesman from the American Enterprise Institute and Brookings Institution, who concluded, "It's the right approach to policy."

Meanwhile, even the flimsy stipulations of the feed bill went unenforced in the United States and Canada. Sixty percent of sampled feeds labeled "vegetable only" were found to contain animal proteins, and more than 80 percent of firms handling feed forbidden to ruminants failed to label it as such. The ban on beef (30 months of age and over) imported from Canada, announced in May 2003 after Canada reported its first native BSE case, was no better enforced. All the steers and heifers in the pen the day Dave Louthan killed his mad cow had Canadian ear tags, he reported; the USDA inspector he'd checked with told him that any Canadian cattle already on this side of the border were safe. In November the USDA dreamed up a "minimal-risk" category that allowed Canada to resume shipping "certain ruminants and ruminant products," which included live cattle *under* 30 months of age and boxed beef from animals of any age. In December, when the United States confirmed that a BSE cow in Washington state had come from Canada, their government tried to soothe worriers by saying that the cow's age of 6½ years guaranteed that it had been exposed to "BSE materials" prior to the 1997 feed ban. The United States then tried to track the cow's "birth cohort" of 141 cows, all of which would have eaten the same feed, some of which might have been shipped to the United States and entered the human food chain. But soon the trail went cold and so did the news. Meanwhile, APHIS (Animal and Plant Health Inspection Service of the USDA) announced that all Canadian cattle would be tagged and tracked throughout the import process, and boasted that opening trade with "low-risk products" in "low-risk countries" would give the United States a "leadership role in fostering trade."

Nevertheless, the big packers like Tyson and Cargill (through the American Meat Institute) filed a lawsuit against the government in December 2004, saying that the existing U.S. ban on older Canadian cattle was arbitrary, capricious, and "scientifically unsupportable." No matter that in 2004 there were at least 300,000 Canadian-born cattle in American herds, part of the thousands of cattle imported annually from Canada and Mexico to keep the giant processing plants in the United States humming. R-CALF had tried a protectionist ploy earlier, in April, seeking an injunction against the USDA's allowing any imports of "bone-in and ground beef" from Canada. But Beef Without Borders was the name of the beef industry's game, especially after NAFTA, and government and industry dealt from the top and bottom of a stacked deck to maintain it. Every time a government agency announced a new "safety" rule, it understood that industry would go to work to lessen or rescind it. The NCBA continued to produce glossy promotional materials intended to "maintain the trust of domestic and international customers." Noncompliance with the feed ban was, to be sure, a "point of vulnerability," but there would be no BSE epidemic and the disease would diminish in time. Instead of increased testing, the USDA implemented what it called a "surveillance program," based on statistical models not meant to test samples but to measure the extent of a "possible" problem. In 2006 APHIS announced that this program had been so successful — in testing 263,115 high-risk cattle, no BSE had been found — that they were going to shut it down altogether as unnecessary.

There was no lack of critics who believed that the government's regulations were far too flimsy. The USDA meat inspectors' union made numerous complaints about the enforceability of existing regulations. The Union of Concerned Scientists complained that the USDA used "unscientific testing standards" to protect a beef industry that had sent its own members to head the agency. In February 2005 the Inspector General of the Government Accountability Office issued a report blasting APHIS for "permit creep," weak processes, vague language, shifting definitions, and capricious decisions. Many products that had been banned in 2003 as high risk, such as beef tongues, had been mysteriously demoted in 2004 to low-risk. Not a single Canadian facility met the minimum stipulated requirements for segregating younger cattle from older cattle, and many feed manufacturers and shippers went not only uninspected but unidentified. As a result, 42,000 pounds of beef products of "questionable eligibility" had been imported from Canada in 2004.

Nonetheless, Secretary of Agriculture Mike Johanns continued to stonewall: "It is the job of the government to do all it can to help maintain and increase the confidence of consumers and make decisions based on science." Senators from Western states upped the pressure on Japan, which had been dragging its heels after a tentative agreement to reopen trade. "It is spilling over from an agricultural issue to a trade issue, which is unfortunate," said Howard Baker with faux naïveté, as if the two were not Siamese twins. Senator Tom Harkin of Iowa remained a lone voice from the legislature in seriously questioning the motives of the USDA in carrying out its responsibilities.

R-CALF had argued all along that it was folly to open the Canadian border as long as the Japanese border was closed because the increased volume of slaughter would only depress prices for American producers. Meanwhile, Australia had happily filled the beef gap in Japan and Korea, doubling its share of the $2.3 billion import market in Japan from 44 percent to 91 percent. R-CALF found support in a variety of individuals alert to the dicey relationship between trade and safety. E. G. Vallianatos, a former analyst with the U.S. Environmental Protection Agency, warned that BSE was not a border matter but a disease of industrialized agriculture everywhere. Dr. Lester Friedlander, a veterinarian and former meat inspector for a packing plant in Pennsylvania who'd been fired for whistle-blowing, told members of Canada's parliament that the United States had had cases of mad cow that it never reported. Dr. Masuo Doi, a retired USDA veterinarian who'd investigated a possible case of BSE in 1997 in Canada, warned that the "right tests were not done" and that the most important samples had gone missing.

Leave it to Cattle-Fax to get to the heart of the matter. They looked at the costs to the industry of newly tightened USDA/FSIS rules at the beginning of 2004 to prevent BSE, which would ban for the first time *all* downer cattle from the human food chain, remove certain Specified Risk Materials better known as SRM (skull, brain, trigeminal ganglia, eyes, tonsils, spinal column, dorsal-root ganglia, distal ileum) from the human food chain, remove mammalian blood and blood products from ruminant feeds, ban poultry litter and plate waste from ruminant feeds, require dedicated lines for mills and renderers that handle prohibited ruminant materials, and increase inspections. The cost to the industry in banning downer cows for human feed would be $50 to $70 million. Increasing Specified Risk Materials would cost another $50 to $70 million. "The changes to the industry are permanent," they warned. "Added uncertainty and extreme volatility will be common." And yet a study commissioned by the Kansas Department of Agriculture concluded that the loss of export markets from BSE ($3.2 to $4.7 billion) could have been covered had the United States agreed to increased testing. We would have regained 25 percent of the Pacific Rim export market by testing 75 percent of U.S. cattle. Or put another way, if we had spent $600 million to test even 25 percent of our cattle, we would have saved billions in regained markets.

On March 2, 2005, a federal district court granted the preliminary injunction sought by R-CALF against easing import restrictions. The industry continued to talk money, citing the $20 to $40 cost per head for every animal processed under tightened tests and rules. They blamed activists and the media for the loss of exports. "The only criteria that seems to matter is perception, and perception has largely been created by activist groups," wailed "Cow-Calf Weekly." While one group of Canadian cattle producers threatened to sue R-CALF, another group brought a $7 billion class-action suit against the Canadian government for not preventing BSE in the first place. In turn, Canadian Prime Minister Paul Martin warned U.S. meat packers that they would pay a price for the border closures, which had cost Canada's cattle industry over $4.5 billion. Canada, he said, will simply have to increase its own processing capacity and compete for European and Asian markets.

In May, Bob Goodlatte, chairman of the House Agricultural Committee, introduced legislation for voluntary labeling as a way to sidestep the mandatory labeling (COOL) that under the last farm bill was supposed to take effect at the end of September. After all, Japan was proposing to drop its demand for 100 percent testing, and the EU and UK were showing signs of easing restrictions, too. By this time, only 180,000 cases of BSE had been found worldwide. Secretary Johanns was so confident that Americans were no longer afraid of BSE that, at the beginning of June, he convened a BSE summit roundtable in Minnesota to discuss reopening the Canadian border for live cattle under 30 months. Designed to reinforce consumer and producer confidence in the United States and to benefit U.S. processors, the summit played to a packed house in St. Paul, with a stacked deck — seven of the nine panel participants were reps for big beef, with a lone representative each from R-CALF and the National Farmers Union.

Just two days later, on June 11, the *New York Times* reported a second possible mad cow in the United States, this one a steer, which showed on the first testing an ambiguous "positive," so the report was sent to Weybridge, England, for further testing. It was very bad timing. Johanns worked hard to reassure Americans that whatever the test results, the questionable animal had never entered their food supply. "There is no risk whatsoever," he crowed. "I'm going to enjoy a good steak." On June 13, however, Johanns was forced to call a press conference to announce that the cow the Department had called "safe" last November had, under this second test — the Western blot test, which was the "gold standard" in England, Europe, and Japan, and had been demanded by Phyllis K. Fong, the Agriculture Department's inspector general — generated a "weak positive." The NCBA jumped in to say that this sort of unprecedented testing created "great anxiety within our industry" and warned of economic losses. What Johanns did not announce was that this mad cow, a Brahman crossbreed, was the first to have been born and bred in the United States. About a week later, he had to confirm a BSE positive for this 8½-year-old downer, which had tested negative under the USDA's standard immunohistochemistry test called the BioRad quick test. Others pointed to problems with the testing of this animal that Johanns omitted: The brain samples had been frozen, the animal's body parts had been mixed with those of others, and no written records had been kept. Critics of U.S. testing methods were not surprised, for this was business as usual; it was the intervention of Inspector General Fong that was extraordinary. Johanns tried to spin the news as positive: Catching one positive mad cow in 388,000 cattle tested proved that "our system works." Critics said, "Nonsense." Johanns complained that Fong had overstepped her bounds in ordering retesting without his knowledge or approval, despite the fact that the Inspector General's office was set up as an independent arm to conduct audits and investigations.

While R-CALF continued to insist on BSE as "a foreign animal disease" that had infected the American herd, the Center for Media and Democracy scolded R-CALF ranchers for choosing the wrong battle. Instead of fighting to keep the border closed, they should have been fighting to institute the kind of testing that Japan was doing. On the other side of the battle, the American Agricultural Economics Association proclaimed: "The human health risk from BSE is probably far lower than the risk of choking on a toothbrush," and urged "a fact-based view of the almost nonexistent public health risk that BSE poses in North America." It was as if America were just a little bit pregnant. On July 14, the Ninth U.S. Circuit Court of Appeals overturned the injunction. Days later, the first load of live Canadian cattle since May 2003 — 27,168 hamburger cows over 30 months old — crossed the border into the United States on July 22, 2005.

R-CALF decided to shift its focus to making COOL mandatory, while the meat industry went to work on Japan. The Senate voted to prohibit Japanese beef as long as Japan banned U.S. beef. But Japanese regulators claimed that half of the twenty mad-cow cases that had been found in Japan would not have been discovered in the United States, where all testing was voluntary, where the only cows tested were ones showing some visual signs of disease that put them in the "highest risk" category, and where even then, only 16 percent in that category were tested. Skeptical of U.S. safeguards and aware of polls that showed popular opposition in Japan to U.S. beef, Japan's Food Safety Commission demanded the right of Japanese officials to conduct on-site inspections of U.S.

plants. South Korean farmers threatened national demonstrations if the ban on U.S. beef were lifted. Secretary Johanns replied that Congress was running out of patience. Canada's response was also testy. "Too often Canada acts like a boy scout in trade disputes," wrote one Canadian editorialist, "while the schoolyard bully south of the border steals our lunch money."

In December Japan finally accepted a shipment of U.S. beef younger than 21 months. Zenshoku, a Korean barbecue chain based in Osaka, had ordered 10 tons of this shipment for their dish called Beef Bowl, which it served adorned with tiny American flags. On January 20, however, in the wake of a public outcry in Japan over news that a shipment of veal from a Brooklyn company contained spinal-column material, Japan reinstated the ban. The NCBA responded, "What's being investigated is a technical violation, not a beef safety issue." The USDA reported that the incident was the result of negligence by the exporter, who didn't realize these products were not eligible for shipment to Japan. "For the Japanese to use this one instance as the basis for saying that they can't trust our entire system and shutting down the market again is extremely frustrating," said Agriculture Chairman Goodlatte, who once again threatened reprisals. But in November, Japanese officials now discovered a box of thymus glands (sweetbreads) that had been shipped as part of 11 tons of beef products from ConAgra/Swift's Greeley plant.

Korea had warned that even when it lifted its ban, beef bones would still be banned. Unfortunately, a popular Korean dish, *bul kal-bi,* is barbecued beef ribs. In December 2006 South Korea suspended imports from a U.S. slaughterhouse after finding seven bone fragments in a 10-ton shipment of beef. In a mind-boggling response, Secretary Johanns announced that he was testing Korea to see whether their "market was sincere, whether it was really open." He said, "These were not huge, huge quantities of beef. They were sent into the marketplace with rigorous inspection here in the United States, delivered over to Korea, and they found a way to reject it." Six months later, Tyson Foods ran aground in South Korea after officials there discovered 290 pounds of beef with bone in, although it was labeled "for domestic use only." Tyson explained that it had shipped the beef produced in its Springdale, Arkansas, plant to a Minnesota company, which had resold it to Midamar Corporation in Cedar Rapids, Iowa. "The producing plant was not the shipping plant," said a spokesman for the USDA, asking that the producing plants be reinstated. In July, Cargill and Swift were in trouble for shipping two boxes of banned beef ribs from plants in Wichita, Kansas, and Greeley, Colorado, in beef shipments that did qualify for Johann's "huge, huge quantities" — 25 tons apiece. "Our review indicates simple human error," explained a Cargill spokesman. Seems a worker put bone-in ribs into a box labeled "boneless beef ribs."

Meanwhile, mad cows had begun to pile up here and abroad. In March 2006 the report came of a third mad cow in the United States, this one a Santa Gertrudis downer in Alabama, over 10 years old, and confirmed positive by the Western blot test now in use by the United States. The NCBA saw only a silver lining: "The animal did not enter the human food or animal feed supply. . . . Your beef is safe." On July 10, Canada confirmed its ninth BSE case (three within the last twelve months), this one a relatively young dairy cow of only 50 months, born five years after the feed ban and detected by a rapid test eight months before the regular Canadian program would have targeted the animal for testing. A week later, Johanns announced that the USDA would reduce its own testing by 90 percent: Its "enhanced surveillance program" had not been designed as a food-safety program and had already done its work by finding only three new cases of BSE in 759,000 cattle tested; by cutting testing from 1000 to 100 cattle a day, the cost of the program would be reduced from $52 to $8 million.

Consumers Union and the Center for Science in the Public Interest questioned the new risk assessment made by the Food Safety and Inspection Service (FSIS) of the USDA: The questioners noted that mislabeling and the mistaken use of proscribed feeds were far more common than the analysis stated; that only a fraction of feed mills were inspected; that visual inspection alone was insufficient to detect 95 percent of BSE-infected animals. "The BSE battle lines are as hardened as those that divide pro-war and anti-war political factions," Dan Murphy noted, as he slammed nitpicking critics of government and the beef industry who rant on about "minuscule risk factors" while millions of beef-eating consumers happily don't care. He explained that since zero prevention is impossible, the best risk-management is what it's always been: "Find cost-effective ways to mitigate risk." He did not mention that of the 112 countries that bought U.S. beef before the discovery in 2003 of BSE, 23 countries have not bought it since.

JOHN STAUBER IS older than I would have thought from his telephone voice, maybe in his fifties, with whitish hair but a boyish grin and manner, clear of skin and eye. He looks like a seventies kid in his backpack and jeans, sturdy and determined, a Wisconsin-born optimist. When we meet, he is suffering from severe hay fever, which does nothing to deter the powers of persuasion that led him to found the nonprofit Center for Media and Democracy and to publish his first book in 1995, *Toxic Sludge Is Good for You*, a scathing indictment of the public-relations industry. "Two hundred years after the American Revolution, there's a new King George, and it's the giant global transnational corporations," he says. "I'm a total believer in the fundamental ideals of democracy, and I work on cutting-edge issues I'm passionate about that are being ignored and hidden."

One of those issues involved Monsanto's selling genetically engineered bovine growth hormone (BGH) for dairy cattle in the 1990s, and it was then that he noticed "this tremendous collusion" between companies and government regulatory agencies. He saw how closely four companies — Monsanto, American Cyanamid (now a division of Wyeth), Eli Lilly, and Upjohn — worked with the FDA and USDA. He made two major Freedom of Information Act investigations of these agencies and "hit the jackpot." He found that the biggest single player in the dairy industry at the time was a tobacco company, Philip Morris/Kraft, and that the biggest dairy-industry players lined right up with the biggest biotechnology players. Together they got BGH milk on the market with no consumer labeling. The public didn't even hear about BGH until a couple of reporters for a Fox affiliate in Tampa Bay got fired when they wrote a story about it. Earlier, when he'd organized in Washington, D.C., a strategy session for a small invited group interested in fighting BGH, he got a call from a woman who said she was with the Maryland Citizens Consumer Council and was a mother concerned for her kids. Later he found she'd given a fake name and actually worked for the PR firm Burson-Marsteller. One of its major clients was Monsanto, for whom it had instituted a major lobbying campaign under the auspices of the Animal Health Institute, essentially an animal-drug lobby. When Stauber mentioned the planted "concerned mom" to someone in the media, he was told, "This is what big PR firms serving corporations do. They infiltrate, they spy, they smear. This is part of the services they offer." After he found that a PR firm called "Direct Impact" was owned by Burson-Marsteller and had pulled a dirty-tricks operation in New York City at a meeting of dairy farmers, he decided to start the Center for Media and Democracy.

BGH led Stauber to BSE. Around 1990, Stauber had gotten a call from a retired vet in Iowa who'd made the connection. Stauber had thought that because Monsanto was using synthetic BGH, instead of collecting it in the usual way from the pituitaries of dead cows, mad cow disease was not relevant to Monsanto's drug. "You don't understand," the vet said. "If you're injecting cows with a drug this powerful, you have to feed them more fat and protein or the cows will take sick, and where does that fat and protein come from?"

"Cows?" John asked.

"Exactly," the vet answered. The use of BGH intensifies the "normal" feeding of rendered cows to cows. Stauber learned that the USDA had begun feeding slaughterhouse waste to cattle as a fat and protein supplement in a big way in the 1980s and had increased the volume every year since. The biggest surprise was a USDA internal memo he came across that said: "If we don't stop this practice of feeding cows to cows, BSE could emerge in the United States." Through the Freedom of Information Act, he found a 1991 USDA document that stated: "With BSE there are two issues where agriculture is vulnerable to media scrutiny. These are the practices of feeding rendered ruminant products to ruminants and risks to human health." What they were worried about was not human health but media scrutiny, how to spin it correctly.

For years Stauber had protested feeding cattle their own waste blood because scientists had long known that blood might transmit mad cow disease. Dr. Prusiner had warned that the American practice of weaning calves on milk replacer containing cattle blood was "a really stupid idea." The United Kingdom had already reported that two people had been stricken with vCJD after receiving blood transfusions. The United Kingdom decided to ban donations from anyone who'd had transfusions since 1980, since they feared that humans with CJD might have contaminated the British blood supply. The United States finally banned Americans from donating blood if they had lived in the United Kingdom during the 1980s or 1990s, but our government has yet to take the simple steps of testing every animal and implementing "a total ban on feeding slaughterhouse waste back to livestock," Stauber says. "The public think they've implemented these steps because the USDA says they have, and that's a lie." Most people outside the animal feed industry, he believes, including USDA vets and officials, are wholly unaware of the massive feeding of cattle to cattle still going on in the United States. In 1990 the National Renderers Association (NRA) admitted the feeding was going on, but said, "What's the big deal?"

"The big deal," John says, "is that now that indigenous cases have appeared in the States, that means we've had mad cow disease in North America for at least a decade."

One of the problems with mad cow is that it belongs to a family called TSE disease, and when you feed slaughterhouse waste back to livestock, you amplify and spread strains that might otherwise have existed only rarely through an entire species. John was a friend of that same Dr. Richard Marsh who'd investigated TSE in Wisconsin mink in 1985. "Every time TSE spreads into a new species," John learned, "you have at least one new strain created, and where it goes, nobody knows." Even after Dr. Prusiner had warned that TSE was a "rogue infectious agent" that could cross species, "We're still feeding pigs to pigs and pigs to cattle and cattle to pigs," John says. "We're weaning calves on cattle blood because it's cheap." He talked of the dangers of chronic wasting disease (CWD) when government agencies that were involved in managing wild deer-and-game farms promoted the use of "supplemental protein pellets" (slaughterhouse waste) so that deer and elk would grow bigger antlers for hunters. CWD is an especially frightening strain to John because it transmits even through saliva. "The nightmare would be CWD spreading to people in a science fiction scenario — a fatal dementia disease with an invisible incubation period spread merely through saliva contact."

As John puts it, "The rendering industry is where the livestock industry and the feedlot industry and the poultry-feed industry all come together." At the end of the day, all those fragmented parts that make up the disassembly line reconnect in the humungous disposals where millions of pounds of animal bone, blood, organs, and tissue are dumped, ground, cooked, and disgorged into a river of sludge that is dried and formed into pellets. But because prions cannot be destroyed by normal heating or freezing or bombarding with X-rays, experimenters have come up with "tissue digestors," in which whole carcasses of diseased animals can be dissolved in lye vats heated to 300 degrees in a process called "alkaline hydrolysis," patented by Waste Reduction Inc. and guaranteed to "liquefy a 1,500-pound cow in six to eight hours." Disgorged from the digestor is a liquid and a residue powder that can be used as fertilizer, but the ideal use would be biomass fuel in a power plant, or so says the company. In England such waste is now burned with fossil fuels to make portland cement. Since a large U.S. meatpacking plant produces 500,000 pounds a day of "risky" waste materials no longer allowed in the food supply, Waste Reduction Inc. proposes creating digestors that would hold 40,000 pounds at a time. Already the U.S. rendering industry produces annually 6.2 billion pounds of meat and bone meal. That's 6 billion out of the 50 billion pounds of total products that the meatpacking industry processes annually, which they boast would fill "a convoy of semi trucks, four lanes wide, running from New York to Los Angeles every year."

"There's so much about prions that we don't know," John says. Scientists now believe that normal proteins sometimes spontaneously misfold and become prions, which produces "a cascading effect" to transform other proteins into prions, as in "spontaneous" CJD. "Yet the government says, 'Wait and see,' instead of forcing the livestock industry to stop risking animal and human health in the name of cheap feed." Even if animal components are removed from feed, agriculture has to be vigilant against new cases because of the long incubation period of prion diseases. "The government keeps fooling the public into believing they've taken the correct steps, but they haven't." There are nearly seven hundred products that have waste cattle parts in them, and more than half of those use cattle protein, Stauber explains, everything from lipstick to drugs. "All my life I thought that when there was a problem, people would want to know about it," Dr. Marsh had told John. "When I realized that in the United States cattle were being fed to cattle, I thought that industry would want me to speak out and warn them. I thought government would want to stop this dangerous practice. I've been very conservative all my life. What I found out was that I was very stupid and naïve." "What I do now," says Stauber, "is investigate why the public is so propagandized."

"WHO'S RESPONSIBLE FOR the new fear of eating?" Paul Krugman asked in a May 21, 2007, editorial in the *New York Times*. Along with the usual suspects — globalization, food corporations, Bush government know-nothings — he named Milton Friedman, who'd called for the abolition of the FDA. Friedman was the model for "'*E. coli* conservatives': ideologues who won't accept even the most compelling case for government regulation." Fear of big government — not of big business — feeds the ideology and mythology of both cattle ranchers and corporate processors, herding them into an unlikely partnership at the expense of those who merely eat the meat. Beneath all the economic rationalizations and defensive posturing of both groups is a deep-seated fear that the rugged individual, maybe even America itself, is no longer in control of his destiny. Mad cow disease got attention because it fed the fear of an alien presence, a threat from outer space. *E. coli*, on the other hand, which many environmental activists fear most, is such a widespread, everyday variety of pathogen that it's easier to ignore or laugh off since it's not inevitably fatal. It's more like the disease next door.

In March 2005 the USDA announced a drop in the number of beef samples that had tested positive for *E. coli*. But watchdog organizations such as STOP (Safe Tables Our Priority) pointed out the flaws in the USDA system that did not test for *E. coli* in ground beef in a way that would protect consumers. As biostatistician and STOP board member Barbara Kowalcyk noted, "If you don't look for something, you're not likely to find it." STOP is a nonprofit grassroots organization founded in 1993 after Jack in the Box hamburgers caused 600 reported illnesses and the deaths of four children. Their grieving parents, including Kowalcyk, came together for solace and information and formed the new group, which declared that the USDA and the meat industry were "like the Wizard of Oz telling Dorothy to pay no attention to what she saw behind the curtain." Just four years after the Jack in the Box deaths, *E. coli* in hamburger patties destined for Burger King caused the largest meat recall in U.S. history: 25 million pounds of ground beef from Hudson Foods in Columbus, Nebraska. "There's always somebody out there trying to downgrade the meat industry," grumbled Dale Collinsworth of the Columbus Area Chamber of Commerce. "I'm sure the people — veggies, is what they call them — I bet they're rejoicing right now." Ten years later, in June 2007, the United Food Group in Vernon, California, had to recall 5.7 million pounds of ground beef for *E. coli* contamination after illnesses were reported in six Western states. On February 17, 2008, a new record was set in the recall of 143 million pounds of ground beef, destined for school lunch programs and processed at Hallmark/Westland Meat Packing Co., in Chino, California, after videotape by the Humane Society documented animal abuse by slaughterhouse workers who were forcing downers to walk so they wouldn't be tested as downers. The recalls don't stop because *E. coli* doesn't.

It wasn't until 1994, a year after Jack in the Box, that the USDA was given the power to recall a product contaminated with *E. coli* if the company did not do so voluntarily. (This power has *still* not been given to any agency over food contaminated with salmonella.) The fact that nobody is in charge of safeguarding the health of the human population of America is simply not credible to most Americans, who remain blissfully unaware of the history of our government agencies.

The USDA was founded in 1862, not to protect consumers, but to promote agriculture, including the production of meat. America was still a farming nation, rather than a society of consumers, and it was natural to fund a government department designed to help farmers produce. Land-grant colleges were founded the same year in the Morill Land-Grant College Act and for the same purpose: to help farmers produce more and to get consumers to eat more. Until this time, individual states had been in charge of any safety problems relating to food, usually some form of food adulteration, and of enacting their own laws against food fraud. Increasingly, as chemical preservatives became dangerous adulterants, citizen "poison squad" volunteers were unable to keep up with "testing" suspect foods by sampling them. In 1906 the Federal Food and Drugs Act was passed to add some regulatory powers to the USDA's Division of Chemistry. The act applied to medical equipment, animal feed, and human food products, with the exception of meat and poultry. The latter were assumed to be already regulated by the 1890 Meat Inspection Act under the USDA, intended to help trade by inspecting animals for export and quarantining imported animals as needed. In 1940 the FDA was moved to the Federal Security Agency and eventually to the Department of Health and Human Services. How the government ranks health and human services is evident in the amount of money allotted to each agency. The FDA, which monitors 80 percent of our food supply, is slotted in 2008 for an annual budget of $1.7 billion; whereas the USDA, which monitors only the remaining 20 percent, is slotted for $17 billion. The byzantine relation between the two agencies is best illustrated by the absurd bifurcation of a hamburger and its bun: The USDA is supposed to cover the meat and the FDA the bread and condiments, but in reality the eater alone is responsible for the safety of the meat he eats because it is up to him to kill any germs that are in it by overcooking it to 155 degrees.

WHAT PRICE CHEAP meat? According to the GAO, the government spends $1.7 billion on food safety annually, but the annual cost of food-borne illnesses is $7 billion. While *E. coli* and mad cow might suggest some urgency in establishing a single federal food-safety department, the beef industry strongly opposes it for the usual reasons. Dan Murphy of the American Meat Institute scoffs at the notion that the cure for government incompetence is more government, a scoffery given teeth by the heckuva job FEMA did on New Orleans after Hurricane Katrina. In 2005 the GAO investigators reported that FDA practices continued to "place U.S. cattle at risk of spreading BSE."

But safer meat costs more. Even after the 1993 *E. coli* outbreak, the industry strongly resisted the HACCP system of meat inspection the government finally instituted in 1998. Instead of visual inspection, HACCP required microbial testing of the finished meat product in spot checks; further, the USDA could now close a plant if its products exceeded allowable salmonella limits. Industry responded quickly. By December 2001, the Fifth Circuit Court of Appeals ruled in favor of Supreme Beef Processors Inc., after it brought suit against the USDA for closing its plant. The company, which had supplied thousands of pounds of ground beef to the public-school system in Texas, had failed the salmonella test three times in eight months. The Appeals Court decided that the presence of salmonella could not serve as an index for other pathogens and that salmonella alone could not render a product "injurious to health." The meat packers had defanged USDA's inspection power in a single stroke, which Senator Harkin noted when he remarked that "the food-safety reforms USDA enacted in 1996 are on life support."

In 2007 the USDA came up with the bright idea of overhauling the entire inspection system, in order to initiate a "risk-based" inspection that would increase inspections for plants with a history of unsafe practices and decrease inspections for plants without. Under Secretary of Agriculture Richard Raymond assured the media that these changes were not "money-driven," but motivated by the desire to reduce food poisoning, which affects 76 million Americans each year, 5,000 of them fatally.

The USDA's jurisdiction, however, has never extended beyond the slaughterhouse to the farm or the feedlot, even though runoff from feedlot manure can get into the water system irrigating lettuce fields nearby, with the danger that those good green leaves will suck up what's in the water and in the soil and carry *E. coli* to vegetarians. Nutrition expert Marion Nestle called the September 2006 outbreak of *E. coli* in the spinach fields of California's Salinas Valley "entirely predictable," saying that it once again "reflects the huge gaps in the nation's century-old and highly dysfunctional food safety system." Neither pasteurization nor irradiation is a reasonable response to the ludicrous breakdown of our industrial food system over something as vulgarly natural as cow shit. To de-euphemize an oft-quoted phrase, "Sterilized shit is still shit."

Ironically, the widespread problem of *E. coli* as a powerful new microbe was created by the intense feeding of corn to cattle. And it can be mitigated by feeding them something else. According to the research of microbiologist James Russell at Cornell University, a diet of too much grain and too little fiber has altered "the ruminal ecosystem" of feedlot cattle. When fed corn, the rumen becomes more acidic in order to digest the grain, and this is exactly the environment that *E. coli* bacteria likes. When the rumen contains grass rather than grain, the bacteria cannot multiply because the ruminal ecosystem is not acidic enough. Dr. Russell advocates simple procedures like adding sodium carbonate and alkali to manure and feeding cattle on hay for a few days before slaughter, which can produce an up to 80 percent drop in *E. coli*. But the industry is as addicted to drugs as it is to corn. In 2007 the FDA reported that it was almost compelled to approve the new antibiotic cefquinome, even though its superpotency might produce resistant strains of a bacterium that causes anthrax and severe diarrhea in humans. Compelled how? By its new "guidance document," which, as a *Washington Post* reporter said, "is more deferential to pharmaceutical companies than is recommended by the World Health Organization." An industry-funded epidemiologist said in rebuttal, "Until you show us a direct link to human mortality from the use of these drugs in animals, we don't think you should preclude their use."

Human intervention is the cornerstone of an industry built on a belief in man's superiority to anything animal or natural. But now that "natural" has become a consumer buzzword, the industry would do well to watch its language, Dan Murphy advises, when he urges leaders to substitute the term "managed production" for "factory farming." Regrettably, factory farming has come to have negative connotations, he says. If only national breeders, feeders, packers, and processors would switch terms, they could convey the message that managed production is like parents caring for their children. "Would any parents concerned about their children's welfare allow them to roam at large? . . . Of course not. We keep our kids indoors, under supervision, living in housing that's temperature controlled and subject to meaningful restrictions on when and where and for how long they can stay outdoors. . . . Does the 'lifestyle' of those animals differ so radically from the day-to-day controls we vigorously impose on our children?"

Meantime, who's watching the stove? The alarums that mad cow disease set off in 2005 were repeated in the shock of polluted pet food from China in 2007. Both problems dramatized the conjugal union of politics and business in providing human and animal food. In their rush to industrialize, China's producers of animal and fish feed had for years been bulking it up with the additive melamine, an inexpensive by-product created by heating coal in enormous vats. "It just saves money if you add melamine scrap," said one manager of an animal-feed factory in Zhangqiu. With fewer U.S. port inspectors than ever before, according to Caroline Smith DeWaal of the Center for Science in the Public Interest, "This open-door policy on food ingredients is an open invitation for an attack on the food supply, either intentional or unintentional."

But despite a rash of scandals over imported animal and human food from China, critics such as Public Citizens' Global Trade Watch have pointed out that the trade problem isn't specific to China, but stems from a model that puts the volume of traded goods over safety. Since the expansion of NAFTA and CAFTA, the value of imported food had doubled to reach $65 billion in 2006. Seafood imports had increased 65 percent. The year before, in 2005, the United States, for the first time in its history, had become a net food importer with a deficit of $370 million.

Contrary to what most Americans believe, the vast majority of imported foods are unexamined and untested. In 2007 the USDA tested only 6 percent of imported foodstuffs of all kinds, including animal feed. Only 11 percent of beef, pork, and chicken is inspected at the border by the USDA. The FDA estimates that pesticide residues on imported foods is triple that of domestic foods, yet trade agreements with foreign countries specify that we rely on foreign rules and inspections for food safety. A new FDA proposal would include "equivalence determination" to permit imports of meat and poultry that do not meet U.S. standards, but can be imported anyway if they meet the standards of the exporting country. The fact that 14 percent of beef consumed in the United States is imported and that 80 percent of that beef goes into hamburger should tell consumers something they don't want to know about the safety of mass-produced ground beef.

For all these reasons, it has long been clear that we need a national animal identification system (NAIS) in order to track animals quickly after a pathogenic outbreak. Yet every food industry in the country dragged its heels over the COOL labeling requirements in the 2002 Farm Bill, which were supposed to become mandatory in late 2004. The USDA beat a rapid retreat, opting for voluntary testing until that second mad cow was discovered and it was forced to respond. Animal identification was now supposed to become mandatory by the beginning of 2008, and would involve registering premises, tagging individual animals, and tracing animal movement. Of course this was harder with cows than with other kinds of livestock because there were so many different kinds of premises scattered here and there across the borders. Who was going to pay for all this registration, and who would have access to the data once it was gleaned? Small ranchers and processors squawked that they'd be put out of business. Large ones squawked about their bottom lines. Everyone squawked about private property, and how what you did with it was supposed to be nobody's business but your own.

In a complete about-face, Johanns announced that the USDA would allow private industry to build and maintain the NAIS database, which the NCBA had been pushing for all along, ostensibly to keep control of the data. But privatizing was really simply one more delaying tactic, as if it was reasonable to tell an industry that for more than a century had gotten together on nothing to get together now and figure it out. By October 2005 only 126,800 premises had been registered, or 6 percent of the 2.2 million premises nationwide involving livestock. "It's like a rodeo out there right now," said an industry source. "All these feedyards have different programs with different paperwork they want producers to sign." Few in Congress complained, but the reliable exception was Senator Harkin, who said in November, "After two years of discussions, USDA has no clear plan for moving forward with a workable system. Producers are getting upset that they still don't know how much the system will cost them and who will run it."

A year later, *Beef* magazine announced that NAIS was "road-kill on history's highway." As the syndicated agricultural journalist Alan Guebert put it in his "Farm and Food File," "The silver bullet used by agbiz and their livestock allies to cripple COOL was — and remains — money." The winners were "the meat packers and confinement operations, who will not have to do individual identification and tracking," announced the *Grassfed Gazette*. "The NAIS is more about marketing than it is about animal health. Foreign markets seek trace-back for consumer confidence." The *Gazette* suggested that a better way to produce consumer confidence was through a direct relation between farmer and consumer and not by increased taxes for the consumer in order to fund "a larger government bureaucracy."

The 2007 Farm Bill includes a measure aimed to enforce the five-year-old labeling law that was passed but never implemented. The new rule applied to beef was supposed to establish three types of labels by the end of 2008. Only cattle born, raised, and slaughtered in the United States could earn a domestic label. Mixed-origin products, as in a Mexican-born cow slaughtered and processed in the United States, would list both countries. Ground-meat products would list all the countries the meat "could be" from. AMI warned producer groups that meat packers would soon be issuing their own directives on what they'd require in the way of affidavits with each load of livestock purchased. Beef producers complained that they were stuck with the burden and the cost of all this paperwork, noting that the vast majority of imported beef went to restaurants, which were in any case exempt from COOL regulation. Everyone wanted to shift the burden of COOL labeling to retailers. The only supporters of the labeling law were producers like R-CALF from Great Plains states, who felt they would benefit from a "Made in America" label. They complained that the current USDA inspection label implied to a consumer that this was a U.S. product, although in 2006 it enabled meat packers to import 3 billion pounds of "a cheaper product and sell it under the reputation of the U.S. cattle industry." Opponents to labeling, like the AMI and NCBA, cried "protectionism," but that was mere distraction from their masterful maneuverings within the corridors of power. Republican Senator Henry Bonilla from Texas, who received hefty campaign funds from the livestock industry, pushed through a bill that prohibited the Department of Agriculture from spending a cent on COOL labeling. If consumers had wanted it, they would have demanded it, he said. A few more poisonings from pet food and fish from China, a few more outbreaks of Asian flu in poultry and swine fever in hogs in China, and maybe they will.

IN HIS *Golden Arches: East,* Harvard's cultural anthropologist James L. Watson uses the Big Mac as an icon of the good and the bad of globalization, and the bad raises the possibility that "in the future, eating a hamburger will be comparable in risk to eating a puffer fish." A few more outbreaks of mad cow ("which is inevitable," Watson says) will demonstrate that industrializing meat production "has ransacked biodiversity, making livestock far more susceptible to disease and various other kinds of problems than ever." Whether you chomp down on your Big Global

Mac in Beijing, Paris, or Dubai, issues of food safety, trade, energy, and power now salt and pepper every bite.

Icons in collision. Today the cowboy of rugged independence collides with the golden arch of total interdependence. What they have in common is Big Global Oil. During the last century, the American myth of endless land was displaced by the myth of endless oil. Drawing the earth's blood, as Basil Geloke and Ray McCormack call it in their 2006 documentary *A Crude Awakening,* had given industrial America its power over the rest of the world. In this country, oil had been so cheap it felt free, and we used it freely to build the transport that built the cities that built the trade that erected the World Trade Towers in New York. Without a moment's hesitation, we fueled our dreams and our skyscrapers with this nonrenewable resource that had taken millions of years to form deep underground, and which we were able to deplete in a single century because we made everything dependent on it. Cheap oil created cheap fertilizer which created cheap corn which created cheap beef. The equation was simple in the extreme, however complex the consequences.

Michael Pollan, our grand expositor of the oil-corn-beef connection, has said, "When you eat meat, you're eating oil." Well, when you eat beef, you're *guzzling* oil. If it takes half a gallon of gasoline to produce a bushel of corn, and if a steer has to eat 25 pounds of corn a day (or around half a bushel) to gain a slaughter weight of 1200 pounds, then that steer will have consumed 35 gallons of oil. Instead of using leaves of grass to harness the sun's energy through photosynthesis without our having to lift a finger, we chose to plow the grass under and spread the earth with cheap petroleum products to grow seeds, not leaves, and to get more and more energy through more and more seeds per plant. That's called increasing yield. Nature gave us a lawn of prairie grass, but we saw it as wilderness because we hadn't planted it. "Corn," Pollan says, "is like this second great American lawn." Because taxpayer money subsidizes this lawn, we also subsidize unintentional corn by-products like obesity from cheap corn sugar, microbes that require drugs, diseases that we can't control. Meanwhile, the lawn controls us by demanding we tend it until we become, as Pollan says, "dupes of our lawns."

The name of the corn game in this century has been "too much is never enough." Quantity was the only goal of the hybrid corn revolution that in the first half of the twentieth century produced the world's first fully industrialized plant, and in the second half the world's first almost fully industrialized animals. We've been "passing half of the corn crop in America through the guts of animals," Pollan says, and through cheap feed have been subsidizing all the big boys in the livestock industry. Cheap feed was an even larger windfall for poultry and pigs. Alan Guebert cites a recent study at Tufts University that shows livestock "feed prices were an estimated 21 percent below production costs for poultry and 26 percent below costs for the hog industry," which brought Tyson, ConAgra, and Smithfield savings of $19.75 billion and allowed them to integrate ever more closely. The economic logic of the "cattle cycle" is based entirely on corn so cheap that it costs less for the beef industry to buy it than for the farmer to grow it. When corn sold for around $2.25 a bushel, it cost around $3 a bushel to grow, but taxpayer subsidies made up the difference. Now the cycle is more like a cyclone, because suddenly corn that was selling for $2.11 a bushel in 2006 sold for $6.12 in May 2008.

Enter ethanol. With the ethanol explosion, corn planting is now the highest it's been since World War II, 25 percent of our cultivated acreage or 73.4 million acres, with projections of 152 bushels of corn per acre. In 2006 ethanol consumed 11 billion bushels, or 20 percent of the nation's corn crop; in the last two years, we've built 31 new ethanol plants and 78 are under construction for 2009. For the first time in sixty-three years, corn is in such demand that packers will be forced to produce 1 billion less pounds of meat in 2007 and Americans will eat 1.7 pounds less per person because they will have to pay more for it. Even so, taxpayers are now subsidizing ethanol through government tax benefits for new refineries to the tune of $7 billion a year. "I think when the consumer figures out that they pay for [ethanol] three times, it might not be so popular," said a Texas cattle feeder for Friona Industries. "They pay for it when they pay their taxes, they pay for it at the pump (with reduced performance and lower gas mileage), and they pay for it again at the grocery store."

Presently, farmers are paid a subsidy of $48 an acre not to raise corn, but the skyrocketing prices that ethanol has brought may tempt farmers to plant anew. Anyone can do the math. It takes one ton of corn kernels to yield 100 gallons of ethanol. It takes 1.5 gallons of ethanol to equal the energy of 1 gallon of gasoline. U.S. gasoline consumption in 2005 was 140 billion gallons. How many tons of corn kernels are required to furnish the equivalent of 140 billion gallons of gas? It's 2.1 *billion* tons, in a new gold rush that pits big packers like Tyson against big grain merchants like ADM. Currently ADM is the biggest ethanol producer, with over one billion gallons per year, and projected earnings in 2007 of $1.3 billion from ethanol alone. Some companies like Cargill are both packers and grain merchants, but Cargill has announced that it intends to increase its ethanol output of 120 million gallons to 7.5 billion gallons by 2012 and five times that amount by 2022. When oil was $70 a barrel, an ethanol plant could earn a profit of $5 a bushel for corn that it bought for $2. But despite shrinking profits in the ethanol industry due to rising corn prices, the NCBA, which has long lobbied for maintaining farm subsidies for corn, suddenly finds itself arguing that subsidies for ethanol are unfair.

No matter how many acres in the United States are planted with corn, the era of cheap corn from cheap oil is over, since oil itself, consumed in ever greater quantities by industrializing countries like China and India, will become ever more expensive. The cattle industry, which has largely ignored environmental consequences in favor of economic laws of supply and demand, is now forced to take note of an ever-expanding "sphere of influence" as oil prices rise. The situation in Iran affects the price of cattle in Omaha just as much as rain or drought or the cyclic size of the national herd. The hue and cry in the industry over the rise in corn prices through ethanol is a form of distraction from deeper fears. The more corn that goes into gas tanks, the less can go into cows' rumens. In 2007 our total of 124 ethanol refineries in the United States produced an average of 6.4 billion gallons a year, and the projection is that new refineries will double that amount by 2009. But even 12 billion gallons a year is scarcely a drop in the bucket to meet our current demand of 120 million barrels *a day,* if we compensate for the depletion of existing oil wells. More is never enough.

Green fuel is supposed to free us from the tyranny of foreign oil barons, but we're trapped in a high-tech fantasy of finding a cheap fuel substitute. Tyson is said to be exploring fat fuel, diesel made from animal fat. There's talk of converting the methane gas of cow manure into bio-diesel fuel, but critics warn that it would be just another way to subsidize agribusiness, producing only "brown power." Some may remember that in the 1930s Henry Ford experimented with producing car bodies from soybeans. That didn't catch on, but other bioplastics did. Entrepreneurs today are looking into glycerin as a substitute feed for cows at about half the price of corn. "Actually it's like feeding sugar to a cow," admits Monty Kerley, professor of "ruminant nutrition" at the University of Missouri–Columbia, and there are questions about how much glycerin a cow can process. While just plain grass for grass-fed beef is now moving full speed ahead — 60,000 grass-fed cattle were marketed in 2006, compared to 5000 in 2000 — that's still less than 1 percent of the nation's supply of beef, and if all our acreage is planted in corn, the cost of grass will also go sky high.

Our new range wars will be oil wars, some predict, since there are still some oil pockets in parts of the globe to be exploited, although at increasingly higher costs. There are also 6 billion people in the world to use it up. Although we in the United States use one-quarter of the world's oil, we are a small population of slightly more than 300 million people. Because we've done such a good job of extracting oil in this country, it seems that our production has peaked. Alternative energy sources like biomass, nuclear, hydrogen, wind, or solar will all have to be done on such a massive scale that they will be impossible to execute if cheap oil remains the dominant model in our heads.

But to change the model of oil, we would have to change the model of industrialism, and that would change our model of growth. We would have to change the model of who we are as humans in relation to the rest of the created world. We would have to think twice about destroying the two-fifths of the world's remaining rain forests in the Amazon with

50 million cattle. We would have to heed the warning that methane gas and nitrous oxide from livestock today produce more global-warming pollution than the carbon dioxide emitted by all transportation vehicles combined — cars, trucks, buses, and planes. We would have to question whether it's a good thing that global meat production is supposed to double from 229 million tons in 2000 to 465 million tons in 2050. We would have to start thinking about relationships instead of objects, synergies instead of commodities, fellow creatures — vegetable, mineral, animal — instead of machines.

Writing about the "unintended consequences of technological progress," George F. Will quotes the Federal Bureau of Soils in 1878: "The soil is the one indestructible, immutable asset that the nation possesses. It is the one resource that cannot be exhausted." He reminds us that in the 1920s a number of wet years led people to expect that the nation's climate had changed for the better and would continue forever. In 1931 the corn harvest that had replaced prairie grass totaled 250 million bushels and was hailed as a technological marvel. In 1932 — just one year later — the dust storms that would create the Great American Dust Bowl showed Americans "how an inch of topsoil produced over millennia could be blown away in an hour." Both soil and oil are variations on the ongoing theme of unintended consequences that shadows America's vision of riding point for progress into a limitless horizon.

For a new people in a new land, freed of Old World broodings over nature's implacability and man's tragic fall from grace into corruption, the myth of progress in an age of reason blinded a population hell-bent on the future. We believed in the first principle of capital: that it was destined to grow. Growth is what money was for, to breed more of it. Corporations existed for the sole purpose of growing money for stockholders. That was one of those self-evident truths of the property-owning class, Marjorie Kelly writes in "The Stockholder Myth," but in making the transition from monarchy to democracy we got only as far as a political democracy, not an economic one. Our colonies were founded by farmers who believed in the sanctity of property and of private enterprise, but as the corporation evolved it became, as Franklin D. Roosevelt said seventy years ago, "a kind of private government which is a power unto itself." Instead of private kingdoms owned by kings, Kelly states, we now have private empires ruled by CEOs, with revenues larger than nation-states and with the power to direct those states.

At the beginning of the twenty-first century, many voices are beginning to question the myths that our parents and grandparents and their grandparents lived by. "Our prevailing economic mythology prompts us to believe that *growth forever* is the only avenue to economic health and well-being," writes Fred Kirschenmann. "This is not an eternal truth but an intellectual construct that needs to be changed because our global ecosystem is limited and continued growth is untenable." He quotes Bill McKibben, in *Deep Economy:* "Growth no longer makes most people wealthier, but instead generates inequality and insecurity. Growth is bumping up against physical limits so profound — like climate change and peak oil — that trying to keep expanding the economy may not just be impossible but also dangerous. And perhaps most surprisingly, growth no longer makes us happy." The myth of growth forever — the myth that unlimited growth is an unmitigated good — has propelled us for four hundred years. But in 1972, a think tank of scientists, economists, businessmen, and politicians from five continents got together in Rome at the behest of a businessman, Aurelio Peccei. As a kind of technological Buffalo Commons, they became the Club of Rome and designed a computer model to predict the consequences of population growth. The result was *The Limits to Growth,* which challenged the "grow or die" maxim of capitalist economics, with its faith-based premise that the earth and its resources are infinite. The Club had argued that while modern Western society has to change its "exploitative attitude toward humans and the earth itself," our market system is designed to perpetuate it.

In 1992 the group reconvened to update their work in *Beyond the Limits: Confronting Global Collapse, Envisioning a Sustainable Future.* What had happened in the intervening twenty years was not quite the economic collapse they'd predicted, but a speeding up of unsustainable practices and a narrowing of choices. They warned that poverty will not be ended by "indefinite material growth," that "the material human economy" must contract, despite the fact that our "whole culture has evolved around the principle of fighting against limits rather than learning to live with them." They warned that our faith in technology continues to divert us from a problem that doesn't have a technological solution: the premise of growth in a system that is finite. The world's exponential growth since 1900 is not a law of nature but a narrative of overgrowth and collapse as resources dissipate in erosion, pollution, and depletion. Instead of invoking the logic of efficiency, we should be praising the logic of sufficiency, as ecological-economist Thomas Princen wrote in *The Logic of Sufficiency* — "seeking enough when more is possible." Instead of more, enough. Instead of sky's the limit, earth's the limit. Instead of develop, restore.

We need a change of heart — and of metaphor. The word "growth" comes from the organic world of cycling and recycling, birth and decay. Despite Einstein's and later physicists' revelations about the universe, as a culture we continue to see the world as a machine, that mechanical deistic universe of unchanging Natural Laws that our eighteenth-century ancestors saw, and that continues to supply us with mechanical metaphors that counter everything meant by growth.

But change is in the wind, and perhaps new scientific research into the heart of life, the gene, will further it. The $73.5 billion biotech industry is based on the mechanistic presumption that "genes operate independently of each other: 'one gene, one protein,'" as Denise Caruso writes in the *New York Times*. She uses a mechanical metaphor to explain how this presumption works: "Proteins are the cogs and the motors that drive the function of cells and, ultimately, organisms," on the premise that each gene carries the information needed to construct one protein. But many scientists now say that genes operate not one on one but in a "complex network," and it's this network that is essential. What happens now to intellectual-property laws that are based entirely on the mechanistic principle of "the industrial gene," 4000 of which have been patented in the United States alone? Genetic engineering and the patents that go with it are defined "in terms of genes acting independently."

What if they don't? What if "the genetic material responsible for conferring antibiotic resistance moves easily between different species of bacteria," which makes inevitable the evolution of supergerms? What if the genetic material of men and animals is so organically interelated that pathogens like prions can move easily between species? What if we've been looking at the universe darkly, through spectacles so myopic we could see only one gene at a time?

◆ Beef: It's What's for Dinner ◆

"Preparing Supper at Roundup Time on the Northern Plains" was based on a photograph by C. D. Kirkland and appeared in *Frank Leslie's Illustrated Newspaper* on November 3, 1888. The typical cattle-trail chuck wagon stored medicines, bedrolls, and bullets, as well as provisions for cooking over an open fire. But few campfire grounds, one imagines, were spread with tablecloth and tableware.

Now, killin' folks and cookin' ain't so very far apart.

— Glen Ohrlin, cowboy poet-singer

◆

IT'S NOT JUST ABOUT THE BEEF, but about the ritual. It's not just a stroll to the Upper East Side of Manhattan, but way across the East River into the unknown wilderness of Williamsburg, Brooklyn, and you have to ride something to get there. You wish it were a horse. A horse and carriage would suit its beginnings in 1887 within sniffing distance of the river, six years before the Williamsburg Bridge was built, when the area was still a bustling waterfront of breweries and warehouses, shipyards and sugar refineries. It was crowded with Irish, Austrian, and German immigrants, among them Carl Luger, who hedged his bets on the food angle by calling it Carl Luger's Café, Billiards and Bowling Alley. It was just as well, since the neighborhood declined once the bridge was built, the rich burghers crossing over to Manhattan and leaving behind working-class slums and tenements. In 1950 Sol Forman, who ate steak at least once and often twice a day at the café, because it was across the street from his factory for stamping metal giftware, bought the place at auction so that he could continue his diet until his death at ninety-eight in 2001.

Whatever he may have done to the myth that steak is bad for you, Sol certainly furthered the mythos of the American steakhouse, which was founded in market centers where cattle were turned into meat. Thomas De Voe, writing in 1862, numbered 1200 butchers "both of the olden and modern times" in the many meat markets of the city and described the driving of cattle to market as a processional: "About 60 carts, accompanied with music, and flags and streamers, conveyed through the streets the 32 head of cattle fattened by Philip Fink of the Washington Market." However secular its format, the modern steakhouse bears vestiges of this ceremony of celebration. It gives meaning to the same animal sacrifice that our most ancient ancestors commemorated by offering the best parts to the gods. In Ulysses' day, the "best" was the fattiest piece of the slain ox, offered up hot and smoking on the altar. Nowadays a chef will slice off and discard the extra fat from the slab of meat he throws on the hot and smoking grill, because now it's trimmed meat that is deemed "best." But it's still an offering, and the scented smoke of its grilling is still meant to tempt whatever gods there be to a feast that echoes, however faintly, all that is heroic, primordial, carnal, and carnivorous in man's eternal urge for blood. "We're all basically animals," Sol is quoted as saying. "We want to eat meat." And in this country, we want to eat beef. Not just any beef, we want to eat steak, because steak for all of us immigrants means America. From the middle of the nineteenth century onward, steak was not only the commonest meal in America, it also represented every man's right to have the best. And while the Great American Steakhouse may have grown out of the inns and taverns and bars of early-nineteenth-century market cities, it was a late-nineteenth-century phenomenon celebrating what was already lost to the new industrialism, a vision of a gutsier time when every man had a right to claim the best, in a wilderness where men were men and meat was red as blood.

In New York City an annual beefsteak orgy had been staged for decades by butchers in a tavern at Shannon's Corner on Catherine Street to reward their favorite sea-captain customers. But by the 1880s and '90s men's eating and drinking clubs allowed newly enriched merchants and Wall Street tycoons to play red-neck primitives at the beefsteak feasts with which this book began, staged in halls made to look like old-time taverns. Just as cowboys anticipated letting go at the end of the cattle drive in an orgy of booze and gals in railroad-town bars, so urban herders of the money market looked forward to letting go at the end of the Wall Street week. The steakhouse is about letting go, about eating and drinking too much, about the joys of carnival excess. The romance of the steakhouse, like the romance of the cowboy, is rooted in a deep American nostalgia for male rituals, the more primitive the better.

When you enter Peter Luger's (Carl's heir Peter, who died in 1941, renamed the restaurant after himself), you walk into a bar — a long wooden bar under bare wooden beams next to a room with bare wooden tables and bench booths and brass chandeliers. You don't ask for a glass of house red or a wine list. You ask for a martini straight up. Or beer — pint or pitcher. The ceilings are tin, the floors strewn with sawdust. You don't ask for a menu, and you don't expect the waiter to introduce himself by name and tell you his life story. The waiters have been here for decades and scorn such guff. The entire ritual was set a century before you walked in the door, and thank god Sol Forman didn't change a thing. Men in shirtsleeves, women in housedresses, huge families packed with fat kids yelling loudly as they tuck in. You relax. You feel good, privileged, king of the fort. Everything is big: the chewy onion rolls, the thick-sliced tomatoes and onions in the salad slathered with Luger's special steak sauce, the 1¾-inch porterhouse sliced and sizzling on a platter so hot it can cook, the sides of German fried potatoes and creamed spinach, the bowl of whipped cream next to the apple strudel or chocolate mousse or pecan pie. You are in for a Big Evening and you pay in cash. Joseph Mitchell in the 1939 *New Yorker* piece "All You Can Hold For Five Bucks" recounted a typical Peter Luger's conversation: "At a table near the kitchen door I heard a woman say to another, 'Here, don't be bashful. Have a steak.' 'I just et six,' her friend replied. The first woman said, 'Wasn't you hungry? Why, you eat like a bird.' Then they threw their heads back and laughed." One 2007 blogger just didn't get it. "The place is a barn," she wrote, complaining about the poor wine list, the lack of menu, the arrogant waiters. "I prefer a finer atmosphere." The American steakhouse was born for no other reason than to give "finer atmosphere" the finger.

The Luger's menu is bare-boned because you're there single-mindedly for steak, not for lamb or salmon, which got added as concessions to the weaker sex. Cowboys don't have choice; it's one gun or two. Here it's Steak for One, Two, Three, or Four, with "Steak for Two" the best cut because it's a bone-in porterhouse with a large filet, so you just double that for Four. The only real choice is rare or, for the hopelessly overurbanized, medium rare. If you want well-done, eat at home. Significantly, creamed spinach is the only green stuff, made tolerable by cream and butter. The potatoes are made tolerable by chopped bacon and onion. But nothing distracts from the platter of meat brought straight from the old Garland broilers set to 500 degrees that guarantee this is something you couldn't easily manage on your home stove or grill. The steakhouse is not meant to simulate home cooking or backyard barbecue. It's a communal feast celebrating superabundance and topsy-turvy, as in Roman Saturnalia or the medieval Land of Cockaigne, where nuns go bottoms up, servants beat their masters, the world flips upside down, and skies rain cheeses and pies and everything your animal gut desires.

What sets the steakhouse apart beyond all else is the quality of the beef, which you cannot buy in a supermarket but may in one of the few remaining butcher shops in cities as large as New York. Top steakhouses, along with upscale white-tablecloth restaurants, skim off the cream of beef stamped USDA Prime, which totals less than 2 percent of the beef market to begin with. Industrial beef cranks out Choice and Select. Within the Prime category, there are varying degrees of quality. Not only is it hard to get Prime beef of the highest quality, it's also hard to get beef that has been properly dry-aged. You need a temperature-controlled aging room for that, not to mention skill and knowledge. When you read stories about Peter Luger's, most of the story is about selecting the beef.

I meet Jody Spiera Storch, granddaughter of Sol, at Walmir Meat, Inc. at 839 Washington Street, in what remains of the old Gansevoort Meat Market. Jody is a vivacious pretty blue-eyed brunette, mother of two young children, not at all the person you'd expect to see poking at half carcasses hung on a rail above the cement loading deck of a meat wholesaler's. But the lady meat buyers of Luger's are a family tradition. It was

Sol's wife, Marsha, who took on the meat buying when Sol bought the restaurant, and it was Marsha who went to a retired government meat grader for instruction. "My grandmother used to bring me here from about age ten on non–school days," Jody said. "She was a really special lady, very regal, she'd come down here in a fur coat, pearls, and a fur hat." Jody dons a white butcher's coat and knit gloves while we talk with Ray DeStefano, a longtime Walmir's worker, who chimes in, "She'd come in her Cadillac, twenty-five years old and had 3000 miles on it."

Grandma Marsha established the matriarchal tradition followed by her daughter Marilyn Forman Spiera, Jody's mother, and now by Jody herself. Jody's father is a surgeon and all her siblings are doctors; they call Jody the Meat Doctor, despite the fact that she thought she wouldn't be able to stand the blood and gore, and in fact after her first visit went vegetarian for a month. She'd gone to Barnard and was set to go to law school, but got distracted by the family business, which turns out to suit her. "I don't like being in an office," she says. "I like being out here with the guys." There are a lot of guys to be out with, since Luger's buys around 10 tons of beef per week, using half a dozen suppliers, three in the Gansevoort Market and the rest at Hunts Point. The restaurant uses at least 600 short loins a week, she says, each serving eight to twelve diners. The short loin is the section just below the steer's bottom rib, about a foot and a half long, which is cut into two or three porterhouses, T-bones, and New York strip or shell sirloins.

"This used to be an old Armour building," Ray says, "Armour meats, Armour foods, used to bring the meat downstairs and we'd cut it up and ship it out. Used to be all meat places here, but money talks and bullshit walks, and now a guy spends $6 million for the building on the corner for a dress shop."

"This is much more fun than Hunts Point, this neighborhood," Jody says.

"The kind of guys that are down here are all fun," Ray says. "They joke around, somebody you'd want to take home. But everything is boxed now, there's not enough top quality to go around, that's why they box it to get rid of it." Jody gets the first selection, Ray adds. "She pays top dollar."

Jody pokes one of the hanging sides. "My grandmother used to call this 'Christmas cattle,' *real* Prime."

Finding real Prime, even when all the carcasses are stamped USDA Prime, turns out to be an exacting task. Jody goes beneath one of the carcasses to touch the exposed thirteenth rib with her finger. "See how silky this is? Good fat, good color." Beware of dark cutters, she warns. Sometimes she'll cut a thin slice off the surface to see if the color beneath will brighten when it's exposed to air, but if it doesn't, she rejects it. Some she rejects because the texture is "ropy" instead of silky or because there's so much outside fat on it that it's "wastey," for the fat will have to be discarded. She inspects the backbone; if the meat's been sliced away, it won't age properly, the flesh will deteriorate faster. The meat she selects she stamps twice with her grandmother's long-handled brass die, which marks "F4F" within a purple ovoid, the stamp of Forman's metal factory.

"The calves used to be very rich, very grainy, but now they rush them, they force-feed them, the grain is stringy, looks like valleys and crevasses, instead of pinpoint marbling," Ray says. "It's all speed feeding now. They've changed the rules on what it takes to be Prime, and it doesn't take that much today."

"In the yield grading we always liked 3s," Jody says. "We never even looked at 2s, but now we're forced to because there aren't enough." She exams a rib on a carcass. "This is a 2, looks very pretty, but I prefer more outside-fat cover because we age them with the kidney and kidney fat on it. The fat protects the meat during the aging period."

"See how the kidneys are bright red on this one?" Ray asks me. "When the kidneys are black, the quality could be there, but the meat isn't going to taste as good. The blood type is different." Jody has moved down the carcass line. "Oh, this is beautiful, silky, marbley — not ropy — heavy like velvet, tiny points of marbling, nice rosy color."

Ray points to another one. "This one's nice, but it's got a small eye."

"Looks a little Choicey to me," Jody tells him. "Not great. This one felt very gummy, rubbery, got a lot of bruises. See where it's yellow? The animal got kicked or something."

"They butt each other," Ray says. "They know they're going to die, so they butt to get out."

"You don't want to get involved with that," says Jody. Of the next one, she exclaims, "This is graded Prime, but my grandmother would roll over if she saw that. This is Prime *crime*."

We step inside Walmir's warehouse to look at the metal trees of short loins, hooked on a central spike like a coat hanger, hanging upside down. Each loin weighs around 45 pounds, Jody says, depending on the size of the kidney, which might weigh 12 to 15 pounds. At Luger's they render the kidney for fat, use some of it for cooking and for suet; the rest gets picked up. Luger's famed aging room, Jody says, is just "a long skinny room with fans blowing on it, nothing weird about temperature, humidity, no set rules. A lot depends on the meat. If it has a lot of thick, heavy marbling, it takes more time than meat with fine flecking. So when the meat comes in, we divide it into lot numbers, then keep logs on everything. Some lot might need an extra week. It's a family business, not a committee. If I see meat very ropy, I'll say, 'This needs a little more time.' A lot of people don't understand what meat should be. They think it should be soft, bland, but it should have a little texture to it."

Besides the quality of the meat, what sets the steakhouse apart from home cooking is the quantity of heat. Typically, steakhouse kitchens go for quick-searing in upright commercial broilers that use infrared or radiant heat. Infrared uses ceramic bricks and is hotter than radiant, but the bricks are more fragile than the cast-iron burners that radiant broilers use. BTUs for either broiler are in the range of 70,000 to 104,000 per deck, which generates a quick sear that can be followed by a finishing oven. Jody and Ray compare the best way to simulate the heat of restaurant grills on home broilers, which are rarely more than 25,000 BTUs tops. Jody suggests preheating the boiler for as long as half an hour, then putting the meat close to the flame, although that creates a real risk of fire. Ray's technique is to take some of the kidney fat, melt it down, brush it on the outside, and put the meat right up to the fire in a broiler pan. "I like it singed, nice and pink in the middle, all those juices locked in."

Ray's been making a living at Walmir's for forty years. His grandfather had a little butcher shop on Houston called DeStefano's, where he was a plumber and his grandmother was the butcher. "I used to have the smallest fingers in the family, so I stuffed the sausage," Ray says. Real butchering he learned in the Army in France, where he'd been sent after he got wounded in Korea.

His sergeant said, "Anybody know how to cut meat?"

"'Yeah, I know.' I didn't, but before you knew it, I took over the place, just for officers and their wives, and stayed there four years, in Orléans, near Paris."

He misses the old days of butchering in the Washington Meat Market. "There were so many jobs around in the sixties," he says. "If you didn't like your boss, you'd go next door and work for the other guy. But now there's only three places left here. Cryovac spoiled everything. I went to visit IBP after they said, 'Come and see how our meat is processed.' They put us up, fed us, gave us a lot of brochures, predicted that by 2010 they're going to have machinery to bone out cattle. Butchering's a dying art. I heard those things and I was getting sick. I love this business. I don't want to go, like, *down,* you know what I mean?"

THERE ARE TWO historic butcher shops still alive and thriving in New York, one downtown and the other up. Downtown, Florence Meat Market at 5 Jones Street was opened in 1936 by Jack Ubaldi, a small place with a corridor in front just big enough to haul in the sides, take them to age in the basement, and cut them by hand in the back room. When I first came to New York in 1949, I lived around the corner from the Florence, and it's a comfort to know it's just as it was: sawdust on the floor, the big butcher block by the display case where thick hands still cut Prime aged meat to order. When he retired in 1976, Jack sold the place to Tony Pellegrino, who came from Trapani in Sicily, arrived at the market in 1962 and was trained by Mr. Jack, as Tony calls him. The current owner is Benny Pizzuco, a man as big and solid as a butcher block, who runs the place with Maria Alava, there since 1985.

I talked to Tony, age seventy-seven, in his apartment around the corner on Sixth Avenue. When he came from Italy in 1958, he got a job in a plastics factory and took classes at night at a free school for butchering on Fourteenth Street, near the Market. He went to work for a Calabrian butcher on Mott Street, where he learned to make sausage. In 1962 he heard that Florence Meat Market was looking for a butcher, and when he saw Jack Ubaldi working, he said to himself, "My god, I don't know nothing." He made deliveries and cleaned up, but Ubaldi said, "Tony, if you like it, you're gonna learn. I learned from German butchers." When Tony got an offer to work for Sloan's supermarket, Mr. Jack asked, "Tony, you wanna be butcher or you wanna be number?" Tony said, "I wanna be butcher." And Jack said, "This is the place." Mr. Jack told him that when he reached sixty-two, "this place is gonna be yours." He reached sixty-two, business was better and better, he stopped talking. When he was sixty-five, he offered to make Tony a partner, but Tony said no partners, paid him $10,000 in cash, and promised to pay the remaining $20,000 a little each month. In six months, he'd paid it all. "I used to work very hard," Tony says. When Mr. Jack retired, he started to teach professional butchers and chefs in the culinary school at New York University.

In butchering, how you handle the meat is very important, Tony says. "I never put my hands on top of the meat when I tie it up nice. It takes two minutes to make it nice, then when you bring the good meat home and open the package, you see a beautiful thing. The eyes eat first, you know." When he began, it was all hanger meat, no boxes. Now it's 90 percent boxes and the quality is not there. Meat needs to breathe, Tony says. They put it in plastic bags and you see all the juices running out. Meat is like a fruit, you have to age it, ripen it. "You take a Prime piece of meat, you take the first slice off and then cut it. You have butter in the mouth. Beautiful." And it's important to know how to buy. He used to go to the wholesaler every day except Saturday. "The train used to come right down there on the tracks, but things change, everywhere. I went to the market for forty-five years, so I learn. When you see the marble is too heavy, the fat is too heavy, this is no good, no good for your heart, no good to eat a piece of fat in the mouth. Too rich, gotta be just right."

After Tony retired in 1996, he bought a little house in Sicily near Trapani. "A lot of meat they buy now in Italy is Argentina, not the same, no compare; the best meat is in New York and Paris." As for Kobe beef, too fat, he won't eat it. "We got educated meat for educated customers," he likes to say. His customers ranged from Jacqueline Kennedy, Luciano Pavarotti, and Pope John Paul to students at the New School and NYU, for whom Mr. Jack invented his "Newport Steak," a less costly cut from the sirloin that sells at $7.29 a pound. "Customers are like my family," Tony says.

If it's Italian Florence downtown, uptown it's Germanic Lobel's, at 1096 Madison Avenue, where I find Evan Lobel working at the long butcher block behind the glass counter with ten other men in butcher's aprons. Evan's father, Leon, died last year at age seventy-seven, one in a long butchering tradition of 160 years, beginning with Nathan Lobel in Austria, who raised beef cattle in the 1840s and added a slaughterhouse. His grandson Morris emigrated to America in 1911 at age seventeen, eventually opening a butcher shop in the Bronx. Nathan's sons, Leon, Nathan, and Stanley, continued the business at the present location, where Evan and his cousins David and Mark carry it on.

At fifty-one, Evan is tall, with gray curly hair and gray whiskers, friendly and at ease with the world, a good thing for a man with daughters aged eight, eleven, and twelve. When I ask him if any of the girls would like to be butchers, he replies tactfully that it would be a wonderful thing for the butchering world, but he's not sure they'd be interested. "Physically it's very challenging, but there are a lot of strong women in the world."

What makes Lobel's beef distinctive in the butchering world is that they buy only "Natural Prime." They mean meat from cattle raised in pastures, free of hormones and antibiotics, given a purely vegetarian diet, and raised and slaughtered under humane practices, from fifty farms on 30,000 acres scattered through the Northeast and Midwest. "We have long-standing relations with both large and small producers," Evan says, "often second or third generations. It's a small world, we know each other, we have to know and trust each other." Most of the beef is grain-finished, but Lobel's online operation also sells grass-finished heritage beef from breeds like Galloway, Hereford, Devon, Highlander. "Green is definitely a movement," Evan says. They added the grass-finished line to diversify their offerings, but he finds that people who want fully green beef tend to eat with their minds. "I eat more with my belly," he says. "I like that burst in your mouth of flavor that corn-fed gives the meat."

The Web site is now 50 percent of Lobel's market, bringing in 400 orders a day. Here you can buy a whole steer or a half, which they will then cut to your desire. A whole steer at 1200 pounds will provide a total primal weight of 325 pounds for $4,868.50. The cuts are flash frozen and then shipped. Evan says that they sell a lot of half carcasses, fewer whole ones. Half or whole carcasses are the sole exception to Lobel's rule of selling fresh beef only, FedExed overnight. "We like to think of ourselves as trendsetters," he says. As with a good steakhouse, Lobel's dry-ages its beef for four to six weeks, including American Wagyu, which it buys from a ranch in Texas. It sells Wagyu mostly for steak tartare, he adds, since they believe this meat is best eaten rare to raw.

"Prime is more of a hot ticket now than ever," Evan says. Although many restaurants and online marketers label their steaks "Prime," that can mean just a Prime cut like a porterhouse, not USDA grade Prime. Prices for the real thing have risen at least 15 percent, but the customer base is younger than ever and more brand conscious, so no matter how high the price, there's heavy demand for the best quality money can buy.

Evan's favorite cut for a backyard barbecue is a porterhouse or T-bone, or a New York strip or triple strip that's 3½–4 inches thick (about 2 pounds), seared first over hot coals, then with pecan wood chips added to the coals, roasted with the lid on over indirect heat for around 25 to 30 minutes. Indoors you can simulate the effect by pan-grilling the meat for a crust and then roasting it at 400 degrees to finish it off quickly. Customers ask him all kinds of cooking questions all the time, he says, but "Please, don't ask me how long you should *braise* the chateaubriand."

THE NAMES RIPPLE like sunlight across the prairie — Jean-Georges Vongerichten, David Burke, Michael Lomonaco, Alan Stillman, Bobby Flay, Tom Colicchio, Wolfgang Puck, Charlie Palmer, Rick Tramanto and

Gale Gand, Jeffrey Chodorow, Bradley Ogden, Laurent Tourondel, Michael Mina. All around the country, but especially in posh spots like Las Vegas, Manhattan, Beverly Hills, and San Francisco, every celebrity chef and restaurateur worth his salt and pepper has opened a steakhouse. Even Wolfgang Zweiner, who waited tables at Luger's for four years and spent another three dozen there as headwaiter, opened a steakhouse in 2004, with two other waiters as partners. "When I started in Luger's," Zweiner says, "it was like a men's club. A woman was not allowed to sit at the bar unless she had an escort. Most evenings there weren't any women there at all; now it's almost equal."

Steakhouses haven't been male-only for almost as long as jeans haven't. But just as jeans make a statement that obliterates distinctions of class and wealth, so the steakhouse makes a statement about the primacy of American Casual: "Hey, guys and gals, it's not about class, it's not about money. You may have to fork over five hundred bucks a head, but you don't have to wear a tie." In restaurants it's the liberating cry of Eaters of the World Unite, it's the faux-prole equivalent of throw off your chains, you huddled masses, and put on jeans — whatever the shape, condition, and status of your body and soul, whether rich or poor, fat or skinny, young or old, CEO or ex-con, movie star or homeless — we're all equal wearing denim or eating steak. Actually the jeans craze is only a half-century old, although it has covered the globe and is a better symbol than McDonald's of the imperial reach of American style. The steakhouse craze arose more slowly in the same period, but it's making up now for lost time. According to CREST research, the sales at casual steak restaurants in America from 1993 to 2000 increased 150 percent. And a more astonishing trend is that one-fourth of "high-end" restaurants in America are now steakhouses, a tabulation made in 2000 before the recent entrance of celebrity chefs into the game. "You don't really need a chef," Wolfgang Puck said of Las Vegas steakhouses before he opened his own. And you need mighty few ingredients. CREST found that there were two reasons for the steakhouse increase: "Most people go out for steak because they either don't want to cook (21%) or they are celebrating a special occasion/holiday (20%)." That would seem to sum up the push-pull attractions of the steakhouse: comfort food on the one hand and something special on the other — eating out because it's just like home and eating out because it's not.

In the last twenty years or so, the country's been mapped by a dozen major chains providing steak for Everyman. These are small chains from 30 to 60 units, like Steak and Ale, Bugaboo Creek Steak House, Hoss's Steak and Sea House. And large chains running from 165 to 900 units, not counting the units in other countries: Lone Star Steakhouse and Saloon, Texas Roadhouse, Sizzler, and Outback, the 800-pound gorilla. At the top of the heap are the "luxury" chains of Smith & Wollensky, the Palm, Morton's, Ruth's Chris. Across the country people value their local historic steakhouses, each with its own aura. There's Cattlemen's Steakhouse in the historic district of Stockyards City within Oklahoma City, which began in 1910 for cowboys, ranchers, packers, and railroad men, and which continues to thrive because the Stockyards is still home to the largest stocker/feeder cattle auction in the world, plus celebratory events like the annual Longhorn Cattle Drive in December and the Stockyards Stampede in June. There's Threadgill's in Austin, which grew from a filling station to a bar in 1933 and got famous for its chicken-fried steak and country music with regulars like Willie Nelson. Of more recent fame is the Hitching Post II, in Buellton, California, in the Santa Barbara Valley, which can trace its roots to 1952 but its glory to the movie *Sideways,* whose Hartley Ostini Highliner Pinot Noir did more than Parker could to change the ways of Merlot man.

If all of these are suitable for family outings, the steakhouse nonetheless thrives on its past reputation for naughtiness, if not downright debauchery. Thus the frequent bordello decor, as in Vongerichten's Prime Steakhouse, which is but the flip side of dark-paneled men's-club decor. In the steakhouse smoke, there's always a whiff of the outlaw, whether cowboy or mobster, rooted in such real events as the gunning down in 1985 of a pair of mobsters at the entrance of Sparks Steak House in New York City, on the orders of John Gotti, when he took over the Gambino family. The Glazier Group in Manhattan puns on the bordello connection in its Strip House, with photos on red-velvet walls of sexy gals in stripper mode. Or there's STK, half steakhouse and half nightclub in the Meat Market district, with the motto "Not your daddy's steakhouse," and the logo of a dame with a raw steak on a meat hook in one hand and a cleaver in the other. If you get bored with visual conceits and want the reality of HBO's *Sopranos*, you can always spring for Robert's Steakhouse in the Penthouse Executive Club on the far West Side, West Forty-fifth Street and Eleventh Avenue, where sizzling cuts of short loin compete with the thonged loins of lap dancers.

Sex and violence spell current steakhouse chic for both sexes. Women, it seems, are turning away from salad as fare for wimps, and declaring their power by choosing steak and red wine. A woman in her thirties, who in her vegetarian teens wore a "Meat is Murder" T-shirt, now works the red-meat line to attract guys. Red meat, steak or burger, sends a message, she says. Hamburgers say this girl is unpretentious, down to earth, real. Steak says she's self-assured, gutsy, worldly. Violence for boys and girls alike is provided by an only-in–New York entertainment called "Beef & Guns," which follows rifle shooting at the West Side Rifle & Pistol Range in Chelsea with a steak dinner at Frank's, which has been serving steaks near the Washington Meat Market since 1912. With your borrowed .22-caliber rifle, you get 150 bullets, and with your steak you get an appetizer, for a fixed price of 98 bucks. The online ad reads: "Today, you are a man."

From a restaurateur's point of view, steakhouses are about making money. Today steakhouses convey glamour in addition to *nostalgie de la cowboy boue,* and price does not seem to matter. Perhaps we're in a period of such affluence, or are driven by a need to believe in an illusion of such affluence, that the more steakhouses we have, the less we seem to care what they cost. Mass-produced steakhouse chains are based on food costs of 40 percent and labor costs of 20 percent, so that the real money lies in the side orders, desserts, and booze — oversize martinis and vintage Cabernets. It's the way movie theaters make their real money— not on the box-office take, but on the popcorn.

In Manhattan the number of steakhouses now totals eighty, up 10 percent from the previous year. Prices rose along with volume. "I don't think our customers have noticed," says the CEO of the Palm Restaurant Group. The Palm is one of the older steakhouse chains, founded in 1926 by John Ganzi and Pio Bozzi from Parma, Italy, a place name which got transliterated into "Palm" when they went to get a license for the little restaurant on Second Avenue they wanted to start in order to feed local artists and writers.

Ruth's Chris chain got its start in a similarly personal way, forty years ago down in New Orleans. When Ruth Fertel found herself divorced with two young sons to raise, she mortgaged her house to buy out a local joint called Chris Steak House. After 1965's Hurricane Betsy, Ruth tirelessly cooked free steaks on her gas broilers for disaster victims and relief workers. When she went to open a branch nearby, the original owner sued to prevent her from using his name, so she added hers. She designed her own extra-hot broilers to sear her meat at the unheard-of temperature of 1800 degrees F. Today Ruth's Chris uses Montague C45S radiant broilers and is the largest luxury steakhouse chain in the world, serving Prime dry-aged beef at 106 locations, although the original site was lost to Hurricane Katrina and the then-publicly-held corporation decided not to restore it.

On the trail of steakhouse entrepreneurs, I went to Grand Central Station to talk to Peter Glazier, head of the Glazier Group, and chef David Walzog, who created the menu uptown for Michael Jordan's: The Steak House and downtown for Strip House in Greenwich Village. Walzog had helped create Tapika restaurant in Manhattan for Glazier, and if that restaurant was a fantasy of the Southwest, Michael Jordan's in the northwest balcony of Grand Central Station, overlooking the vast concourse and looking up at the cyclorama of stars, is a fantasy of sports celebrity topped with men's-club power. The Cowboy in the form of a basketball superhero meets the Machine in surely one of the grandest temples the railroad industry in this country ever built in its own honor. Eating steak here celebrates that union.

The idea, David said, was to apply the white-tablecloth mentality of seasonally fresh, quality ingredients to the steakhouse, and move away from the standard men's-club mentality. "We wanted to go after Peter Luger's because that was the quintessential steakhouse of New York," said Peter in admiration. "They packaged the look, the waiters, the mystique of the stoves, the lady who picks out the meat — it's all packaging." For Jordan's, they began with the meat, in a relentless number of tastings, different vendors, ages, breeds — twenty-five people blind-tasting forty different strip steaks at a time. Some were wet-aged, some dry-aged, some grass-fed, some grain-fed. Over a period of four or five months, they narrowed the forty steaks down to twelve, then six. To their surprise, they found that the marketing labels of certified breeds like Hereford, Black Angus, Sterling Silver was a variant that mattered, David said. Their meats had great texture and silkiness even before they were aged, and even if they weren't stamped USDA Prime.

They had to check that their butchers were sending them the best of the best of whichever certified breed. They went for Prime 21-day dry-aged beef not as a taste decision, Peter said, but as a marketing one. "We put the extra money into the best cuts so that people would know we had only the highest quality." For them, the best cattle turned out to be Hereford from Nebraska, corn-fed 22 miles southeast of Omaha and slaughtered in Chicago. Their purveyor in New Jersey butchers and ages the meat to their exact specifications. At least I think he's in New Jersey. David and Peter have a running joke about the Tapika Mountains in Colorado that Peter used to say was where the name of the restaurant Tapika came from when they got tired of customers asking. There were no mountains, Peter said. He just liked the sound of the word. (It sounded vaguely Sioux, but is actually a Swahili word.) So now their wholesale purveyor, Peter says, is in the Tapika Mountains — three miles west of the Meadowlands.

"We knew we wanted a steak with a crispy outside, well charred and seasoned so the juices would stay in the middle," Peter says. "But we also had to design the service, the atmosphere — a fine-service steak restaurant in a nice atmosphere, great wine. We're trying to redefine what a steakhouse is." When they opened Michael Jordan's in 1997, David says, he served salads with heirloom tomatoes and other summer seasonal vegetables, but he soon learned that people come to a steakhouse because they want only certain items. So he kept the tomatoes, but dropped the heirloom. "Some of my chef-y kind of things we had to pull back on," he says. "Some people wanted tweaky ingredients applied to a steakhouse, but the masses weren't ready for it."

Peter adds, "We've gone a step further than other steakhouses in saying the chef is important to the process. I mean, who's the chef at Peter Luger's? What a name chef brings is expertise in the cooking. We're ratcheting it up." Same goes for the service. Their waiters look like old-time servers, but their service is much better, and so is the relationship between the front and back of the house. "I didn't know how complicated a service it is," says David. "So many variables — the cut, temperatures, side dishes — to bring everything to the table at the same time is a little more intense." David's theory about what counts most in a steakhouse is the eater's expectations. "Everyone's got their own definition of a great steakhouse and that's built in, whether it's when your father got a raise or whether it's how your momma used to cook. People recognize what they grew up on, and they know what they want. Beyond money things like the opulence of the nineties with big wines, big meat, big spending, people go to steakhouses because it puts them in the driver's seat. You have choices. *Your* choices. The chef does not dictate what you eat."

Peter agrees. "In a steakhouse people can eat what they want, and what they want here are Herefords from the Tapika Hills. We should call up Jean-Georges and ask, 'Are your cows Tapika-fed?'" I could hear the gears clicking on the new Glazier Group packaging as we sat analyzing Cowboy nostalgia in the temple of the Machine.

The United Steaks of America

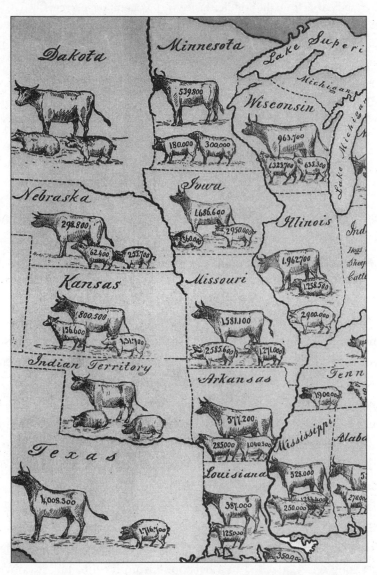

"Map of the United States Showing the Farm Animals in Each State" was published in 1878 in Decatur, Illinois, by H. W. Hill Co. The numbers of livestock printed on each animal in these Midwestern states are already impressively high.

— *From the Geography and Map Division, Library of Congress*

A mighty porterhouse steak an inch and a half thick, hot and sputtering from the griddle; dusted with fragrant pepper; enriched with little melting bits of butter of the most unimpeachable freshness and genuineness; then the precious juices of the meat trickling out and joining the gravy, archipelagoed with mushrooms; a township or two of tender, yellowish fat gracing an outlying district of this ample county of beefsteak; the long white bone which divides the sirloin from the tenderloin still in its place.

— Mark Twain, while touring Europe in 1878

◆

STEAK IS NOT a dish but a geography — a country, or at least a county as Twain says, with gravy lakes and fat townships and a bone fence — an analog on-the-plate of the land of the free and the home of the brave that prides itself on good eats rather than high cuisine. In fact, our word "steak" evolved from *stik*, Old Norse for stick, and for meat stuck on a stick, *steik*, which is as close to caveman cooking as you can get. A steak means No Pot Needed, only fire. That keeps steak masculine, at home on the open range, not the cast-iron one indoors. Consequently, steak is not about recipes but about hunting, hunting down that really good piece of cow, whether by mail or green-market or supermarket or one of the few remaining butcher shops or, if you're lucky, from a friend who raises his own.

If you think of a cow with a body like your own, you'll find all the parts, but in different proportions and often with several different names, which confuses identification. If you think of a cow's primary muscles as a very long series attached to a backbone from head to tail, it's obvious that the front and rear muscles, where the cow's legs are, will have worked the hardest. Therefore, the tenderest and fattiest meat will lie in between and along the back. Between the shoulder (chuck) and rump (round) are the rib section and the extended loin section. The loin muscles between rib and hip bones are so extended that we divide that section in two: the short loin, right next to the ribs, and the sirloin, between short loin and round, constituting the back and side muscles directly above the animal's loins. To the rear are the large muscle groups that make up the rump, or round. The tenderloin is a long horizontal muscle that lies just under the larger muscle of the sirloin and extends into the short loin. If we can think of the animal's short loin as equivalent to our own dorsal muscle along the backbone at our waistline, then the animal's flank is equivalent to our abdominal muscle in front. Just above our abdominal muscle is our diaphragm, which in a cow we call the plate. This stretches between the flank and the brisket, which in our body is equivalent to our chest. Looking at the diagram of a cow, we see the rib section above the plate, and the extended loin above the flank. Flank and plate are thin muscles that get more exercise than back muscles, but not as much as shoulder and rump. Conclusion: The poshest cuts will come from rib and loin, for the good reason that they are the tenderest.

As a fat-lover, if I had a single choice of steak I'd choose the rib eye (right next to the short loin), because it combines fat with chewiness, which creates what I perceive as juiciness and flavor and, okay, *umami*.

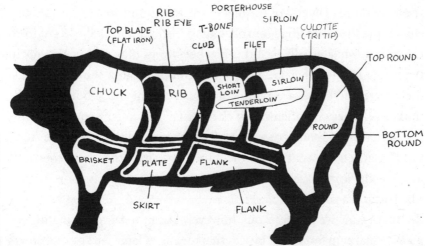

DRAWING BY TUCKY MACKENZIE

Club steak (sometimes called Delmonico, after New York's famed nineteenth-century restaurant) is cut next to the rib end of the short loin, sometimes with bone in and sometimes without, but its "eye" is close in quality to the rib eye. Shell or strip steak (also called New York strip, Kansas City strip) is cut from the short loin without the backbone or any part of the tenderloin, and therefore is a classic steak for one person. Porterhouse is certainly my favorite cut when serving more than one person because it's the American Ur-steak in terms of size, drama, complexity, and communality. Cut from the rear end of the short loin, it's got everything you want: a big T-shaped bone (a cross section of the backbone with its long vertebra) that separates a large top-loin muscle from the smaller tenderloin. Both muscles are enclosed in a nice rim of fat that curves around a little tail of meat like a Cajun *lagniappe,* an extra dividend. You can get a porterhouse cut 2 to 3 inches thick, so that you can slice it on each side of the bone as if you're carving up a Thanksgiving turkey. It's a showpiece. A T-bone steak, cut with that same-shaped bone from the center of the short loin, has a smaller piece of tenderloin. The tenderloin is my least favorite among costly cuts because it has no fat and no chewiness — often no more texture than a wet marshmallow — but it's convenient for slicing into rounds because it has no bone. The chateaubriand ("the aristocrat," as a 1935 magazine called it) was popular in the nineteenth century as a double-thick steak cut from the center of the tenderloin. (The rest of the filet toward the thinner end provided filet steaks, and the Frenchified tournedos and filet mignons.) Steaks cut from the sirloin, while usually flavorful in a beefy way, often disappoint me in the eating because they are usually cut thinner than a short-loin steak, their sacroiliac bones are more complicated than the T-bone, and the muscle is leaner and often much chewier (in fact, often tough). For me, they lack the flavor burst of fat. Sirloin steak is usually cut from the "top," but a relatively new cut called the tri-tip is a small muscle in the "bottom" of the loin muscle near the hip, and is considerably more tender. The tri-tip is a good buy.

By the time we get to sirloin, however, I want to start marinating the meat to make up for less fat by external means. A large part of that cow is still available for good-tasting steaks, but you have to work a little harder than just throwing the meat on the grill. Of these, round steaks cut from the top of the round are more tender than the eye of the round near the bottom because the top gets worked less than the muscles attached to hip and leg. But the round is not about tenderness, and therefore not good for grilling anyway, unless you take a top round (the tenderest) or an eye of round (often used for thin-cut minute steaks) and tenderize it for a couple of days in a marinade with an acid in it. Still, why bother? Any part of the round makes a very good roast. The same goes for a slice of chuck as a steak, for even though it has a lot more flavor than the round because its fibers are nice and fatty, it's also full of connective tissue that needs either to be ground into burgers or cooked long and slow as a roast. The flatiron is a recently devised name for a top blade steak (from the chuck), which has had the connective tissue removed and is full of flavor. The flatiron joins traditional cheaper cuts like skirt (from the plate), hanger, and flank steaks, all of them flavorful and easy to cook, but requiring a marinade for a few hours or overnight for tenderizing. (The hanger steak is a relatively thin muscle known as the "hanging tender" because when the carcass is cut up, this part of the diaphragm is literally left hanging in one piece from the last rib.) London broil is not properly a cut, but a method of marinating a flank or round steak before grilling.

TO SAY YOU have to find a piece of well-aged meat is like saying you have to find a risk-free hedge fund. I mean dry-aged meat. Wet-aged is "a crock," says meat expert Bruce Aidells with Western candor. "The meat sits in its own juices — blood, really — and that doesn't help the flavor at all. Wet-aged beef tastes *wet*, not juicy." In my own taste testing at home, I can always pick out the dry-aged from the wet, in comparable cuts. As *Wine Spectator* columnist Sam Gugino says, "It's the difference between skim milk and whole milk." Since dry-aged beef loses moisture in the drying, the result is a more concentrated, beefier, more aromatic flavor, and there's less moisture loss in the cooking. Dry aging also increases tenderness through the work of enzymes over a period of two to three weeks, but it's not easily done at home unless you have a temperature-controlled chill room, and of course you have to pay more.

Once you've got your dry-aged beef, how to cook it? For me a steak that is not rare is not a steak, just as a well-done hamburger is an oxymoron that should be forbidden by law and punished by hanging. But how rare is rare? *Muy, très,* very, says I, what the French call *bleu,* or black-blue. *The Meat Buyer's Guide,* the Bible of the Meat Processors Industry, calibrates very rare at 130 degrees F., rare at 140 degrees F., medium rare at 145 degrees F., medium at 160 degrees F., well done at 170 degrees F., and very well done at 180 degrees F. My advice is to throw out the thermometer, since these temperatures are based on USDA guidelines and are dictated by keep-from-being-sued safety, rather than by taste. I'd subtract at least 10 degrees temperature from each of those categories and call anything above medium rare way overdone. Remember that raw beef, whether fancied up into steak tartare or just gnawed off the bone, has been thought tasty since beef eating began, and it's only in these latter days of industrial decadence that raw commodity beef, especially that which is ground into slurry at the processors, has been rendered unsafe.

But the glory of steak is the dramatic conflict between the raw and the cooked, between the outside — crusty, "caramelized," richly browned — and the inside tenderly pink as a baby's bottom. That's what makes every bite of a steak dramatic, as opposed to the one-dimensional slices of a beef roast. It's a contradiction like a Baked Alaska, and the trick is to get these opposite effects simultaneously from the same piece of meat. The first step is to make sure the meat is at room temperature before you start. Whether you've bought it fresh or frozen is of less importance than its temperature at the moment of cooking. (If frozen, be sure to thaw it in the refrigerator — no quick hot-water bath — in order to conserve its juices as much as possible in the thawing.) Next, make sure that the surface of the meat is dry. Pat it well with paper towels or a kitchen towel on both sides, or place it uncovered on a rack over a pan in the refrigerator for a day or two, turning it a couple of times, for extra dryness to guarantee a really crusty crust. Just before you cook it, press grains of sea salt and lots of freshly ground pepper into both sides. Or, press in a mixed-spice rub with Asian flavors like Szechuan peppercorns, anise, cloves, cinnamon, fennel; or with Mexican flavors like ground ancho, chipotle, cumin, coriander, oregano.

Now you're ready to cook. On an outside grill, you can get good high heat by piling the hot coals in the middle until they turn to gray ash. You can sear the meat a couple of minutes on each side, then, if the meat is thick and needs slower cooking for the interior, move the steak away from the hot center. How hot is hot? What your great-grandmothers did in baking bread in a hearth was to use the hand test; after they'd swept out the hot coals, they stuck a hand into the oven: "An oven in which the bare hand and arm can not be held longer than to count twenty moderately, is hot enough." Chris Schlesinger, in *License to Grill*, advises a similar hand test for a modern grill: Put your hand five inches above the hot ashes in a grill and if you can hold it there less than a second, you've got a really hot fire; two seconds is medium hot; three to four is medium, five to six is low.

One grilling trick is to brush the steak with olive oil on both sides after initial searing because the oil transmits heat and flavor into the interior of the flesh. How do you tell when it's the degree of rareness you want? Chefs press the top of the meat with a forefinger to test the amount of resistance. (The more it cooks, the firmer it gets.) But they also test with a knife, making a small cut to reveal the interior ("nick and peek"), and ignoring that little drop of juice that leaks out. As I say, forget the meat thermometer on a steak: By the time you've poked the interior and the mercury has risen and you try to read the damn thing, the meat has probably already overcooked. The main thing is to remove the meat *before* it reaches the doneness you want, because it will continue cooking as it rests, and it should rest off the heat for a good five minutes before slicing. As the muscle relaxes, juices retreat into the interior from the surface, where they've been drawn by the heat. Remember: There is no such thing as exact timing because every grill is going to be different and so is the person using it. Lobel's suggests for a one-inch steak a total of 10 minutes for rare, 15 for medium, 20 for medium well, but all yardsticks are rough because the ground is uneven. There's no substitute for your own experience and the way to get it is to do it. The risks are small. If you think the steak's done and a guest cringes in disgust at a raw interior, you can always toss the meat back on the grill. If a steak's done more than you like, well, you can always whip up a little steak sauce of butter or oil with a dash of Worcestershire and some chopped herbs and garlic — anything to ease the pain.

Sometimes reading a recipe is as good as actually cooking up the thing yourself. Here's a quintessential grilled ribeye, of substantial size, adapted from *The Niman Ranch Cookbook: From Farm to Table with America's Finest Meat* that I lick my chops over word by word:

✤ Rib-Eye Steaks with Thai Basil and Mint Sauce

4 fresh dry-aged rib-eye steaks, ¾ pound each
⅔ cup extra-virgin olive oil
¼ cup minced garlic (about 12 cloves)
1 tablespoon firmly packed fresh Thai basil leaves, chopped
1 cup firmly packed fresh mint leaves, chopped
1 tablespoon fresh thyme leaves, chopped
Minced zest and juice of 1 lemon
1 tablespoon sugar
1 tablespoon Dijon mustard
Kosher salt and freshly ground black pepper

Prepare and light a charcoal grill for direct cooking. Bring the steaks to room temperature. Heat the olive oil in a saucepan over medium heat. Add the garlic and cook, stirring, for 1 to 2 minutes, until aromatic. Stir in the basil, mint, thyme, and lemon zest. Remove from heat. Combine the lemon juice and sugar in a small bowl and stir until the sugar dissolves. Whisk in the mustard and then the herb mixture.

When the grill is hot (when the coals are red and glowing but there isn't any flame), season the steaks on the cooking grate directly over the coals and spread a spoonful of the herb mixture over each steak. Cook uncovered for 4 to 5 minutes. (If there are flare-ups, move the steaks to the edge of the grate to prevent burning.) Turn the steaks and again spread a spoonful of the sauce over each steak. (You will have some sauce remaining for serving.) Cook uncovered for 4 to 5 minutes longer for medium rare; the timing will depend on the thickness of the steak. Transfer to a cutting board and let rest for 5 minutes. Salt and pepper to taste. Serve whole or cut across the grain into slices. Offer the remaining herb mixture as a condiment at the table.

Today most of us don't have the luxury or the challenge of grilling our meat over an outdoor campfire, chuck wagon style. But there are still some cowboys who do, and Jim Hodges, the lead cowboy and horse trainer who cooked me up a steak at the George Ranch in Richmond, Texas, is one of them. Says Jim, "Look for a USDA Prime steak, marbled with equal spatters of tiny dots, and for a jelly-type wiggle when you shake it," to be sure the meat is fresh. He prefers the wide, thin cuts chuck-wagon cooks used to serve, bone in, because "you could eat them easily while holding the steak in your hand." However, he says, "No campfire is complete without the venerable Sir Loin, picked by a keen eye, rubbed with rich spices, served on a Texas-sized platter, and savored under a star-studded sky."

✢ Jim's "Pecos Bill" Sirloin

2- to 3-pound sirloin steak, no more than 1¼-inch thick

For the marinade:
1 cup olive oil
¾ teaspoon sea salt
¾ teaspoon freshly ground black pepper
¾ teaspoon paprika
4 cloves garlic, crushed

For the spice rub:

2 teaspoons smoked paprika (La Vera Dolce is a good brand)

2 teaspoons sea salt

1 teaspoon freshly ground black pepper

½ teaspoon turmeric

3 teaspoons chopped parsley

Pound the steak with a meat-tenderizing hammer until thin and pliable. Mix ingredients of the marinade and marinate the meat overnight, or at least 6 to 8 hours, in the refrigerator. Remove from the marinade and rub both sides of the steak well with the mixed ingredients of the spice rub. Refrigerate again for 2 to 4 hours, then bring to room temperature when ready to cook. Place steaks on hottest part of the grill and cook quickly, turning once only, with heavy tongs. Lift onto the platter, then cut steak into portions and serve with a spoonful of Jim's grilled corn garnish for an extra whiff of Texas ranchero cooking.

❖ Jim's Grilled Elote Garnish

4 large ears sweet corn in their husks

4 tablespoons mayonnaise

3 to 4 teaspoons fresh lime juice

¼ cup grated cotija or parmesan cheese

1 teaspoon ground ancho chili

½ teaspoon ground red chili pepper

½ teaspoon ground cumin

¼ teaspoon salt

Before cooking the steak, grill the corn in the husk over hot coals, turning frequently, until the husks are evenly charred (12 to 15 minutes). Remove from the fire and remove the husks as soon as they are cool enough to handle. Cut the kernels from the cobs into a large flat pan and mash them into a mush with the bottom of a heavy glass. Place them in a bowl with the other ingredients and mix well.

But what if you don't have an outdoors? What if you don't even have a grill? For the past twenty-five years I've been grill-less in Manhattan, where in any case fire laws prohibit charcoal fires even on fire escapes. Most of us have oversensitive smoke alarms and domestic ranges with low BTU broilers, which are no substitute for charcoal or gas-fired grills. Forget the broiler. I get far better heat and far better control with a cast-iron ridged grill pan, to which I've become addicted. The parallel ridges will mark the food in the familiar grill pattern that says, "Eat me, I'm delicious, I've been grilled!" and that allows for excess fat to drain away from the meat surface.

That paragon of contemporary French haute-chefdom, Alain Ducasse, isn't interested in the grill marks, or in draining away the fat. He recommends cooking his favorite cut, the rib eye, on top of the stove in a pan, first searing its rim of fat by holding the steak vertically with tongs, in order to add some fat to the pan at the outset. Then he adds "a nice chunk of butter" to the pan, along with some large unpeeled cloves of garlic. Fat carries the garlic flavor into the meat as well as infusing some heat. When the steak is cooked, Ducasse rests it "for at least half as long as it took to cook." He cooks a 1½-inch rib eye about 10 minutes a side over not "very" high heat, which would mean a rest of 10 minutes. But I still want those grill marks because we eat first with our eyes and we taste what we see. So my method is to use two pans: a grill pan for the quick searing of the fat rim and top and bottom sides; then a second preheated plain cast-iron skillet with the butter and garlic in it (I crush the garlic flat, skin and all, with the side of a knife), to which I transfer the seared meat and finish it off in the garlic butter. For me the extra pan is worth the trouble because I love garlic butter almost as much as I love steak.

·   ·   ·

CLEARLY, COOKING STEAK is an arena for rugged individualism, and written-down recipes counter the whole spirit of steak as improvised theater in the open air, on the road, on the run. The fun of looking at steak recipes in historical American cookbooks is to track whether the inflection is British, French, or Mexican. As befits an English-speaking nation, the body of our printed cookbooks before World War I reflect the culinary traditions as well as the language of the British, and therefore of indoor hearths. Amelia Simmons's 1796 *American Cookery* provides no steak but only a roast of "Cow beef" (more tender and juicy than Ox) hung over "a brisk hot fire." But Mary Randolph's 1824 *The Virginia House-wife* delivers a finely detailed recipe for "Beef Steaks," cooked on the hearth on a gridiron.

> The best part of the beef for steaks, is the seventh and eight ribs, the fat and lean are better mixed, and it is more tender than the rump if it be kept long enough; cut the steaks half an inch thick, beat them a little, have fine clear coals, rub the bars of the gridiron with a cloth dipped in lard before you put it over the coals, that none may drip to cause a bad smell, put no salt on till you dish them, broil them quick, turning them frequently; the dish must be very hot, put some slices of onion in it, lay in the steaks, sprinkle a little salt, and pour over them a spoonful of water and one of mushroom catsup, both made boiling hot, garnish with scraped horse radish, and put on a hot dish cover. Every thing must be in readiness, for the great excellence of a beef steak lies in having it immediately from the gridiron.

Mrs. Randolph's demand for a hot platter and some kind of "gravy" is more than a nicety. As culinary historian Karen Hess explains, until the iron stove came in, the English in Virginia roasted their meats as they did in England, on a spit roast at the hearth, or on a gridiron, in *front* of the fire itself, from which hot coals could be raked as needed. With spit roasting, a drip pan was always placed beneath the roast. As gridirons became more popular, any juices lost in grilling meats could be made up for with a sauce, or gravy, which would help distinguish a civilized

British dish from the cruder methods of the Natives. William Wood describes in *New Englands Prospect* in 1634 how gravy was lost in the Native way of "laying the Meat itself upon the Coals, [or] by laying it upon Sticks rais'd upon forks at some distance above the live Coals, which heats more gently, and drys up the *Gravy;* this they, and we also from them, call Barbecueing."

In *Miss Parloa's Kitchen Companion* of 1887 Maria Parloa gives instructions for beefsteak so fine-tuned that they might appear in a current copy of *Gourmet:*

> A steak or chop, properly broiled, should have a thin, well-browned crust. Beyond this crust the meat should be red and juicy, hardly a shade rarer at the centre than near the surface. The common mode of cooking a steak is to keep it over the coals until one side is rather well done; then to turn it and treat the other side in the same manner. The steak, when cut into, will, if thick, be found well done about one-third through on each side and almost raw in the centre.

Mrs. D. A. Lincoln, better known as Mary Lincoln, cuts to the chase in her method for "Broiled Steak" in her *Boston School Kitchen Text-Book* of 1894:

> Wipe, trim off the superfluous fat, and remove the bone. Grease the gridiron with some of the fat. Broil over a clear fire, turning every ten seconds. Cook 3 or 4 m. if liked rare; longer, if well done. Serve on a hot platter, season with salt, and butter and pepper, if desired.

Lincoln paved the way for an extremely ambitious pupil, Fannie Farmer, who in her *Boston Cooking-School Cook Book* of 1896 goes to town with complete instructions on the primal cuts of a side of beef, the chemical composition of different cuts, and nearly two dozen recipes for them, including a number of positively luxurious French sauces — Maître d'Hôtel, Bordelaise, Henriette, Chiron, Mirabeau, and Victor Hugo — which had the delicate balance, and the central ingredients, of a Béarnaise with a dollop of English horseradish. For "Beefsteak à la Hugo," she instructs:

Wipe a porterhouse steak, broil, and serve with Victor Hugo Sauce: Cook one-half teaspoon finely chopped shallot in one tablespoon tarragon vinegar five minutes. Wash one-third cup butter, and divide in thirds. Add one piece butter to mixture, with yolks two eggs, one teaspoon lemon juice, and one teaspoon meat extract. Cook over hot water, stirring constantly; as soon as butter is melted, add second piece, and then third piece. When mixture thickens, add one-half tablespoon grated horseradish.

The intertwining of British and French names and methods came to a head in the mid-nineteenth century, when dishes began to be named for celebrities. A *filet de boeuf,* for example, standard French for the tenderloin, was elevated to glamour when it was renamed for the Vicomte de Chateaubriand, who in his *Génie du Christianisme* (1802) and a trio of novellas set in America's Deep South, created the mold for Romanticism. Today, a chateaubriand still suggests a whiff of French grandeur, particularly when a pat of butter is transformed into a Béarnaise, as offered by William Rice in *The Steak Lover's Cookbook.*

❖ Chateaubriand with Béarnaise Sauce

1 center-cut beef tenderloin (about 1¼ pounds), cut 1½ to 2 inches thick
1 tablespoon vegetable oil, preferably corn oil
Salt

Béarnaise Sauce
2 tablespoons dry white wine
1 tablespoon white wine vinegar, preferably tarragon flavored
1 tablespoon chopped fresh tarragon leaves
1 tablespoon minced shallots (optional)
white pepper, to taste
1 egg yolk

1 tablespoon fresh lemon juice

salt, to taste

2 or 3 drops hot pepper sauce, preferably Tabasco

1 cup melted unsalted butter, hot

At least 45 minutes before cooking, remove the steak from the refrigerator, and let it come to room temperature. Pat it dry, coat lightly with vegetable oil, and set aside. Preheat the oven to 450°F. Heat a large ovenproof skillet, preferably cast iron, over medium-high heat. Sear the tenderloin until browned on one side, about 3 minutes. Turn, season with salt, and sear the second side for 3 minutes more. Transfer the skillet to the oven and roast the steak about 12 minutes for medium-rare and 14 minutes for medium. Transfer the steak to a cutting board and let it rest for 4 to 5 minutes before carving.

Two purely British beefsteak dishes which survived an Atlantic crossing were beefsteak puddings and pies as well as steak with oysters. An 1854 recipe of Miss Eliza Leslie's for "A Beef Steak Pot-Pie" shows off British home-style cooking at its best, with "fine, tender beef steaks" cut in pieces, stewed with butter and flour for gravy, mixed with boiled white potatoes and enclosed in a thick crust of either suet or butter in proportions that suggest a delicious flakiness: half as much suet or butter as flour. "Stewed" beefsteaks was also a favored British preparation, with tougher cuts like rump steaks simmered in gravy until tender and flavored with onions and mushrooms.

A latter-day descendant of stewed beefsteak was a special treat in my family during the Depression and the only form of beef I ever ate except for hamburger, whose texture it resembled. This was my father's Swiss steak, accomplished with the aid of the newfangled pressure cooker, which magically transformed anything with texture into pap for babes and old folks who had to gum their food rather than chew it. This recipe from the *Good Housekeeping Cook Book* of 1955 is very close to my memory of Dad's pressurized steak, except he pounded his meat thin with a wooden mallet, not a saucer edge, and he would have just thrown in the vegetables.

✧ Swiss Steak

1½ lb. round steak, cut 1½-inch thick
¼ cup flour
1 teaspoon salt
¼ teaspoon pepper
2 tablespoons fat or salad oil
4 green pepper rings, ¼-inch thick
4 onion slices, ¼-inch thick
4 tomato slices, ½-inch thick
3 tablespoons tomato juice, water, or cooking sherry

Trim excess fat from beef; score beef on both sides with sharp knife; cut into 4 equal pieces. Mix flour, salt, pepper: pound into beef, using edge of heavy saucer. In hot fat in pressure cooker, brown beef quickly. On each piece of beef, place 1 pepper ring with onion slice inside it and tomato slice on top. Sprinkle vegetables lightly with more salt and pepper. Add tomato juice. Cook at 15 lb. pressure 25 to 30 min. as manufacturer directs. Reduce pressure immediately. Thicken gravy if desired. Makes 4 servings.

One form of steak stewed in gravy that gained brief popularity on this side the Atlantic from around the 1930s to the 1950s was that stalwart of British pub fare, steak and kidney pie. Louis de Gouy in the *Gold Cook Book* of 1947 offers a splendidly hearty dish that I hope will not be lost to posterity in these days of "instant gourmet."

✤ Beef and Kidney Pie Old Scotch Style

Sear quickly on both sides in a little hot fat 1½ pounds of round steak, cut into slices ¼-inch thick and 3 inches long. Wrap each slice around a small strip of bacon and a stub of kidney, making a tight roll, and securing with a toothpick. Combine ¾ teaspoon of salt, ½ scant teaspoon of black pepper, ⅛ teaspoon each of clove, thyme, marjoram, allspice and cinnamon, all ground, and ½ cup of bread flour, and toss the meat rolls in this. Stand them on end, tightly packed, in a deep pie dish; sprinkle the remaining spice-flour mixture over with 2½–3 tablespoons of grated onion. Gently and carefully pour 2½ cups of beef stock or condensed or concentrated canned beef bouillon over the whole; add 1 small bay leaf. Cover and set the dish over a very gentle flame or in a slow oven (300 degrees F.) for 1 hour. Then pour in ¼ cup of sherry wine; add 2 hard-cooked egg yolks, diluted with a very little milk, being careful not to close the slashes, and bake in a moderate oven (375 degrees F.) 25–30 minutes, or until pastry is delicately browned. Serve at once.

Another British favorite, steak and oysters, was an early version of Surf 'n' Turf. Fannie Farmer gives us this delectable combination, though just to be clear, you'd want to sear the meat on both sides and make sure not to overcook the oysters:

✤ Beefsteak with Oyster Blanket

Wipe a sirloin steak, cut one and one-half inches thick, broil five minutes, and remove to platter. Spread with butter and sprinkle with salt and pepper. Clean one pint oysters, cover steak with same, sprinkle oysters with salt and pepper and dot over with butter. Place on grate in hot oven, and cook until oysters are plump.

In 1896 this would not have been the costly dish it would be today, because a century ago oysters were so cheap they were often a freebie in city saloons to tempt men in for strong drink. In America in the 1940s, the name "carpetbag steak" got attached to a steak stuffed with oysters, but there's no need for that complication. It's much simpler to pan-sauté oysters (about eight per steak) very quickly in butter and to pour all those good juices over your previously grilled steak.

Steak Diane, popular in America in the 1950s, but clearly a version of the French steak *au poivre*, is best remembered for its name. To season a cut of meat with lots of pepper is as old as Roman cuisine, but Sauce Diane, named for the Greek huntress Diana and therefore associated with game like venison, made it into the Escoffier lexicon when a Sauce Poivrade was enriched with truffles, cream, and brandy, which provided the opportunity for some restaurant pyrotechnics. Ingredients vary — calvados or bourbon instead of cognac, green peppercorns instead of black — as do methods, but usually the steak is pounded thin, so that the focus is all on the sauce, as in this recipe from Michael Lomonaco's *The "21" Cookbook:*

✤ Traditional Steak Diane

2 tablespoons unsalted butter
4 (6-ounce) shell steaks, butterflied and pounded with a meat
  tenderizer to ¼-inch thick
Salt and freshly ground black pepper to taste
3 tablespoons chopped shallots
2 ounces fine brandy
¼ cup white wine
1 teaspoon hot prepared English mustard
¼ cup beef stock
4 tablespoons heavy cream
3 tablespoons chopped fresh chives

Since each pounded, flattened steak should have a large circumference, it will be necessary to cook the steaks one or two at a time, setting each aside on a warm platter as you finish those that remain.

Preheat the oven to 350°. On top of the stove, heat a large, heavy skillet over medium heat. Add ½ tablespoon butter to the hot pan and heat until it begins to foam. Season the beef with salt and pepper. Add the first steak and sear, cooking no more than 1 to 2 minutes before turning it over and allowing another minute on the second side. Remove the steak from the pan to a warm ovenproof platter. Repeat with the remaining butter and the remaining steaks.

After the fourth steak has been cooked and removed from the pan, add the shallots and cook 2 minutes, until translucent. Lower the heat, move the pan away from the stove, and cautiously add the brandy. Being careful not to flame the brandy, return the pan to the stove, and allow it to cook off. Add the white wine to the pan, raise the heat, and bring quickly to the boil. Stir in the mustard. Allow this to cook 1 minute before adding the beef stock. Cook 1 minute more. Add the cream. Bring just to the boil. Remove from the heat and stir in the chives.

Place the ovenproof platter of steaks in the oven 1 to 2 minutes to reheat them very quickly before placing them on individual dishes and topping them with some of the Diane sauce.

A homier form of steak cooking derives from using cheaper cuts, pounded thin, cut in strips or not, breaded or floured, grilled or fried in a hot skillet, and served with gravy. It's the bread-crumb coating and the butter "gravy" that helps define this as an English method to the author of the *Mexican Culinary Dictionary* of 1888, in a recipe that translates as follows:

✤ Beefsteak English Style

You need a good piece of red top-round steak. Cut the piece of meat into strips, each about 1 inch thick (or you can buy the steaks already cut from the meat market). Take steaks and trim the excess fat and nerves. Pound steaks to tenderize them with the flat side of a wood or metal kitchen hammer and make it round in shape. Put salt and pepper on both sides of the steak. To bread the meat, first put melted butter in a bowl and soak the meat. Then bread it on both sides with breadcrumbs. Put it on the grill. To serve, melt some butter, mash pieces of parsley and a little touch of lemon juice, then pour it over the steaks.

———————

German immigrants to Texas in the nineteenth century brought in their tradition of Wiener schnitzel for batter-fried veal and pork and applied it to beef, but the British gravy tradition superseded all. The result was tenderized steaks, cutlets, cube steaks, or "minute steaks," pounded thin as chicken breasts, fried crisp as Southern fried chicken, then topped with boatloads of cream gravy to produce classic "chicken-fried" steak. Threadgill's in Austin is famed for a classic version of this dish, where they dip their beef cutlets in a thick batter before frying in a lot of oil in a hot cast-iron skillet. I prefer an even homier version that uses buttermilk for the batter and lard for the oil. Some Texans season their gravy with Tabasco and Worcestershire sauce, but others just grind in a cloudburst of black pepper.

✣ Texas Chicken-Fried Steak with Cream Gravy

1 pound top or bottom round steak (fat removed)
¾ cup flour
½ teaspoon salt
½ teaspoon smoked paprika
¼ teaspoon black pepper
1 large egg
⅓ cup buttermilk
¼ to ⅓ cup lard (or vegetable oil) for frying

For the cream gravy:

2 tablespoons pan drippings

2 tablespoons flour (or use flour left from dipping)

2 cups milk (Milk is traditional, but substituting 1 cup chicken stock plus 1 cup heavy cream tastes awfully good.)

Salt and pepper to taste

Cut the steak into four pieces and tenderize them vigorously with a meat mallet (or the rim of a metal plate). On a plate mix together the flour, salt, paprika, and pepper. Dip the cutlets in the flour and shake off excess flour. ·

Beat the egg well with the buttermilk. Dip each cutlet into the egg mixture, then back in the flour mix, then set aside.

In a heavy cast-iron skillet, melt the lard to make it about ½-inch deep in the pan. Heat the fat until hot but not smoking. (You can test it by flicking in a drop of water, which should sizzle and pop.) Fry each cutlet quickly, turning to brown on each side. Lower heat and cook 2 to 3 minutes more until meat seems cooked through. Remove cutlets to a warmed plate and keep warm.

Pour off all but two tablespoons of the pan drippings. Sprinkle on the flour and stir it in well to brown, scraping up any browned bits on the bottom. Gradually add the milk, stirring constantly as the flour thickens. A wooden spoon is the best tool for this maneuver. Bring to a simmer, season to taste, and stir well for 4 to 5 minutes until gravy is the thickness you like. Immediately pour over the steaks.

———————

A cream gravy enriched with cheese gives us Philadelphia's famed cheese steak, which has managed to retain its historic authenticity in places like Judy Wick's White Dog Café, using citified baguettes or hoagie rolls rather than country biscuits.

✣ White Dog Café's Philly Cheese Steak

2 tablespoons olive oil

2 large yellow onions, thinly sliced (about 4 cups)

2 large Portobello mushroom caps, thinly sliced (about 3 cups)

1½ teaspoons salt

1 pound trimmed flank steak, sliced as thinly as possible (preferably on a slicer)

½ teaspoon freshly ground black pepper

1½ cups grated pepper-Jack cheese

2 soft-crusted long baguettes, or 4 Italian-style hoagie rolls

Preheat oven to 400°F.

Heat the oil in a large non-reactive sauté pan set over medium high heat. Add the onions and cook until soft, about 5 minutes. Add the mushrooms and 1 teaspoon of the salt and sauté until tender, about 5 minutes. Add the flank steak and the remaining ½ teaspoon salt, and the pepper and sauté until the meat is cooked through about 5 minutes more.

Remove the pan from the heat. Sprinkle the cheese over the top, cover the pan and set aside until the cheese melts, around 5 minutes.

Meanwhile, slice the baguettes lengthwise. Place, cut side down, on a baking sheet, and toast in the oven until crisp, 4 to 5 minutes.

Fill the baguettes with the meat and cheese. Cut each into two portions. Serve immediately — with or without ketchup.

————

British culinary traditions, however, were only the domesticated half of American steak cooking, The more important tradition for America was outdoor cooking of a far simpler sort, practiced by Native Americans for thousands of years before cattle came to be mixed with game and before the gridiron or iron skillet replaced green sticks and wooden planks. But just as the Spanish changed the nature of hunting by introducing cattle to the New World, so they modulated native campfire cooking by their own ranching traditions, which suited a continent where mobility mattered. Spain used oil rather than animal fat or butter, and liked high flavorings from plants and herbs that grew easily in Mediterranean heat. While the Spanish brought garlic and onions to the Americas, they returned with tomatoes and red peppers, to create delicious marinades and sauces, just as their neighbors did along all the lands that bordered the Mediterranean. The habit of flavoring food with sauces blended well with the food that the Conquistadors found when they stormed Teotihuacán and discovered the elaborate cuisine of Montezuma. Aztec cuisine was, like French cuisine, built upon sauces, hundreds and hundreds of sauces for their basic staple of corn, supplemented with game and other proteins. The central Aztec cooking method was an open fire, their central tool a ceramic *comál* (or griddle), the kind you see today all over Mexico. Just as Spaniards intermarried with Indians to beget the generations of mestizos that have built the Mexican nation, so they intermarried their cuisines to beget *criollo* cooking, which spread into the United States as a ranchero tradition, a form of community cooking wholly unlike the chef-oriented kitchens of Britain and France.

The abundance of Mexican beef astonished English visitors in the nineteenth century, but they deplored the fact that the meat was universally overcooked, which they attributed to bad butchers. In fact, local butchers cut thin steaks to order for local customers who preferred their meat well done. "Mexicans abhorred the dripping, rare filets served in Europe," writes historian Jeffrey M. Pilcher, "and cut their meat in thin strips, pounding and marinating to tenderize them." To a nation of carvers, like the British, this method seemed to reek of poverty or, at best, demeaning thrift. To a culture given to finger food, however, how an animal was butchered was less important than utilizing every part of the animal that could be cut into small pieces and wrapped in a tamale or tortilla. Montezuma's society was structured into royalty and peasants, and only the former feasted in a banquet room with food and ceremonies as elaborate as the Sun King's at Versailles. The rest of the populace improvised their meals, as feudal peasants had in Europe. When beef in Mexico became part of the diet even of the peasantry, the ranchero culture retained the structure of a feudal landlord and serfs, and among the serfs, cutting beef into strips had the effect of making all cuts equal for the working classes.

Improvised finger food and equal portions turned out to fit the American cowboy's needs as much as Mexican saddles and lariats did, and cowboys assimilated cooking traditions from *vaqueros* and transformed them into Western style. American cowboys wanted their meat well done, too, regarding rare meat as a perversion of the effete East. There are books full of folksy cowboy responses to rare beef, as in "I've seen cattle hurt worse than that live." The same taste for well-done beef pervades the heartland of America even today, as any traveler from the coasts knows from gut-wrenching experience. I can explain it only as a lingering nostalgia for a time when categories — East and West, city and country, foreign and American, elite and prole — were more clear-cut, and when "raw" meant disgustingly barbaric and inedible, and "cooked" meant civilized and well-done. But Western cowboy cooking differed from heartland cooking, and from most of America until the last forty years, in its embrace of chilies, garlic, and other strong flavors, as well by the habit of cutting meat in small pieces. One cowpuncher from Colorado in 1883, when asked why the cook spoiled steaks by cutting them up and frying them in black grease, answered that if a cowboy got a broiled piece of meat, he "might walk off with a whole steak, eat of it what he could and throw the rest away." Frying bits of meat in gravy not only made the meat go further, but guaranteed each got a share.

Fresh steak was in any case a luxury for cowboys or early settlers. Cathy Luchetti's *Home on the Range: A Culinary History of the American West* includes an account by Oliver Nelson, self-described "Freighter, Camp Cook, Cowboy, Frontiersman" in 1880 of the chuck-wagon fare he cooked up on his days on the Chisholm Trail:

> A couple of days after I came, they killed a beef. Hamlet hollered, "Cook, come jerk the beef.". . . I went out and cut the meat in strips three inches wide and one inch thick. Then I stretched ropes from posts, hung the strips on to dry, and built a smudge to keep the flies off. We fried this jerked beef in tallow and ate it dry; but some cooks boiled it, thickened it with flour, and seasoned it with salt

and plenty of pepper to make a dish called jowler, which was said to be awful fine.

Jerky, like barbecue, is a good example of the melding of indigenous food preparations with Spanish ones. (The word *jerky* comes from *charqui,* a Quechuan word for dried meat that Conquistadors found in Peru, just as the word *barbecue* comes from Taino *barbicao,* meaning a large grill for cooking food over an outdoor fire pit.) But jerky was more obviously travel food. Edward Abbey supplies a jerky recipe for travelers backpacking into the wilderness, which involves pinning strips of highly seasoned beef to "a line in the hot sun." For city dwellers, Elaine Hubbell suggests in her contribution to *Canyon Cookery* how to make beef jerky by laying strips of brined meat on oven racks and drying them for 3 to 6 hours at a temperature of 150 degrees with the door slightly open. "When the meat is very dark and dry and cracks sharply, but does not break when bent, it is ready." It will also keep for a year.

Carne seca was simply the Spanish name for jerky, but it was almost always flavored with hot chilies, which were also a good preservative. José Ramon Pico, nephew of Pio Pico, who became California's governor for a year in 1845, remembers in 1899 the Christmas fiestas they staged at the family ranch near Mission Santa Clara:

> In killing so many cattle there was more meat than could be eaten or sold, and the choices parts of the beef were cut into long strips, dipped in a strong boiling brine full of hot red peppers, and then hung over rawhide lines to dry in the sun, making it a very appetizing and nutritious food known as *carne seca,* which is used during the rest of the year for preparing the delicious enchiladas and chili con carne.

Mexican rancho tradition was strong in all our states bordering Mexico, but it thrived best in Texas and California. Jacqueline Higuera McMahan, as her name suggests, traces her ancestry back to a triple great-grandfather, Ignacio Higuera, who followed in the footsteps of Captain Juan Bautista de Anza on his expedition from Mexico into California. His descendants occupied Rancho Los Tularcitos for 130 years in Santa

Clara Valley, on the east side of San Francisco Bay, even as their original land grant dwindled to a 15-acre plot with an alley of olive trees. In *Rancho Cooking*, she writes warmly of family celebrations when her grandfather took over the role of *asador*, the man in charge of the outdoor fire and grill, and the meats that would be cooked thereon. Her family's *carne asada* was classic in method and ingredients, marinating flank steak in oil, vinegar, and herbs and serving it with a spicy red chile salsa, or in Californio vernacular *sarsa*, meaning a good chunky salsa.

✣ Carne Asada

4 pounds flank steak or tri-tip
8 garlic cloves
1 tablespoon sea salt
¼ cup minced parsley
3 tablespoons dried oregano
1 to 2 teaspoons crushed red pepper
2 teaspoons freshly ground black pepper
½ cup red wine vinegar, depending on the amount of meat
¼ cup fruity olive oil, depending on the amount of meat

Make a dry seasoning paste by chopping together garlic, salt, parsley, oregano, red and black peppers (a food processor will do it). Place meat in a bowl, rub the paste over all the meat surfaces, sprinkle with the vinegar and oil, cover and refrigerate at least 2 hours or overnight. Bring the meat to room temperature while you prepare the fire (they often use almond wood on top of hardwood charcoal) until it's reduced to white embers. Sear the meat over the hottest part of the fire, then raise the grate or spread the coals and grill over medium heat. Turn meat about every 8 minutes and brush with marinade halfway through (flank steaks will take 20 to 25 minutes). After removing meat from grill, let it rest 10 minutes. Cut across the grain. Serve with a good chunky salsa.

Skirt steak, which is better marbled than flank, has long been the favorite cut for a favorite dish, fajitas. In fact, the word *fajita* means a girdle or sash, which is what the diaphragm is. As Melissa Guerra points out in *Dishes from the Wild Horse Desert*, the muscle is in two layers, one attached outside the ribs and the other attached inside the ribs. The inside layer is the "true" hanger steak, but the temptation to double the meat lumps them both under the name. Melissa likes to serve fajitas with a *pico de gallo* ("rooster's beak") that is a favorite of her husband's family, whose ranch is next door.

❖ Fajitas, or Grilled Skirt Steak

One 2-pound skirt or hanger steak
Salt and pepper
8 to 12 corn tortillas

Preheat an outside grill or inside broiler or cast-iron skillet or stovetop griddle. Season steak on both sides with salt and pepper. Grill 5 to 10 minutes on each side, depending on meat thickness. Allow meat to rest for 10 to 20 minutes. Slice fajitas across the grain into ½-inch strips and serve with warm tortillas and *pico de gallo*.

❖ Pico de Gallo con Aguacate

1 cup minced white onion
½ pound tomatoes, seeded and chopped (or use tomatillos)
½ avocado, peeled, pitted and cubed
1 ounce (about 4) Serrano chiles, stems removed, minced
2 tablespoons minced cilantro
Salt to taste

Combine ingredients in a mixing bowl.

Flank steak is leaner, slightly thicker, and slightly tougher than skirt steak and is sometimes still called by the ridiculous name "London broil," an American invention to give a little class to a cheaper cut. It lends itself to marinating in oil, garlic, and lime, plus "jerk" or other seasonings — before throwing it on the barbecue. An alternative to marinating is pounding a flank steak very thin, as butcher Jack Ubaldi of the Florence Meat Market does in his *Meat Book,* when he treats flank steak in an Italian way, as he might a scallopini of veal, rolling a thin layer of meat around a hefty stuffing and braising it. The cut slices look like a galantine.

✣ Butterflied and Stuffed Flank Steak Sicilian Style

1 flank steak, 2 to 2½ pounds
Salt, freshly ground pepper
½ pound veal, ground
½ pound pork, ground
2 eggs
6 slices of pancetta or bacon, cut into small pieces
1 tablespoon chopped parsley
3 tablespoons grated *pecorino romano* cheese
¼ pound salami, sliced
¼ pound provolone, sliced
4 hard-boiled eggs, split in half lengthwise
2 tablespoons oil
2 tablespoons butter
1 onion, sliced
1 cup dry red wine
1 16-ounce can peeled plum tomatoes with the juice
1 pound fresh shelled or frozen peas

Lay the flank steak on your workspace and butterfly it with the knife running parallel to the fibers. Open it up like the leaves of a book. Flatten with a pounder and season it with salt and pepper. Mix the ground meats, eggs, pancetta, parsley, and grated cheese together and season with pepper. Spread the meat mixture evenly all over the flank steak. Place the salami slices over the mixture, then the provolone. Place the hard-boiled eggs along the flank steak. Roll the flank up with the fiber of the meat so that you have a long roll.

In a flameproof casserole, heat the oil and butter. Heat the onion and the meat and let brown on all sides. Add the wine, reduce a bit, then add tomatoes.

Cover casserole and cook very slowly in a preheated 350° oven for 1 hour and 30 minutes. Add the peas and cook another few minutes until they are done. Serve the steak on a serving platter, covered with some of the sauce.

An alternate way to cook a stuffed flank steak is to wrap it in an extra-large piece of aluminum foil. Make a small hole at one end for the steam to escape. Place it in a roasting pan and cook in a preheated 350° oven for 1 hour. Open the foil and cook for another 10 minutes. Carve the stuffed steak against the fibers.

Now that Asian fusion has become mainstream American cooking, we find a multitude of recipes for flank, round, and chuck steak, flavored typically by the Asian triad of salt, sweet, and spicy hot, then cooked typically in a quick stir-fry with other ingredients. In Asia, meat is precious, as revealed both in the way it's cooked and preserved. Throughout China, Japan, Korea, Vietnam, Laos, Indonesia, the Philippines, "Asian jerky," or sun-dried beef, is as universal as rice. Spices that flavor also preserve and the main element that distinguishes Asian jerky from American jerky is that of sweetness. A recipe from Laos for dried beef ("Sien Savanh") uses sugar, along with garlic, ginger, sesame, black pepper, and soy. A recipe from Vietnam for dried beef ("Thit Bo Kho") uses honey, along with lemon grass, chile peppers, soy, and nuoc mam. In both countries, beef strips are laid flat on a rack or tray and dried in the sun, or nowadays in the oven or dehydrator.

Recently, I found crisp strips of dried beef ("Tapa") in a salad at a Soho restaurant in Manhattan named Cendrillon, owned by a Philippine couple who happily unite a scholar with a chef, Amy Besa and Romy Dorotan. Amy explained that the name "Beef Tapa" had nothing to do with the word or tradition of Spanish *tapas* (in Spanish, *tapa* means lid, or cover), but with the Sanskrit word *tapas*, which means heat. In the Philippines meats from wild animals such as boar and deer were sun-dried millennia before the word was applied to beef. Traditionally, Amy says, beef tapa is a breakfast dish where the meat is paired with garlic-fried rice (*sinangag*) and fried eggs (*itlog*). You'll find it on a menu shortened to *Tapsilog*.

✣ Cendrillon's Beef Tapa

2 pounds flank steak

For the marinade:
½ cup soy sauce
½ cup mirin (sweetened rice wine)
Juice of 2 limes
½ cup rice vinegar
1 tablespoon garlic, minced
¼ cup sugar
1 tablespoon freshly ground black pepper

Slice the steak thinly, in ⅛-inch slices, across the grain. Combine remaining ingredients and marinate the beef at least an hour or overnight. Remove slices and lay them flat on wire racks on pans. Air-dry the slices using an electric fan, for about an hour. Cover a large skillet with a film of oil and fry the slices over medium heat until they crisp. Serve with garlic-fried rice and fried eggs.

———

One of the early introducers of Asian-flavored beef to the American palate was Craig Claiborne. In 1961, in *The New York Times Cookbook,* Claiborne had to explain to American readers that "teriyaki" came from the words *teri,* meaning glaze, and *yaki,* meaning grill. But in these early days of Asian-food exploration, Japan was too distant by far, so Claiborne explained that teriyaki was "Hawaiian for steak marinated in soy sauce, garlic and ginger and broiled, preferably over charcoal."

❖ Teriyaki

---

2 pounds sirloin steak, about ¼ inch thick
1 tablespoon finely chopped fresh ginger, or 2 teaspoons powdered
ginger
2 cloves garlic, chopped fine
1 medium onion, chopped fine
2 tablespoons sugar
1 cup soy sauce
½ cup sherry

Cut the steak into thin slices or strips. Combine the ginger, garlic, onion, sugar, soy sauce, and sherry and pour the mixture over the meat. Let stand one to two hours. Thread the meat on skewers and broil quickly on both sides over charcoal or in a preheated broiler. Serve hot.

Another major introducer of Asian-flavored beef to the American palate during the same period was Grace Zia Chu, who gave us *The Pleasures of Chinese Cooking* in 1962. A little sugar, a little sherry made palatable the otherwise strange-sounding sauce for what has become a classic of Chinese-American cooking — a stir-fry of thin beef strips, flavored with oyster sauce thickened with cornstarch. It seems quaint today that Chu had then to explain that water chestnuts came in a can and oyster sauce in a bottle and that both could be purchased in Chinese food stores. Her trick of freezing the meat in order to cut it very thin is still a useful one.

✣ Flank Steak in Oyster Sauce

12 ounces flank steak

8 water chestnuts

3 tablespoons bottled oyster sauce

1 tablespoon dry sherry

½ teaspoon sugar

2 tablespoons peanut or corn oil

2 teaspoons cornstarch

Cut flank steak into long, inch-wide strips and freeze for about 4 hours. Slice steak against the grain about ⅛-inch thick. Slice water chestnuts into ¼-inch pieces. Mix the oyster sauce, sherry, sugar, and cornstarch in a bowl and set aside. Heat the oil in a wok or a heavy frying pan for about 2 minutes over a high flame. Add the steak slices and stir immediately; continue to stir until oil covers all the surfaces and the meat turns a whitish color. Add water chestnuts and mix well. Stir in the sauce mixture; it will thicken gradually. When the steak is thoroughly mixed with the sauce, serve at once.

———————————

Since green beef, our original pasture-fed and -finished beef, is a different kind of animal from commodity corn-fed beef, we must cook it differently. The animal has exercised its muscles differently and probably longer, and those muscles will have far less fat, inside and out. Without fat, the meat will cook much more quickly. The American Grassfed Association estimates 30 percent less cooking time for grassfed. "Fat in the meat gives you a great deal of cushion against overcooking," a Brazilian chef has said. "Meat with little to no fat has no such cushion and so requires more skill." If you cook grass-fed beefsteaks beyond medium rare, they will be much too dry, and you'll be apt to blame it on the meat rather than the cook. If well-done is the only way you like beef, then save yourself money, buy a cheaper cut than rib or loin, and braise whatever cut you're using at a low, slow temperature, in some liquid to add moisture. Most rules for cooking grass-fed steaks stipulate that they should be cooked at a lower heat than usual, lest they become dry and tough. I'm wary of all such rules except one: When grilling a grass-fed steak you must pay close attention every moment it's on the fire, because it is not generic, it is one of a kind. In my experience, every steak that has been raised artisanally is different from its fellows, and that's one of its pleasures. Commodity beef is like jug wine; grass-fed beef, and especially from heritage breeds, is like boutique wines from small vineyards individually fashioned according to season, locale, *terroir.* Instead of looking for uniformity, we look for individuality. Instead of recipes, we look for guidelines; instead of rules, suggestions.

It's the particulars that matter to the palate. I once talked to a cheese man on a small farm in Ireland and asked him for a round of his cheddar. He asked whether I wanted cheddar made from morning or afternoon milk. The taste depended on when they'd been milked, as well as in which meadow they'd been feeding. R. W. Apple, reporting on Scottish chefs for the *New York Times,* claimed that chef Clive Davidson in Linlithgow, west of Edinburgh, served the best steaks in Europe. These were from Angus beef hung for three weeks. But which steaks he served on any given night depended entirely on which cuts were ripe, "which cuts were in season." Trapped by our industrial mind-sets, we're not used to contemplating variations in aging and cooking times, dependent on each singular piece of meat. But there's no reason that beef shouldn't be as interestingly varied and complex as wine.

Since the muscles of grass-fed beef are tougher on the tongue, the Grassfed Association recommends a hand tool for tenderizing: the

Jaccard meat tenderizer. This does a slightly different job from the handheld wooden mallet with which my father smashed the meat for his Swiss steaks into a pulp. The Jaccard has a series of metal needles held in a handle so that you can puncture the flesh on its entire surface without smashing it; this is a hand version of the automated electric blade tenderizer used by commercial processors. The device is useful on a cut like round steak, when you want to keep the cut thick, but I haven't found it necessary or even desirable on Prime cuts, not as long as I still have teeth to chew with. I far prefer to tenderize by marinating lean-and-mean cuts like sirloin or chuck and to baste Prime cuts with olive oil and butter, which also helps flavor and speeds browning. Because grass-fed beef tends to have more intense flavor than corn-fed, it stands up well to strongly flavored marinades and spice rubs. (When braising a grass-fed cut from the chuck or round, the AGA advises reducing the oven temperature by 50 degrees from your usual corn-fed braising or roasting temperature, because again the meat will cook more quickly.)

At the kitchen of La Cense Ranch, when I was out in Montana, I worked with chef Shanna Pacifico, who'd come with me from Savoy Restaurant, to test timing on different grass-fed cuts. We found cooking times were the same on an outside gas grill and an inside stove-top skillet using a medium-high flame. We tried first a ¾-inch strip steak and then a 1¼-inch rib eye, and found the cooking times to be the same by adding just one more minute to each category for the thicker rib eye. When cooking steaks in the skillet, Shana basted the meat with butter while they were cooking to transmit heat, flavor, and juiciness.

Timing for a ¾-inch strip steak:

1. Super rare, "black-blue": 2 minutes each side, 3 minutes rest (crisp seared exterior, velvety cool interior, full flavor)
2. Rare: 3 minutes each side, 5 minutes rest (crisp exterior, warm bright red interior, still tender, slightly more cooked flavor)
3. Medium rare: 4 minutes each side, 5 minutes rest (crisp exterior, pink interior, texture much chewier)

4. Medium: 5 minutes each side, 5 minutes rest (thicker exterior crust, interior still pinkish, chewy and less juicy)
5. Well-done: 8 minutes each side, 5 minutes rest (meat dried out and wasted)

Wagyu beef requires even more care in the cooking than grass-fed, but for opposite reasons: Instead of being very lean, it is very fat. This time it's not the feed but the breed. Wagyu means simply Japanese cow (wa = Japanese, gyu = cow), so it's not a purebred but a generic term for many strains that were crossbred for generations until a century ago, when they began to be linebred for specific traits. The result is singular because the history of beef in Japan is singular. Eating meat was prohibited for a thousand years before 1868, for both religious and practical reasons: Buddhist precepts reinforced the need to prevent draft animals from being killed for meat. In 1868, with the Meiji Restoration, when the new emperor opened Japan to the West, he also lifted the ban on eating meat, although it took another century for a significant diet shift toward beef in the general population. The heaviest beef eaters today are those in the Kinki region southwest of Tokyo, where most Wagyu in Japan are raised: *Omi* in Shiga Prefecture, *Matsusaka* in Mie Prefecture, and *Kobe* in Hyago Prefecture. Kobe is the name we attach to Japanese cattle only because Kobe is a port where the major commercial beef processors are located and where most Japanese beef is shipped from.

The fact that beef was so long forbidden in Japan has added to Wagyu's mystique as a ritual folk art, in which each cow guzzles beer and is massaged daily with sake. Those who raise Matsusaka, and who claim that it is the very best Wagyu, say that they select only females, fatten them on fodder, tofu lees, wheat, and sometimes beer; spray their hides with a homebrew called *shochu*, massage them with straw brushes, and play soft music to calm them. That may be, but the larger truth is that Japan has so little land and so little grain that massage has to substitute for exercise and an intensified local-protein diet substitutes for corn. At the same time, cattle in Japan are highly valued and cared for accordingly. Beer helps stimulate flagging appetites depressed by summer heat and humidity. Massaging relieves stress and stiffness in cramped quarters. Sake or *shochu* brushed on their hides increases skin softness, which some relate to the quality of the meat within.

Although the Japanese government carefully guards its appellation of "Kobe" beef, ironically most Kobe beef today is from Wagyu crossbreeds raised in Australia and America, where there is plenty of land and grain, and where the cattle are sent back to Japan to be processed and labeled. There are about forty-five American Kobe beef ranchers in the United States today, the largest being Snake River Farms, a subsidiary of Agri Beef Co., which was started in 1968 by Robert Rebholtz, Jr. and is still a family-owned company that has found a sizable niche within the niche market of noncommodity beef. Sizable means a herd of around 6,000 head (in 2004), producing 3 million pounds of meat, and where they used to sell exclusively to Japan, they now sell half their product in the United States. They crossbreed Japanese Black with Black Angus and feed them on barley, wheat straw, alfalfa hay, and Idaho potatoes for about four times as long as the usual fattening period for commodity beef. That's one reason for the quadruple price of American Kobe. In Japan Wagyu sells for at least $300 a pound; here it's anywhere from $40 to $80 a pound; a 10-ounce strip steak from Snake River Farms will cost $75. Instead of being tethered with a nose ring, cattle at Snake River Farms graze pasture freely until they are a year old. "After that," their marketing director explains, "they are not allowed to graze in order to limit exercise and promote soft, tender muscles." As one reporter writes, "Just like a fine wine, it's not truly Kobe until it's time."

What "truly Kobe" means in America is cattle with at least 51 percent Wagyu, fed for a longer period of time, and genetically geared to marble more and better than other breeds. Genetically, Kobe fat is of a different kind, most of it monounsaturated rather than saturated. Because of the quantity and quality of its interior fat, Kobe cooks 35 percent faster than standard Prime, and it's easy to destroy the web of marbled muscle under heat that dissolves the fat so quickly that it oozes out. Think of Kobe as foie gras, and you will automatically cook it carefully. While some experts, including Lobel's, advise that Kobe steaks be grilled at slightly lower temperatures than ordinary Prime to avoid melting the fat, I prefer a crisp exterior, which means a quick sear over a hot flame before it is whisked away from the heat. Again, think of the contradictions of a Baked Alaska: hot on the outside, cool within.

You can make Kobe the centerpiece of the Japanese hot-pot dish called "Shabu Shabu," or "swish, swish," in which thin strips of beef are swished for a moment in a savory broth flavored with vegetables, noodles, and tofu. You will need chopsticks for swishing the beef in and out quickly and for dipping all of the swished ingredients into the sauce. You'll also need a cooking pot that will sit on a tabletop burner unit.

❖ Snake River Farms American Style Kobe Beef — Shabu Shabu

24 ounces Kobe beef cut in paper-thin strips
3 ounces sliced enoki mushrooms
6 ounces sliced carrots, zucchini, or spinach
3 ounces dried clear noodles (harusame or maroni noodles)
1 small napa cabbage, sliced
1 block firm tofu, cut in 1-inch cubes

1 bottle ponzu sauce
2 ounces green onions, chopped

Stock
1 large piece of konbu, or dried kelp (optional)
1 large pinch bonito flakes (optional)

If beef is frozen, thaw in the refrigerator according to directions before cooking. Soak the noodles in cold water until soft; drain. Arrange beef, sliced vegetables, tofu, and cold noodles on individual serving plates and set them around the table. Mix ponzu sauce and green onions in a small saucer for each diner.

For the stock, boil konbu and bonito flakes in 6 cups water for 10 minutes on the tabletop cooking unit or the stove. (If desired, substitute chicken bouillon cubes.) Remove the konbu from the broth before cooking the raw ingredients.

Bring broth to a light boil. Each diner adds his raw ingredients to the broth with his chopsticks and cooks to desired doneness, then dips them into the ponzu sauce.

———————

Of course you don't have to cook Kobe at all. This is one form of beef, like grass-fed, that you can eat raw, simply with good sea salt and lots of black pepper, chopped as steak tartare or sliced as carpaccio or sashimi with a dip of soy, dashi broth, and green onion. You don't want to overwhelm but merely enhance the delicacy of the meat, so if in doubt go light on the usual ingredients for a tartare, which is simply ground beef held together by a highly seasoned and textured mayonnaise.

❖ Wagyu Steak Tartare

1½ pounds American Kobe sirloin, finely chopped

3 anchovy fillets, chopped

1 tablespoon chopped onion

1 tablespoon capers, rinsed

2 tablespoons chopped parsley leaves

1 large egg yolk

2 teaspoons Dijon mustard

1 teaspoon Worcestershire sauce

1 teaspoon cognac

2 tablespoons olive oil

½ teaspoon black pepper

Tabasco to taste

Toast points

With a sharp knife, chop the meat as fine as you can and then chop again. (A processor will turn this beef to mush.) Next chop the anchovies, onion, capers, and parsley until they are uniform in size. In a large bowl beat the egg yolk with the mustard, Worcestershire, and cognac. Gradually beat in the olive oil until the mixture thickens. Add pepper and Tabasco. Add the meat and chopped ingredients and mix well but very gently with your hands to keep the meat light and air-filled. Form gently into four to six patties and top each with a toast point set upright.

WHAT BETTER WAY to end this book than with a recipe for eating beef raw? And how American that the beef should be from a hybrid cow that reconfigures East and West in a mating of Japanese Kobe with Anglo Angus in Texas or Idaho. But to eat meat raw you have to trust the source, as if you'd pampered that steer for many months on sweet meadow grass and yourself took a hand in transforming him into meat in order to feed your hunger. Human hunger, born in the head and heart as well as the gut, includes a longing for the land to last longer than we do, a longing to respect our fellow creatures, a longing to reconcile the violence of death with the dream of justice. Images eat reality, and we feed our hunger for power and glory more than our need for nutrients when we eat steak.

ACKNOWLEDGMENTS

PERMISSIONS ACKNOWLEDGMENTS

ENDNOTES

SELECTED BIBLIOGRAPHY

INDEX

ACKNOWLEDGMENTS

———————————◆———————————

The older I get, the more grateful I am for the team effort needed to put together a book like this. My largest debt, as always, is to Becky Saletan, an editor who is one of a kind and that kind an endangered species; and to Gloria Loomis, who as a literary agent is of like quality and endangerment. Their friendship and patience over many years have meant more than they know.

Friends are indispensable and I'm indebted to far too many to name, but those whose gifts of time, skill, and knowledge helped push this project along, in manifold and unexpected ways, are Griselda Warr, Katherine Weber, Daphne Derven, Marion Nestle, Martha Taylor, Michael Pollan, Dan Barber, Eugenia Bone, Sandy Walcott, Peter Hoffmann, Gary Nabhan, Deborah Madison, Melissa Sweeney, Dorothy Lyman, Nina Planck, Nancy Bundt, Madeleine Corson, Glenna Campbell, Sandy Johnson, James Oseland.

Traveling the country, I was helped by a huge variety of people with special arts and crafts, from cowboy bootmaking to cattle insemination. Whenever I could, I've named them in the text, but there are many more I'd like to name. For me, their images are linked intimately with places. In Colorado, there were Elizabeth Wright Ingraham, Dick Hansen,

Michael McCarthy, Ivan Wilson, Robbie Baird LeValley, Peggy Ford, Alan Bates, J. Daryl Tatum, Mark Gustafson, Don Anderson, Russ Moss, Trent Horton. In Texas and the Southwest, Peggy Grodinsky, Mike Risica, Rocky Carroll, Patricia Patterson, Clifton Caldwell, Deborah and Jim Bill Anderson, Nathan and Cathy Melson, Carol Ellick and Joe Wheat, Joe Taylor. In Oregon, Mike Bentz, the Harrells — Edna, Bob and Becky — Dan and Jo Warnock, Lowell and Mary Forman, Clair and Patti Pickard. In Montana, Eric Stenberg, Skip Hoagland, Daryl and Steve Kroon. In California, Mike and Sally Gates, David Evans.

For research, I've been aided by many of the best and brightest in New York University's Food Studies program: Jennifer Berg, Ellen Fried, Johanna Kolodny, Joy Santofler, Diana Pittet, Berthsy Ayide, Christina Ciambriello, Jenny Fiedler, Mary Beth Brookby, David McIntyre, Jaime Harder, James Feustel.

For other special kinds of help I'm indebted to Jean Kidd, Judith La-Belle, Nancye Good, Charlotte Buchen, Peggy Tagliarini, Karen Schloss, Brenda McDowell, Mary Bartz, Carrie Balkrom, Don Bixby, Aundrea Fares, Olivia Bonom, Danielle DiGiacomo, Amy Besa, Romy Dorotan, Dwight Lee.

Finally, I have a long-standing debt to Paul Fussell, who long ago taught me the profession of reading and writing, and the pleasures of both.

PERMISSIONS ACKNOWLEDGMENTS

ENDNOTES

———— ♦ ————

The Cowboy and the Machine

3 *marrow of political freedom.* "Mad Cows and Englishmen," *New Yorker,* April 8, 1996.

   vanquish the effeminate French. A full workup on the symbolic power of meat is provided by Nick Fiddes, *Meat: A Natural Symbol* (London & New York: Routledge, 1991). For the symbolic power of beef in England, see Ben Rogers, *Beef and Liberty: Roast Beef, John Bull and the English Nation* (London: Chatto & Windus, 2003).

   the very flesh of the French soldier. "Steak and Chips," *Mythologies* (London: Jonathan Cape, 1972, translated by Annette Lavers from the 1957 French edition).

6 *power that clothes violence in virtue.* Richard Slotkin has explored this territory in two notable books: *Regeneration through Violence: The Mythology of the American Frontier, 1600–1860* (Middletown, CT: Wesleyan University Press, 1974) and *Gunfighter Nation: The Myth of the Frontier in Twentieth-Century America* (New York: Atheneum, 1992).

   the eating of cows. Kim Severson said it best in "Bringing Moos and Oinks to the Food Debate," *New York Times,* July 25, 2007: "Although animal-rights groups and chefs might agree that farm animals need to be treated with more care, one side wants to put those animals on the grill and the other wants to simply hang out with them."

Beefy Boys

9 "*All You Can Hold for Five Bucks.*" *New Yorker,* April 15, 1939.

10 *tonight's boys to shame.* Ben Rogers, *Beef and Liberty: Roast Beef, John Bull and the English Nation* (London: Chatto & Windus, 2003).
horror of horrors — table linen. Charles Michener, "The Mess Hall," *New Yorker,* February 19 & 26, 2001.

11 *the beefsteak is American.* "The Supremacy of Beefsteak," *The Nation,* December 26, 1923.

13 *84.3 pounds per person.* For these and later statistics, see "Factors Affecting U.S. Beef Consumption." www.ers.usda.gov/publications/ldp/oct05/ldpm13502/.
putative American warrior. Baker quoted by Warren Belasco, *Meals to Come: A History of the Future of Food* (Berkeley & Los Angeles; London: University of California Press, 2006). See especially his first chapter, "The Stakes in Our Steaks."
symbol of machismo. Quoted by Jeremy Rifkin in his chapter "Meat and Gender Hierarchies" in *Beyond Beef: The Rise and Fall of the Cattle Culture* (New York: Dutton, 1992).
roast food death. Quoted by Rifkin in the same chapter.

14 *250 slaughterhouses and meat packers.* Edwin G. Burrows and Mike Wallace, *Gotham: A History of New York City to 1898* (New York: Oxford University Press, 1998).

15 *waving red flags in front of the freight trains.* Sarah Maslin Nir, "Under the Skin of the Big Apple," May 10, 2007, at Times Online. http://www.travel.timesonline .co.uk/tol/life_and_style/travel/destinations/usa/articles.
melancholy reminder of change. A thumbnail history with historical images and contemporary maps can be found at "Save Gansevoort Market: A Walking Tour" (2002). http://www.gvshp.org/walktour/walktour.htm.
meatpackers probably think we're crazy. Quoted by Lincoln Anderson, "Instead of meat, High Line will offload artistas at Dia museum," *The Villager,* volume 74, number 54 (May 18–24, 2005).

18 *trade and violence.* Russell Shorto, *The Island at the Center of the World: The Epic Story of Dutch Manhattan and the Forgotten Colony That Shaped America* (New York: Random House, 2004).
began to crowd lower Manhattan. George M. Welling, "The United States of America and the Netherlands"; also Jan Folkerts, "The Failure of West Indian Company Farming on the Island of Manhattan," essays at the website "From Revolution to Reconstruction . . . an HTML project," initiated by the Department of Humanities Computing, University of Gröningen, the Netherlands. http://www.let.rug.nl/~usa/E/newnetherlands/nlxx.htm.
de wal, or Wall Street. Jimmy M. Skaggs, *Prime Cut: Livestock Raising and Meatpacking in the U.S., 1607–1983* (College Station, TX: Texas A&M University Press, 1986).

19 *along drover trails to London.* Terry G. Jordan, *North American Cattle-Ranching*

Frontiers: Origins, Diffusion, and Differentiation (Albuquerque, NM: University of New Mexico Press, 1993).

"milch cows" throughout Europe. Virginia D. Anderson, *Creatures of Empire: How Domestic Animals Transformed Early America* (Oxford & New York: Oxford University Press, 2004). Anderson's book is vital to understanding how differently Native Americans and colonial conquerors viewed man's relation to animals and to the land. She notes the potential for violence at the heart of every livestock dispute.

20 *shipped to the West Indies.* James E. McWilliams, *A Revolution in Eating: How the Quest for Food Shaped America* (New York: Columbia University Press, 2005).

assist the settlers in their work. Quoted by Jordan, *North American Cattle-Ranching Frontiers.*

killed merely for tallow and hides. John Rouse, *The Criollo: Spanish Cattle in the Americas* (Norman, OK: University of Oklahoma Press, 1977). Rouse traces the historic evolution of this breed throughout the Americas.

G for guerra, or war. Harold McCracken, *The American Cowboy* (Garden City, NY: Doubleday, 1973).

21 *beef and pork were commodities of the city.* William Cronon, *Nature's Metropolis: Chicago and the Great West* (New York: W. W. Norton, 1991).

Putting Meat on the American Table: Taste, Technology, Transformation (Baltimore: Johns Hopkins University Press, 2006).

22 *slaughterhouses within 200 yards of his house. The Market Book: containing a historical account of the public markets of the cities of New York, Boston, Philadelphia and Brooklyn, with a brief description of every article of human food sold therein, the introduction of cattle in America, and notices of many remarkable specimens* (New York: printed for the author, 1862).

awaiting designation as a landmark site. For a detailed history of the Hudson Yards, see "Appendix K-Archaeological Resources" (2003). http://www.nyc.gov/html/dc[/pdf/hyards/app_k_archaeolgical_text_fgeis_final.pdf. A personal glimpse of the Cow Tunnel is given by ZippyTheChimp Jan. 27–28, 2006, at http://www.wirednewyork.com/forum/archive/index.php/t-8314.html.

23 *like water up a straw. Great Plains* (New York: Picador, 2001).

speckled cattle and the festive cowboy. Quoted by Frazier in *Great Plains.*

Chicago for slaughtering and packing. Skaggs, *Prime Cut.*

ice in straw-lined chests. "Slaughterhouse to the World" (2005). http://www.chicagohs.org/history/stockyard/stck1.html.

24 *35 million in 1900.* Edward E. Dale, *The Range Cattle Industry: Ranching on the Great Plains from 1865 to 1925* (Norman, OK: University of Oklahoma Press, 1930).

"handicraft methods" of a traditional peasantry. Siegfried Giedion, *Mechanization Takes Command: A Contribution to Anonymous History* (New York: Norton, 1975).

26 *the infallibility of technology. New York Times,* December 10, 2003.

Breaking the Wild

31 *1000 tons of venison a year.* U.S. deer production is increasing at the rate of 25 to 30 percent annually, with around 25,000 red deer harvested per year in the United States and Canada.

35 *settlers to the west coast of Florida.* John Rouse, *The Criollo: Spanish Cattle in the Americas* (Norman, OK: University of Oklahoma Press, 1977).

36 *600,000 acres to a single claimant.* Don Graham, *Kings of Texas: The 150-Year Saga of an American Ranching Empire* (New York: John Wiley & Sons, 2003).

37 *with nothing to stand on.* Ibid.

descendants of enterprising Anglo-Mexican marriages. Dan Butler and Frank Yturria shared lands and bloodlines from their great-grandfather, Daniel McGraw. He'd been adopted by a native of Matamoros, Francisco Yturria, who'd made his fortune with Richard King by running cotton past the Union blockade through Brownsville. Francisco bought a 200,000-acre land grant, Punta del Monte, and enlarged it by marrying land-rich Felicitas Trevino. As the couple was childless, they adopted both Daniel McGraw and a Mexican girl, Isabel, who married another Mexican, Miguel Garcia. Francisco disapproved of the marriage and cut Isabel from his will. At her father's death, Isabel Garcia claimed her share of the land and, to make peace, the Yturria family agreed to split the property down the middle. Everything to the east of the railroad would be Yturria's, everything to the west Garcia's. That's why today the descendant cousins Dan, Francisco, and Monica (Garcia) live on adjoining ranches separated by rail lines.

land grant to her father that dated from 1767. As the McAllens tell the story in their family history, Salome's first husband was another émigré Britisher named John Young. A merchant in Brownsville, Young had an assistant he'd rescued from jail. This was John McAllen, who'd emigrated to New York in 1845, become a surveyor in Tehuantepec, and was on his way to the California Gold Rush when Young found him. At Young's death, McAllen married the boss's widow. They came in waves, says descendant Jim McAllen: Spanish settlers in the 1740s, Mexicans in the 1840s, Anglos in the 1850s. See *I Would Rather Sleep in Texas: A History of the Lower Rio Grande Valley & the People of the Santa Anita Land Grant* (Austin: Texas State Historical Association, 2003).

cookbook author and television chef. Dishes from the Wild Horse Desert: Norteño Cooking of South Texas (Hoboken, NJ: John Wiley & Sons, 2006).

39 *woman rancher named Randee Fawcett. Dallas Morning News.* January 3, 2005.

not cattlemen but "land managers." Graham, *Kings of Texas.* http://www.king-ranch.com/legend.htm; http://www.tsha.utexas.edu/handbook/onlinearticles/view/KK/apk1.html.

40 *vermin, to be exterminated.* Graham, *Kings of Texas.*

better-paid Anglo cowboys. Jack Weston, *The Real American Cowboy* (New York: Schocken, 1985).

42 *Kleberg settled it.* Ibid.

land-grant claim against King. Major William Chapman had been a partner with King in the original Rincón de Santa Gertrudis grant. At his death in 1879, Chapman's widow claimed half interest in the land. King testified in court that Chapman had signed over his half of the property to King, who could not produce the deed. Over 100 years later, Chapman heirs renewed the suit in 1995, but lost their case. The archives of King Ranch remain closed.

45 *ignorant, uneducated and desperate.* "Migrants Sue Vigilantes for Violent Assaults," Southern Poverty Law Center: http://www.splcenter.org/center/splreport/article. June, 2003.

47 *sister runs the village deli.* Bryan's mother, a spry seventy-three, lives across the brook and up the hill on land her husband's great-grandfather settled in 1800 when he came from Edinburgh by way of the Carolinas. Her father's old farm has just been bought by "foreigners," a doctor and his wife from Boston.

49 *small-scale and integrated.* Bryan's farm is typical of what's happened to the American family farm after a century and a half of industrialism. Today, half of all farm income is produced by 1 percent of our farms; 90 percent earn less than $20,000 a year. Although an America of small family-owned subsistence farms lives on in Jeffersonian myth and environmentalist rhetoric, in fact subsistence farming is largely an oxymoron. While some factory farms are still owned by families who've pooled their lands and resources, most are the megalithic farms owned by industrial corporations which also own the seeds and the chemicals to produce megalithic monocrops. In this economic hierarchy, most farm workers are hired serfs. Organic, sustainable farming, however, has made notable inroads, and Vermont has been true to its name and its heritage of independence in searching for ways to go green. See the New England Livestock Alliance, Vermont Fresh Network, Vermont Grass Farmers Association.

50 *long enough to get it out of their system.* Sandi's concern is personal because the women in her family are allergic to penicillin. When her mother was on a chicken diet to lose weight, she became ill. Sandi switched her to free-range chicken, despite the extra cost, and "she picked right up." As for hormones, Sandi worries about why kids are so big today: "There's a couple of kids at school built like redwoods. Next to their mothers, these kids are humongous."

51 William Cronon, *Changes in the Land: Indians, Colonists, and the Ecology of New England* (New York: HarperCollins, 1983).
cattell to maintayne it. "General Observations," 1629. Quoted by Cronon.
visible by enclosure and manurance. Virginia DeJohn Anderson, *Creatures of Empire: How Domestic Animals Transformed Early America* (New York: Oxford University Press, 2004). Courses in American history should begin with a careful reading of this transformative book.

52 *agents of empire.* Ibid.
he should be killed. William Bradford, *Of Plymouth Plantation 1620–1647,* ed. Samuel Eliot Morison (New York: Alfred A. Knopf, 1991). Quoted by Anderson.

like a cloud of light. Quoted by Don D. Walker, *Clio's Cowboys: Studies in the Historiography of the Cattle Trade* (Lincoln: University of Nebraska Press, 1981).

American West in the minds of the colonists. The Culture of Wilderness: Agriculture as Colonization in the American West (Chapel Hill: University of North Carolina Press, 1996).

from Barbarism to Civilitie. Quoted by Warren J. Belasco, *Meals to Come: A History of the Future of Food* (Berkeley: University of California Press, 2006).

53 *kept Cattle in New-England.* Quoted by Anderson.

55 *meat is for home consumption.* Ninety percent of beef cattle raised in Vermont is sold within the state.

any meat or bone left together. The rule was designed for processing commercial beef after the discovery of mad cow disease in this country impacted global trade. The failure of some processors to comply fully shut down the renewal of trade with Japan in January 2006 after an interim of three years and the loss of billions of dollars.

56 *game . . . is that it's seasonal.* There are special hazards to cutting game. Sandi first asks a hunter, "Where'd you shoot it?" If it's gut shot, she must work faster and sometimes the hunter will lie. It's costly to hunt moose: $25 to get into the lottery and $1,200 if you win a permit. Some guys have been waiting ten years for a permit.

58 *the dead language of commodity.* Frieda Knobloch, *The Culture of Wilderness* (Chapel Hill: University of North Carolina Press, 1996).

59 *streamlining the whole with polished steel.* Fairbanks scales are so widely used globally that they're said to weigh each week a total of a million million pounds of material.

St. Jesus and Long Coming. Center of Rural Studies, University of Vermont. http://www.crs.uvm.edu.

offset by an upturn in another. Ron Chernow, *Alexander Hamilton* (New York: Penguin Press, 2004).

60 *any Scripture of Nature.* Quoted by Mark D. Mitchell, *St. Johnsbury Athenaeum: Handbook of the Art Collection* (St. Johnsbury, VT: Trustees of the St. Johnsbury Athenaeum, 2005).

industrialization had rendered virtually obsolete. Ibid.

Playing Cowboy

63 *less need to go on to Abilene.* The Handbook of Texas Online. http://www.tsha.utexas.edu/handbook/online/articles/FF/dif4_print.html.

64 *men were cheap but cattle cost money.* Jack Weston, *The Real American Cowboy* (New York: Schocken, 1985).

65 *decimation of cattle herds simply for hides.* D. L. Frazier, "How Roping Came to Be." *Cowboy Magazine,* September 2004. Frazier notes that the sixteenth-

century slaughter of cattle in Mexico resembles the nineteenth-century slaughter of buffalo in the United States.

Hero of the Mexican Bull Ring. Richard Slatta, *The Cowboy Encyclopedia* (New York: W.W. Norton & Co., 2002).

Bedouins on their Arabian steeds. The term for this style is *jinetea*, as noted by Slatta, which indicates its Arabic origin. See Gary Nabhan, "Chasing Alice Ann: Echoes of Arabic Across the Sonoran Desert Borderlands," *Arab/American: Landscape, Culture, and Cuisine in Two Great Deserts* (Tucson: University of Arizona Press, 2008). Nabhan finds many traces of Arabic words, sieved through Spanish, in the cowboy lingo of the Southwest today — e.g., a good horseman is called *jinete*, from Arabic *zeneti*; "hackamore"derives from Arabic *sakima*. See also Robert Smead, *VocabularioVaquero/CowboyTalk: A Dictionary of Spanish Terms from the American West* (Norman, OK: University of Oklahoma Press, 2004).

coronation of Alfonso VIII. Mario Carrión, "The Spanish Fiesta Brava: Historical Perspective and Definition." http://www.coloquio.com/toros/bullhist.html.

66 *amalgam of Old and New Spain.* David Dary, *Cowboy Culture: A Saga of Five Centuries* (New York: Alfred A. Knopf, 1981).

jousting and then to cavalry fighting. Slatta gives a condensed history of rodeo competitions in *The Cowboy Encyclopedia.*

68 *murdered in his bed.* Ian Frazier, *Great Plains* (New York: Farrar, Straus & Giroux, 1989).

69 *denim, denim and more denim.* Guy Trebay, *New York Times,* August 7, 2005.

71 *Edison in New Jersey in 1894.* See *New York Times* review of Louis Warren's *Buffalo Bill's America,* December 22, 2005.

72 *Mulhall . . . Madison Square Garden.* http://www.cowgirls.com/dream/cowgals/mulhall.htm.

Ladies Bucking Horse Champion. Eric V. Sorg, "Annie Oakley," *Wild West* magazine, February 2001.

73 *railroad lands for themselves.* Robert V. Hine and John M. Faragher, *The American West: A New Interpretive History* (New Haven: Yale University Press, 2000).

fraudulently by or for corporations. Jack Weston, *The Real American Cowboy* (New York: Schocken Books, 1985).

74 *therefore ripe for lynching.* For a fully illustrated account, see "Johnson County War, From Wyoming Tales and Trails." http://www.wyomingtalesandtrails.com/johnson.html.

75 *conform to patrician ideals.* Both hero and villain are wealthy capitalists in *Chisum* (1970), but John Wayne is the benign paternalistic rancher, not the greedy one.

might reach as much as $500. Weston, *The Real American Cowboy.*

77 *The Arizona Bandit.* For a photograph, see http://www.legendsofamerica.com/PicturePages/PP-Outlaws-4-P.

78 *ballet dance with death.* Carrión, "The Spanish Fiesta Brava."

The New Range Wars

84 *they knew little about ranching.* First off, the Davieses hired a full-time irrigator, who had come with his family twenty years ago from Mexico, so that his wife is now the ranch cook and his eldest son the head buckaroo.

88 *spirit in every page without knowing.* Interview in *St. Louis Post-Dispatch*, quoted by Tom Farley, "Canyons, Cowboys, and Cash: Walt Whitman's West." *Mickle Street Review,* issue 17/18, 2006. http://www.micklestreet.rutgers.edu/pages/Scholarship/Farley.htm.
vast masses of men and families. Quoted by Farley from Walt Whitman's *Specimen Days* (1882).

89 *England's cottage sensibility.* Whitman did respond to something unique in the "unbounded scale, unconfined" prairies some two thousand miles square in the center of the nation, something anti-European, something which "seems fated to be the home both of what I could call America's distinctive ideas and distinctive realities." "The Prairies, And an Undeliver'd Speech," *Specimen Days.*
settlements for markets and tools. Bruce Chatwin, *What Am I Doing Here?* (New York: Viking Press, 1989).

90 *virtues that undergird personal independence.* "Mr. Jefferson comes to town: Thomas Jefferson's aversion to urban life," *Public Interest:* Summer 1993.
eruption of forces totally new. Quoted by George Will.

91 *control the land that depends on it.* Wallace Stegner, *Beyond the Hundredth Meridian: John Wesley Powell and the Second Opening of the West* (Boston: Houghton Mifflin, 1954).
soled and saddled into Crimea on American bison. Richard Manning, *Against the Grain: How Agriculture Hijacked Civilization* (New York: North Point Press, 2004).

92 *the titles granted were fraudulent.* For the chilling sequence by which public lands became private, see Jeremy Rifkin, *Beyond Beef: The Rise and Fall of the Cattle Culture* (New York: Dutton, 1992).
civilizing power of private property. For a full text of the Dawes Act, see http://www.nebraskastudies.org.
reduced some herds by 70 percent. Charles F. Wilkinson, *Crossing the Next Meridian: Land, Water, and the Future of the West* (Washington, D.C.: Island Press, 1992).

93 *fix the terms on which its property may be used.* Ibid.
understaffed, underfunded, and underpowered. Ibid.

94 *solely an economic problem.* Aldo Leopold, *A Sand County Almanac* (New York: Oxford University Press, 1949).

95 *land without spoiling it.* Quoted by Verlyn Klinkenborg, "Aldo Leopold's Odyssey: 2006," *New York Times,* November 5, 2006.

96 *tend to go out the window.* Stacy's view was predictive of Measure 37, a property-rights law Oregon passed in 2004, which in effect countermanded the statewide program of regulating land use. The new measure stated that the state government must pay compensation to a property owner whose land was reduced in value through land regulations.

98 *each constitutes a wholly different culture.* All shades of the political spectrum

are involved: the Sierra Club on the left is matched by Stewards of the Range on the right. Earlier enviro slogans like "No Moo by '92" and "Cattle Free by '93" are countered by current rancher battle cries like "Unite to Fight," which joins three defenders of property rights: Stewards of the Range, American Land Foundation, and Liberty Matters.

Circling the Wagons

101 *considered radical by ranchers and farmers.* Twenty years later, the idea of ecosystems has so permeated our language that we find books on how to make money by their metaphoric use: "Discover how the economy is like an ecosystem and money is a token we use to represent calories of energy in the ecosystem." See Thomas J. Elpel's *Direct Pointing to Real Wealth: Thomas J. Elpel's Field Guide to Money* (HOPS Press, LLC, 2000). http://www.hollowtop.com.
time . . . controls overgrazing. Quoted by Allan Savory in *Holistic Resource Management* (Washington, D.C.: Island Press, 1988).

102 *destruction of our common ground.* In 1936 government surveys found that overgrazing had depleted 52 percent of our rangeland; in 1980, 85 percent of the land had lost more than half its potential vegetation. See Richard Manning, *Grassland: The History, Biology, Politics, and Promise of the American Prairie* (New York: Viking, 1995).
2 billion tons each year. See "Lessons from the Land Institute." http://www.landinstitute.org.
skeptics as well as converts. Skeptics refer to the Wizard of Oz in the Kingdom of Savory. See Lynn Jacobs, *Waste of the West: Public Lands Ranching* (self-published, 1992), especially chapter 12. Available online at http://www.wasteofthewest.com.

103 *but 50 of which supply cattle.* Niman sold his brand at the end of 2007 and now raises cattle, sheep, and goats on his Bolinas ranch.

105 *to keep the old industrial system going.* See Kirschenmann's columns in the "Leopold Letter: A Newsletter for the Leopold Center for Sustainable Agriculture," available online at http://www.leopold.iastate.edu. See especially "Farming: . . . 'an industry like any other?'" Summer 2002, volume 14, number 2.
the uniqueness of each situation. Allan Savory, "Re-Creating the West . . . One Decision at a Time," in *Ranching West of the 100th Meridian: Culture, Ecology, and Economics,* ed. by Richard Knight, Wendell Gilgert, and Ed Marston (Washington, D.C.: Island Press, 2002).
they moved West. Paiutes had once thrived in this part of the Great Basin until shunted into the Malheur Indian Reservation in 1872 and told to become farmers. Their lands became public domain for settlers and the Pacific Livestock Company. By the turn of the century, sheepherders had denuded the range.

107 *natural-food stores in Colorado.* Stephen M. Voynick, *Riding the Higher Range: The Story of Colorado's Coleman Ranch and Coleman Natural Beef* (Saguache, CO: self-published by Glenn Melvin Coleman, 1998).

108 *quantifying profits at the producing end.* See Peter Donovan's comprehensive interview with Doc and Connie Hatfield, "Oregon Country Beef: growing a solution to economic, environmental, and social needs," *Patterns of Choice,* 2000, available online at a Web site dedicated to holistic management. http://www.managingwholes.com. For the current business structure of Coleman Natural Beef, see Susan Moran, "The Range Gets Crowded for Natural Beef," *New York Times,* June 10, 2006.

111 *then trucked to the slaughterhouse.* By 2008, Oregon Country Beef had to change its name to Country Natural Beef because it now includes 125 member ranches in 12 western states, running 103,000 cows on 6.5 million acres. Half its production goes to Whole Foods; it has also allied itself to institutional distributors like Bon Appetit and Sodexho, concerned with issues of sustainability and humane stewardship. It has added a new feedlot and processing plant in Hereford, Texas, with the aim of keeping regional connections.

117 *a relatively small region, or locale.* Niman substitutes for "locale" the term "local," to describe livestock raised in appropriate environments, but not necessarily for local consumption.
society to match the scenery. High Country News. http://www.hcn.org.

119 *Turner Reserve Grassfed Bison.* http://www.tedturner.com.

Buffalo Commons

124 *covered with Hair like a Lion.* See Tae Ellin, "Where the Buffalo Roam . . . Again," *Culinary Historians of New York* newsletter, volume 18, number 2, Fall 2005.

125 *native plant species have a relationship.* Annie Proulx, *That Old Ace in the Hole: A Novel* (New York: Scribner, 2002).
much as we do with air or water. "The Buffalo Commons: Metaphor as Method," *Geographical Review,* issue 4, October 1999.

134 *WAAAUUUGGGHHHH!* Sam died on June 9, 2006.
an attempt to domesticate their wildness. Yote Risa, "Buffalo Resistance in Yellowstone," *Earth First! Journal,* Summer 2004. See also http://www.wildrockies.org/buffalo.
what are effectively parked cars. Jim Robbins, "Critics of Montana Hunt Say Bison Aren't Fair Game," *New York Times,* October 17, 2005.

135 *as Choctaw or Arapaho.* Lisa Anderson, "How Buffalo Ted Hunts Bison Bucks," *Insight on the News,* June 28, 1999.

Greening Beef

137 *real food rots.* Joel Salatin, *Holy Cows and Hog Heaven: The Food Buyer's Guide to Farm Friendly Food* (Swoope, VA: Polyface Inc., 1995).

shoot-out with the machine. Todd Purdum, "High Priest of the Pasture," *New York Times* magazine, May 1, 2005.

138 *influential family farms in America.* Michael Pollan, "Sustaining Vision," *Gourmet,* September 2002. Pollan devotes a chapter in *Omnivore's Dilemma* to Salatin as a model for New Wave farming in the anti-industrial mode.

139 *physical nutrition feeds spiritual health.* See http://www.westonaprice.org.

140 *Kurtis, down in Sedan, Kansas.* Chicago's Swedish Covenant Hospital announced in 2006 that all beef in patients' meals would be grass-fed beef from the Kurtis ranch. "Wholesome and healthy foods play such a vital role in patient recovery," said hospital spokesman Ann Bagel Storck. "Grass-fed beef processor makes it onto hospital menu," *Meatingplace,* November 29, 2006. http://www.meatingplace.com.

141 *we don't connect the two ends.* In the last five years, prairie has been blacktopped by suburbs all the way along Route 24 from Colorado Springs to the Matheson turnoff, 55 miles to the southeast. In the words of Russell Baker, "The condos get so dense out in those 'burbs that the deer have to run through hot tubs."

142 *means literally "there-his-land."* Lasater is probably a Basque name, and the Spanish connection was reinforced by the ranchland of Castella de La Mota that Ed Lasater began to acquire in the 1890s. Dale has written his family's history in *Falfurrias: Ed C. Lasater and the Development of South Texas* (College Station, TX: Texas A&M University Press, 1985).

143 *at least for a day. Knowledge Rich Ranching* (Ridgeland, MI: Green Park Press, 2000).

145 *1400 pounds, and in the southern, 1200. Stockman Grass Farmer,* July 2002.

146 *changed the source of the inputs, Nation says. Stockman,* September 2006.

147 *pastures and his cows. Salad Bar Beef* (Swoope, VA: Polyface Inc., 1995).

Good Breeding

151 *far smaller than commercial beef breeds.* Jim Bill Anderson, in Canadian, Texas, is the only rancher in the country to raise Corriente for meat. He describes them thus: triangular-shaped heads, hips higher than shoulders which puts a sway in their backs, horns that sit wide on their polls. Their muscles have a higher percentage of red than white muscle fibers: white fibers burn carbohydrates for quick energy, red use inner muscular lipids for slow and enduring energy. Herefords are sprinters, Corriente are long-distance runners.

on the plains of Andalusia. James MacDonald, *Food from the Far West: or, American Agriculture with Special References to the Beef Production & Importation of Dead Meat from America to Great Britain* (London & Edinburgh: William P. Nimmo, 1878). See http://www.chla.library.cornell.edu.

152 *self-reliance and initiative.* Quoted by Frieda Knobloch, *The Culture of Wilderness: Agriculture as Colonization in the American West* (Chapel Hill: University of North Carolina Press, 1996).

and for much the same reasons. In 1742 Benjamin Tomkins in Herefordshire mated a bull calf (from a cow named Silver) with two cows, Pidgeon and Mottle, and thereby founded the Hereford breed.

herd was established in upstate New York. It was Henry Clay of Kentucky who first imported Herefords to the United States in 1817 and two men in New York, William Sotham and Erastus Corning in Albany, who established Herefords as an American breed.

two rather than four years. North Carolina Agricultural Research Service, North Carolina State University. See http://www.ww4.ncsu.edu.

Aberdeen into the Aberdeen-Angus. At the hands of William McCombie of Tillyfour, England, called "the Great Preserver."

154 *meeting of the ALBC in Florida.* In 2004 the ALBC met jointly with the Florida Cracker Cattle Association at Withlacoochee State Forest, amidst pines, palmettos, and moss-dripping oaks. Unusual cattle country, until you think of the Mormons' giant Deseret Ranch near Orlando.

156 *ropers are a different culture, Ginny says.* Denny Gentry in Albuquerque started U.S. Team Roping Championships in the 1980s, when he devised a scoring system for ropers working in pairs, one of whom might be a skilled vet and the other a kid. There's big money in roping, and Ginny cites a neighbor kid who won a truck and trailer before he was old enough to drive.

159 *animal life in the borderlands region.* See R. Randall Schumann, "The Malpai Borderlands Project: A Stewardship Approach to Rangeland Management," at http://www.geochange.er.usgs.gov/sw/responses/malpai.

The Smell of Greeley

174 *$155 was collected from each.* Peggy A. Ford, "The History of Greeley, Colorado." http://www.ci.greeley.co.us.

175 *set up an osteopathic practice.* My grandfather, among early graduates of the S. S. Still College of Osteopathy founded in 1898 in Des Moines, Iowa, was attracted to Dr. A. T. Still's conservative-progressive logic that because the human body had been designed by an All-wise Creator, it was therefore "a perfect machine."

176 *survived for a century and a half, with slight variations.* See http://www.stetson.com.

181 *cornfields in Kansas and Nebraska.* For a condensed history of the Monfort operation in relation to ConAgra, see Perry Swanson, "The Company," *Greeley Tribune,* May 26, 2002. For a broader history of the cattle feeding industry, see http://www.answers.com/topic/beef-cattle-feedlots.

A. D. Anderson and Currier Holman. See http://www.fundinguniverse.com/company-histories/IBP-Inc-Company-History.html.

182 *acquiring Swift Independent Packing Company.* Swanson, "The Company."

traced to beef at the Greeley plant. Michael Scherer, "U.S. Department of Agriculture (USDA) Captured by Meatpacking Industry," *Mother Jones*, December 2003.

183 *ten sites in five states.* "Cattle Feeding Got Bigger — Lots Bigger," *Beef* magazine, March 14, 2005. See Beef Stocker Trends, http://www.beefstockerusa.org.
to make 26 billion pounds of beef. http://www.answers.com/topic/beef-cattle-feedlots.
the largest meat conglomerate in the world. Tom Johnston, "Brazilian firm to buy Swift, become world's biggest meat conglomerate," http://www.meatingplace.com. May 29, 2007. ·

184 *put our cows on drugs.* The industry position on drugs is outlined by the American Feed Industry Association Web site under the category "Safe Feed/Safe Food": http://www.afia.org/about/html. See also its trade journal, *Feedstuffs*. The environmentalist position is outlined well by the Ohio Environmental Council at http://www.theoec.org. See its "Position Paper on Antibiotic Resistance and the Role of Animal Agriculture."
transform grass into protein. Frontline: "Modern Meat"; interviews: Michael Pollan/PBS. http://www.pbs.org/wgbh/pages/frontline/shows/meat/interviews/pollan.html.

185 *chlortetracycline, oxytetracyline, sulfamethazine.* For an industry take on the issue, see Sally Schuff, "Brown unveils legislation to phase out antibiotics," *Feedstuffs Magazine*, March 4, 2002.
92 percent of feedlot managers implant these routinely during the initial processing at the lot. "The Use of Drugs in Food Animals: Benefits and Risks," published by National Academy Press (Washington, D.C., 1999). For more recent information on the use of antibiotics, see the Web site of a coalition of medical and environmental groups called "Keep Antibiotics Working: The Campaign to End Antibiotic Overuse" (KAW): http://www.keepantibioticsworking.com. In August 2005, they noted the "First Ever FDA Ban on Antibiotic Use (Cipro) in Factory Farms." See also their *Factsheet: Antibiotic Resistance and Animal Agriculture.*

186 *New York Times in 2002. Sunday Magazine* section, March 31, 2002.

188 *get all their food from foreign countries.* One example: The region of Querétaro northwest of Mexico City is now burgeoning with mega-cattle feedlots and factory farms for chickens and hogs.

Slaughterhouse Blues

192 *three-day workshop, Beef 101.* Because it's part of the university's Extension Service, anyone with the money to pay for it can apply to "Beef 101: Everything You Wanted to Know About Beef."

200 *in one generation, an extraordinary feat.* See "A Biography of America: Industrial Supremacy." http://www.learner.org/biographyofamerica/prog14/transcript/page03.html.

always wanted their beef fresh. For detailed biographies of Armour and Swift, see http://www.answers.com.

201 *tethered to a natural product.* Roger Horowitz, *Putting Meat on the American Table: Taste, Technology, Transformation* (Baltimore: Johns Hopkins University Press, 2006).

almost entirely of human parts. Ibid.

neither the body nor the face of humans. Giacosa quoted in "A Biography of America: Industrial Supremacy."

83 percent of the slaughtering/processing segment. Statistics are for 2007. See "The issues: slaughterhouses and processing," at http://www.sustainable.org/issues/processing/index_pf.html.

46 percent of the marketing segment. Statistics are for 2004. See Mary Hendrickson, "Trends in Concentration in Agribusiness and Food Retailing," http://www.tacd.org/events/meeting7/m_hendrickson.ppt#259. Her charts clarify the vertical integration of chemicals, fertilizers, seeds, meat production, meat processing, and (in one case) grocery-shelf foods at ADM, Cargill, and ConAgra.

202 *cattle to IBP between 1994 and 2002.* See David R. Moeller, "The Problem of Agricultural Concentration: The Case of the Tyson-IBP Merger," *Drake Journal of Agricultural Law,* volume 8, 2003. http://www.law.drake.edu(center/aglaw)?pageID=agPublications#Center Publications.

203 *over 99 percent of the people of the country.* Quoted by Callicrate, "Reining in the Big Meat Packers," *Cattlemen's Legal Fund News,* February 22, 2002. http://www.nobull.net/CattlemenLegal/news.

putting them out of business. Interview with Candace Krebs, *Beef Today* magazine, November/December, 2000.

if the market had been truly open. See Elizabeth Becker, "Jury Awards Ranchers $1.28 Billion from Tyson," *New York Times,* February 18, 2004.

204 *with its captive inventory of big money, won.* Clint Peck headlined the event for *Beef* magazine, "U.S. Supreme Court Dumps Pickett v Tyson," April 4, 16, 2006.

not just another economic activity. See "Court Fines Tyson Foods $1.3 Billion for Swindling Cattle Ranchers," February 2004, at http://www.organicconsumers.org.

corporate outlaw. Cattlemen's Legal Fund News, January 31, 2004.

205 *hide harmful practices from public scrutiny.* "Challenging Concentration of Control in the American Meat Industry," 117 *Harvard Law Review* 2643, document.8, June 2004.

put big feeders and packers on its board. See Jim Eichstadt, "R-Calf USA Challenges Beef Establishment," *The Milkweed,* August 2005. http://www.themilkweed.com/Milkweed%20archives.htm.

206 *minimal standards for food safety.* In March 2006, Creekstone filed a lawsuit against the USDA to challenge its ban on voluntary testing and to challenge the NCBA's concurrence. "If testing is allowed at Creekstone," the NCBA president had said, "we think it would become the international standard and the domestic standard, too." Testing each cow might increase the cost of beef 10 cents per pound.

207 *in bed with the Big Four.* "Jolley: Five Minutes with Brian Schweitzer," interview September 30, 2005, at http://www.cattlenetwork.com.

208 *beef that the big packers slaughter is inspected.* Because the United States consumes far more beef than it produces, it is the world's largest beef importer, largely of live cattle to be processed in the United States.

209 *how long a steak has been on a supermarket shelf.* For consumer response, see Julie Schmit, "Carbon monoxide keeps meat red longer; is that good?" *USA Today,* October 30, 2007. For industry response, see a study by researchers at the University of Illinois and Tyson Fresh Foods, Inc. on beef strip steaks in the *Journal of Muscle Foods,* volume 18, number 1, January 2007.

211 *pressure off middle meats (loin and rib).* Cattle Today Online, October 2004. http://www.cattletoday.com.

212 *bringing suit against it.* In 2004 R-CALF challenged the legality of the checkoff program.

Riding Point for the Industry

221 *the new outbreak of BSE. New York Times,* October 27, 2004.

223 *than any other single item today to our industry.* An invaluable resource is NCBA's centenary volume, written by Charles E. Ball, *Building the Beef Industry: A Century of Commitment* (Denver: National Cattlemen's Foundation, 1998).

   in the category of Consumer Education. The *Beef Training Camp Manual* defines beef types as follows: Conventional beef is grain-finished. Natural beef is "minimally processed, contains no additives." Grass-finished beef is "not necessarily Certified Organic," tends to grade Select, produces more waste than grain-finished, is not more nutritious, is less tender, has a different taste "like game meat." Certified Organic beef costs more and is not proven to be healthier or more nutritious. Branded beef "delivers a promise to the consumer" from a company that has set up a unique program specifying grade, age, and size.

224 *"vertical coordination," and "vertical alignment."* Harlan Ritchie, "What Are the Market Targets for Beef?" http://www.beef.org, August 9, 2004. (Ritchie is a meat scientist at Michigan State University.)

   vertical integration of the poultry and pork industries. "Cow-Calf Weekly," August 1, 2001. The Weekly is the e-newsletter of *Beef* magazine. http://www.beefmagazine.com.

226 *these public lands belong to all of us. They do not!* Brock quoted in Ball, *Building the Beef Industry.*

227 *cost U.S. taxpayers $2 billion.* "Cattle Ranchers Sue to Stop Government Slaughter of Dairy Cows," *New York Times,* April 9, 1986.

   possesses great strengthening powers. Quoted by Harvey Levenstein, *Revolution at the Table: The Transformation of the American Diet* (New York: Oxford University Press, 1988).

Marshall in "Cow-Calf Weekly" in 2006. September 23, 2006. Marshall, a CSU graduate and an editor of "Cow-Calf Weekly," founded *The Seedstock Digest* in 2000.

228 *household editors, agricultural colleges and others.* Thomas E. Wilson's address to the 1922 convention after a disastrous drop in meat consumption.

229 *including the prion theory of BSE.* Milloy is a FoxNews.com columnist and adviser to a number of free-enterprise organizations funded by oil companies.
a favorite whipping boy. Schlosser responded to the accusation that he's hurting American ranchers in an interview in Callicrate's *Ranch Foods Direct Newsletter,* August 5, 2006: "Right now your meat cannot be sold in Japan and cannot be sold throughout the European Union and that is because of the policies of the USDA and the big meatpacking companies which have given American meat a bad reputation. . . . I think American beef is terrific, and it saddens me profoundly that all of the policies have given it a bad reputation in the major core countries where we should be exporting. . . . We should have the best food safety policies in the world . . . [We don't] because of the industry but not because of me." http://www.ranchfoodsdirect.com/_RFDNewsletter/2006.
queen of the "Nanny Culture." See the Web site of the Center for Consumer Freedom, created by lobbyist Rick Berman: http://www.activistcash.com.
these radical, domestic elements. Spring 2005.

230 *appears regularly at Meatingplace.com.* http://www.meatingplace.com, "the Internet Home of Meat Marketing and Technology."
the evil meat industry — by any means necessary. August 19, 2005.
singled out for persecution throughout time. "Cow-Calf Weekly," June 2, 2006.
sponsored by corporate livestock groups. A speaker at the convention's Issues and Activism session warned, "The Internet has become the latest, greatest arrow in our quiver of social activism. Advocacy groups have an advantage on the Internet because they share information." Confirming his fear is the fact that the activist satiric film *Meatrix* has now been downloaded by over 10 million people.

231 *the right question at the right time.* The phrase was given political currency in 1984 when Walter Mondale used it successfully to counter the repeated mantra of "new ideas" recited by his rival Gary Hart.

233 *in favor of the defendants.* The case of *Johanns, Secretary of Agriculture, et al. v. Livestock Marketing Assocation et al.* was argued on December 8, 2004, and decided on May 23, 2005. See full text at http://www.caselaw:lp.findlaw.com.

234 *for its indifference to live cattle.* December 17, 2004.

235 *scholarly publications he's written since.* Scanga, along with other members of his Department, contributed to "The 2000 National Beef Quality Audits: Views of Producers, Packers, and Merchandisers on Current Quality Characteristics of Beef," funded by the beef-checkoff program of the CBB and NCBA.

236 *accounts for only "a very small proportion."* "The Meat Tenderness Debate" is explored in detail for the general reader at http://www.naturalhub.com/buy_food_meat_tenderness.htm.
industry's answer is palatability. See, for example, a Department of Animal Sci-

ences' study, "Relationships of consumer sensory ratings, marbling score, and shear force value to consumer acceptance of beef strip loin steaks," *Journal of Animal Science,* November 2003.

the economist who devised them. William Vickery devised what's known to economists as "sealed-bid auctions."

237 *a brief summary.* G. C. Smith, "Red vs. White Muscle Fibers in Beef," printed for classroom use.

239 *trying to shove all the data into it.* In *The Harvard Brain,* volume 7, Spring 2000.

those calves are raised for beef. Anne Raver interview, "Qualities of an Animal Scientist: Cow's Eye View and Autism," *New York Times,* August 5, 1997.

243 *not a machine or just an economic entity.* "Transferring results of behavioral research to industry to improve animal welfare on the farm, ranch and the slaughter plant," in *Applied Animal Behaviour Science* 81, 2003.

sound of metal clanging and clanging. NPR profile, "Temple Grandin and how she's brought big changes in the treatment of cattle in slaughterhouses as an inspector for McDonald's," on *All Things Considered,* Washington, D.C., April 29, 2002.

244 *they're not posts or machines.* Quoted in *New York Times,* August 5, 1997.

so that people themselves don't get corrupted. NPR profile.

246 *increase efficiency and productivity.* "Keynote Address: Animal agriculture and emerging social ethics for animals," *Journal of Animal Science,* March 2004.

247 *to emerge as the 'good guys.'* Ibid.

Mad Cows and Ethanol

249 *blog entry on Corrente.* http://www.correntewire.com.

diseased animals, to live animals. FDA summaries of feed restrictions in relation to BSE can be found in the March-April 2001 *FDA Consumer* magazine: Linda Bren, "Trying to Keep 'Mad Cow Disease' Out of U.S. Herds," http://www.fda.gov/fdac/features/2001/201_cow.html. Also see report from April 2001 at http://www.fda.gov/ola/2001/bse0401.html. For the continuing issue of downer cattle in the food chain, see Libby Quaid, "Mad cow back on the menu?" June 17, 2005, AP report at http://www.nodowners.org.

250 *her brain was just gone.* Quoted by D. T. Max, "The Case of the Cherry Hill Cluster," *New York Times Sunday Magazine,* March 28, 2004.

it won him a Nobel Prize. Sheila Jasanoff, *Science at the Bar: Law, Science, and Technology in America* (Cambridge: Harvard University Press, 1995).

was still fresh in their minds. For an early alert to the danger of these libel laws, see Donella H. Meadows, "Veggie Libel Suits Are Meant to SLAPP Free Speech," *Global Citizen,* January 22, 1998, at http://www.pcdf.org/meadows.SLAPP.htm.

from apples to hamburgers. For a history of these laws, see A. J. Nomai, "Food disparagement laws: A threat to us all," *Free Heretic Publications,* 1999. http://www.geocities.com/CapitolHill/Lobby/1818/3_2.VeggieLibel.htm.

251 *before the California State Senate in February 2004.* See Dave Louthan, "They

Are Lying About Your Food," http://www.counterpumch.org/louthan1202004
.html, January 20, 2004; "AR-News: (US) Dave Louthan Speaks Out on Mad
Cow Disease," http://www.lists.envirolink.org/pipermail/ar-news/week-of-
mon20040517/025244.html; Donald G. McNeill, Jr., "Man Who Killed the Mad
Cow Has Questions of His Own," *New York Times,* February 3, 2004; "Inter-
view with Dave Louthan and Dr. Michael Greger," http://www.mikehudak
.com/Radio/RadioDirectory.html, February 23, 2004; Charlette LeFevre and
Philip Lipson, "Mad Cow Mysteries Solved Dave Louthan — Mad Cow Killer
Has the USDA by Its Bullhorns," http://www.seattlechatclub.org/news.html,
March 9, 2004.

252 *activists out there picketing were strange.* Skarbek, trained in statistics, had been
a CPA, worked for the IRS, ran her own accounting business, and had published a book, *Planning Your Future: A Guide for Professional Women.*

feed reform through the FDA. Jonathan Kwitney (*Wall Street Journal* reporter),
in his book, *Vicious Circles: The Mafia in the Marketplace* (1979), details Mafia
connections to the beef industry in the 1960s and 1970s: the Mafia bought
downer cows in Wisconsin — site of Dr. Marsh's studies of TSE where downer
cows were used as feed — faked the USDA stamp in their own slaughterhouses, and distributed "stinger meat" to their wholesalers in New York and
Philadelphia.

disease was transmissible by blood. See recent papers at http://www.lib.bioinfo
.pl/auth:Collinge,J.

but come from eating animals. Donald G. McNeil, Jr., "Research in Italy Turns
Up a New Form of Mad Cow Disease," *New York Times,* February 17, 2004.

253 *cases of BSE and CJD have spread.* It's now believed that CJD was the actual
cause of death of George Balanchine in 1983: Lawrence K. Altman, "The Doctor's World: The Mystery of Balanchine's Death Is Solved," *New York Times,*
May 8, 1984.

mad cow–related deaths in the United Kingdom. For a list of articles and up-
dates on major interrelated prion diseases, see Dr. Michael Greger's reports at
http://www.organicconsumers.org/madcow.cfm.

special risk materials from being added to cattle feed. For a summary of government responses to BSE from 1998 to 2004, see the USDA's online report of its
Foreign Agricultural Service, FASonline, at http://www.fas.usda.gov/info/BSE/
bse.html. See also an overview of BSE in 2001 by U.S. Department of Health
and Human Services at http://www.hhs.gov/news/press/2001pres/01fsbse.html.
The USDA's "Factsheet on BSE" at its APHIS Web site keeps changing, as does
the name of the Web site itself. APHIS's report of October 1998, "BSE response
plan summary," is no longer available. See instead "FDA Bovine Spongiform
Encephalopathy Emergency Response Plan Summary," created December 2003
and revised April 2004, at http://www.fda.gov/oc/opacom/hottopics/default
.htm. For a 2006 "Bovine Spongiform Encephalopathy (BSE) Ongoing Surveillance Plan," see http://www.aphis.usda.gov/newsroom/hot_issues/bse/
surveillance/BSE_disease_surv.shtml.

cattle blood and fat, along with downer cattle. Downer cattle were first banned as human food in 2003; the USDA sought to ease that ban in 2005 for cattle under 30 months of age.

prohibited material in cattle feed. Marion Nestle, *Safe Food: Bacteria, Biotechnology, and Bioterrorism* (Berkeley: University of California Press, 2003).

allow them to test their own herd. http://www.creekstonefarms.com.

endanger consumer confidence. Dan Murphy, "The Vocal Point," http://www.meatingplace.com, April 14, 2006. Canada had a similar case with Tender Beef Co-op, where the Alberta government opposed the company's testing program on the grounds it would anger the United States. http://www.foodsafetynetwork.ca, August 2004.

cattle declared to be BSE were not. http://www.organicconsumers.org/madcow/BSE7601.cfm, July 6, 2001.

254 *they don't want that.* Dave Ranney, "Beef Giants & USDA Prevent Small Slaughterhouses from Testing for Mad Cow Disease," *Kansas Journal-World,* January 2, 2005.

we now call mad cow disease. Jonathan Weissman, " 'Promiscuous Prion' Yields Clues to Infection Across Species Barriers" (originally published in *Nature,* March 8, 2001), available at http://www.sciencedaily.com, March 12, 2001.

convergent molecular signatures. "Prion Diseases and the BSE Crisis," *Science* magazine, 2003. http://www.sciencemag.org/feature/data/prusiner/245.dtl.

Prusiner had predicted twenty years earlier. The link continues to be studied. See, for example, Kevin J. Barnham et al., "Delineating common molecular mechanisms in Alzheimer's and prion diseases," *Trends in Biochemical Sciences,* volume 31, issue 8, August 2006.

255 *42 percent of those over eighty-five will contract it.* See Mickey Z., "Mad Cow: This Is Your Brain on Meat," in OpEdNews, Newton, PA, August 22, 2007, at http://www.mickeyz.net.

256 *right approach to policy.* Robert Hahn, director of AEI-Brookings Joint Center for Regulatory Studies, is quoted by David E. Sanger, "Mr. Deregulation's Regulations: Stuff of Politics, Mad Cows and Suspect Dietary Pills," *New York Times,* December 31, 2003.

failed to label it as such. http://www.consumersunion.org, July 18, 2003.

leadership role in fostering trade. Watchdog Alan Guebert called it "USDA's mad cow 'circus act,' " in the *Globe Gazette,* January 9, 2005. http://www.globegazette.com. Guebert claimed that this "undermines every argument the agency has ever made against the mandatory country of origin labeling." FoodRoutes Final Word, January 7, 2005. http://www.foodroutes.org.

257 *Canadian-born cattle in American herds.* According to a former director of Canadian Livestock Generics quoted in the *New York Times,* January 6, 2004.

the disease would diminish in time. They cited an updated and much-quoted 2003 Harvard Risk Assessment Report.

banned in 2003 as high risk. "High risk" meant specifically any bone marrow or tissue from the brains, skulls, spinal columns, and spinal cords (plus trigeminal and dorsal-root ganglia, eyes, tonsils, and small intestines) of cattle 30 months and older. The industry's 1994 high-tech system of Advanced Meat Recovery (AMR), hydraulic-pressured "rubber fingers" designed to squeeze muscle tissue from beef bones, has made implementation of this rule problematic.

258 *imported from Canada in 2004.* The report notes the difficulty in divided responsibilities: The USDA is responsible for detecting disease in cattle; the FDA is responsible for animal feed. The full report can be accessed at http://www.usda.gov/oig/whatsnew.htm 2/18/2005. An abstract is available at http://www.gao.gov/docdblite/summary.php?.

make decisions based on science. Quoted from his keynote address in March 2005 to Nebraska's annual Governor's Agricultural Conference.

as if the two were not Siamese twins. Quoted in the *New York Times,* April 21, 2005.

44 percent to 91 percent. Daniel Goldstein's report, January 3, 2005. http://www.bloomberg.com.

a disease of industrialized agriculture everywhere. This Land Is Their Land: How Corporate Farms Threaten the World (Monroe, ME: Common Courage Press, 2006).

the most important samples had gone missing. CBC News, "Concerns Raised About 1997 U.S. Mad Cow Tests," April 13, 2005. http://www.cbc.ca/story/canada/national/2005/04/12/usbse050412.html.

259 *saved billions in regained markets.* From a report in the *Kansas City Star* quoted in "Cow-Calf Weekly," April 30, 2005.

260 *enjoy a good steak.* T. Christian Miller, "2nd Mad Cow Possible; US Sees 'No Risk,'" *Los Angeles Times,* June 11, 2005.

warned of economic losses. Donald McNeil, Jr. and Alexei Barrionuevo, "For Months, Agriculture Department Delayed Announcing Result of Mad Cow Test," *New York Times,* June 26, 2005.

no written records had been kept. Ibid.

261 *critics of U.S. testing methods were not surprised.* Scott Kilman, "Mad Cow Test on U.S. Animal Sparks Concerns," *Wall Street Journal,* June 13, 2005.

critics said, "Nonsense." Andrew Martin, in "USDA Stance on Mad Cow a Tough Sell," *Chicago Tribune,* June 27, 2005, noted the absurdity of Johanns's message "that a teensy bit of mad cow disease — which turns the brains of cattle to mush — is little cause for alarm."

had infected the American herd. R-CALF Cattle Update at http://www.cattlenetwork.com, July 12, 2005.

the kind of testing that Japan was doing. Reuters, August 17, 2005.

risk that BSE poses in North America. "Report critical of Canadian border closing," *Choices,* July 13, 2005, http://www.drovers.com.

only 16 percent in that category were tested. Inspector General's report, 2004.

on-site inspection of U.S. plants. http://www.meatingplace.com, November 4, 2005.

262 *if the ban on U.S. beef were lifted.* http://www.meatingplace.com, November 30, 2005.

schoolyard bully . . . steals our lunch money. "No More Mr. Nice Guy," *Brandon Sun,* December 8, 2005.

adorned with tiny American flags. New York Times, January 7, 2006.

contained spinal-column material. http://www.meatingplace.com, January 25, 2006.

not a beef safety issue. http://www.meatingplace.com, January 23, 2006.

once again threatened reprisals. http://www.agriculture.house.gov, January 31, 2006.

they found a way to reject it. http://www.meatingplace.com, December 7, 2006.

263 *producing plants be reinstated.* http://www.meatingplace.com, June 20, 2007.

your beef is safe. "Cow-Calf Weekly," July 1, 2006.

reduced from $52 to $8 million. http://www.home.hetnet.nl/~mad.cow/2006/jul06/usdalesstests.htm.

assessment by the Food Safety and Inspection Service (FSIS). "*Our Mission:* The Food Safety and Inspection Service (FSIS) is the public health agency in the U.S. Department of Agriculture responsible for ensuring that the nation's commercial supply of meat, poultry, and egg products is safe, wholesome, and correctly labeled and packaged." http://www.fsis.usda.gov.

95 percent of BSE-infected animals. http://www.meatingplace.com, July 28, 2006.

millions of beef-eating consumers happily don't care. Ibid.

266 *how to spin it correctly.* Documented in Stauber and Sheldon Rampton, *Mad Cow U.S.A.: Could the Nightmare Happen Here?* (Monroe, ME: Common Courage Press, 1997).

a really stupid idea. Quoted by Diane Farsetta at http://www.prwatch.org, September 7, 2005.

contaminated the British blood supply. "Risk of mad cow disease to dental patients investigated," *Daily Telegraph,* September 1, 2005.

267 *and the poultry-feed industry all come together.* The USDA/FDA's attempts to distinguish ruminant feeds from nonruminant feeds were entirely unrealistic from the beginning of their 1997 "feed reform."

1500-pound cow in six to eight hours. "With Diseased Animals Disposal Isn't Simple," *New York Times,* January 6, 2004.

New York to Los Angeles every year. Jim Hodges, president of AMI Foundation, quoted by Libby Quaid, "Gaps Remain in U.S. Defense vs. Mad Cow," *Los Angeles Times,* June 17, 2005.

268 *the most compelling case for government regulation.* "Fear of Eating," *New York Times,* May 21, 2007.

269 *you're not likely to find it.* http://www.safetables.org, March 15, 2005.

they're rejoicing right now. Pam Belluck, "The Tangled Trail That Led to a Beef Recall," *New York Times,* August 24, 1997.

illnesses were reported in six Western states. http://www.meatingplace.com, June 11, 2007.

so they wouldn't be tested as downers. The video can be accessed at Hub Pages http://www.hubpages.com/hub/USDA-Beef-Recall-Hallmark-Westland-Meat-Packing-beef-recalled.

270 *get consumers to eat more.* See "Meat: Questions of Safety," in Warren Belasco, *Meals to Come: A History of the Future of Food* (Berkeley: University of California Press, 2006).

Department of Health and Human Services. John P. Swann, "History of the FDA," http://www.fda.gov/oc/history.

271 *U.S. cattle at risk of spreading BSE.* See report for February 2005, at http://www.gao.gov. See also the Meat Section of Belasco, *Meals to Come.*

reforms USDA enacted in 1996 are on life support. "Evaluating the inspection system: supreme beef v. USDA," Frontline's Modern Meat. http://www.pbs.org/whbh.

272 *5,000 of them fatally.* http://www.wjz.com, February 22, 2007.

highly dysfunctional food safety system. "The Spinach Fallout: Restoring Trust in California Produce," *Mercury News,* October 22, 2006.

sterilized shit is still shit. See Carol Tucker Foreman, "Sterilized poop is still poop," *Consumer Reports,* March 1998.

produce an up to 80 percent drop in E. coli. James B. Russell and Graeme N. Jarvis, "Practical Mechanisms for Interrupting the Oral-fecal Lifecycle of Escherichia coli," *Journal of Molecular Microbiology Biotechnology,* 2001. See also J. B. Russell, F. Diez-Gonzalez, G. N. Jarvis, "Symposium: Farm Health and Safety: Invited Review: Effects of Diet Shifts on Escherichia coli in Cattle," *Journal of Dairy Science,* 2000 (83:863–73).

273 *we don't think you should preclude their use.* Rick Weiss, "FDA Rules Override Warning About Drug," *Washington Post,* March 4, 2007.

we vigorously impose on your children? "The Vocal Point: Tearing down the 'factory farm' fallacy," http://www.meatingplace.com, January 20, 2006.

either intentional or unintentional. David Barboza and Alexei Barrionuevo, "Filler in Animal Feed Is Open Secret in China," *New York Times,* April 30, 2007.

274 *the standards of the exporting country.* See "The True Cost of Food Safety," http://www.citizen.org, July 26, 2007.

275 *different paperwork they want producers to sign.* Beef: Stocker Trends, October 23, 2005.

who will run it. Beef: Stocker Trends, November 28, 2005, 86.

276 *list all the countries the meat "could be" from.* Renae Merle, "Bill Calls for Meat to be Labeled by Origin," *Washington Post,* July 26, 2007. See also John Gregerson at http://www.meatingplace.com, July 30, 2007.

277 *steer will have consumed 35 gallons of oil.* Michael Pollan, *The Omnivore's Dilemma: A Natural History of Four Meals* (New York: Penguin Press, 2006).

dupes of our lawns. Interview with Matthew MacLean, "When corn is king," *Christian Science Monitor,* October 31, 2002.

278 *to integrate ever more closely.* See Alan Guebert, "Sir Isaac Newton meets Congress."

152 bushels of corn per acre. "Cow-Calf Weekly," March 6, 2007.

pay for it again at the grocery store. Burt Rutherford, "Ethanol's Effects on Cattlemen Offers Many Unknowns," *Beef* magazine, June 1, 2007.

279 *Tyson against big grain merchants like ADM.* "For Good or Ill, Ethanol Boom Reshapes Heartland Economy," *New York Times,* June 25, 2006.

$1.3 billion from ethanol alone. http://www.meatingplace.com, July 25, 2007.

280 *producing only "brown power."* Nicolette Hahn Niman, "A Load of Manure," *New York Times,* March 4, 2006.

how much glycerin a cow can process. http://www.meatingplace.com, May 29, 2007.

rain forests in the Amazon with 50 million cattle. George Monblot, "The price of cheap beef: disease, deforestation, slavery and murder," *The Guardian,* October 18, 2005.

281 *229 million tons in 2000 to 465 million tons in 2050. Christian Science Monitor,* February 20, 2007.

the one resource that cannot be exhausted. George F. Will, "Dust Bowl is reminder of our environmental impact," *Washington Post,* April 29, 2007.

282 *and with the power to direct those states.* Marjorie Kelly, "The Stockholder Myth," *Earth Island Journal,* Autumn 2000, reprinted at http://www.thirdworldtraveler .com, August 5, 2004.

global ecosystem is limited and continued growth is untenable. Leopold Letter, Summer 2007, volume 19, number 2.

market system is designed to perpetuate it. Club member Keith Suter, "Fair Warning? The Club of Rome Revisited" — an interview for the Slab Lab. http://www.abc.net.au/science/slab/rome/default/htm, March 10, 2006.

283 *seeking enough when more is possible.* Thomas Princen, *The Logic of Sufficiency* (Cambridge, MA: MIT Press, 2005).

Denise Caruso writes in the New York Times. "RE: Framing: A Challenge to Gene Theory, a Tougher Look at Biotech," July 1, 2007.

Beef: It's What's for Dinner

287 *Philip Fink of the Washington Market.* Thomas De Voe, *The Market Book* (New York: Augustus M. Kelley, c1862, reprint 1970).

We want to eat meat. Douglas Martin's obituary, "Sol Forman, 98, Owner of Famed Steakhouse," *New York Times,* November 27, 2001.

reward their favorite sea-captain customers. Michael Batterberry and Ariane R. Batterberry, *On the Town in New York: From 1776 to the Present* (New York: Scribner, 1973).

288 *threw their heads back and laughed. The New Yorker,* April 15, 1939.

297 *now it's almost equal.* Alex Witchel, "After 40 Years, a Waiter Is the Boss," *New York Times,* April 28, 2004.

you need mighty few ingredients. R. W. Apple, Jr., "In Vegas, Scouting the Choicest Cuts," *New York Times,* December 28, 2003.

celebrating a special occasion/holiday (20%). NPD FoodWorld CREST Research, http://www.beef.org/documents/Beef%20Bytes%20Restaurants.pdf.

299 *she's self-assured, gutsy, worldly.* Allen Salkin, "Be Yourselves, Girls, Order the Rib-Eye," *New York Times,* September 9, 2007.
oversize martinis and vintage Cabernets. NPD FoodWorld CREST Research.
CEO of the Palm Restaurant Group. Florence Fabricant, "Demand and Costs Rise for Best Cuts," *New York Times,* May 23, 2007.

The United Steaks of America

307 *wet-aged beef tastes wet, not juicy.* Quoted by Sam Gugino, "Dry-Aged Beef: Try a Little Tenderness," *Wine Spectator,* April 30, 1999.
difference between skim milk and whole milk. Ibid.
unless you have a temperature-controlled chill room. 34 to 38 degrees F., humidity 50 to 75 percent, plus a room spanking clean and free of rats and roaches.

308 *the outside — crusty, "caramelized."* We now know that instead of "caramelize" we're supposed to use the term "the Maillard reaction" to describe what creates the flavors in browning meats: Under heat a chemical reaction takes place between an amino acid and a "reducing sugar" like glucose. "Caramelizing" refers only to what happens to sugars under heat.

309 *than to count twenty moderately, is hot enough.* The Buckeye Cookbook: Traditional American Recipes as Published by the Buckeye Publishing Company, 1883 (facsimile edition, New York: Dover Publications, 1975).

313 *would mean a rest of 10 minutes.* "Steak with Style: Easy Does It," *New York Times,* January 27, 2002.

314 *hung over "a brisk hot fire."* American Cookery (New York: Oxford University Press 1958, facsimile of the first edition of 1796, reprinted by Dover, 1984). The title page reads: "American Cookery, or the Art of Dressing Viands, Fish, Poultry, and Vegetables, and the Best Modes of Making Pastes, Puffs, Pies, Tarts, Puddings, Custards and Preserves, and All Kinds of Cakes, from the Imperial Plumb to Plain Cake, Adapted to this Country, and All Grades of Life. By Amelia Simmons, an American Orphan. Published according to Act of Congress." Hartford: Printed by Hudson & Goodwin. For the author. 1796.
having it immediately from the gridiron. (Columbia: University of South Carolina Press, facsimile of first edition of 1824, plus material from editions of 1825 and 1828, edited by Karen Hess, 1984.)

315 *we also from them, call Barbecueing.* (Amherst: University of Massachusetts Press, 1977, paperback reprint 1994.)
and almost raw in the centre. Miss Parloa's Kitchen Companion, 21st edition (Boston, MA: Dana Estes & Co., 1887).
and butter and pepper, if desired. Mrs. D. A. Lincoln, *Boston School Kitchen Text-Book. Lessons in cooking for the use in public and industrial schools,* copyright 1887 (Boston: Roberts Brothers, 1891).

316 *add one-half tablespoon grated horseradish.* Fannie Farmer, *Boston Cooking-School Cook Book* (Boston: Little, Brown and Company, 1896).

317 *half as much suet or butter as flour.* Eliza Leslie, *New Receipts for Cooking* (Philadelphia: T. B. Peterson, 1854).

318 *Makes 4 servings.* Dorothy B. Marsh (ed.), *The Good Housekeeping Cook Book* (New York & Toronto: Rinehart & Company, 1955).

319 *Serve at once.* Louis P. De Gouy, *The Gold Cook Book* (Philadelphia & New York: Chilton Company, 1947; enlarged and revised 1948).
cook until oysters are plump. Fannie Farmer, *Boston Cooking-School Cook Book.*

321 *then pour it over the steaks. Nuevo Cocinero Mexicano en forma de Diccionario* 1888, facsimile edition (Mexico, D. F.: Miguel Angel Porrua Grupo Editorial, 1992).

325 *pounding and marinating to tenderize them. ¡Que vivan los tamales! Food and the Making of Mexican Identity* (Albuquerque: University of New Mexico Press, 1998).

326 *cattle hurt worse than that live.* Quoted by B. Byron Price, *The Chuck Wagon Cookbook* (Norman: University of Oklahoma Press, 2004).
but guaranteed each got a share. Ibid.
Home on the Range: A Culinary History of the American West (New York: Villard Books, 1993).
which was said to be awful fine. For a fuller account by Nelson, see *The Cowman's Southwest, Being the Reminiscences of Oliver Nelson, Freighter, Camp Cook, Cowboy, Frontiersman in Kansas, Indian Territory, Texas and Oklahoma, 1878–1893* (Glendale, CA: Arthur H. Clark Co., 1953).

327 *does not break when bent, it is ready.* A collection of historical recipes from Montana's Bridger Canyon (Bozeman, MT: Bridger Canyon Women's Club, 1978).
Quoted in "Christmas in California Before the Gringo Came," *San Francisco Call,* December 7, 1899.

334 *and so requires more skill.* Quoted by Allan Nation, *The Stockman Grass Farmer,* October 2005.

335 *which cuts were in season.* Quoted by Apple in "Scotland's New Chefs Take Its Riches to Heart," *New York Times,* June 25, 2003.

337 *where most Japanese beef is shipped from.* John W. Longworth, "The History of Kobe Beef in Japan," under Meat Digest: The History of Kobe Beef, http://www.luciesfarm.com/artman/publish/article_37.php.

338 *it's not truly Kobe until it's time.* Carole Kotkin, "Wagyu Beef — Safe, Succulent and No Longer Rare," *Wine News Magazine,* September 9, 2004.

SELECTED BIBLIOGRAPHY

◆

Useful Trade and Organization Journals

Amber Waves: The economics of food, farming, natural resources, and rural America: www.ers.usda.gov/amberwaves
Acres U.S.A.: A voice for eco-agriculture: www.acresusa.com
American Grassfed Association Newsletter: www.americangrassfed.org
American Livestock Breeds Conservancy News: www.albc-usa.org
AMN News: A newsletter for members of the American Meat Institute: www.meatami.com
Beef Magazine: www.beefmagazine.com; www.beefcowcalf.com
BeefSpotter: The Feedlot Atlas: www.beefspotter.com
Chefs Collaborative Newsletter: www.chefscollaborative.org
Drovers: www.drovers.com
Eatwild guide: www.eatwild.com
Feedlot Magazine: www.feedlotmagazine.com
Feedstuffs: The weekly newspaper for agribusiness: www.feedstuffs.com
The Quivira Coalition Journal: www.quiviracoalition.org
Food and Foodways: www.tandf.co.uk/journals
High Country News: www.hcn.org
Lean Trimmings: Newsletter for members of the National Meat Association: http://nmaonline.org
Leopold Letter: Newsletter of the Leopold Center for sustainable agriculture: www.leopold.iastate.edu
Meating Place: Meat marketing and technology: www.meatingplace.com
National Cattlemen's Beef Association: www.beef.org; www.beefUSA.org

Organic Bytes: Organic Consumers Association newsletter: www.organicconsumers
.org
Range: www.rangemagazine.com
R-CALF USA newsletter: www.r-calfusa.com
Render: The national magazine of rendering: www.rendermagazine.com
The Snail: A journal of Slow Food USA: www.slowfoodusa.org
Small Farmer's Journal: www.smallfarmersjournal.com
The Stockman Grass Farmer: www.stockmangrassfarmer.net
Sustainable Food News: www.sustainablefoodnews.com
Western Farmer-Stockman: www.westernfarmerstockman.com
Western Livestock Journal: www.wlj.net
Weekly Livestock Reporter: www.weeklylivestock.com
World Watch Institute Magazine: www.worldwatch.org

Cowboy Magazines and Books

MAGAZINES

American Cowboy, Cowboys & Indians, Cowboy Magazine, Guns of the Old West, Horse & Rider, Shoot! Magazine, True West, Western Horseman, Wild West

PHOTO ESSAY BOOKS

Allard, William Albert. *Vanishing Breed: Photographs of the Cowboy and the West.* Boston: Little Brown, 1982.
Beard, Tyler, and Jim Arndt. *The Cowboy Boot Book.* Salt Lake City, UT: Gibbs-Smith Publisher, 1992.
Hall, Douglas Kent. *Working Cowboys.* Fort Worth, TX: Holt Rinehart & Winston, 1984.
Pattie, Jane. *Cowboy Spurs and Their Makers.* College Station, TX: Texas A&M Press, 1991.
Stoecklein, David R. *Cowboy Gear: A Photographic Portrayal of the Early Cowboys and Their Equipment.* Ketchum, ID: Dober Hill, 1993.
———. *The Cowboy Hat.* Ketchum, ID: Stoecklein Publishing, 2006.
———. *The Western Buckle: History, Art, Culture, Function.* Ketchum, ID: Stoecklein Publishing, 2003.
Wittliff, Bill. *Vaquero: Genesis of the Texas Cowboy.* Austin, TX: University of Texas Press, 2004.

Useful Background Books

Abbey, Edward. *The Monkey Wrench Gang.* Philadelphia: Lippincott, 1975.
Abbott, E. C. "Teddy Blue," and Helena Huntington Smith. *We Pointed Them North: Recollections of a Cowpuncher.* New York: Farrar & Rinehart, 1939. Reprint: Norman, OK: University of Oklahoma Press, 1955.

Adams, Andy. *The Log of a Cowboy: A Narrative of the Old Trail Days.* Boston: Houghton Mifflin, 1903. Reprint with introduction by Thomas McGuane. Boston: Houghton Mifflin, 2000.

Adams, Ramon F. *Cowboy Lingo: A Dictionary of the Slack-jaw Words and Whang-doodle Ways of the American West.* Boston: Houghton Mifflin, 1936. Reprint Boston: Houghton Mifflin, 2000.

Akerman, Joe A., Jr., and Brenda J. Elliott, Joe Knetsch, Cecil A. Tucker II, eds. *Florida Cattle Frontier: Over 400 Years of Cattle Raising.* Kissimmee, FL: Florida Cattlemen's Association and Florida Cracker Cattle Association, 2003.

Amberson, Mary Margaret McAllen, James A. McAllen, and Margaret H. McAllen. *I Would Rather Sleep in Texas: A History of the Lower Rio Grande Valley and the People of the Santa Anita Land Grant.* Austin, TX: Texas State Historical Association, 2003.

Anderson, Virginia DeJohn. *Creatures of Empire: How Domestic Animals Transformed Early America.* New York: Oxford University Press, 2004.

Atherton, Lewis. *The Cattle Kings.* Bloomington, IN: Indiana University Press, 1961.

Avery, Dennis T. *Saving the Planet with Pesticides and Plastics: The Environmental Triumph of High-yield Farming.* Washington, D.C.: Hudson Institute, 2000.

Ball, Charles E., Susannah S. Borg, and Hugh S. Sidey, *Building the Beef Industry: A Century of Commitment, 1898–1998.* Denver: National Cattlemen's Foundation, 1998.

Batterberry, Michael, and Ariane R. Batterberry. *On the Town in New York: The Landmark History of Eating, Drinking, and Entertainments from the American Revolution to the Food Revolution.* New York: Routledge, 1999.

Belasco, Warren J. *Meals to Come: A History of the Future of Food.* Vol. 16. Berkeley: University of California Press, 2006.

Berry, Wendell. *What Are People For?* New York: North Point Press, 1990.

Bingham, Sam. *The Last Ranch: A Colorado Community and the Coming Desert.* New York: Pantheon Books, 1996.

Bone, Eugenia. *At Mesa's Edge: Cooking and Ranching in Colorado's North Fork Valley.* Boston and New York: Houghton Mifflin, 2004.

Brisbin, James S. *The Beef Bonanza, or, How to Get Rich on the Plains: Being a Description of Cattle-growing, Sheep-farming, Horse-raising, and Dairying in the West.* Philadelphia: J. B. Lippincott & Co., 1885. New edition: Norman, OK: University of Oklahoma Press, 1959.

Brown, Mark H., and W. R. Felton. *Before Barbed Wire: L. A. Huffman, Photographer on Horseback.* New York: Henry Holt, 1956.

Brox, Jane. *Clearing Land: Legacies of the American Farm.* New York: North Point Press, 2004.

Burnham, Frank. *Rendering: The Invisible Industry.* Fallbrook, CA: Aero Publishers Inc., 1978.

Carlson, Laurie Winn. *Cattle: An Informal Social History.* Chicago: Ivan R. Dee, 2001.

Coetzee, J. M. *The Lives of Animals.* Princeton, NJ: Princeton University Press, 1999.

Cronon, William. *Changes in the Land: Indians, Colonists, and the Ecology of New England.* New York: HarperCollins, 1983.

———. *Nature's Metropolis: Chicago and the Great West.* New York: W. W. Norton, 1991.

Crosby, Alfred W. *Ecological Imperialism: The Biological Expansion of Europe, 900–1900.* Cambridge, UK: Cambridge University Press, 1986.

Dale, Edward E. *The Range Cattle Industry: Ranching on the Great Plains from 1865 to 1925.* Norman, OK: University of Oklahoma Press, 1930.

Dary, David. *Cowboy Culture: A Saga of Five Centuries.* New York: Alfred A. Knopf, 1981.

De Voe, Thomas F. *The Market Book: Containing a historical account of the public markets of the cities of New York, Boston, Philadelphia and Brooklyn, with a brief description of every article of human food sold therein, the introduction of cattle in America, and notices of many remarkable specimens.* New York: Printed for the author, 1862.

Dobie, J. Frank. *The Longhorns.* Boston: Little Brown, 1941. Reprint Austin, TX: University of Texas Press, 1982.

Eisnitz, Gail A. *Slaughterhouse: The Shocking Story of Greed, Neglect, and Inhumane Treatment Inside the U.S. Meat Industry.* Amherst, NY: Prometheus Books, 1997.

Fiege, Mark. *Irrigated Eden: The Making of an Agricultural Landscape in the American West.* Seattle and London: University of Washington Press, 1999.

Fiddes, Nick. *Meat: A Natural Symbol.* London: Routledge, 1991.

Fox, Nicols. *Spoiled: The Dangerous Truth About a Food Chain Gone Haywire.* New York: Basic Books, 1997.

Franz, Joe B., and Julian E. Choate, Jr. *The American Cowboy: The Myth and the Reality.* Norman, OK: University of Oklahoma Press, 1955.

Frazier, Ian. *Great Plains.* New York: Farrar, Straus & Giroux, 1989.

French, Philip. *Westerns: Aspects of a Movie Genre.* London: Secker & Warburg, 1973. Revised edition including *Westerns Revisited.* Manchester, UK: Carcanet Press, 2005.

Giedion, Siegfried. *Mechanization Takes Command: A Contribution to Anonymous History.* New York: Oxford University Press, 1948.

Gladwell, Malcolm. *The Tipping Point: How Little Things Can Make a Big Difference.* Boston: Little Brown, 2000.

Graham, Don. *Kings of Texas: The 150-year Saga of an American Ranching Empire.* New York: John Wiley & Sons, 2003.

Grandin, Temple. *Thinking in Pictures: My Life with Autism.* New York: Vintage Press, 1996. Expanded edition, 2006.

———. *Livestock Handling and Transport.* New York: Oxford University Press, 2000.

——— and Catherine Johnson. *Animals in Translation: Using the Mysteries of Autism to Decode Animal Behavior.* New York: Scribner, 2005.

Hine, Robert V., and John M. Faragher. *The American West: A New Interpretive History.* New Haven, CT: Yale University Press, 2000.

Horowitz, Roger. *Putting Meat on the American Table: Taste, Technology, Transformation.* Baltimore, MD: Johns Hopkins University Press, 2006.

Jackson, Wes. *Becoming Native to This Place.* Lexington, KY: University of Kentucky, 1994.

Jasanoff, Sheila. *Science at the Bar: Law, Science, and Technology in America.* Cambridge, MA: Harvard University Press, 1995.

Jordan, Teresa. *Riding the White Horse Home: A Western Family Album.* New York: Pantheon Books, 1993.

Jordan, Terry G. *North American Cattle-ranching Frontiers: Origins, Diffusion, and Differentiation.* Albuquerque, NM: University of New Mexico Press, 1993.

Klitzman, Robert. *The Trembling Mountain: A Personal Account of Kuru, Cannibals, and Mad Cow Disease.* New York: Plenum Press, 1999.

Knobloch, Frieda. *The Culture of Wilderness: Agriculture as Colonization in the American West.* Chapel Hill, NC: University of North Carolina Press, 1996.

Korten, David C. *When Corporations Rule the World.* Bloomfield, CT: Kormarian Press, 1995.

Kwitny, Jonathan. *Vicious Circles: The Mafia in the Marketplace.* New York: W. W. Norton, 1979.

Lasater, Dale. *Falfurrias: Ed C. Lasater and the Development of South Texas.* College Station, TX: Texas A&M University Press, 1985.

Leopold, Aldo. *A Sand County Almanac.* New York: Oxford University Press, 1949.

Levenstein, Harvey A. *Revolution at the Table: The Transformation of the American Diet.* New York: Oxford University Press, 1988.

Lieber, James B. *Rats in the Grain: The Dirty Tricks and Trials of Archer Daniels Midland.* New York: Four Walls Eight Windows, 2002.

Living in the Runaway West: Partisan Views from Writers on the Range. Compiled by the editors of *High Country News.* Golden, CO: Fulcrum Publishing, 2000.

Lomax, John A. *Songs of the Cattle Trail and Cow Camp.* New York: MacMillan Co., 1939.

Lutz Newton, Julianne. *Aldo Leopold's Odyssey: Rediscovering the Author of A Sand County Almanac.* Washington, D.C.: Island Press, 2006.

Lyman, Howard F., with Glen Metzer. *Mad Cowboy: Plain Truth from the Cattle Rancher Who Won't Eat Meat.* New York: Scribner, 1998.

Macdonald, James. *Food from the Far West: or, American agriculture, with special references to the beef production and importation of dead meat from America to Great Britain.* London & Edinburgh: William P. Nimmo, 1878.

Manning, Richard. *Against the Grain: How Agriculture Hijacked Civilization.* New York: North Point Press, 2004.

———. *Grassland: The History, Biology, Politics, and Promise of the American Prairie.* New York: Viking, 1995.

Marx, Leo. *The Machine in the Garden: Technology and the Pastoral Ideal in America.* London: Oxford University Press, 1964.

McCoy, Joseph G. *Historic Sketches of the Cattle Trade of the West and Southwest.* Kansas City, MO: Ramsey, Millett & Hudson, 1874.

McCracken, Harold. *The American Cowboy.* Garden City, NY: Doubleday & Co., 1973.

McCumber, David. *The Cowboy Way: Seasons of a Montana Ranch.* New York: HarperCollins, 1999.

McDowell, Robert. *Cowboy Poetry Matters: From Abilene to the Mainstream.* Ashland, OR: Story Line Press, 2000.

McKibben, Bill. *Deep Economy: The Wealth of Communities and the Durable Future.* New York: Times Books, 2007.

McMurtry, Larry. *Lonesome Dove.* New York: Simon & Schuster, 1985.

McWilliams, James E. *A Revolution in Eating: How the Quest for Food Shaped America.* New York: Columbia University Press, 2005.

Meadows, Donella H., Jørgen Randers, and Dennis L. Meadows. *Beyond the Limits: Confronting Global Collapse, Envisioning a Sustainable Future.* Mills, VT: Chelsea Green Publishers, 1992.

Montgomery, M. R. *A Cow's Life: The Surprising History of Cattle and How the Black Angus Came to Be Home on the Range.* New York: Walker Publishing Co., 2004.

Morgan, Dan. *Merchants of Grain.* New York: Viking Press, 1979.

Nabhan, Gary Paul. *Cross-pollinations: The Marriage of Science and Poetry.* Minneapolis, MN: Milkweed Editions, 2004.

Nation, Allan. *Knowledge Rich Ranching.* Ridgeland, MI: Green Park Press, 2000.

Nestle, Marion. *Food Politics: How the Food Industry Influences Nutrition and Health.* Berkeley, CA: University of California Press, 2002.

———. *Safe Food: Bacteria, Biotechnology, and Bioterrorism.* Berkeley, CA: University of California Press, 2003.

North American Meat Processors Association. *The Meat Buyer's Guide.* Reston, VA: 1997.

Ozeki, Ruth L. *My Year of Meats.* New York: Penguin, 1998.

Pilcher, Jeffrey M. *¡Que Vivan los Tamales!: Food and the Making of Mexican Identity.* Albuquerque, NM: University of New Mexico Press, 1998.

Pollan, Michael. *The Omnivore's Dilemma: A Natural History of Four Meals.* New York: Penguin Press, 2006.

Powell, John Wesley. *The Exploration of the Colorado River and Its Tributaries.* Washington, D.C.: Government Printing Office, 1875. Reprint of *The Exploration of the Colorado River and Its Canyons.* New York: Penguin Books, 1987.

———. *Report on the Lands of the Arid Regions of the United States.* Cambridge, MA: Harvard Common Press, 1983.

Princen, Thomas. *The Logic of Sufficiency.* Cambridge, MA: MIT Press, 2005.

Proulx, Annie. *That Old Ace in the Hole: A Novel.* New York: Scribner, 2002.

Pyle, George. *Raising Less Corn, More Hell: The Case for the Independent Farm and Against Industrial Food.* New York: PublicAffairs/Perseus Books, 2005.

Pukite, John. *A Field Guide to Cows: How to Identify and Appreciate.* Guilford, CT: The Globe Pequot Press, 1996.

Rath, Sara. *The Complete Cow.* Stillwater, MN: Voyageur Press, 1998.

Rhodes, Richard. *Deadly Feasts: Tracking the Secrets of a Terrifying New Plague.* New York: Simon & Schuster, 1997.

Rifkin, Jeremy. *Beyond Beef: The Rise and Fall of the Cattle Culture.* New York: Dutton, 1992.

Rogers, Ben. *Beef and Liberty.* London: Chatto & Windus, 2003.

Rollin, Bernard E. *Animal Rights and Human Morality.* Buffalo, NY: Prometheus Books, 1981.

Roosevelt, Theodore. *Ranch Life and the Hunting Trail.* New York: The Century Co., 1888. Reprint: Lincoln, NE: University of Nebraska Press, 1983.

———. *The Winning of the West.* 2 vols. London and New York: Putnam's Sons, 1889.

Rouse, John. *The Criollo: Spanish Cattle in the Americas.* Norman, OK: University of Oklahoma Press, 1977.

Salatin, Joel. *Salad Bar Beef.* Swoope, VA: Polyface Inc., 1995.

———. *Holy Cows and Hog Heaven: The Food Buyer's Guide to Farm Friendly Food.* Swoope, VA: Polyface Inc., 2004.

Savage, William W., Jr. *The Cowboy Hero: His Image in American History and Culture.* Norman, OK: University of Oklahoma Press, 1979.

Savory, Allan. *Holistic Resource Management.* Washington, D.C.: Island Press, 1988.

Schell, Orville. *Modern Meat: Antibiotics, Hormones, and the Pharmaceutical Farm.* New York: Random House, 1984.

Schlosser, Eric. *Fast Food Nation: The Dark Side of the All-American Meal.* Boston: Houghton Mifflin, 2001.

Scully, Matthew. *Dominion: The Power of Man, the Suffering of Animals, and the Call to Mercy.* New York: St. Martin's Press, 2002.

Shorto, Russell. *The Island at the Center of the World: The Epic Story of Dutch Manhattan and the Forgotten Colony That Shaped America.* New York: Random House, 2004.

Sinclair, Upton. *The Jungle.* New York: Jungle Publishing Co., 1906.

Skaggs, Jimmy. *Prime Cut: Livestock Raising and Meatpacking in the U.S., 1607–1983.* College Station, TX: Texas A&M University Press, 1986.

Slatta, Richard. *Cowboys of the Americas.* New Haven, CT: Yale University Press, 1990.

———. *The Cowboy Encyclopedia.* New York: W. W. Norton & Co., 2002.

Slotkin, Richard. *Regeneration through Violence: The Mythology of the American Frontier, 1600–1860.* Middletown, CT: Wesleyan University Press, 1974.

———. *Gunfighter Nation: The Myth of the Frontier in Twentieth-Century America.* New York: Atheneum, 1992.

Slywotzky, Adrian. *The Art of Profitability.* New York: Warner Books, 2002.

Smith, Henry Nash. *Virgin Land: The American West as Symbol and Myth.* Cambridge, MA: Harvard University Press, 1950.

Stanley, David, and Elaine Thatcher, eds. *Cowboy Poets & Cowboy Poetry.* Urbana, IL: University of Illinois Press, 2000.

Stanton, Bette L. *Where God Put the West: Movie Making in the Desert; A Moab-Monument Valley Movie History.* Moab, UT: Canyonlands Natural History Association, 1994.

Starrs, Paul F. *Let the Cowboy Ride: Cattle Ranching in the American West.* Baltimore, MD: Johns Hopkins University Press, 1998.

Stauber, John C., and Sheldon Rampton. *Toxic Sludge Is Good for You: Lies, Damn Lies, and the Public Relations Industry.* Monroe, ME: Common Courage Press, 1995.

————. *Mad Cow U.S.A.: Could the Nightmare Happen Here?* Monroe, ME: Common Courage Press, 1997.

Stegner, Wallace E. *Beyond the Hundredth Meridian: John Wesley Powell and the Second Opening of the West.* Boston: Houghton Mifflin, 1954.

Stull, Donald D., and Michael J. Broadway. *Slaughterhouse Blues: The Meat and Poultry Industry in North America.* Belmont, CA: Thomson/Wadsworth, 2004.

Thomas, Heather Smith. *Storey's Guide to Raising Beef Cattle: Health, Handling, Breeding.* North Adams, MA: Storey Books, 1998.

Twain, Mark. *Roughing It.* Hartford, CT: American Publishing Co., 1872.

Vallianatos, E. G. *This Land Is Their Land: How Corporate Farms Threaten the World.* Monroe, ME: Common Courage Press, 2006.

Verman, Glenn R. *The Rawhide Years: A History of the Cattlemen and the Cattle Country.* New York: Doubleday, 1976.

Vestal, Stanley. *Queen of Cowtowns.* New York: Harper & Row, 1952. Reprint of *Dodge City: Queen of Cowtowns.* Lincoln, NE: University of Nebraska Press, 1972.

Voisin, André. *Soil, Grass and Cancer: The Link Between Human and Animal Health and the Mineral Balance of the Soil.* New York: Philosophical Library, 1959.

Voynick, Stephen M. *Riding the Higher Range: The Story of Colorado's Coleman Ranch and Coleman Natural Beef.* Saguache, CO: Glenn Melvin Coleman, 1998.

Waldman, Murray, and Marjorie Lamb. *Dying for a Hamburger: Modern Meat Processing and the Epidemic of Alzheimer's Disease.* Toronto: McClelland & Stewart, 2004.

Walker, Don D. *Clio's Cowboys: Studies in the Historiography of the Cattle Trade.* Lincoln: University of Nebraska Press, 1981.

Watson, James L. *Golden Arches East: McDonald's in East Asia.* Palo Alto, CA: Stanford University Press, 1997.

Webb, Walter Prescott. *The Great Plains.* Boston: Ginn, 1931. Reprint: Lincoln, NE: University of Nebraska Press, 1981.

Weston, Jack. *The Real American Cowboy.* New York: Schocken, 1985.

Wilkinson, Charles F. *Crossing the Next Meridian: Land, Water, and the Future of the West.* Washington, D.C.: Island Press, 1992.

Wister, Owen. *The Virginian, a Horseman of the Plains.* New York: Macmillan, 1902. Reprint: New York: Scribner, 2002.

Wright, Will. *The Wild West: The Mythical Cowboy and Social Theory.* London: Sage Publications, 2001.

Worster, Donald. *Under Western Skies: Nature and History in the American West.* New York: Oxford University Press, 1992.

————. *A River Running West: The Life of John Wesley Powell.* New York: Oxford University Press, 2001.

Selected Cookbooks

Arnold, Samuel P. *Eating Up the Santa Fe Trail*. Niwot, CO: University of Colorado Press, 1990.

————. *The Fort Cookbook: New Foods of the Old West from the Famous Denver Restaurant*. New York: HarperCollins Publishers, 1997.

Besa, Amy, and Rory Dorotan. *Memories of Philippine Kitchens*. New York: Stewart, Tabori & Chang, 2006.

Bryant, Tom, and Joel Bernstein. *A Taste of Texas Ranching: Cooks & Cowboys*. Lubbock, TX: Texas Tech University Press, 1995.

The Buckeye Cookbook: Traditional American Recipes as Published by the Buckeye Publishing Co., 1883. New York: Dover Publications, facsimile edition 1975.

Canyon Cookery: A Gathering of Recipes and Recollections from Montana's Scenic Bridger Canyon. Bozeman, MT: Bridger Canyon Women's Club, 1978.

Chu, Grace Zia. *The Pleasures of Chinese Cooking*. New York: Simon & Schuster, 1962.

Claiborne, Craig. *The New York Times Cook Book*. New York: Times Publishing Co., 1961.

Conlin, Joseph R. *Bacon, Beans, and Galantines: Food and Foodways on the Western Mining Frontier*. Reno, NV: University of Nevada Press, 1987.

Cox, Beverly, and Martin Jacobs. *Spirit of the West: Cooking from Ranch House and Range*. New York: Stewart, Tabori & Chang, 1996.

De Gouy, Louis P. *The Gold Cook Book*. Philadelphia & New York: Chilton Company, 1947; enlarged and revised 1948.

Guerra, Melissa. *Dishes from the Wild Horse Desert: Norteño Cooking of South Texas*. Hoboken, NJ: John Wiley & Sons, 2006.

Farmer, Fannie Merritt. *The Boston Cooking-School Cook Book*. Boston: Little Brown, 1896.

Fearnley-Whittingstall, Hugh. *The River Cottage Meat Book*. Berkeley, CA: Ten Speed Press, 2007.

Hatfield, Connie, and Doc Hatfield, eds. *Oregon Country Beef Family Ranch Cookbook*. Brothers, OR: Oregon Country Beef, 2004.

Hawkins, Arthur. *The Steak Book: How to Buy, Prepare, Cook, and Serve*. Garden City, NY: Doubleday & Co., 1966.

Hayes, Shannon. *The Grassfed Gourmet Cookbook: Healthy Cooking and Good Living with Pasture-raised Foods*. Hopewell, NJ: Eating Fresh Publications, 2004.

Henderson, Fergus. *The Whole Beast: Nose to Tail Eating*. New York: Ecco Press, 2004.

Jamison, Cheryl Alters, and Bill Jamison. *Rancho de Chimayo Cookbook: The Traditional Cooking of New Mexico*. Boston: Harvard Common Press, 1991.

Leslie, Eliza. *New Receipts for Cooking*. Philadelphia: T. B. Peterson, 1854.

Lincoln, Mary J. *Boston School Kitchen Text-Book: Lessons in Cooking for the Use of Classes in Public and Industrial Schools*. Boston: Roberts Brothers Publishers, 1891.

Lobel, Evan, Stanley Leon, and Mark Lobel. *Prime Time: The Lobels' Guide to Great Grilled Meats.* New York: Macmillan, 1999.

Lomonaco, Michael, and Donna Forsman. *The "21" Cookbook.* New York: Doubleday & Co., 1995.

Luchetti, Cathy. *Home on the Range: A Culinary History of the American West.* New York: Villard Books, 1993.

Marsh, Dorothy B., ed. *The Good Housekeeping Cook Book.* New York: Rinehart & Co., 1955.

May, Lily, and John Spaulding, eds. *Civil War Recipes: Receipts from the Pages of Godey's Lady's Book of 1860.* Lexington, KY: University of Kentucky Press, 1998.

McElfresh, Beth A. *Chuckwagon Cookbook.* Denver, CO: Sage Books, 1960.

McMahan, Jacqueline H. *California Rancho Cooking.* Lake Hughes, CA: Olive Press, 1983.

McMahan, Jacqueline Higuera. *Rancho Cooking: Mexican & California Recipes.* Seattle, WA: Sasquatch Books, 2001.

Nathan, Joan. *The New American Cooking.* New York: Alfred A. Knopf, 2005.

Niman, Bill, and Janet Fletcher. *The Niman Ranch Cookbook: From Farm to Table with America's Finest Meats.* Berkeley, CA: Ten Speed Press, 2005.

Nuevo Cocinero Mexicano en forma de Diccionario 1888. Facsimile edition, Mexico, D. F.: Miguel Angel Porrua Grupo Editorial, 1992.

Parloa, Maria. *Miss Parloa's Kitchen Companion.* Boston: Dana Estes & Company, 1887.

Price, Byron B. *The Chuck Wagon Cookbook: Recipes from the Ranch and Range for Today's Kitchen.* Norman, OK: University of Oklahoma Press, 2004.

Randolph, Mary. *The Virginia House-wife: Method Is the Soul of Management.* Washington, D.C.: Davis and Force, 1824. Facsimile edition with materials from editions of 1825 and 1828, ed. by Karen Hess. Columbia, SC: University of South Carolina Press, 1984.

Rice, William. *A Steak Lover's Cookbook.* New York: Workman, 1997.

Robinson, Jo. *Pasture Perfect: The Far-reaching Benefits of Choosing Meat, Eggs, and Dairy Products from Grass-fed Animals.* Washington, D.C.: Vashon Island Press, 2004.

Schlesinger, Chris, and John Willoughby. *License to Grill.* New York: William Morrow & Co., 1997.

———. *How to Cook Meat.* New York: HarperCollins, 2000.

Simmons, Amelia. *American Cookery, or the art of dressing viands, fish, poultry and vegetables, and the best modes of making pastes, puffs, pies, tarts, puddings, custards and preserves, and all kinds of cakes, from the imperial plumb to plain cake. Adapted to this country, and all grades of life.* Hartford, CT: Hudson & Goodwin, 1796. Facsimile edition, New York, NY: Oxford University Press, 1958.

Ubaldi, Jack, and Elizabeth Crossman. *Jack Ubaldi's Meat Book: A Butcher's Guide to Buying, Cutting, and Cooking Meat.* New York: Collier Books, 1991.

Wicks, Judy, Kevin Von Klause, Elizabeth Fitzgerald, and Mardee Hardin Regan. *The White Dog Café Cookbook.* Philadelphia: Running Press, 1998.

INDEX